EDUCATION
OF THE
AFRICAN AMERICAN
ADULT

Recent Titles in
Contributions in Afro-American and African Studies

Visible Now: Blacks in Private Schools
Diana T. Slaughter and Deborah J. Johnson, editors

From a Caste to a Minority: Changing Attitudes of American Sociologists Toward
Afro-Americans, 1896–1945
Vernon J. Williams, Jr.

African-American Principals: School Leadership and Success
Kofi Lomotey

Class and Consciousness: The Black Petty Bourgeoisie in South Africa, 1924 to 1950
Alan Gregor Cobley

Black Novelist as White Racist: The Myth of Black Inferiority in the Novels of Oscar
Micheaux
Joseph A. Young

Famine in East Africa: Food Production and Food Policies
Ronald E. Seavoy

Archetypes, Imprecators, and Victims of Fate: Origins and Developments of Satire
in Black Drama
Femi Euba

Black and White Racial Identity: Theory, Research, and Practice
Janet E. Helms, editor

Black Students and School Failure: Policies, Practices, and Prescriptions
Jacqueline Jordan Irvine

Anne, the White Woman in Contemporary African-American Fiction: Archetypes,
Stereotypes, and Characterizations
Anna Maria Chupa

Wines in the Wilderness: Plays by African-American Women from the Harlem
Renaissance to the Present
Elizabeth Brown-Guillory, editor and compiler

Education
of the
African American
Adult

AN HISTORICAL OVERVIEW

Edited by
Harvey G. Neufeldt
and
Leo McGee

CONTRIBUTIONS IN AFRO-AMERICAN
AND AFRICAN STUDIES,
NUMBER 134

Greenwood Press
NEW YORK • WESTPORT, CONNECTICUT • LONDON

Library of Congress Cataloging-in-Publication Data

Education of the African American adult : an historical overview /
edited by Harvey G. Neufeldt and Leo McGee.
    p. cm. — (Contributions in Afro-American and African
studies, ISSN 0069–9624 ; no. 134)
  Includes bibliographical references.
  ISBN 0–313–25972–0 (lib. bdg. : alk. paper)
  1. Afro-Americans—Education—United States—History. 2. Adult
education—United States—History. 3. Literacy programs—United
States—History. 4. Afro-Americans—Vocational education—United
States—History. I. Neufeldt, Harvey G. II. McGee, Leo.
III. Series.
LC2741.E38 1990
374′.008996073—dc20   89–25925

British Library Cataloguing in Publication Data is available.

Library of Congress Catalog Card Number: 89–25925
ISBN: 0–313–25972–0
ISSN: 0069–9624

First published in 1990

Greenwood Press, 88 Post Road West, Westport, CT 06881
An imprint of Greenwood Publishing Group, Inc.

Printed in the United States of America

The paper used in this book complies with the
Permanent Paper Standard issued by the National
Information Standards Organization (Z39.48–1984).

10 9 8 7 6 5 4 3 2

Contents

Preface

Education has been highly valued in the African American community. As V. P. Franklin points out in his study on black self-determination, the black community associated education, including literacy, with advancement, self-determination, and freedom.[1] As a minority group confronting racism and subordination, adult education became increasingly important.

Despite the fact that adult education looms large in the history of African American education, little mention is made of this fact by most standard histories of American education or adult education. Historians have noted that some adult slaves taught themselves to read, and some were highly skilled craftsmen. Mention is made of the hunger for literacy exhibited by the ex-slaves during the 1860s. But once the historian moves beyond the early years of the Reconstruction era, the only major story worth telling seems to be the African American's experience in the more traditional setting of elementary and secondary schools and colleges. Malcolm Knowles' standard history of the American adult education movement devotes little space to the black adult education movement except for a brief mention of the efforts to educate ex-slaves and the promotion of educational activities of the National Association for the Advancement of Colored People and the Urban League. Absent in the index of his book are Booker T. Washington, Tuskegee Institute, Hampton Institute, Jessup Wagon, George Washington Carver, *Journal of Negro Education*, Negro, Black, or African American. Alain Locke is included but only as one of the former presidents of the American Association of Adult Education.[2]

The purpose of these essays is to highlight some of the efforts by both blacks and whites in promoting adult education for the African American community. Although the essays are grouped chronologically, they are not intended to provide a comprehensive history. Space precludes the inclusion of other topics that are not covered, topics such as the Negro conventions before the Civil War, the Negro press in the nineteenth century, the Negro county agent, and the extension work by the land grant colleges. The role of the black church is mentioned in several essays but merits further analysis. Nor is any attempt made to examine the training of black professional adult educators.

The term adult education is used in these essays in a nontechnical sense. Huey Long provides one workable definition in the preface of his study of adult education.[3]

"In its broadest sense, education of adults can be used to include all systematic efforts of adults to obtain knowledge or skills." This would include literacy and job training, but also instruction in religion, race history, health, and civic consciousness. It includes activities provided in formal classrooms, but also activities by fraternal organizations and efforts to educate through the press, radio, and television.

Part I highlights adult education efforts in antebellum society. L. H. Whiteaker's focus is on the education of a small percentage of slaves, those who were trained as skilled craftsmen and those who taught themselves to read and write. Elizabeth Ihle describes the efforts of nineteenth-century African Americans to improve their own education as they functioned in groups organized to meet other needs of their daily lives. Ihle concludes that by 1860, blacks outside the South had established social structures that offered adult education in civic, intellectual, and spiritual forms. Access to them was limited, however, to those who were somewhat economically secure.

The Civil War and Reconstruction period witnessed a flurry of educational activities within the African American community. These activities are addressed by two essays in Part II. Bobby Lovett describes the heightened educational efforts during the Civil War years, during which time some one-half million blacks were exposed to some formal education. Ron Butchart analyzes conflicting goals in black adult education as he examines five institutions and a distinctive curriculum that evolved during the 1860s.

Part III focuses on institutional, governmental, and voluntary association efforts in black adult education since the 1890s. Emphasis is placed on educational activities and programs initiated by and for black adults in northern and southern as well as rural and urban communities.

Tuskegee Institute was an early leader in promoting the extension work concept. Felix James describes the activities of Booker T. Washington and George Washington Carver as they sought to establish a model for blacks all over the world.

The Negro press long served as an important adult educational institution. The periodical press was especially important in the education of the small black middle class. Michael Fultz highlights the emphasis of the press on service, education, social uplift, justice, and morality.

Three writers focus on adult education activities of and programs initiated by governmental and black fraternal, religious, and voluntary associations during the early twentieth century. V. P. Franklin concludes that black self-help activities were important to the African American community, whether the programs were undertaken by voluntary efforts or promoted by the government. He points out that the black communities' support for literacy training or specialized educational opportunities reflected their core values of self-determination and education. Lillian Williams highlights the educational activities and programs of the YMCA, the YWCA, and black fraternal organizations. Williams, along with Cynthia Neverdon-Morton, analyzes the role of educational programs for black women as they confronted the issues of gender and race.

Literacy education has been an important component of black adult education. Two essays discuss literacy programs in the southern states. James Akenson and Harvey Neufeldt focus on the literacy movement in Alabama and South Carolina from 1915 to 1930, underscoring its conservative goals, limited financial support, and modest outcomes. Sandra Ohlendorf describes a literacy program initiated in the South Carolina Sea Islands with very different goals. The citizenship schools deliberately embarked on a program to link literacy with political and individual empowerment, with first-class citizenship.

Governmental programs for adult education are analyzed in the final two essays. Nancy Grant's study of federal programs during the Depression and World War II, including the programs in the Works Progress Administration, the Civilian Conservation Corps, the National Youth Administration, agriculture, and the Tennessee Valley Authority, reveals the extent to which adult education served different functions based on race attitudes. Grant argues that in the main, these programs failed to provide a significant change in opportunities for blacks, especially opportunities in vocational training. Edwin Hamilton surveys several manpower training programs during the 1960s and 1970s. Although many programs had a disproportionately high black enrollment, this was not true for those programs that provided comprehensive skills training.

The story of black adult education is a remarkable story of a minority community confronting the issue of race. It is a story worth telling. It is hoped that these essays will stimulate interest and research in this topic.

Harvey Neufeldt
Leo McGee

NOTES

1. V. P. Franklin, *Black Self-determination: A Cultural History of the Faith of the Fathers* (Westport, Conn.: Lawrence Hill & Co., 1984).

2. Malcolm S. Knowles, *A History of the Adult Education Movement in the United States* (Malibar, Fla.: Robert E. Krieger Pub. Co., 1977, revised).

3. Huey Long, *New Perspectives on the Education of Adults in the United States* (London: Croom Helm, 1987).

I
BLACK ADULT EDUCATION BEFORE 1860

1

Adult Education within the Slave Community

L. H. Whiteaker

Education broadly defined as acquisition of knowledge can be obtained in a multitude of settings, formal and informal. In this sense, adult education of black slaves began the moment they made contact with the people condemning them to slavery and continued unabated as they entered into their new environment in North America. If education is more narrowly defined to be the transference of distinct skills from one person to another in some kind of "school" setting, adult education for slaves took shape on two levels: the training of skilled workers and the teaching of reading, writing, and other elementary subjects.

Concerning skilled workers, it is very likely that some of the slaves in the seventeenth and eighteenth centuries brought with them to America skills that they had already acquired in Africa. Cotton weaving had developed in the Sudan hundreds of years before Europeans became involved in the slave trade, and reports of African craftsmanship in metalworking helped to bring the Portuguese to the West African coast. Various African societies produced well-made hoes and other farm implements and engaged in making leather and handicrafts.[1]

Some of these skills African craftsmen passed on, no doubt, to fellow slaves, but it was the acute need for skilled workers on the New World plantations that provided a greater avenue for the education of the slaves. The flow of skilled mechanics from Europe to the North American colonies in the seventeenth and eighteenth centuries was not sufficient to meet the needs of plantations or the newly emerging villages and towns. This shortage in skilled laborers also led to craftsmen charging higher prices for their goods and services; this situation, not surprisingly, caused many colonial people to seek additional sources of skilled workers.[2]

White, indentured servants—some already trained in crafts and others apprenticed to craftsmen—were one source of skilled labor, but the problem with these workers was that they could not be depended on after their service time (about five years) was completed. Slaves, by the very nature of their lifetime service, thus became a more certain source of skilled laborers and a more reliable one, providing, of course, that enough craftsmen and tradesmen were available to train the slaves. Even in the seventeenth century, when relatively few slaves had arrived in the English colonies, planters, merchants, and other businessmen from South Carolina to New England were beginning to instruct their slaves in the trades.[3]

Plantations, in particular, depended on slave craftsmen. Often isolated from towns and cities and sometimes without an adequate supply of manufactured goods from Europe, plantations had to function as industrial villages, producing nearly every item and offering every service necessary for the plantation's agricultural production. At various times plantation owners needed carpenters, blacksmiths, coopers, tanners, cobblers, wheelwrights, harnessmakers, butchers, cabinetmakers, bricklayers, stonemasons, silversmiths, spinners, weavers, seamstresses, tailors, cooks, and many other kinds of trained workers. As early as 1649 the training of such skills was under way, as one Virginia planter noted that he had taught forty blacks on his plantation to spin and weave cloth and to make shoes. As another example, a New Jersey planter reported in the 1670s that he was using skilled slaves to make iron.[4] This kind of "school" for slaves was born of necessity but was not wide open.

The training of slave craftsmen ranged from the very casual to the most intentional. Some slave boys and men began as assistants to slave blacksmiths, carpenters, and other workers and gradually learned the trade; the same was true of slave women as they learned spinning, sewing, and cooking skills from more experienced slaves or even from their plantation mistresses. In other instances, though, slaveowners singled out slave men to be apprenticed to white artisans to learn a particular skill. In one case, for example, a planter paid a white machinist $500 to train a slave in his craft and then used the slave to supervise and to repair all machines on the plantation.[5]

The age at which such training began varied from plantation to plantation. Some owners followed the general scheme of apprenticing their slaves at the age of nine or ten, whereas others waited until the slaves were young men or women before starting their training. James W. C. Pennington, once a slave in Maryland, recalled that he became a stonemason apprentice at the age of nine but later, as an adult, received training to become a blacksmith.[6]

Opportunities to train as a skilled worker seem to have been welcomed by most slaves. Undoubtedly, some were forced to learn a particular skill, but others believed that almost any trade was preferable to field work. Indeed, the acquisition of skills excused slaves from agricultural drudgery and was a powerful incentive for them to seek training rather than to wait for their owners to choose them for it.[7]

With the training also came a rise in status in the slave community. Frederick Douglass, for example, recalled that the blacksmith, cartwright, shoemaker, and cooper on his plantation were revered for their skills (as well as their age), and others noted that slaves and planters alike considered slave craftsmen to be superior in many ways to field hands. Adding to this sense of esteem was the slaves' knowledge that as skilled workers, they had a greater ability to direct their own work and display their talents. Being a skilled worker, the slave craftsman found it easier to avoid being "alienated" from his labor.[8]

Various incentives also existed for slaveowners to train slaves in the crafts. In addition to filling the industrial need left by the shortage of white artisans, slave craftsmen, many owners realized, were capable of being employed the year round. No seasonal fluctuations hampered skilled workers, and when the craftsmen had no work on the plantation, there was the prospect of hiring out the slaves to other planters or nearby businessmen.[9]

Another strong incentive for training slaves was their increased value once training was completed. Slaves were often advertised with descriptions of their skills—descriptions that also justified the prices being asked. As a rule, prices of skilled slaves were about double those asked for field hands.[10]

Some planters, though, did have reservations about crafts training for their slaves. George Mason, for instance, contended that the presence of slave craftsmen discouraged the immigration of white artisans, who feared competition from the slaves, and still others agreed with Adam Smith's argument that a slave who could never acquire property would never be as motivated (or as skilled) as a white artisan. Finally, there were always some who feared that the slave's "education" would make him or her dangerous, with the learning making the slave more conscious of his or her status and perhaps awakening a desire for more knowledge and a higher status.[11]

Some evidence exists that slave craftsmen in the towns and cities were more difficult to control and were more feared than those on the plantations. Towns and cities, like plantations, had suffered from the white artisan shortage, and as early as the mid-seventeenth century, city residents were training slaves in the crafts. The apprenticeship system provided most of the training, with slaveowners often paying white craftsmen to train the slaves. Also, the white artisans themselves often bought slaves to be trained in their trades.[12]

What towns and cities lacked most were the isolation and degree of control that many plantations had. A large number of urban slaves were hired out by their owners to work for others as barbers, blacksmiths, carpenters, or other craftsmen, with the owners receiving most, if not all, of the wages and fees earned. This somewhat loose arrangement gave the slaves even more control over their work and the amount of time they spent doing it. Cash gifts, above their fees, also enabled some of the slaves to save money and even enabled a few to buy their freedom. Otherwise, some slaves used their spare time and extra money to indulge in the vices that the cities offered. Owners were particularly concerned about the slaves' gambling and drinking.[13]

A measure of independence when coupled with the craftsmen's skills awakened another fear in some city residents. Could not a craftsman's heightened sense of self-worth and acquired skills enable him to fashion weapons and exert the leadership to cause slaves to revolt against their bondage? Some whites, for this very reason, opposed slave education, and fragmentary evidence indicates some basis for this concern. A revolt planned for the eastern shore of Virginia involved a slave blacksmith who had forged more than 300 spearheads for the uprising, and some of the leaders of the 1741 "conspiracy" in New York City were reportedly slave craftsmen.[14]

Ultimately, though, slaveholders on plantations and in the cities alike kept on training slaves for the arts and crafts. They overcame their fears of loss of control and their other doubts in return for adding value to their slaves and receiving the benefits of their skills. It should be noted, however, that the best estimate is that at no time in the history of slavery did more than 5 percent of the slaves fit into the skilled worker category. Indeed, as the nineteenth century progressed, the percentage of skilled workers on the plantations actually declined.[15]

By the second decade of the nineteenth century, several factors hindered the development of black craftsmen. For some time white artisans in cities such as Charleston had complained to city officials about slave competition, but by the 1810s this opposition was not as important an influence on slave education as were the developments of better transportation and Northern factories. From this time onward many planters chose to purchase factory-made barrels, cloth, shoes, and other industrial items and have them delivered to their plantations rather than to have slaves spend several years learning to make these things.[16] In fact, as the need for skilled slaves declined, many found that the only kind of formal education now left was the quest for literacy, and this learning to read and write proved to be the most difficult part (as well as the most dangerous) of the educational process.

Concern about the formal education of slaves first arose in the Puritan colonies of New England in the seventeenth century. Religion seems to be the main reason the Puritans wanted their slaves to be able at least to read, because Puritans believed in each person having some knowledge of the Bible. In Massachusetts, Connecticut, and New Hampshire, therefore, slave-owners—if not encouraged by the authorities—were not hindered by any law from making their slaves literate.[17]

In 1674 the Reverend John Eliot, famed for his missionary work with the Indians, called for the establishment of a school for slaves. Education, he contended, would not only be an act of Christian charity, but also help to destroy the ignorance that bound the slaves' souls. After Eliot's death, which came before he could set up a school, Eliot's friend Cotton Mather continued his interest in slave education and in 1717 opened a charity school for Indians and blacks. This school taught children and adults to read the scriptures and learn catechisms.[18]

Other advocates of slave education came from still other religious groups. Quakers had begun to form antislavery opinions as early as the 1670s, and as part of this stand against slavery called for the slaves' education. Quakers wanted the slaveowners to take responsibility for this, but they also made some attempts to provide teachers for the slaves. Likewise, the Society for the Propagation of the Gospel, founded in 1701 for the Anglican church, not only sent missionaries to the slaves, but also strongly encouraged missionaries and slaveowners to teach the slaves to read and write. Particularly in the New England colonies, several ministers working for or with the Society opened schools for slaves—children and adults alike.[19]

In the Southern colonies, where slavery had, by the eighteenth century, become far more important than in the North, slaveowners viewed education as a menace to the slave system. South Carolina and Georgia set the tone for the South by early on passing legislation to suppress teaching slaves to read and write. South Carolina's law in 1740 stated:

Whereas having slaves taught to write, or suffering them to be employed in writing, may be attended with great inconveniences; Be it therefore enacted by the authority aforesaid, That all and every person or persons whatsoever, who shall hereafter teach, or cause a slave or slaves to be taught, to write, . . . every person and persons, shall, for every offense, forfeit the sum of one hundred pounds current money.[20]

In 1770 Georgia, influenced by the South Carolina law, passed its statute imposing a twenty-pound fine on anyone instructing a slave in reading and writing.[21]

The South Carolina emphasis on writing instruction arose, to a great extent, from slaveowners' fears that slaves who could write would forge passes and use them to escape. As time passed reading also became a target because of the fear that slaves would find literature that would incite them to rebel. What this literature was specifically, slaveowners seldom said, but they became particularly wary after news arrived in the early 1800s of slave rebellions on Hispaniola. They seemed to sense that reading was a dangerous skill for a subjugated person to acquire.[22]

Events of the 1830s brought even more attempts to stop slave education. Nat Turner's rebellion in 1831 involved a slave with at least some ability to read, and reawakened the fear that rebel slaves were most likely to be led by educated ones. The suppression of the Turner rebellion not only brought on restrictions on slave movement and gatherings, but also resulted in further penalties for teaching slaves to read and write. In 1834, for example, South Carolina imposed a fine of $100 and imprisonment for six months on any white person involved in slave instruction and threatened free blacks and slaves with whippings and fines for committing the same offense.[23]

The abolition movement, beginning about the same time as the Turner rebellion, became another source of worry for slaveowners. Fear of abolitionist literature reaching the slaves led to more antieducation laws. In 1830 authorities in Georgia found David Walker's "An Appeal to the Colored Citizens of the World" in Savannah, causing the legislature to strengthen the laws prohibiting slave education. In 1835 North Carolina outlawed all public instruction of slaves, and in 1847 Missouri also made it illegal to teach blacks. Indeed, by the 1840s nearly every slave state had a statute forbidding slave instruction, and in those that did not have such laws public opinion was almost as effective in eliminating educational opportunities.[24]

Despite these attempts to suppress slave education, many blacks continued to receive instruction. In some instances, slaveowners themselves ignored the laws and taught at least some of their slaves. Some did this out of benevolence; others did so because they needed slaves assisting them in their businesses to be able to read, write, and keep accounts. White children also from time to time ignored the laws (and public opinion) and taught their slave playmates and servants to read and write.[25]

More important, once slaves learned the basic subjects, many of them took control of the educational process and began to teach fellow slaves. Slave fathers and mothers taught their sons and daughters, and they, in turn, instructed others. One former slave recalled that he had learned to write by watching a slave friend make his letters. Still another retrieved discarded correspondence and copied the writing onto scrap paper, in effect, teaching himself to read and write.[26]

The more daring slaves opened clandestine schools. Frederick Douglass, eager to impart his knowledge to fellow slaves, began with two pupils and, as word spread, soon had over twenty men learning their letters and enrolled in his makeshift sabbath school. Avoiding a setting that might provoke white suspicions, Douglass and his pupils had to meet "under the trees," pretending that they were meeting for purely social purposes. Another former slave recalled that he had operated a clandestine night school for slaves on St. Helena Island, and still another remembered that on his plantation, an elderly slave taught others after the white people had retired for the night.[27]

Slaves knew of and sometimes felt the penalties that the quest for literacy could entail. Some plantation children and workers informed on slaves caught trying to read and write, and other slave students were discovered by their owners. Whippings and confinement were the usual punishments meted out, but these were often coupled with dire threats of greater punishments. Titus Barnes, for example, after being discovered practicing his writing, had his mistress threaten to maim his right arm. Still another slave found that his learning to spell was so upsetting to his mistress that she threatened to kill him.[28] Slaves attempting to educate themselves received throughout the slave era beatings, loss of privileges, and even mutilations.

Because of slaveowners' efforts to suppress slave literacy, and perhaps because of the dangers to slaves themselves, few slaves, relatively speaking, learned to read and write. W. E. B. Du Bois estimated that only 5 percent learned to read by 1860. Eugene Genovese, in a more recent study, contends that this figure may be too low but does not insist that the percentage was that much higher.[29]

Altogether then, perhaps 5 percent of the slaves became literate and 5 percent or so became skilled workers. Because many of the slave craftsmen were also literate, though, this does not mean that 10 percent received education, but that somewhere between 5 and 10 percent did.

The importance of adult education within the slave community, however, lies not in the small numbers of slaves who received instruction, but in another area. Slaves, whether carpenters learning their trade or house servants learning to weave or students meeting under a tree to learn reading and writing, seem to have gained enormous self-esteem from their learning efforts and also seem to have received the esteem of most of their fellow slaves. Pride in craftsmanship and pride in making letters and reading words produced, not surprisingly, pride in oneself. However small a movement it was for the slave, education did produce a movement up the social scale. Slaves knew this (just as slaveowners feared it), and thus it was only fitting that it was from the skilled slaves and the literate that black leadership arose when slavery ended in the 1860s. Education, as people such as Frederick Douglass and Booker T. Washington could attest, had been for many slaves the first step toward freedom.

NOTES

1. Leonard Price Stavisky, "Negro Craftsmanship in Early America," *American Historical Review* 54 (January 1949):315–316; Eugene D. Genovese, *Roll, Jordan, Roll: The World the Slaves Made* (New York: Pantheon Books, 1972), 389.

2. Stavisky, "Negro Craftsmanship," 317–318; Marcus Wilson Jernegan, *Laboring and Dependent Classes in Colonial America, 1607–1783* (Chicago: University of Chicago Press, 1931), 11.

3. Jernegan, *Laboring and Dependent Classes*, 11.

4. Stavisky, "Negro Craftsmanship," 318.

5. Anthony Gerald Albanese, *The Plantation School* (New York: Vantage Press, 1976), 149, 152.

6. James W.C. Pennington, *The Fugitive Blacksmith; or, Events in the History of James W.C. Pennington, Pastor of a Presbyterian Church, New York, Formerly a Slave in the State of Maryland, United States* (London: Charles Gilpin, 1849), 4.

7. Albanese, *Plantation School*, 148.

8. Ibid., 147–149; Genovese, *Roll, Jordon, Roll*, 393.

9. Leonard Stavisky, "The Origins of Negro Craftsmanship in Colonial America," *Journal of Negro History* 32 (October 1947):423–424.

10. Ibid., 424; Eugene P. Southall, "Negroes in Florida Prior to the Civil War," *Journal of Negro History* 19 (January 1934):80–81.

11. Stavisky, "Origins of Negro Craftsmanship," 421–422; Genovese, *Roll, Jordan, Roll*, 393.

12. Thad W. Tate, *The Negro in Eighteenth-century Williamsburg* (Charlottesville: University Press of Virginia, 1965), 68.

13. Genovese, *Roll, Jordan, Roll*, 393.

14. Ibid.; Stavisky, "Origins of Negro Craftsmanship," 422–423.

15. Genovese, *Roll, Jordan, Roll*, 389–390.

16. Ibid.

17. Lorenzo Johnston Greene, *The Negro in Colonial New England, 1620–1776* (New York: Columbia University Press, 1942), 236.

18. Ibid., 237–238.

19. Ibid., 239–240.

20. William Goodell, *The American Slave Code* (New York: American and Foreign Anti-slavery Society, 1858), 319.

21. Albanese, *Plantation School*, 131, 133.

22. Genovese, *Roll, Jordan, Roll*, 561–562.

23. Albanese, *Plantation School*, 132–133.

24. Ibid., 133, 135; Donnie D. Bellamy, "The Education of Blacks in Missouri Prior to 1861," *Journal of Negro History* 59 (April 1974):149.

25. Thomas L. Webber, *Deep Like the Rivers: Education in the Slave Quarter Community, 1831–1865* (New York: W. W. Norton & Co., 1978), 131–133; Genovese, *Roll, Jordan, Roll*, 563.

26. Webber, *Deep Like the Rivers*, 133–134.

27. Ibid., 133; Genovese, *Roll, Jordan, Roll*, 564.

28. Webber, *Deep Like the Rivers*, 134.

29. Genovese, *Roll, Jordan, Roll*, 563.

2

Education of the Free Blacks before the Civil War

Elizabeth L. Ihle

Before the Civil War various kinds of adult education were available to free American blacks in many parts of the country. The bulk of it came in indirect forms; little evidence has emerged that would indicate an extensive network focused directly on intellectual and cultural development. Instead, free black adults largely improved their own education as they functioned in groups organized to meet other needs of their daily lives. The amount of their access differed dramatically based on their position in the community, their economic status, and their geographical location. This chapter documents those variations and relates them to larger social configurations and movements of the times.[1]

BEFORE 1800

Adult education for free blacks was largely a nineteenth-century phenomenon, but its seeds were sown in the late 1700s. Evidence of early organization points largely to Philadelphia, where adult education surfaced first in 1787 in the form of the Free African Society, the first chartered Negro organization in the country. Its purpose was to uplift its members and others of the black community; accordingly, the group regulated marriages, taught thrift, tried to improve the morals of its members, and served as a forerunner of moral improvement societies in a number of other cities. It opposed singing and dancing, maintaining that the society should help the needy of the race.[2]

Another function that the Free African Society served was that of a beneficial club. This type of organization, the most numerous of all antebellum black organizations, was designed primarily to provide security for member blacks whose employment was frequently seasonal, unstable, and ill-paid. Members paid a weekly stipend, usually 25 cents, to the club in return for assurance of help for their families in cases of unemployment, illness, or death. Distribution of benefits was usually directed by a club committee.[3]

The clubs increasingly attracted people of the same kind (e.g., members of the same church or workers in the same trade). By overseeing members' morals and lifestyles, a beneficial club could exercise control over its disbursements. Consequently, many of the beneficial clubs soon limited their memberships to people perceived to be appropriate to maintenance of the club's financial health.[4]

Other cities witnessed the establishment of similar groups. In New Orleans the Perseverance Benevolence and Mutual Aid Association was created in 1783. Boston had the Boston African Society in 1796, and New York City had an association that maintained a church site and a burial plot. Another pre–1800 Philadelphia benevolent society was the Benevolent Daughters, established in 1796.[5]

Beneficial clubs in Charleston most strikingly illustrated the role of skin color and social class in membership. The most prestigious of the city's beneficial clubs was the Brown Fellowship Society, established in 1790 and open only to free mulattoes. Limited to fifty members who paid a $50 initiation fee and monthly dues, the society provided a minimum of $1.50 a week to members too ill to work, a $60 annuity for indigent widows and orphans, and burial in the society's burial grounds, benefits substantially higher than those of similar groups. It attracted Charleston's most outstanding mulatto citizens. The next year free Africans formed Free Dark Men of Color; its membership, limited to thirty-five, was not so well to do as those in the Brown Fellowship. It paid widows an annuity of only $12 and maintained a burying ground next to that of the Brown Fellowship but separated by a stout fence.[6]

Although regulation of morality was often a function of the beneficial societies, a few groups were organized primarily as agents of moral improvement. Philadelphia's Society for the Suppression of Vice and Immorality, established in 1809, is an outstanding example. Other similar moral improvement groups included temperance societies and Bible groups.[7]

Separate black religious groups grew slowly in North America. Unlike other immigrants, who brought their church with them and established it immediately on the new soil, blacks first needed to establish a sense of identity before breaking away from white mainstream religion. Only three small black churches emerged before 1790. The growth after that date was stimulated by whites' increasing discomfiture with black membership and blacks' growing reluctance to continue tolerating discrimination in seating, communion, and church leadership.[8]

Philadelphia's Free African Society began to assist in the establishment of black religion in 1798 when two of its founders, Richard Allen and Absalom Jones, were asked to move to segregated seating in the formerly integrated St. George's Methodist Church. The society collected funds and built a church. Although Allen wanted a Methodist church, the society voted to make the church Episcopalian, and Absalom Jones agreed to be its first priest. Whites objected to him because of his lack of training, and for a number of years relations were strained between the white Episcopalian churches and the new African Church of St. Thomas. When it emerged from the society, the church established two beneficial societies of its own, the Female Benevolent Society of St. Thomas and the male African Friendly Society of St. Thomas.[9]

The next black church in Philadelphia was the root of what eventually became the first separate black denomination in the country. Richard Allen thought that Methodism better suited blacks than Episcopalianism because of the former's strong antislavery stance, simple preaching, and emotional services. Consequently, he formed his own church, the Bethel African Methodist Episcopal (AME) Church.[10]

Another black organization with eighteenth-century roots was the fraternal order. The earliest black lodge was a Masonic one established by Prince Hall in Boston in 1775. Others were founded in Providence and Philadelphia in the 1790s. These groups had literary, beneficial, social, and philanthropic purposes.[11]

1800–1830

Everywhere except in the South the first three decades of the nineteenth century witnessed steady growth in black organizations and a greater variety of adult educational opportunities. Beneficial groups and black churches increased, and a black newspaper and literary societies were started.

The number of beneficial societies grew rapidly in the opening decades of the nineteenth century and they continued their multipurpose functions of providing aid to their members and directing and improving members' lifestyles. Next to the church perhaps, these societies provided more of a sense of identification to the black communities than any other group. Some of the stronger ones offered talks about black heroes, discredited popular conceptions about black inferiority, and provided forums for emerging black community leaders.[12]

New York witnessed the organization of one of the most prominent of these societies, the New York African Society for Mutual Relief, which attracted a socially distinguished clientele. Organized in 1808, beginning its work in 1809, and incorporated in 1810, it became one of the wealthiest of all such groups. It amassed so much income from rental property that membership dues comprised only a tenth of its income. Its wealth was also augmented by the fact that its sixty-five members were so carefully chosen that it had little need for disbursements. Because of this, historian Leonard P. Curry suspects that "its true purposes were more social than beneficial—a conclusion bolstered by its 'inordinate influence in the Negro community.' "[13]

Other societies started as well. In 1809 the Woolman Benevolent Society was organized in Brooklyn. Baltimore had a similar group by 1821, and Providence had two such societies by the late 1820s, the Young Men's Union Friendly Association and the Mutual Relief Society. Philadelphia witnessed the foundation of the Daughters of Africa in 1821. Its minutes reveal that its savings fund covered the burial expenses of a member's husband and made a disbursement to a sick member's family. Like numerous other societies, it was concerned about the conduct of its members, and on one occasion it expelled a member for stealing.[14]

Some of these groups served others as well as themselves. The African Marine Fund in New York, while stressing good behavior for all its members, also proposed a school for black children in 1810. Another similar group in New York, the Society among the Free People of Colour, proposed a similar school in 1812. The Minors' Moralist Society of Charleston, organized in 1803, supported five free colored orphans.[15]

Other groups developed that were solely devoted to charity. African Dorcas societies in both Philadelphia and New York distributed clothing to the needy. The Philanthropic Society of Pittsburgh, established in 1834, relieved black indigents.[16]

Black churches continued to grow also in the first three decades of the 1800s as their denominations split from their white precursors; forms of Methodism were the most popular, followed in order by Baptist, Presbyterian, and Episcopalian denominations.

The AME denomination was one of the most rapidly expanding. It separated from Methodist authority in 1816, becoming the first independent black denomination in the country with the merger of Richard Allen's Bethel AME Church in Philadelphia and another church in Baltimore. Other congregations were soon started throughout the Northeast. In Charleston, Morris Brown started an AME church that had attracted 3,000 members by 1822 when it was destroyed as an unfortunate result of the uncovering of the Denmark Vesey plot. By 1850 every major city except Charleston had an AME church. Another black Methodist denomination, the AME Zion group, established itself as a separate denomination in 1822. Despite Methodism's appeal, not all Methodist church groups affiliated with black denominations.[17]

The Baptists were the second most popular denomination, appealing because of the simplicity of their administrative structure, congregational independence, and simpler ordination procedures. Boston boasted a black Baptist church by 1805, New York by 1807, and Philadelphia by 1810. All were small congregations, but the Philadelphia church owned land by 1817. Baptist churches later spread to Albany, New Orleans, and St. Louis before a major growth spurt occurred in the 1830s.[18]

Philadelphia was also the home of the first black Presbyterian church, founded in 1807 by John Gloucester, a friend of Richard Allen's. It had a building by 1811 and served, as did the Bethel AME church, as a center for the Underground Railway. The Second African Presbyterian Church of the same city was founded in 1824, when some members were displeased with the selection of the minister at the first church. Despite the establishment of the two Philadelphia churches, this denomination spread more slowly than the previous two. One reason may have been that black ministers were in short supply because of ordination requirements.[19]

Episcopalianism was the fourth-ranking denomination in popularity with antebellum blacks, but growth remained slow between 1800 and 1830. New York witnessed the establishment of its first black Episcopal church in 1809, but it did not get a building for another ten years. Like the Presbyterians, it had difficulty locating a sufficient number of clergy.[20]

Blacks in the South were generally affiliated with white churches, albeit in a secondary role, since slave states regarded separate black churches as sources of possible sedition. Free blacks and slaves, however, did not necessarily mingle in church and sometimes sat in separate sections. Blacks and whites in some churches had separate activities; in Charleston's Episcopal churches, for instance, black members supported a white missionary on the west coast of Africa.[21]

There were class distinctions among the church membership. W. E. B. Du Bois noted that in Philadelphia, Episcopalians tended to be well-to-do; Presbyterians were the older, simpler set of respectable Philadelphians; the AME appealed to the laboring class; and the Baptists attracted servant girls and their young men. It is highly likely that a similar set of class distinctions could be found in any city with a number of churches.[22]

Regardless of denomination, the churches assumed similar functions. They served as social centers, shapers of political opinions and racial consciousness, incubators of black leaders, and regulators of morals; in a few cases they even expelled members who continued their misbehavior. In taking on these roles, the black churches served as the most far-reaching agencies of black adult education in antebellum United States. Their influence provided succor to an oppressed people: "In a world where every lever of power was held by a white hand and every symbol of authority was white, the separated church stood as a towering monument to the zeal, strength, and determination of the American Negro—a black rock casting a cooling shadow in a harsh desert of whiteness."[23]

Black Americans developed other organizations in response to blacks' status throughout the country. Again, Philadelphia was the center of much of this activity. Even before 1800 the Free African Society had petitioned Congress on several occasions concerning the slave trade. In 1806 Absalom Jones, Richard Allen, and James Forten drafted a petition to Congress seeking modifications to the Fugitive Slave Act of 1793, and a number of anti-slavery groups developed throughout the Northeast. A most active one was in New Haven, Connecticut, and both New York and Philadelphia had several. By 1830 about fifty such groups existed. There was also concern about efforts to remove all blacks from North America. A mass meeting was held at Bethel Church in 1817 to protest plans of the American Colonization Society to deport blacks to Africa.[24]

Before 1830 most blacks were still so concerned with their survival that they chose to direct their excess energy toward the churches and beneficial societies that enhanced their security. Consequently, the first part of the nineteenth century witnessed the birth of a few black organizations whose purposes were intellectual enhancement. The most common types of the intellectual organizations were literary and debating societies, although lyceums, oratory, and prose reading groups were also organized. Boston had a debating society and Brooklyn a reading club by 1825; Philadelphia had a reading room group by 1828, the Colored Reading Society for Mental Improvement.[25]

Many societies, both beneficial and literary, were limited to one sex. The former, which were frequently organized around trades, naturally sparked the interest of many black women working outside the homes as maids, laundresses, and cooks. In some areas women organized and joined beneficial societies more frequently than men, but men's societies were likely to be more prosperous.[26]

Fraternal lodges, which also functioned in some cases as literary societies, continued to grow. Boston's Prince Hall Grand Lodge chartered a lodge in New York in 1812 and three others by 1825. The First Independent African Grand Lodge of Pennsylvania, which had been formed with four subordinate lodges in 1815, established the Social Lodge in Washington in 1822 and the Friendship Lodge in Baltimore in 1825.[27]

Toward the end of the nineteenth century's first three decades, black Americans developed another highly important form of adult education: the newspaper. *Freedom's Journal* printed its first weekly issue in New York City on March 16, 1827. Its editors were James B. Russworm, the first black college graduate (Bowdoin) in the United States, and the Rev. Samuel Cornish. Declaring that "useful knowledge of every kind, and every thing that relates to Africa, shall find a ready admission into our columns," the newspaper solicited $3 annual subscriptions up and down the East Coast. The newspaper ceased publication in 1829, possibly because of the opposing opinions of its editors regarding the African colonization movement, but two months later Cornish began the short-lived *The Rights of All.*[28]

The growth of organizations in the early nineteenth century was largely confined to the North because many Southern states had laws that restricted gatherings of blacks or that barred free blacks from associating with slaves. Although upper-class free blacks in major cities like New Orleans and Charleston were only tangentially affected because of their well-established connections to influential whites, these laws limited the establishment of official organizations. Although schools for free black children were sometimes tolerated, they were often actually illegal.[29]

1830–1860

Many of the organizations that had their roots in previous decades continued to grow everywhere in the pre–Civil War decades except in the South, where conditions became more repressive, even for free blacks. To the already established outlets of adult education were added black anti-slavery societies. Philadelphia, always the leader in black cultural affairs, was sufficiently sophisticated in numbers and kinds of black adult educational outlets by 1840 that one observer described the city as having an upper class "large enough to be composed of distinct circles, divided into no less than four Protestant denominations and numerous delegating, beneficial, masonic, and literary associations."[30]

Although many beneficial societies organized in the previous period, their real growth spurt occurred after 1830. Records of beneficial societies can be located in cities where none had previously been found. Albany, for example, was the home of the Female Lundy Society in the 1830s, and a similar group could be found in Cincinnati. Washington's first such organization can be traced to the 1850s.[31]

New societies, sometimes more specialized, appeared in other cities. Philadelphia witnessed in 1839 the establishment of the Agricultural and Mechanical Association of Pennsylvania and New Jersey, designed to help people move into trades. The function of another group, the Agricultural Emigrant Association, was to establish a settlement in Montana for those wishing to escape from an urban America into a rural one. By 1848 the city's blacks ran Lebanon Cemetery, in which people could buy lots. Charleston's mulatto citizens organized the Friendly Moralist Society in 1839, while the city's Free Dark Men of Color changed its name to the Humane Brotherhood.[32]

Societies with moral and philanthropic missions continued to organize. In Philadelphia the Association for the Moral and Intellectual Improvement of the People of Color started in 1837. Its mission was to visit black families in order to encourage the education of their children. In Charleston the Christian Benevolent Society was founded in 1839 to aid sick and impoverished people of color. Like similar groups, however, its resources were meager; between 1839 and 1856 it assisted seventy persons and spent only $1,228. In New Orleans the Christian Benevolent Society was founded in 1839 to assist the poor. The Colored Female Benevolent Society of Louisiana was also organized in the same city in 1846, not only to relieve the sick and bury the dead, but also to suppress vice and inculcate virtue.[33]

After 1830 another form of moral improvement emerged: black temperance societies. Two early leaders were Jehiel Beman and his son Amos. In 1833

Jehiel helped to found a society in Middletown, Connecticut, and three years later his son was an organizer of the state temperance group. In 1842 the Connecticut temperance group joined with those in three other states to form the States Delavan Union Temperance Society of Colored People. Although these groups' primary concern was temperance, they also discussed "slavery, education, a national convention, employment offices for the colored, [and] the importance of the mechanical arts and of agriculture to Negroes."[34]

Churches continued their expansion, resulting in more than 100 separate religious congregations disbursed in fifteen cities by 1850. Other denominations besides the "big four" appeared as well, although often in short-lived forms. Before the Civil War, black congregations of Dutch Reformed, Lutheran, Unitarian, Disciples of Christ, and Catholic congregations surfaced at least briefly.[35]

Methodists continued as the largest denomination; by midcentury there were about sixty Methodist churches in urban areas, two-thirds of whom were allied with one of the black-controlled denominations. Although congregations continued to grow, membership grew at a slower pace.[36]

The Baptists experienced a major growth spurt in the 1830s with the appearance of new black congregations in Cincinnati, Washington, Louisville, Baltimore, and Buffalo; a black Baptist church in Detroit was organized in 1836, although it did not own a building until 1857. Second congregations appeared in New York, Philadelphia, and Providence. In Philadelphia, by the 1840s, the Baptist denomination was associated with migrants from the South.[37]

Presbyterians continued to gain ground, especially in the 1840s. Congregations were formed in Baltimore, Brooklyn, Buffalo, Cincinnati, Louisville, Pittsburgh, and Washington. Philadelphia got its third Presbyterian church and New York, its second. The limited supply of black ministers stimulated the establishment of a short-lived academy in Philadelphia to train them.[38]

Episcopalianism remained the smallest of the four largest denominations. Providence got a black Episcopalian congregation in 1839 and Brooklyn, in 1846. Philadelphia got its second Episcopal church in 1847. In the South, Charleston established a separate but subordinate black congregation in 1849, and New Orleans authorized its black Episcopalians to hold separate services in the 1850s.[39]

The 1830-through-1860 period showed major growth in literary organizations, and most seemed longer-lived than the ones begun previously. Two important societies were formed in 1833. The one in New York, the Phoenix Society, attracted men who became national black leaders, such as newspaper editor Samuel E. Cornish and abolitionist David Ruggles. The society developed discussion groups, a lecture series, a library, and reading rooms. It had subordinate ward societies that performed the same function on lower levels. Simultaneously, the Philadelphia Library Company of Colored Persons opened. By 1838 its 150 members met in the basement of the St. Thomas African Episcopal Church and housed their 600-volume library there. Pittsburgh blacks founded a literary club in 1832, the Pittsburg [sic] African Education Society, and also Providence witnessed the start of a literary club in 1833.[40]

Especially among the literary groups, sometimes a society for men had a female counterpart. For example, in Philadelphia men had, shortly after 1830, the Banneker Society, the Rush Library Company and Debating Society, and the Demosthenian Institute, while women organized the Minerva Literary Society and the Edgeworth Society. The Minerva Society met weekly, and members read their original compositions. Women's groups, however, did not usually hold debates, since argument was not considered an appropriate aspect of female character. Meeting topics were often stereotypical, with women hearing talks on moral improvement and the influence of the woman on family life, and men discussing current issues of the day. It is likely that many protests and petitions of the day were formed at these meetings.[41]

Two Philadelphia groups had a scientific interest. The Gilbert Lyceum, established in 1841 and open to both sexes, studied both literary and scientific topics. The Banneker Institute, named after the black mathematician and astronomer Benjamin Banneker, established in 1854, discussed literary and scientific topics and also those of particular interest to blacks. Although membership was open to both sexes, only male members could vote.[42]

Little evidence exists of similar groups in the South. One exception is a group of seventeen New Orleans mulatto poets, who published an anthology of their poetry, *Les Cenelles: Choix de Poesies Indigenes* (Cenelle: Selection of Native Poetry), in 1845. Probably financed by the poets themselves, their friends, and their families, the book contained eighty-five poems with themes of melancholy, death, suicide, nature, and thwarted love. The book was preceded by a short-lived literary journal in 1843, *L'Album Litteraire, Journal des jeunes gens, amateurs de Litterature*, edited by a white man and whose main contributors were mulattos.[43]

Newspapers continued to spread so rapidly that by 1865, about fifty black newspapers had been founded; most were published weekly, focused on abolitionism, and did not last long. Among the more famous were *The Colored American*, begun in New York in 1837 and edited by Samuel Cornish and Philip A. Bell, and Frederick Douglass' *North Star*, which began publication in 1847. Readers of black newspapers were largely, but not entirely, black, and the tradition of passing newspapers from reader to reader makes total readership hard to estimate.[44]

Three events mark the advent of militant abolitionism in the 1830s: the publication of William Lloyd Garrison's *The Liberator*, the insurrection of Nat Turner, and the appearance of David Walker's *Appeal*. This third event had special significance for blacks. Walker, a free North Carolina black who had moved to Boston, urged both free and enslaved blacks to end slavery. His essay caught the attention of many Americans and helped to galvanize blacks into cooperating with whites in the establishment of the American Anti-Slavery Society. Its declaration of sentiments was drawn up in Philadelphia, and five blacks served on its first board of managers.[45]

Blacks were particularly active in the formation and maintenance of vigilance committees, which helped to facilitate slaves' successful escapes. The committees raised money to assist fleeing slaves and frequently supplied them with food, shelter, and clothing as they made their way to freedom. The first was established in 1819 in Baltimore, which was an early stop for fleeing slaves. New York established a similar committee in 1835 and Philadelphia, two years later. These groups often had socially prominent blacks as their leaders.[46]

Neither the North nor the South was a particularly hospitable place for blacks, particularly in the decades just before the Civil War. Southern states sought ways of removing free blacks from their soil and placed restrictions on the ones who remained as a means of tightening the security of their slaves. Wealthy free blacks in Charleston, increasingly fearful of being enslaved themselves, sent their families outside the state to ensure their safety. In numerous states black preachers were forbidden to preach and schools for free blacks were closed. Texas passed a law in 1840 that required free blacks to leave the state within two years, but later it amended the law to allow blacks to stay if they were already residents when Texas won its independence from Mexico. The North witnessed outbreaks of violence in Ohio in 1830, several places in New York in 1834 and 1839, and in Pennsylvania, where trouble occurred in Philadelphia in 1834, 1835, and 1842 and in Pittsburgh in 1839. Pennsylvania also limited voting rights to white males in 1838.[47]

Partly as a result of these mounting troubles, blacks held a series of national conventions beginning in the 1830s. The first occurred in Philadelphia in 1830, and others were held up until the Civil War. Attended mainly by blacks from the seaboard states and supported by a number of whites, these conventions passed resolutions urging the creation of more black organizations that would defend blacks' civil rights and spoke out against restrictive laws and on various incidents of violence. One meeting in 1843, for instance, in Buffalo concerned itself with enfranchisement and equal rights. It passed resolutions against colonization and pro-slavery churches. Another in 1853 tried to establish a structure of local societies with dues of 1 cent per week paid to a national council and to organize national committees to address manual labor schooling, a protective union, business relations, and publications. Little came of the plan, however.[48]

WHAT WAS LEARNED

By the time the Civil War broke out, blacks outside the South had well-established social structures that offered adult education in civic, intellectual, and spiritual forms. However, access to it was limited to those who were economically secure enough to have sufficient time and initiative to take advantage of it. In a racially oppressive United States these societies grew and flourished.

From churches, societies, and other organizations free adult blacks were able to improve their education and well-being. They learned to take pride in their cultural heritage despite the many negative connotations placed on it in a largely white society. They used these groups to enhance their confidence and self-images with presentations about their African heritage. Through churches, moral improvement groups, and beneficial societies they developed consensus on appropriate behavior and living standards. Many of their societies helped them to develop self-protection as the groups provided a means for collective action against laws and acts of violence directed toward them. Free blacks learned from their groups to survive and progress by using the system of government and business to further their own well-being.

The history of free black adult education demonstrates steady growth and an increasing complexity of organization from the late 1700s to the Civil War. The organizations formed in this period offered a firm foundation for future development of black adult education in the latter half of the nineteenth century.

NOTES

1. Sometimes discussing free blacks' adult education necessitates the use of nineteenth-century distinctions among the race that were then common. In addition to differentiating between free and enslaved blacks, a closer examination of black community life, especially in the South, necessitates more detailed terminology on which social judgments were commonly made. The descriptor African generally referred to people without noticeable traces of white blood; the terms mulatto, colored, and brown were commonly used to describe people with mixed ancestry of black and white. Because these distinctions were critical to the degree to which blacks (in today's sense) were exposed to adult education, the terms above will be often used in this essay. When discussing both African and "colored" people of the nineteenth century, the term black will be used.

2. Allen B. Ballard, *One More Day's Journey: The Making of Black Philadelphia* (Philadelphia: ISHI Publications, 1984), 5, 42.

3. Leonard P. Curry, *The Free Black in Urban America 1800–1850: The Shadow of the Dream* (Chicago: University of Chicago Press, 1981), 197–98; Ballard, *One More Day's Journey*, 41.

4. Curry, *Free Black in Urban America*, 199.

5. Ibid., 197.

6. Michael P. Johnson and James L. Roark, *Black Masters: A Free Family of Color in the Old South* (New York: W. W. Norton & Co., 1984), 212–213; Marina Wikramanayake, *A World in Shadow: The Free Black in Antebellum South Carolina* (Columbia: University of South Carolina Press, 1973), 81.

7. Curry, *Free Black in Urban America*, 204.

8. Ibid., 174–175.

9. Ballard, *One More Day's Journey*, 41–42.

10. Ibid., 47.

11. Curry, *Free Black in Urban America*, 210.

12. John L. Rury, "Philanthropy, Self-help, and Social Control: The New York Manumission Society and Free Blacks, 1785–1810," *Phylon* 46 (1985):238.

13. Daniel Perlman as quoted by Curry, *Free Black in Urban America*, 198.

14. Daughters of Africa Minutes, 1822–1838. #8 American Negro Historical Society Papers, 1790–1901, the Historical Society of Pennsylvania, Philadelphia.

15. Rury, "Philanthropy," 239; Johnson and Roark, *Black Masters*, 222.

16. Curry, *Free Black in Urban America*, 203; Arnett G. Lindsay, "The Economic Condition of the Negroes of New York Prior to 1861," *Journal of Negro History* 6 (April 1921):190–199.

17. Ballard, *One More Day's Journey*, 47–49; Curry, *Free Black in Urban America*, 178–180.

18. Curry, *Free Black in Urban America*, 184; *Sketches of the Higher Classes of Colored Society in Philadelphia by a Southerner* (1841). Reprint. Afro-American History Series, ed. Maxwell Whiteman (Philadelphia: Merrilew and Thompson, 1841). Philadelphia Rhistoric Publications. Library Company of Philadelphia.

19. Ballard, *One More Day's Journey*, 50; William T. Catto, "A Semi-centenary Discourse Delivered in the First African Presbyterian Church Philadelphia, May 1857" (Philadelphia: Joseph M. Wilson, 1857). Curry, *Free Black in Urban America*, 187.

20. Curry, *Free Black in Urban America*, 189–190.

21. Michael P. Johnson and James L. Roark, eds., *No Chariot Let Down: Charleston's Free People of Color on the Eve of the Civil War* (Chapel Hill: University of North Carolina Press, 1984), 50.

22. Du Bois as cited by Ballard, *One More Day's Journey*, 50.

23. Curry, *Free Black in Urban America*, 194–195.

24. Ballard, *One More Day's Journey*, 66; John Hope Franklin, *From Slavery to Freedom: A History of Negro Americans*, 5th ed. (New York: Alfred A. Knopf, 1980), 186.

25. Curry, *Free Black in Urban America*, 204.

26. Ibid., 199.

27. Ibid., 209; Ballard, *One More Day's Journey*, 63.

28. Lindsay, "Economic Condition of the Negroes," 199; Lionel C. Barrow, Jr., "Our Own Cause: Freedom's Journal and the Beginnings of the Black Press," *Journalism History* 4 (Winter 1977–1978):119, 121.

29. Annie Lee West Stahl, "The Free Negro in Ante-bellum Louisiana," *Louisiana Historical Quarterly* 23 (April 1942):305; John Hope Franklin, *The Free Negro in North Carolina, 1790–1860* (New York: Russell & Russell, 1969; rpt. Chapel Hill: University of North Carolina Press, 1943), 163.

30. *Sketches.*

31. Curry, *Free Black in Urban America*, 198.

32. Ballard, *One More Day's Journey*, 64; Johnson and Roark, *Black Masters*, 213.

33. Johnson and Roark, *Black Masters*, 222; Wikramanayake, *World in Shadows*, 85; Curry, *Free Black in Urban America*, 203.

34. Robert A. Warner, "Amos Gerry Beman—1812–1974, a Memoir on a Forgotten Leader," *Journal of Negro History* 22 (April 1937):200–221.

35. Curry, *Free Black in Urban America*, 190.

36. Ibid., 180.

37. Frank B. Woodford and Arthur M. Woodford, *All Our Yesterdays: A Brief History of Detroit* (Detroit: Wayne State University Press, 1969), 156; Curry, *Free Black in Urban America*, 184; Ballard, *One More Day's Journey*, 51.

38. Curry, *Free Black in Urban America*, 187.

39. Ibid., 189.

40. Ibid., 204; Franklin, *From Slavery to Freedom*, 188–189; Ballard, *One More Day's Journey*, 60; Edward Raymond Turner, *The Negro in Pennsylvania: Slavery, Freedom, Servitude, 1639–1861* (New York: Arno Press; rpt. American Historical Association, 1911), 132.

41. Curry, *Free Black in Urban America*, 200, 206–207; *Sketches*, 107–108.

42. Ballard, *One More Day's Journey*, 60; *Sketches*, 109–110; American Negro Historical Society Papers #4748 1853—Joseph C. White, Jr., Historical Society of Pennsylvania.

43. Patricia Brady Schmit, "Cultural Treasure Acquired," *The Historic New Orleans Collection Newsletter* 5 (Fall 1987):2–3.

44. Henk La Brie III, "Black Newspapers: The Roots Are 150 Years Deep," *Journalism History* 4 (Winter 1977–1978):111.

45. Franklin, *From Slavery to Freedom*, 187.

46. Ibid., 188; Curry, *Free Black in Urban America*, 229.

47. Johnson and Roark, *Chariot*, 130; James M. Smallwood, *Time of Hope, Time of Despair: Black Texans During Reconstruction* (Port Washington, N.Y.: Kennikat Press, 1981), 23; Franklin, *From Slavery to Freedom*, 174; Ballard, *One More Day's Journey*, 73.

48. Franklin, *From Slavery to Freedom*, 175; Warner, "Amos Gerry Beman," 207, 212.

II

BLACK ADULT EDUCATION DURING THE CIVIL WAR AND RECONSTRUCTION

3

Black Adult Education during the Civil War, 1861–1865

Bobby L. Lovett

From the beginning of the peculiar institution of slavery, formal education for America's slaves had always been limited. However, because of the Revolutionary War, which encouraged a decline of slavery as well as a reform movement in public education and an evangelist movement during the first forty years of the nineteenth century, Americans developed a more moderate attitude toward educating blacks. By 1830 most Northern blacks were free men and women and could attend some of the local schools. Before 1861 free blacks had quite limited access to institutions of higher education until Lincoln University (1854) in Pennsylvania and Wilberforce University (1856) in Ohio were founded to accommodate them. The African Methodist Episcopal (AME) Church as well as white religious denominations were largely responsible for providing education for Northern blacks. A few white Northern schools, including Oberlin University in Ohio, admitted and matriculated free blacks before 1860.

In the American South, however, technological and political developments caused a resurgence of slavery during the first half of the nineteenth century. Consequently, Southerners began to express conservative attitudes about either educating or emancipating the slaves. Especially after 1831 in the South, most efforts to educate the slaves became taboo. By 1860 only 1,695 of the 7,300 free blacks in Tennessee could read and write, and only 52 blacks were enrolled in Tennessee schools. Throughout the South perhaps less than 4,000 blacks attended schools when the Civil War began.[1]

Ironically, religion before and after the Civil War served as a conduit for delivering education to African Americans. Except for a Southern evangelical movement which began during the 1820s to Christianize and pacify the large slave population, slaves and free blacks would not have had any access to formal education in the antebellum South. Mainly, this Southern evangelical movement was a direct response to the phenomenal growth of abolitionism in the North after 1830—about the time slaveholders had successfully silenced the post–Revolutionary War period's antislavery movement in the South. The Southern evangelical movement was meant to pacify the large, potentially rebellious slave population by teaching them the nonaggression principles of Christianity and, in some cases, to read the Bible. Southern church leaders wanted to demonstrate to Northerners the humanitarian and Christian-like character of the institution of slavery. Even though the spread of religion to the slaves was a Southern white man's scheme to further oppress blacks, the blacks benefited from the plan because perhaps thousands of them were exposed to Bible readings in the Baptist, Methodist, Catholic, and other sabbath schools.

Moreover, because of this display of Southern religious humanitarianism, in Southern cities like Baltimore, Charleston, Nashville, New Orleans, and Richmond, some free blacks were permitted to operate small schools for their children. Often these free black classes operated covertly with the knowledge of the city's elite whites—the free blacks' allies—but with little publicity and without poorer, nonslaveholding whites knowing about the existence of these schools. For example, when whites decided to move against the prosperous free blacks of Nashville during the city's race riot of 1856, a vigilante committee shut down the black schools.

However, slaves and free blacks frequently gained the rudiments of education through their own ingenuity. Many slave children learned to read and write through working in the house with a Christian mistress. Others learned to read by being a companion to a white child, sometimes accompanying the white child to school. These early efforts focused on educating mostly black children in the rudiments of reading, writing, and arithmetic.

Because the slave codes forbade teaching slaves to read and write and because most free blacks had been excluded from whatever public education existed in the states, adult blacks as well as black children needed to be educated when the war began in 1861. Of the nearly 4 million slaves who lived in fifteen slave states and the District of Columbia, only 5 to 10 percent were barely literate. Most of the country's 488,000 free blacks lived in the rural areas of the slave states, where they, too, suffered exclusion and discrimination relative to access to education. At least in the urban areas some 20 percent or more of the slaves were literate and half of the free blacks could read and write.

Few Southern blacks had formal higher education when the war began, although a number of them had enough education to provide some leadership in educating the former slaves. In some rare cases blacks obtained higher education in the South. At least two blacks attended Nashville's Franklin College, a Christian Church (Disciples of Christ)–affiliated institution in which the proprietor tutored the blacks in private lessons. Two of the blacks educated at Nashville's Franklin College, Daniel Wadkins and Samuel Lowery, and at least one who was educated in that city's free black schools,

James T. Rapier, became teachers and leaders for the freedmen during the
Civil War years. Wadkins founded a school for blacks; Lowery became a black
missionary in the Civil War South; and Rapier became Alabama's first black
congressman.[2] Thus the foundation for black education during the Civil War
years was laid by the elements of religion and slavery in antebellum times.

The Civil War was the sociomilitary event that transformed Southern
society and affected the educational development of blacks in profound ways.
As a consequence of the Civil War, African American education underwent
dramatic changes—indeed a revolution. Indubitably, the Civil War served
as a sociomilitary catalyst for the rapid social transformation of ignorant slaves
into literate men and women. Especially in the southern areas of the country
occupied by the Union Army, black leaders, Northern missionaries, and
federal authorities began the massive task of bringing formal education to
thousands of slaves and former slaves (children and adults). Religion and
churches would continue to be important elements in the education of blacks.

Notwithstanding most ordinary thinking, blacks were not only the beneficiaries of this revolution, they were also the initiators of educational
change. Like their northern white counterparts, black leaders viewed education as an essential aspect for uplifting the former slave race and transforming
a dependent black society into a successful, respectable one. This was the moti-
vating theme of black adult education during the Civil War years.

Black and white educators often differed about what kind of education
was best for black people. Many Northerners wanted black men and women
to learn "domestic science"—sewing, cooking, cleaning houses, small trade
and crafts, morality, and the simple rudiments of reading, 'riting, and 'rith-
metic. Black men sought an education that would prepare them to compete
with whites. During the 1850s, for example, the Annual National Colored
Men's Conventions held in the North had proposed agricultural and industrial
training for blacks. This theme was continued by more than thirty State
Colored Men's Conventions held in southern states beginning in 1865. In
black Nashville the leaders went as far as forming the Colored Agricultural
and Mechanical Association and founding the Tennessee Manual Labor
University, which emphasized agriculture, industrial trades, and Christian
principles. When national black leaders, including Frederick Douglass and
John Mercer Langston, visited Nashville, New Orleans, and other freedmen
communities beginning in 1864, they spoke not only about thrift and morality, but also about agricultural and industrial education as well as basic
literacy to uplift the race. By the 1860s the national economy was shifting
from an emphasis on agriculture to a focus on industrialization, and blacks
would have to be prepared to participate in that economic society.

For black men and women, education was protection against racial discrimination. Even the educated black leaders firmly held the philosophy
that people could differentiate between "low-class" and "high-class," but
regardless of color, they would not discriminate against people of the same

education and social class. The educated free blacks, mulattoes, and slaves
believed that until the black masses—women, men, and children—were rid
of their ignorance, all blacks would be continuously embarrassed, ridiculed,
and discriminated against. Consequently, educating the adult blacks as well
as black children was of utmost importance during the Civil War years.

Free blacks were involved in the first efforts to establish schools in the
Civil War South, often before the Northern missionaries could fully organize
white teachers to instruct the freedmen. The earliest extension of education
to adult blacks took place in the East, where the Union Army first invaded
and occupied slave territories. On September 3, 1861, the American Missionary Association (AMA) opened a freedmen's school at Hampton, Virginia.
The teacher was a free black, Mary S. Peake. Charlotte Forten, a wealthy
free black, journeyed from the North to open a school in September 1862
in a brick Baptist church in the Sea Islands.[3] Some of the first black classes
to open during the war years were entirely supported by blacks. In Nashville
black preacher Daniel Wadkins opened a school in the fall of 1862, barely
six months after Union occupation had started. Six black-operated schools
opened in Nashville before the first missionaries arrived in the city.[4] The
pupils in these schools ranged from children to young adults.

Educated blacks felt a keen responsibility to educate fellow blacks. In
Nashville, Samuel Lowery, a free black, returned from Ohio to his place of
birth to serve as a missionary and teach black soldiers in the 2nd U.S. Colored
Light Artillery, Battery A. Lowery was a minister in the Christian Church
(Disciples of Christ) and a lawyer. Another free black traveled to Mississippi
to establish a school. Richard H. Cain and Francis L. Cardozo, among other
free blacks, traveled into the South to help educate the freedmen. Ex-
President John Tyler's former slave opened a school in the basement of
Tyler's Hampton, Virginia, mansion before any Northern missionaries were
on the scene. Free blacks realized that racial oppression caused blacks—
slave and free—to have a common identity and a common goal of achieving
racial equality. To express her concern for black awareness and comradeship
with fellow blacks, and although she was wealthy and well educated, Charlotte Forten included black history and lessons about Haiti's Toussaint L'Ov-
erture when teaching the freedmen of South Carolina's Sea Islands.[5] Forten's
lessons about Toussaint were not mere children's stories; they were lectures
to illustrate black heroes and raise the self-image of grown black men and
women who were made to feel inferior because of their experiences in
slavery. Tennessee's earliest black teachers included men and women: Alfred
Anderson, Amos Beaman, E. C. Branch, Samuel Lowery, Horatio Rankin,
Maria Robinson, John M. Shelton, Molly Tuggle, and Daniel Wadkins.
When the American Baptist Home Mission Society started the "Baptist
College" (Roger Williams University) for black preachers in Nashville in
1864, one of the teachers was black, as were two of the institution's founders
and trustees, local preachers Randall B. Vandavall and Nelson G. Merry.[6]

Most early black educators were self-made men and women who educated themselves, and were probably illiterate throughout most of their childhood. Therefore, black teachers were sensitive to the need to teach grown men and women to read and write. No one ridiculed older blacks for attending school. Blacks believed that no man was too old to learn. Annie L. Casper, a teacher at Murfreesboro, Tennessee, reported that an eighty-five-year-old freedman learned the alphabet in two days so he could "read a chapter in the Bible."[7]

Ordinary black men and women also established schools for the freedmen during the war years. Field hands in a plantation near Selma, Alabama, erected a schoolhouse near where they worked and hired a teacher.[8] Blacks built their own schoolhouse out of logs in a Memphis, Tennessee, contraband camp and diligently attended classes after working all day. In many other places the illiterate freedmen took the initiative to build a schoolhouse and hire a teacher. In Natchez, Mississippi, black women opened three schools for freedmen. In some places, like Knoxville, Tennessee, and Savannah, Georgia, the freedmen formed school associations and taxed themselves to support classes for adults and children. Ultimately, many types of people and various groups contributed to the education of black adults during this period of U.S. history. Historian John Hope Franklin wrote: "The people responsible for establishing these schools—Northerners and Southerners, whites and blacks—made a most significant contribution to the adjustment of Negroes coming out of slavery."[9]

The black church was instrumental in promoting education among black women and men during the Civil War years, mainly because many black church organizations already existed in the South. As a result of the afore-mentioned southern evangelist movement among the slaves, many quasi-independent black church congregations were organized after 1830. These churches were under the control of white congregations and existed in most of the slave states. Nashville had five quasi-independent black church congregations by 1862. Three of these congregations had their own church buildings, which were used for freedmen schools during the war. In New Orleans, Louisville, and other southern towns the black preachers and the black church buildings readily accommodated the first classes for freedmen schools. The Reverend James Lynch started a school for freedmen in Savannah, Georgia, under the auspices of the AME Church.[10]

The AME Church was heavily involved in delivering religion and education to the South's black population. It was founded in the late 1780s, when Northern free blacks rebelled against racial practices in a Methodist Episcopal church. The African Methodists, however, were banned from the South because after the Nat Turner slave rebellion of 1831, Southerners feared the influence of free blacks among the slave population. But when the Union Army began to occupy the South, the AME Church eagerly began to evangelize the region's blacks.

Adult education was a necessary part of the AME Church's program for the freedmen. The AME Church required its ministers to be literate and encouraged education among the membership of newly organized churches. Some illiterate slave preachers refused to permit AME missionaries to address their congregations for fear of losing their leadership positions in a newly organized church. Still, the AME officials strongly believed that the black man must be educated in order to survive in a hostile South. Before many Northern white churches could form and send their freedmen's missions into the South, the AME Church sent black missionaries to major Southern cities that were under the Union Army's occupation. Bishop Daniel Payne received permission from the War Department to visit cities in occupied parts of Virginia and Tennessee in 1863. By December he had organized AME churches as far west as Nashville.[11]

Bringing education and religion to slaves was not an easy task for a black denomination. The AME Church had to fight battles with Northern white Methodists in the quest to gain a foothold in black Southern churches. For a time in 1863 the War Department granted exclusive control of abandoned Methodist Episcopal Church, South church buildings to the white Methodist Episcopal Church of the North. These churches abandoned by pro-Confederate ministers included 200,000 black members and many quasi-independent black congregations and attached slave missions. The AME Church succeeded in getting President Abraham Lincoln to overturn the War Department's decision, thus allowing the AME Church to continue to become a powerful force in providing religion and education to Southern freedmen.[12]

Beginning in 1865, the African Methodists became an important force in providing political education to the South's freedmen. AME ministers were directly involved in the impetus to energize the freedmen to gain and exercise their political rights. James Lynch, among other AME ministers, helped to organize the State Colored Men's Conventions, which became the main black political forums before the freedmen gained the franchise in the South. These Colored Men's Conventions continued for more than twenty years, even after black men became a vital part of the Southern Republican party.

A larger force in providing adult education to the freedmen during the war years was the white Northern church. Soon after the Union Army pacified a certain territory, white Northern churches, abolitionists, and missionaries seized the opportunity to take education to the Southern slaves. By war's end the South was invaded by dozens of mission societies that soon put the black-owned schools out of business because the missionary schools were better financed and often offered free tuition. In Nashville, for example, some fifteen mission societies operated in the city.

Although most of the freedmen welcomed the white Northern teachers, some learned, native free black teachers resented competition from white missionaries. In several cases during the early war years black teachers and white missionaries clashed as both sought to use the same black churches for classes. Sometimes the missionary teacher was forced to leave a black church building and locate the mission school near a contraband camp, where the Union Army officials gave preference to the white educators. In Nashville the John G. McKee school, which was supported by the United Presbyterian Church's Mission Society, was forced out of the First Colored Baptist Church. Then this same freedmen's school had to move from the First Colored Christian Church when black teacher Daniel Wadkins complained. The McKee School moved three times because of jealous black teachers who were already conducting classes on the sites. The blacks often won the tug of war. Yet the whites simply raised funds in the North and built their own facilities. To demonstrate the advantages of financial backing by whites, the McKee school's founders raised money and built a school to handle 800 students as well as night and industrial classes for adults and instruction for black men in the nearby Tennessee State Prison.[13]

There were some advantages to this rivalry and competition between local black teachers and Northern mission teachers. First, many more black students were served because of schools operated by black and white educators. Second, improved facilities and better financing enabled Northern missionaries to extend educational services to black adults, whereas the smaller black private schools included few adult pupils. To illustrate, by 1865, Nashville had fifteen freedmen schools, seventeen teachers, and 1,155 pupils. Throughout the South in Union-occupied territories, similar statistics could be quoted for black education.[14]

Was education for black adults a major focus of educators during the Civil War years? Indeed, partly because an emphasis on adult education among blacks was an inevitable result of slavery, a peculiar institution of human bondage that relied on skilled black labor but forbade the slaves to read and write. This condition existed partly because of negrophobia among the ill-educated whites of the South and partly because of the Southern tradition of anti-intellectualism during antebellum times when slaveholders possessed most of the fertile lands and opposed real estate taxes to support public education even for whites. The elite, wealthy whites and their mostly poor compatriots opposed education for blacks.[15]

Another reason for the focus on black adult education was the attitude of most of the Northern whites who favored a limited education for the adult and adolescent slaves. Yet they never intended to provide blacks enough education to compete with whites. They hoped that adult blacks would receive a minimal education and practical training but remain in the South. This attitude was developed in part because by 1860 more than 1.3 million whites had migrated from the South to better economic opportunities in the West and Midwest, where, unfortunately, they imported negrophobia and further infected Northerners with the disease of racism. An American Freedmen's Commission report stated: "Even in the North this prejudice [against educating blacks] existed among some of the avowed friends of the freed people, and it is a singular fact that one of the early Freedmen's Aid Societies was rent asunder by the unwillingness of a part of its members to cooperate in any movement looking toward the education of the Negro."[16] Thus the impetus for black education, adult and otherwise, had to come from blacks and liberal Northern whites.

As a result of past Southern denial of education to the slaves and the current desire of Northerners to give the former slaves a limited education, the freedmen's schools had to admit children and adults to the classes. An entire race of people, regardless of age, had to be educated. On one large South Carolina plantation the schools opened at twelve noon and closed at three in the afternoon to permit children to go to the field; after the day's work was completed, black adults came to the school.[17] The adults often took their spelling books to the fields to study during periods when the workers rested from the heat of the day. Because of work schedules, opposition from employers, and an unpromising future in the South, many black adults dropped the classes. Yet in many places—especially in urban areas, night schools were operated two to three hours a day, and night industrial classes instructed adult freedmen to sew, cook, and clean homes ("domestic science"). The opportunity to learn some of the simplest domestic tasks had been denied to many of the female slaves who served as field hands. Because 90 percent of the slaves were illiterate when the war began, the freedmen's schools often taught adults and children in the same classes. The ages of the students in Savannah, Georgia's freedmen's schools ranged from five years to over twenty years old.[18]

Despite the racial prejudices harbored by many Northern whites, the Northern missionaries were foremost in the effort to educate the South's black adults; and they had good reason for their efforts. Early in the war the abolitionists argued that blacks were fit to be educated morally and intellectually. Northerners rushed to organize freedmen's societies after the Union Army invaded Southern soil because the founders of these missions believed that the black and the white Southerners were morally and culturally backward. The missionaries felt a keen religious duty to reform all Southerners and supply them with popular intelligence and morality. Thus most of the Civil War schools for blacks included lessons from the Bible and religious instruction.[19] Historian Jacqueline Jones writes: "The freedmen's teachers and sponsoring societies viewed their work as a natural, benevolent continuation of the war."[20]

The Northerners tried to transform black men and women by teaching them to farm better, improve their morals, live with frugality, respect manual labor, and exercise political power. Even the establishment of the Freedmen's Savings and Trust Company Bank by Congress in 1865 was meant to teach adult blacks how to save money and invest in farms. Unfortunately, this banking enterprise failed partly because of fraud heaped on the freedmen. However, the missionaries generally played no cruel tricks on the freedmen, and these Northerners continued to educate freedmen until after the turn of the twentieth century.

The missionaries' success among the freedmen was partly due to the natural combination of religion and education, which complemented each other and jointly impacted the intellectual development of the blacks. Most of the former slaves were already accustomed to religious services, and in fact either had had churches of their own in many towns or had taken part in the invisible, secret churches operated by slave preachers. Such was the case in slave preacher Dick Ham's church, which secretly met in Nashville's Buck's Alley. Before the war many adult slaves and free blacks learned to read in the sabbath schools, like Nashville's First Colored Baptist Church, which began in 1848 as a slave mission of the white First Baptist Church congregation.[21] Near Beaufort, South Carolina, mission teacher Elizabeth H. Botume observed that some freedmen learned to read in Sunday schools held after church services. She reported: "I started the first Sunday brimful of courage. When we reached the schoolhouse we found a crowd of eager and expectant men, women, and children. . . . The older people were also glad to come to Sunday school when it suited their convenience."[22] Near Port Royal, South Carolina, almost the whole adult black population attended Sunday schools.[23]

Throughout the slave states, schools for freedmen children and adults were organized increasingly as the war progressed. In May 1864 Sunday and regular schools were started by an Army chaplain for blacks near Huntsville, Alabama. Missionaries had not settled into the northern Alabama area, where the Union Army's hold on the territory was still shaky. In the border states, on the other hand, the mission groups, the Union Army, and, ultimately, the Freedmen's Bureau operated schools for the blacks by 1865. Night classes for black adults began in Lawrence, Kansas, in December 1861.[24] In Washington, D.C., where only 678 blacks attended schools in 1860 and 33.6 percent of the adult blacks were illiterate, the federal government allocated funds to establish freedmen schools in 1862, although the mission schools enrolled most of the city's black pupils. When a contraband camp was established outside Washington at Arlington, Virginia, the American Tract Society opened a day school for children and night classes for employed black adults. The Tract Society extended its freedmen educational activities into the West and to Nashville, where it established a school in the Edgefield contraband camp. The society used *Freedmen's Primer* and later published a newsletter, *Freedmen*, for black students.[25]

One of the leading missionary societies to foster adult black education was the AMA. It was founded in 1846 when three missionary societies united at an Albany, New York, meeting. The majority of AMA workers were Oberlin College students who supported that institution's antislavery tradition. Because it originated out of the abolitionist movement, the AMA had a natural propensity to help the freedmen. The AMA and other Northern mission societies shared the philosophy that education of the former slaves was a lasting way to socially elevate the former slaves. The AMA established its first freedmen's school at Fort Monroe in September 1861, and by 1864 it had 250 teachers in freedmen's schools. This association crowned its work among the blacks in December 1865 by founding Fisk Free School, which opened its doors in Nashville just eight months after the war ended. Fisk's students' ages ranged from seven to seventy years. The school was chartered as Fisk University in 1867.[26]

The Union Army also played an important role in the education of adult blacks. Blacks worked for the Union Army from the beginning of the war. Usually they were forced (impressed) laborers. When President Lincoln issued his preliminary Emancipation Proclamation on September 22, 1862, to take effect on January 1, 1863, fugitive slaves from Virginia to Tennessee began to flood the Army's camps. The number of blacks within Union Army lines grew by the tens of thousands as the Army advanced deeper into southern slave territories. Soon a few of the Union Army generals saw the need not only to work and house the contrabands, but also to provide rehabilitative services, including education. On January 15, 1862, General William T. Sherman requested authority to place teachers in his military department to prepare the blacks for freedom and independence. Because of pressures from Northern abolitionists, Lincoln not only made slavery a moral issue, but also authorized the induction of slaves into the Union Army in early 1863. Northerners supported the organizing of black regiments because this move further allayed their fears that former slaves would be unable to defend themselves.[27]

Orders to recruit black troops were often accompanied with directives to establish schools for blacks. One such directive was issued by the Army in the Gulf in 1863. A similar order to establish regimental schools was issued by Adjutant General Lorenzo Thomas in the western theater of Arkansas, Kentucky, Mississippi, and Tennessee in September 1864. George L. Stearns, an abolitionist and the commissioner for the recruitment of United States Colored Troops (USCT) in Tennessee, quickly established schools for black regiments in Nashville, Memphis, other parts of Tennessee, and parts of northern Alabama.[28] Stearns ordered the chaplains to teach the black soldiers and appointed William F. Mitchell of the Pennsylvania Freedmen's Aid Association to help in this effort. Mitchell's task was to establish freedmen's schools throughout the Army's Department of the Cumberland— middle Tennessee and northern Alabama.[29] Until the end of the war, the Army's schools were the only classes for blacks in many southern localities.

Black men eagerly sought and supported education during the war years. Historian Joseph Thomas Wilson noted: "The esteem in which education was held by the soldiers of the Black Phalanx, can be judged of best by the efforts they made to educate themselves and to establish a system of education for others of their race."[30] A regimental school was organized at the

Benton Barracks near St. Louis, Missouri. Later black employees and patients at a nearby military hospital were enrolled in a school. A year after the war former members of the USCT organized Lincoln Institute (Lincoln University) at Jefferson City, Missouri.[31] Two brothers who were born in North Carolina returned from their free haven in Ohio and volunteered to teach the freedmen in Sunday classes near Norfolk, Virginia. One of the brothers served in the 2nd USCT Regiment.[32]

The Union Army started schools for black men for a practical reason—to teach the black soldiers to read and write. Illiteracy was a problem because about 95 percent of the USCT troops were mostly illiterate former slaves, not free blacks. Some rudiments of literacy were needed to train noncommissioned officers (e.g., corporals and sergeants) for the companies and regiments. The Army tried to remedy the educational problem by using whites as commissioned officers (and sometimes for noncommissioned positions) in black regiments and by recruiting literate free blacks from the North and South to help fill black regiments. In middle Tennessee hundreds of free blacks were recruited from Ohio to help fill black artillery regiments. Although 13,000 blacks served in black regiments in the Nashville–middle Tennessee area, only approximately 200 native free blacks of military age in the area could read and write. In Memphis, Tennessee, there were thirteen regimental schools for 1,549 regularly attending black soldiers.[33]

Adult illiteracy was not solely a Southern black problem. At least half of the white Confederate soldiers were illiterates, and many Northern blacks could neither read nor write. Thus the commanders of the Northern black regiments also understood the need for regimental schools. The problem was so massive that the Army solicited help from both within and outside its ranks. In the Deep South the Army gave some missionary agents positions as commissioned officers (lieutenants) to operate schools for black soldiers. By giving mission teachers the rank of lieutenant, the Army nullified the authority of prejudiced lower-ranking officers who preferred that blacks not be given time off to learn to read and write. The black soldiers were taxed to help defray the cost of purchasing books and other materials. Members of the 55th USCT Regiment taxed themselves $1 a month to buy books in Memphis, where the black soldiers could be seen reading their spelling books while on duty along the eastern shore of the Mississippi River.[34] The Army made extensive use of chaplains to provide instruction to black adults. Especially as a consequence of instruction from Army chaplains, many black soldiers learned to read and write well enough to earn promotions to corporal and sergeant.[35]

The Army's contribution to black adult education was significant because nearly 180,000 black men served in the military during the Civil War. The positive impact of their contributions was certainly felt in Kentucky, Louisiana, and Tennessee, where more than 20,000 black men enrolled in the Union Army. Yet the difficult task for missionaries and black teachers was not to bring instruction to black soldiers. The real task was to educate ordinary men and women among the slave population.

In South Carolina, where the rebellion began and where less than 5 percent of the blacks could read in 1863, blacks benefited foremost from the missionaries' educational operations. The first systematic attempt to provide education for fugitive slaves was at Port Royal, South Carolina, where the Union Army occupied the Sea Islands in November 1861 and took control of nearly 10,000 slaves. This was the first plantation territory to fall into Union hands. Edward Pierce, a Treasury agent, secured the help of several mission societies to begin schools at Port Royal in March 1862. By 1864 thirty schools enrolled 3,000 pupils at Port Royal.[36] Soon the Port Royal experiment spread throughout occupied areas in South Carolina, where thousands of black children and adults were introduced to formal education. Again, blacks were among the many mission teachers. Susie King Taylor escaped from slavery in Georgia and later taught black soldiers in South Carolina.[37] In some towns black women attended industrial schools, where they sewed and made clothes from discarded Army garments and cloth donated by Northerners. By the summer of 1865 Charleston had five night schools for adult blacks.[38] Although the number of adults attending the schools tended to decrease after the first year of freedom, the desire of black adults to have their children educated seemed to grow stronger as Reconstruction progressed.[39]

In neighboring North Carolina and Tennessee, Union occupation also brought educational benefits to the freedmen. Army chaplains held evening schools for the adult contrabands. Almost all black contrabands were slaves, although North Carolina and Tennessee had a significant number of free blacks, of whom about 57 percent were literate in 1861.[40] Especially in Tennessee, large numbers of fugitive slaves lived in contraband camps near towns and Union army forts. These concentrations of black population made it easier for the Union Army to gather laborers and soldiers and for the missionaries to educate and provide other services. During the fall of 1862 Lucinda Humphrey, a nurse from the North, opened a school for black employees of an Army hospital in Memphis, Tennessee.[41] Undoubtedly this missionary school included many women as pupils because black women provided a great deal of the labor force for military hospitals in occupied Tennessee.

Equal work and equal benefits were a tradition in black society. Black women had been a significant part of the labor force during slavery, when they worked side by side with the men in the fields. The Union Army continued that social tradition by working black women—but not white women—on hard labor projects, including building forts and railroads. Hundreds of black women were impressed along with black men and children to build the Northwestern Railroad in middle Tennessee in 1863–1864. Additionally, black women pushed wheelbarrows, washed clothes, cooked meals, and drove wagons during the construction of Fort Negley, the largest Union Army fort west of Washington, D.C. Like the men, the women earned $10 a month.[42]

Consequently, black women also became the beneficiaries of adult education when black men benefited from Yankee educators. In many of the Union-occupied towns of the South the mission schools taught black women the art of domestic service, including cooking, cleaning house, and sewing. In some cases the local office for the Bureau for the Commission for the Recruitment of United States Colored Troops provided a service to place black women in the homes of Union Army officers and other whites.[43]

Later there would be consequences of these Civil War developments in black education. Black women not only got an equal start in the schools with black men, but also would dominate the graduating classes in southern black high schools near the turn of the twentieth century, when segregation laws and white racist practices limited the occupational outlook for young black men. Partly because the Army and the missionaries confined the training of black women to "domestic science" after the war, the black women would find themselves restricted to housekeeping jobs in large southern cities like Memphis, Charleston, Richmond, and New Orleans. Whether they wanted to or not, black women would dominate the domestic service jobs in racially segregated Southern society for generations to come; precisely because of this dim prospect of employment, black families increasingly sent the female child (more often than the male child) to normal schools and colleges to become a teacher rather than to work in a house where a black woman was vulnerable to the sexual advances of white men.

Black progress in adult education was difficult during the war years. Confederate raiders frequently burned down the freedmen's schoolhouses. Terrorists harassed the teachers, and employers intimidated black workers who attempted to attend day or night classes. Most problematic for the Army were native whites in the Union Army who sometimes destroyed black schoolhouses because they resented the fact that the blacks were being educated while some poor whites remained illiterate. Amos McCollough, a black teacher at Magnolia, South Carolina, was told to close the school or it would be burned down.[44] In some areas the white mission teachers had to live with black families rather than be isolated and vulnerable to constant death threats. In Tennessee and other places in the South the Freedmen's Bureau spent money to rebuild a number of schoolhouses burned by nightriders. The Bureau raised money by taxing blacks (aged one to fifty-five years) and charging the pupils a $5 tuition fee.[45] Indeed, black adult attendance at these schools declined after 1865, especially after Union Army occupation ended.

Yet adult education became an accepted reality in the black community. At least 366 freedmen's societies had operated in the South during the war and for years thereafter to realize this development. Perhaps one-half million blacks—adults and children—had been exposed to some formal education by 1865. As a result, an education system was established in southern black communities. In 1865 Tennessee reported 51 schools, 105 teachers, and 7,360 students in the black communities.[46] Throughout the South at least 500 teachers were in the freedmen's schools at war's end.[47]

More important, black adult education continued in the form of colleges for the freedmen. In 1865 the AMA founded Atlanta University, and organized the forerunner of Fisk University. Also in 1865 the American Baptist Home Mission Society helped to establish Virginia Union University and Shaw University.[48] The next year this same Society chartered Nashville's "Baptist College" under the name Roger Williams University.[49] These and other former freedmen's schools continued to include grammar and grade school lessons for the many young black men and women who came ill-prepared to do high school– and college-level work.

NOTES

1. Carter G. Woodson, *The Education of the Negro Prior to 1861* (New York: Arno Press, 1968), 219, 220, 224–225.

2. See Loren Schweninger, *James T. Rapier and Reconstruction* (Chicago: University of Chicago Press, 1978).

3. Charlotte Forten, "Life on the Sea Islands," *Atlanta Monthly* 13 (May-June 1864):588–589, 591–594, 666–667, in Thomas R. Frazier, *Afro-American History: Primary Resources*, 2nd ed. (Chicago: Dorsey Press, 1988), 129–137; John W. Blassingame, *Black New Orleans: 1860–1880* (Chicago: University of Chicago Press), 25–47.

4. George W. Hubbard, *History of the Colored Schools of Nashville* (Nashville: Author, 1872), 6–7.

5. Bell I. Wiley, *Southern Negroes, 1861–1865* (Baton Rouge: Louisiana State University Press, 1965), 262, 264–265, 281; Leon F. Litwack, *Been in the Storm So Long: The Aftermath of Slavery* (New York: Random House, 1979), 494–495; David Mills and Bobby L. Lovett, "Samuel and Peter Lowery, a Profile Essay." Paper presented at the 4th Annual Local Conference on Afro-American Culture and History, Nashville, 1985, 1–2.

6. Amos G. Beaman to G. Whipple, The Amos Beaman Papers, Beinecke Library at Yale University, New Haven, quoted in Joe Richardson, "The Negro in Post-Civil War Tennessee: A Report by a Northern Missionary," *Journal of Negro Education* 35 (1965):419–424; Memphis *Bulletin*, January 7, 1865; Hubbard, *History of the Colored Schools in Nashville*, 1–17; Gilbert E. Govan and J. W. Livingood, "Chattanooga Under Military Occupation, 1863–1865," *Journal of Southern History* 17 (1951):23–37; J. W. Alvord, *Report on Schools and Finances, 1865–1866* (Washington, D.C.: Government Printing Office, 1866), 1–18.

7. *Second Annual Report of the Western Freedmen's Aid Commission* (Cincinnati: WFAC, 1865), 40, quoted in Paul D. Phillips, "A History of the Freedmen's Bureau in Tennessee" (Ph.D. diss., Vanderbilt University, 1964), 179, 187.

8. Litwack, *Been in the Storm So Long*, 475.

9. John Hope Franklin, *From Slavery to Freedom: A History of Negro Americans*

(New York: Alfred A. Knopf, 1980), 219; see Leo McGee, "Adult Education for the Black Man in America, 1860–1880: An Historical Study of the Types" (Ph.D. diss., Ohio State University, 1972).

10. William Edward B. Du Bois, *Black Reconstruction in America, 1860–1880* (New York: Atheneum, 1935, 1977), 645.

11. Clarence Earl Walker, *A Rock in a Weary Land: The African Methodist Episcopal Church During the Civil War and Reconstruction* (Baton Rouge: Louisiana State University Press, 1982), 21, 51, 75, 79, 84–85; Daniel A. Payne, *Recollections of Seventy Years* (New York: Arno Press, 1968), 154–156; see also Ralph E. Morrow, *Northern Methodism and Reconstruction* (East Lansing: Michigan State University Press, 1956), and A. F. Beard, *A Crusade of Brotherhood* (Boston: Pilgrim Press, 1909).

12. Walker, *Rock in a Weary Land*, 21, 51, 75, 79, 84–85.

13. *History of the Freedmen's Mission of the Presbyterian Church, 1865–1902* (Knoxville, Tenn.: Presbyterian Church, 1902), 1–8, 81.

14. Clinton B. Fisk, Report on Schools, October 1, 1865, in the List of Letters Relating to Seized Lands and Properties, and Report, 1864–1869, Freedmen's Bureau Records, Record Group 105, Tennessee, National Archives and Record Service, Washington, D.C.; Benjamin Brawley, *A Social History of the American Negro* (London: Collier Books, 1921), 247, 253–254, 265–266.

15. Carter G. Woodson, *The Education of the Negro Prior to 1861* (Washington, D.C.: Associated Publishers, 1919), 240; Robert S. Bahney, "Generals and Negroes: Education of Negroes by the Union Army, 1861–1865" (Ph.D. diss., University of Michigan, 1965), 31; Kelly Miller, "The Education of the Negro," in *Report of the Commission of Education of the Years 1900–1904*, 2 vols. (Washington, D.C.: Government Printing Office, 1902), I, 748.

16. *The Results of Emancipation in the United States of America* by a Committee of the American Freedmen's Commission, quoted in Du Bois, *Black Reconstruction*, 245–246.

17. Du Bois, *Black Reconstruction*, 645.

18. Ibid.; Robert E. Purdue, "The Negro in Savannah, 1865–1900" (Ph.D. diss., University of Chicago, 1971), 33, 129, 132.

19. Blassingame, *Black New Orleans*, 25–47.

20. Jacqueline Jones, *Soldiers of Light and Love: Northern Teachers and Georgia Blacks, 1865–1873* (Chapel Hill: University of North Carolina Press, 1980), 15, 162.

21. B. L. Lovett, unpublished manuscript on black Nashville, 1780–1930 (Nashville 1988), 161.

22. Elizabeth H. Botume, *First Days Amongst the Contrabands* (Boston: Lee & Sheppard Publishers, 1893), 100, 102.

23. James M. McPherson, *The Struggle for Equality: Abolitionists and the Negro in the Civil War and Reconstruction* (Princeton, N.J.: Princeton University Press, 1964), 165.

24. Du Bois, *Black Reconstruction*, 645–667; John B. Meyers, "The Education of the Alabama Freedmen During Presidential Reconstruction, 1865–1867," *Journal of Negro Education* 40 (1971):163–171; Victor B. Howard, "The Struggle for Equal Education in Kentucky, 1866–1884," *Journal of Negro Education* 46 (1977):305–328; Albert Castel, "Civil War Kansas and the Negro," *Journal of Negro History* 51 (1966):125–138.

25. John V. Cimprich, *Slavery's End in Tennessee, 1861–1865* (University: University of Alabama Press, 1985), 79; Melvin R. Williams, "Blacks in Washington, D.C."

(Ph.D. diss., Johns Hopkins University, 1975), 81–82, 115, 119, 241; Felix James, "The Establishment of the Freedmen's Village in Arlington, Virginia," *Negro History Bulletin* 33 (April 1970):223.

26. Richard B. Drake, "The American Missionary Association and the Southern Negro, 1861–1888" (Ph.D. diss., Emory University, 1957), 1–4, 10, 36, 58, 130, 154; Joe M. Richardson, *A History of Fisk University, 1865–1946* (University: University of Alabama Press), 2–3, 7, 59, 78.

27. Phillips, "History of the Freedmen's Bureau in Tennessee," 8; see V. Jacque Vogue, *Free But Not Equal: The Midwest and the Negro During the Civil War* (Chicago: University of Chicago Press, 1967); Brawley, *Social History of the American Negro*, 253–254.

28. Wiley, *Southern Negroes*, 265, 269, 270.

29. Bahney, "Generals and Negroes," 198–199; William B. Armstrong, "Union Army Chaplains and the Education of the Freedmen," *Journal of Negro History* 52 (1967):104–115.

30. Joseph T. Wilson, *The Black Phalanx: A History of the Negro Soldier in the United States in the Wars of 1775–1812, 1861–65* (Hartford, Conn.: American Publishing Company, 1890), 503; see also John W. Blassingame, "Negro Chaplains in the Civil War," *Negro History Bulletin* 27 (October 1963):22–23; J. T. Wilson, *Emancipation: Its Cause and Progress from 1481 B.C. to A.D. 1875* (New York: Negro Universities Press, 1882, 1969), 212–213.

31. Bahney, "Generals and Negroes," 198–199.

32. Earle H. West, "The Harris Brothers: Black Northern Teachers in the Reconstruction South," *Journal of Negro Education* 48 (1978):126–138.

33. Bobby L. Lovett, "The Negro's Civil War in Tennessee: 1861–1865," *Journal of Negro History* 60 (1976):37–54.

34. John W. Blassingame, "The Union Army as an Institution for Negroes, 1862–1865," *Journal of Negro Education* 34 (1965):152–159; see also U.S., the Negro in the Military Service of the United States, 1639–1886, 5 rolls, microfilm, Record Group 94, National Archives and Record Service, Washington, D.C.; see Robert Cowden, *A Brief Sketch of the Organization and Services of the Fifty-ninth Regiment of the United States Organization and Services of the Fifty-ninth Regiment of the United States Colored Infantry* (Dayton, Ohio: State Historical Society, 1883), 60–61.

35. Armstrong, "Union Army Chaplains and the Education of the Freedmen," 104–115.

36. See Joel Williamson, *After Slavery: The Negro in South Carolina During Reconstruction, 1861–1877* (Chapel Hill: University of North Carolina Press, 1965); Edward L. Pierce, *The Negroes at Port Royal: Report of E. L. Pierce, Government Agent, to the Honorable Salmon P. Chase, Secretary of the Treasury* (Boston: R. F. Wallcut, 1862); Willie Lee Rose, *Rehearsal for Reconstruction* (New York: Bobbs-Merrill Co., 1964); William H. Pease, "Three Years Among the Freedmen: William C. Gannett Under the Port Royal Experiment," *Journal of Negro History* 42 (1957):98–117.

37. James M. McPherson, *The Negro's Civil War: How American Negroes Felt and Acted During the War for the Union* (New York: Random House, 1965), 139–141.

38. Bahney, "Generals and Negroes," 31, 89, 175.

39. Williamson, *After Slavery*, 233, 236.

40. See Horace James, *Annual Report of the Superintendent of Negro Affairs in North Carolina, 1864* (Boston: W. F. Brown & Co., 1865); Sing-Nan Fen, "Notes on the

Education of Negroes in North Carolina During the Civil War," *Journal of Negro Education* 36 (1967):24–31; Wiley, *Southern Negroes*, 261–294.

41. L. Humphrey to A. Fiske, Memphis, January 1, 1863; L. Humphrey to the AMA office, Memphis, May 19, 1863, in the American Missionary Association papers, Amistad Center, New Orleans.

42. Bobby L. Lovett, "Nashville's Fort Negley: Symbol of Blacks' Involvement with the Union Army," *Tennessee Historical Quarterly* 61 (1982):3–22.

43. Nashville *Daily Union*, November 29, 1865.

44. Litwack, *Been in the Storm So Long*, 487–488.

45. Du Bois, *Black Reconstruction*, 644–645.

46. Phillips, "History of the Freedmen's Bureau in Tennessee," 177.

47. McPherson, *Struggle for Equality*, 172.

48. Mary Frances Berry and John W. Blassingame, *Long Memory: The Black Experience in America* (New York: Oxford University Press, 1982), 26.

49. Ruth M. Powell, *Ventures in Education with Black Baptists in Tennessee* (New York: Carlton Press, 1979), 18–19.

4

Schooling for a Freed People: The Education of Adult Freedmen, 1861–1871

Ronald E. Butchart

One of the more striking features of Southern black education during the American Civil War and the early years of Reconstruction is the fact that the struggle for education for the freedmen was, almost by definition, adult education.[1] As in perhaps no other era of black education, during those perilous and portentous days, little distinction was made between the education provided to black adults and that provided to black children. The primary concern among those who sought to control and direct the schooling of the freedmen was the black adult, the women and men just emerging from the house of bondage. And Southern black adults, by their actions, were most responsible for the variety of schools that emerged in the South, serving both black children and white children, by the declining years of Reconstruction.

Adult ex-slaves were the focus of freedmen's education for obvious reasons. They were the historical actors of the moment. The education of children might tell in a generation or two, but white America claimed to see a problem more urgent than a generation's intervention could remedy. "Without some help, direction, and restraint," wrote one group of Northern whites in early 1862, "these unhappy creatures . . . may sink into a deeper misery than even they have known, and become not only vicious, but ungovernable and very dangerous." It was the adults, trained under the lash, that the freedmen's aid societies sought to influence. Francis Wharton appealed for support for the Protestant Episcopal Freedmen's Commission in terms common to much of the dialogue on freedmen's education. The North, he argued, had "removed from negro labor the impetus of compulsion, and not yet applied to it the impetus of intelligence and conscientious motive; and, unless the last impetus be applied, we can expect nothing but wreck." John W. Alvord, the Freedmen's Bureau Superintendent of Education, had black adults in mind when he remarked that "this great multitude," if denied education, would "quickly sink into the depravities of ignorance and vice; free to be what they please...carried away with every species of evil."[2] Freedmen's education, then, at least in its early years, was concerned foremost with Southern black adults; the education of the rising generation was not slighted, but neither was it the first issue. The two were virtually never distinguished.

Adult ex-slaves were also the historical actors in another immediate sense, but one overlooked by their white contemporaries and by their subsequent historians. That is, they were not merely the passive objects of schooling. On the contrary, they demanded education, for themselves and for their children, and they created the means to appropriate the knowledge they needed for the social and productive relations being created by emancipation. As the freedmen in one organization described themselves in 1867, "here is a race just escaped out of a worse than Egyptian bondage; and, almost as soon as the shackles have fallen from their limbs, they set themselves to organize a great system of education for their people." "Great efforts are made" by the freedmen, wrote the Freedmen's Bureau Assistant Commissioner for Alabama in 1867, "to support their children while in school, and among themselves primers are found in every situation, laid away for use during the intervals of labor." A teacher for the New England Freedmen's Aid Society wrote:

Old and young are eager to learn. When I go into their cabins, I find the mothers in the midst of their children trying to learn from *them* what *they* have learned during the day. Very often I see men and boys who have to work in the cotton-field from sunrise till dark, sitting under a tree studying a Primer during the few moments of rest they are allowed after dinner. And it is wonderful how much they will learn in these ways.

Contemporary accounts were filled with reports of similar incidents.[3] Clearly, schooling was sought, and schooling was given. Yet, just as emancipation yielded "one kind of freedom" in the economic arena, and not necessarily that kind which the African American sought, so the struggle for knowledge yielded one kind of schooling, not demonstrably that kind which held the greatest promise of black freedom.[4]

At least five distinct institutions and a distinctive curriculum evolved in the decade after the bombardment of Fort Sumter, created by and for the freedmen. Each of those educational responses concealed a tension over ends. For many Northern white sponsors, for instance, through education the freedmen were "to be disposed of by us, either to our great benefit, or our immeasurable loss—perhaps ruin." Or, as Edward S. Philbrick wrote, the freedmen's aid movement had to wield firm paternalistic control "if we mean to make men of them." Yet for the freed slave a contradictory assumption was at work, revealed in William Robinson's exclamation: "How eagerly [the freed slave] embraces the first opportunity to emancipate him-self!"[5] For the former, emancipation was a white project, with schools serving as a means to control and channel emancipation's social and political effects with an eye toward white prerogatives. For the latter, emancipation might well transcend white agendas; the lust for learning symbolized independence from white domination. Schools were central to both projects, but embodied frequently divergent aims.

Between those conflicting views of education, race, and society there hangs a tale, one that illuminates an important corner of the grave story that played itself out in the 1860s and 1870s. It is a story touching the disposition of power in post-bellum America. We shall pursue it here by exploring the institutions and curriculum of adult black education, and the roles of black women and men in shaping portions of that education. That exploration may allow us to point toward some understanding of the role of a conflicted insti-tution—schooling for an oppressed people—in contributing to historical pro-cesses.[6]

The most pervasive and most far-reaching form of adult education was the traditional setting of teacher and schoolhouse. Although usually thought of as the setting for children's education, for much of the 1860s the black schoolhouse in the South lacked age-specificity. Reports from throughout the South remarked that schools "were highly prized and eagerly attended by old and young." Drawings and engravings from the period depict crowded classrooms filled with adults of all ages studying beside children and youths. A convention of freedmen's aid societies, referring to the adult community, remarked: "It is a cause for gratitude . . . that, as they come forth from their long night of thralldom to take a new position in the world, this people manifest this passion to read." One of the few reports that gives information on age, detailing attendance at schools supported by secular aid societies in Cincinnati and Chicago, indicated that more than 35 percent of the 7,463 students in those schools in 1866 were over sixteen years of age. The largest Quaker group involved in freedmen's education reported an age range of five to forty-five in its schools.[7]

The use of the primary school classroom for adult education declined in the years immediately after the close of the war, however. Comments on "the men and women 'fighting with the letters,' " or "the poor old worn white head bent over its pages" began to disappear from reports and letters. In a variety of ways, teachers communicated the expectation that day school was for children. Simultaneously, new regularities and dependencies in eco-nomic roles for adult freedmen, often resulting in less discretionary time than they expected (and less than they had a right to expect) in a state of freedom, meant that they would need to seek other means of extending their learning.[8]

As some freedmen made their way into classrooms, others, particularly young black men, gained their first contact with formal education in the

Union Army. There, escaped slaves and men freed by the Emancipation Proclamation served first as laborers and later as soldiers. At their own behest, and with the occasional assistance of chaplains and literate Northern soldiers, they found the time to struggle toward literacy. Arnold T. Needham, chaplain with the 13th Illinois Volunteer Infantry, observed one of hundreds of such incidents:

Since being settled in this camp, a number of the negroe [sic] cooks—assisted and encouraged by the soldiers—have procured primers and applied themselves to the acquirements of reading and spelling. They have come to me from time to time for aid; and having put up a small log-house, I gather about 15 or 20 around me each afternoon, to teach their dormant ideas how to shoot.[9]

Likewise, S. G. Swain, a second lieutenant in a black regiment, wrote to his sister that the black soldiers were "very anxious to learn," although the Army worked them extremely hard on fatigue and guard duty. In many companies, black troops received formal instruction, frequently paying $1 or more a month out of their meager Army pay, but most literacy training in the Army appears to have been more informal: "Negro servants of officers studied at the campfires of fellow servants," Congressman T. D. Eliot reported. But whether formal or informal, this schooling was not insignificant. Eliot estimated that by the end of the war, 20,000 black soldiers "could read intelligently, and a much larger number were learning the first lessons."[10]

For a brief time white educators spoke of the education of black soldiers as "the mightiest lever in the elevation of the race." They would return to the black community as leaders, "the heroes, the models of admiration and imitation." They had "arms in their hands, the physical guarantee of permanent freedom, and our schools will arm their minds with knowledge." But the idea of armed and educated freedmen evoked images of independence and assertiveness out of keeping with the evolving perceptions of white Americans after the war. During the early years of Reconstruction, the Freedmen's Bureau, particularly, softened the image and idea of education within the black troops. It was enough that these newly literate men should aspire to be teachers. Alvord asserted that many freedmen's teachers were returning soldiers, and at least one Bureau official convinced local Army authorities to establish night school for black soldiers with the intention of enticing them to become teachers in the freedmen's schools when they left the service.[11]

Night schools were a third mode of instruction available to the freedmen. Developing simultaneously with the freedmen's use of the primary classroom and the emergence of schooling in the black regiments, night schools became the more usual means to adult literacy in mid-decade. They were frequently taught by the same teachers who spent their days teaching in the regular school, responding to the freedmen's overwhelming demand for adult education. William Burgess, one such teacher, wrote from Yorktown, Virginia:

"I have ninety men and women every evening, and am obliged to turn away a great many, but they do not more than half of them go away; they stand round the window, and some say their lessons in concert with those inside, they are so anxious to learn." A white teacher in New Orleans taught an evening class of 100 freedmen ranging in age from twenty to seventy years; an observer of his classroom asserted that "with the right kind of teachers, . . . the adults may be bro't to the knowledge & use of letters more rapidly than the children." A young black teacher from Geneva, New York, assisted by two other teachers, found himself with a day class of more than 170 students, with another fifty-six adults asking for class every evening and on Saturdays.[12]

Nathan Condol's ratio of day to night students—about one-third as many night as day students—appears to have been representative in 1866, but thereafter those proportions declined. The American Missionary Association (AMA) reportedly taught nearly 29,000 day students and 9,800 night students in 1867; two years later the respective numbers were 23,000 and 4,000; by 1871 fewer than 10,000 students attended AMA day schools, compared with 873 night students. However, by that latter date, formal modes of secondary and postsecondary schooling were in place serving adult freedmen. Surveying the South in 1867, the Freedmen's Bureau found that 23 percent of freedmen's schools reporting were night schools; by 1870, 10.5 percent were night schools. A combination of forces contributed to the erosion in the number of night schools and adult students in them: a declining willingness on the part of teachers to put in the sacrificial hours required to teach both day and night school; increasing educational opportunities in other institutions; and decreasing financial and temporal resources on the part of the freedmen to invest in schooling after days of agricultural labor.[13]

A further factor in the decline in night schools was, undoubtedly, the growing institutionalization of black education and the resulting growth of a fourth form of adult education, formal secondary schooling. Various forms of secondary education emerged in the second half of the 1860s. They included advanced classes within the freedmen's schools; academies, institutes, and high schools; normal schools or, more frequently in the early years, normal classes within existing schools; and the pioneer black colleges, which until the 1870s at least, provided more secondary and preparatory training than higher education.[14]

Teacher training was by far the most important activity of freedmen's secondary training in this decade. The aid societies were painfully aware that they could not muster the resources necessary to provide Northern teachers for all the demand generated by the freedmen. They needed to create a cadre of Southern black teachers as quickly as possible. Further, the more liberal, primarily secular organizations were committed from the beginning to fostering indigenous, self-educating black communities. For them, training black teachers in decentralized, community-centered normal

classes in day schools was the surest way to put the power of education in
the hands of the black community.[15]

On the other hand, more powerful groups put forward a more limiting
agenda. For them the issue was not to unleash power, but to control it. The
Methodist Episcopal Freedmen's Aid Society put the issue bluntly.
"Whoever furnishes the educators of a people, controls the current of
thought," it declared in 1869, "and molds future generations." These groups
built specialized teacher training institutions, centralized, removed from the
communities they were ostensibly to serve. As James D. Anderson has demonstrated for a later period, these schools strove to nurture a corps of teachers
imbued with a conservative social and political perspective, in the conviction
that, as W. D. Siegfried put it at the time, teacher training would thereby
"mould the minds which are in turn to mould the masses of the South."
The rapid expansion of teacher training among the freedmen in the late
1860s reflected, meanwhile, the demand from the freedmen themselves for
the opportunity to educate their own people.[16]

The fifth form of black adult education developed during the 1860s was
the industrial school. Although the least important form of education in terms
of its availability—there were probably never more than fifty industrial
schools, and by 1869 only seventeen were still in operation[17]—it was important for two reasons. First, the industrial school was the only institution
for adult freedmen's education for which there seems to have been no demand from the freedmen. It was purely a product of the imagination of white
sponsors of freedmen's education, and as such may reveal much about the
content of their vision. Second, although distinct from the much-debated
industrial education that came to dominate thinking about education for
African Americans subsequent to the era of freedmen's education, these
industrial schools carried the seed of that later heresy.

The industrial schools served exclusively women and girls, teaching them
sewing and other aspects "of the useful arts of housewifery." Only in "some
of the schools," according to John Alvord, were "lessons also given in reading
and writing." Their curious name apparently came not from any sense that
they prepared their inmates for industrial pursuits, but rather from their
intention "to teach habits of industry." Never mind that the ex-slaves had,
through their unrequited toil, built the sugar, cotton, and tobacco economies;
Northern whites were convinced that they lacked the "careful habits, the
notions of economy, and the feelings of self-reliance" they would need if
they were to be integrated into a free labor economy. The industrial schools
intended to remedy that apparent deficiency.[18]

The industrial school also had its perfectly practical side. The clothing that
was made by the women was sold, helping to defray the costs of aiding the
freedmen. Further, it provided a "satisfactory method of equalizing the burden" of Northern charity "by allowing those who are able, among the colored
people, to contribute their portion." The industrial schools appear to have

drawn their inspiration from the similarly named industrial schools in England and Europe, institutions intended to teach order and industriousness to the urban poor, and whose curriculum for girls and women was sewing. Indeed, one group of English Quakers sent George Dixon to the Southern states with the express purpose of establishing industrial schools, although the idea seems to have preceded his visit by three or more years.[19]

The institutional response to black adult education, then, embraced five distinct forms of schooling. A further feature of adult freedmen's education was not institutional, but curricular. Many of the freedmen's educators rejected the traditions of the Northern common school, with its efforts to provide a schooling that was common to all. They sought instead to develop a specific curriculum peculiar to the emerging black schools, a distinctive curriculum that reflected the fears and fantasies of its authors' imaginations. Significantly, while the institutional response, excepting industrial schools, was as much a response to freedmen's demands as to white intentions, the curricular response came solely from the educators.

The curricular response came remarkably swiftly. The earliest effort to educate Southern blacks behind Union lines dates from late months in 1861; the major secular organizations emerged in the early months of 1862. Yet the American Tract Society (ATS), the primary publisher of school papers and textbooks for the freedmen, was printing its first tracts for the black schools in February 1862. It claimed then to have twenty-four titles in press "which we have got up on purpose for them." Within a year the society had gone beyond tracts, publishing books intended for the freedmen's schools. At least thirteen titles appeared, including spellers, primers, a set of three graded readers, and didactic books intended to counsel adult freedmen in matters of religion, politics, conduct, and culture. Additionally, a monthly school paper, *The Freedman*, came from the tract society's presses beginning in 1864. These materials were supplied free of charge, or for nominal cost, making them attractive even to teachers who might have hesitated over their racial and ideological tone.[20]

The extent to which freedmen's education was viewed as adult education can be seen clearly in the curricular material produced by the ATS. The primers and readers occasionally had pictures and stories aimed at a child's experiences and imagination, but the bulk of the material, and virtually all of the didactic books, spoke to adults. They portrayed the Southern black adult community in negative, stereotypic racial images, and contrasted its imputed habits with the graces and sensibilities presumably practiced by whites, both Northern and Southern. Intended to mold consciousness and behavior along racially, economically, and politically conservative lines, the messages this material gave to African Americans emerging from racial slavery was unlikely to promote independence or power.[21]

There were freedmen's educators who dissented from using special curricular materials for the freedmen. There were also writers who created a less didactic, more positive literature for the freedmen. Leaders of the American Freedmen's Union Commission deplored ATS publications, asking,

Are not the so-called Freedmen to learn the same language, spell the same words, and read the same literature as the rest of us? Then why in the name of common sense not learn out of the same primers? If we wish to abolish these odious caste distinctions from our laws, why ingrain [them] in our educational system by the very titles of our books?

Restating the basic tenet of the common school tradition, the Commission asserted that the freedmen were "entitled . . . to nothing inferior or different from that used by the rest of us." Longtime abolitionist Lydia Maria Child edited *The Freedmen's Book*, a remarkable collection of writings by and about African Americans. The book had the explicit intention of engendering racial pride and fostering high aspirations. In marked contradiction to the ATS material, the book affirmed the intellectual and moral equality of the races. Similarly, the African Civilization Society, a Northern black organization, sought to compete with ATS's monthly school paper. The Society's *Freedmen's Torchlight* followed the same format as *The Freedman*, but its content diverged sharply. It openly advocated black pride and black control of freedmen's education.[22]

Yet these dissenters had little impact. The ATS and the freedmen's education organizations supporting it ignored the plea for equality in curricular material. Its publication had the warm support of the Freedmen's Bureau Commissioner, Gen. O. O. Howard; the Bureau's Superintendent of Schools, John W. Alvord, ordered numerous copies "for adults in the night schools." Meanwhile, Child's book seems never to have been acknowledged, and certainly never endorsed, by officials of the Bureau or leaders of the more conservative wing of the freedmen's education movement. Meanwhile the *Freedmen's Torchlight* failed for lack of adequate financing.[23]

Education for adult Southern blacks has never experienced a more dramatic period of change than the decade of the 1860s. In that short time, in the midst of civil upheaval and economic chaos, emancipation, war, and reconstruction, blacks and a variety of white allies created opportunities for literacy and enlightenment unprecedented in the history of any oppressed people. However, nothing so momentous as the reallocation of power in postslavery society could be uncontested, and the form and content of those opportunities were unmistakably contested terrain, even among those struggling for schooling. What we have seen here was not the final disposition of the contest, but only the preliminary skirmishes in one corner of a much larger arena. They were crucial skirmishes, however, in which the black community marked itself as a central player, and in which, simultaneously, whites sought to define the meaning of literacy and enlightenment in ways that shifted the contest onto terrain more conducive to continued hierarchical social organization. The future of adult Southern black education would be mediated for the next century by the institutional and curricular patterns hammered out in that decade. Central to that mediation was the use of the institutions and curriculum to achieve black aspirations, on the one hand, or to deflect and redefine those aspirations in line with white agendas. The question of whether black adult education would be wielded for full emancipation or a redefined domination was posed but not resolved in the first decade after legal emancipation.

NOTES

1. This aspect of freedmen's education has, however, largely escaped specific notice in the literature. On freedmen's education, see Ronald E. Butchart, *Northern Schools, Southern Blacks, and Reconstruction: Freedmen's Education, 1862–1875* (Westport, Conn.: Greenwood Press, 1980); Robert C. Morris, *Reading, 'Riting and Reconstruction: The Education of Freedmen in the South, 1865–1870* (Chicago: University of Chicago Press, 1981); Jacqueline Jones, *Soldiers of Light and Love: Northern Teachers and Georgia Blacks, 1865–1873* (Chapel Hill: University of North Carolina Press, 1980); Samuel L. Horst, *Education for Manhood: The Education of Blacks in Virginia During the Civil War* (Lanham, Md.: University Press of America, 1987). James D. Anderson, *The Education of Blacks in the South, 1860–1935* (Chapel Hill: University of North Carolina Press, 1988), 4–25, provides an excellent summary.

2. "Address to the Public by the Committee on Correspondence of the Educational Commission," circular [Boston, February 20, 1862]; Francis Wharton, "Address by the Rev. Francis Wharton, LL.D., Delivered in St. Paul's Church, Brookline, and other Churches, during the Month of December, 1865," in Protestant Episcopal Freedmen's Commission, *Occasional Paper. January 1866* (Boston: George C. Rand & Avery, 1866), 6–7; J. W. Alvord, *Fifth Semi-Annual Report on Schools for Freedmen, January 1, 1868* (Washington, D.C.: Government Printing Office, 1868), 7; see similarly *National Freedmen* 2 (April 1866):122–123; *Twenty-Fourth Annual Report of the American Missionary Association* (New York, 1870), 15 (hereafter AMA, *Annual Report*); AMA, *18th Annual Report* (1864), 15; *National Freedmen* 1 (July 1985):202; *Report of Brevet Major General O. O. Howard, Commissioner Bureau of Refugees, Freedmen, and Abandoned Lands, to the Secretary of War, October 20, 1869* (Washington, D.C.: Government Printing Office, 1869), 12–13; *Freedmen's Record* 3 (May 1867):80; *Second Annual Report of the Baltimore Association for the Moral and Educational Improvement of the Colored People* (Baltimore: J. B. Rose, 1866), 12.

3. Georgia Educational Association, "A New Plan for Educating the Freedmen of the South," circular (n.p., [1867]: Bureau of Refugees, Freedmen, and Abandoned Lands, *Report of the Assistant Commissioner for Alabama, 1867* (n.p.: Barrett and Brown, [1866]), 12; *Freedmen's Record* 2 (July 1866):133; see also, for example, James D. Anderson, "Ex-Slaves and the Rise of Universal Education in the New South, 1860–1880," in *Education and the Rise of the New South*, ed. Ronald K. Goodenow and Arthur O. White (Boston: G. K. Hall & Co., 1981), 1–25; Roberta Sue Alexander, "Hostility and Hope: Black Education in North Carolina During Presidential Reconstruction, 1865–1867," *North Carolina Historical Review* 53 (April 1976):esp. 113–114, 123–125.

4. Cf. the oddly simplistic formula urged in Eric Foner, "Reconstruction Revis-

ited," *Reviews in American History* 10 (December 1982):87; see also Eric Foner, *Reconstruction: America's Unfinished Revolution, 1863–1877* (New York: Harper & Row, 1988), 96–102, 147–148. The quotation is from the conclusion and the title of Roger L. Ransom and Richard Sutch, *One Kind of Freedom: The Economic Consequences of Emancipation* (New York: Cambridge University Press, 1977), 198.

5. E. N. Kirk, "Address of E. N. Kirk," AMA, *22nd Annual Report* (1868), 97; Philbrick to Edward L. Pierce, 27 March 1862, Correspondence of the Fifth Special Agency Relating to Port Royal, South Carolina, National Archives; Robinson quoted in Wilbert Harrell Ahern, "Laissez Faire Versus Equal Rights: Liberal Republicans and the Negro, 1861–1877" (Ph.D. diss., Northwestern University, 1968), 124.

6. There was, arguably, a further form of freedmen's education that we will not explore here. That was the very conscious effort to use controlled "experiments" in free labor as a means to train Southern black labor, such as at Port Royal, South Carolina, and Davis Bend, on the Mississippi River, or the more general "schooling" that the freed people received when they were thrown headlong into a society suddenly bereft of its mode of labor mobilization, but without the mechanisms and belief structures of any alternative mode of productive relationships. That complicated story reaches well beyond the scope of this study, and has been the subject of many important studies. See, among others, Willie Lee Rose, *Rehearsal for Reconstruction: The Port Royal Experiment* (New York: Vintage, 1964); Steven Joseph Ross, "Freed Soil, Freed Labor, Freed Men: John Eaton and the Davis Bend Experiment," *Journal of Southern History* 44 (May 1978):213–232; Richard Paul Fuke, "A School for Freed Labor: The Maryland 'Government Farms,' 1864–1866," *Maryland Historian* 16 (1985):11–23; Ronald L. F. Davis, *Good and Faithful Labor: From Slavery to Sharecropping in the Natchez District, 1860–1890* (Westport, Conn.: Greenwood Press, 1982); Eric Foner, *Nothing but Freedom: Emancipation and Its Legacy* (Baton Rouge: Louisiana State University Press, 1983); Foner, *Reconstruction*, 35–76. For the purposes of this essay, education will be more narrowly defined to include only those institutions whose purposes were the advancement of literacy and numeracy.

7. *First Annual Report of the Educational Commission for Freedmen, May, 1863* (Boston: Prentiss & Deland, 1863), 11; for representative illustrations, see Robert F. Horowitz, "Land to the Freedmen: A Vision of Reconstruction," *Ohio History* 86 (Summer 1977):197; or Morris, *Reading, 'Riting and Reconstruction*, illustrations following p. 169; *American Freedman* 1 (May 1866):27; *First Report of the Executive Board of the Friends Association of Philadelphia and Its Vicinity, for the Relief of the Colored Freedmen* (Philadelphia: Friends Freedmen's Association, 1864), 23; *Minutes of the Convention of Freedmen's Commissions, Held at Indianapolis, Indiana, July 19 and 20, 1864* (Cincinnati: Methodist Book Concern, 1864), 24.

8. *Third Series of Extracts from Letters of Teachers and Superintendents of the New England Freedmen's Aid Society*, circular (Boston, 1863), 2; Richard L. Morton, ed., "Life in Virginia, by a 'Yankee Teacher,' Margaret Newbold Thorpe," *Virginia Magazine of History and Biography* 64 (1956):185. On the impact of the postbellum economy on black adults' control over leisure or discretionary time, see Leon F. Litwack, *Been in the Storm So Long: The Aftermath of Slavery* (New York: Alfred A. Knopf, 1979), 336–449; Ransom and Sutch, *One Kind of Freedom*, 40–105.

9. Arnold T. Needham to W. W. Patton, March 8, 1864, Needham Correspondence, Chicago Historical Society.

10. S. G. Swain to Lucy Ann Swain, April 12, 1864, Swain Collection, Wisconsin

Historical Society; William F. Allen, "Diary," November 6, 1864, Wisc. Hist. Soc.; *Report of Hon. T. D. Eliot, Chairman of the Committee on Freedmen's Affairs, to the House of Representatives, March 10, 1868* (Washington, D.C.: Government Printing Office, 1868), 22; see also *Freedom: A Documentary History of Emancipation, 1861–1867*, Series II, in *The Black Military Experience*, ed. Ira Berlin et al. (Cambridge: Cambridge University Press, 1982), 611–632. Among secondary sources, see Dudley Taylor Cornish, "The Union Army as a School for Negroes," *Journal of Negro History* 37 (October 1952):368–382; John W. Blassingame, "The Union Army as an Education Institution for Negroes, 1861–1865," *Journal of Negro Education* 34 (1965):152–159; Warren B. Armstrong, "Union Chaplains and the Education of the Freedmen," *Journal of Negro History* 52 (April 1967):104–115.

11. AMA, *18th Annual Report* (1864), 23; Alvord, *4th Semi-Annual Report, July 1867*, 18; William F. Messner, *Freedmen and the Ideology of Free Labor: Louisiana, 1862–1865* (Lafayette: University of Southwestern Louisiana, 1978), 164–168; Alton Hornsby, Jr., "The Freedmen's Bureau of Schools in Texas, 1865–1870," *Southwestern Historical Quarterly* 76 (April 1973):13.

12. Burgess quoted in "To the Women of New York Yearly Meeting," from Mary S. Wood, New York Monthly Meeting of Women Friends, circular letter, February 1864; S. W. Magill, report to Executive Committee, AMA, March 3, 1864, American Missionary Association Archives, item #86965, Amistad Research Center, New Orleans (hereafter: AMA #); N. T. Condol to M. E. Strieby, March 26, 1867, AMA #72248. Curricular emphases of night schools can be inferred from Alvord, *4th Semi-Annual Report* (July 1867), 79, among other sources. The extent of night schools throughout the 1860s, and the number of teachers who worked in them in addition to day school responsibilities, can be measured from the monthly reports that teachers returned to their sponsors and to the Freedmen's Bureau; although no researcher has attempted to quantify that material, my impression from working with several hundred of the reports is that freedmen requested and received night schools in at least one-third of the locations in which Northern-supported schools operated.

13. *American Missionary* 11 (July 1867):157; *American Missionary* 15 (May 1871):101; Alvord, *4th Semi-Annual Report* (July 1867), 5; Alvord, *6th Semi-Annual Report* (July 1868), 4–7; Alvord, *8th Semi-Annual Report* (July 1869), 6–10; Alvord, *10th Semi-Annual Report* (July 1870), 4–7; see similarly *Fifth Annual Report. New York Branch Freedmen's Union Commission* (New York: American Freedman, 1867), 12; [U.S. Army], *Report of the Board of Education for Freedmen, Department of the Gulf* (New Orleans: True Delta, 1865), 6.

14. See Alvord, *6th Semi-Annual Report* (July 1868), 59–67; Butchart, *Northern Schools, Southern Blacks, and Reconstruction*, 164–166; Morris, *Reading, 'Riting and Reconstruction*, 160–161; Joe M. Richardson, *Christian Reconstruction: The American Missionary Association and Southern Blacks, 1869–1890*. (Athens, Ga.: University of Georgia Press, 1986), 108–119.

15. *National Freedmen* 1 (July 1865):203; *Freedmen's Record* 1 (August 1865):129; *American Freedman* 2 (November 1867):307; *American Freedman* 3 (July 1869):7; William F. Mitchell, "A Simple Plan for the Organization of Normal Schools, or Normal Classes . . . ," undated, in "Printed Circulars Issued by AFUC," American Freedmen's Union Commission Papers, Cornell University.

16. *Third Annual Report of the Methodist Episcopal Freedmen's Aid Society* (Cincinnati: Western Methodist Book Concern, 1869), 7; *American Missionary* 11 (January

1867):11–12; James D. Anderson, "Northern Philanthropy and the Training of the Black Leadership: Fisk University, a Case Study, 1915–1930," in *New Perspectives on Black Educational History*, ed. Vincent P. Franklin and James D. Anderson (Boston: G. K. Hall & Co., 1978), 97–112; Anderson, *Education of Blacks in the South*, 33–78; W. D. Siegfried, *A Winter in the South, and Work among the Freedmen* (Newark, N.J.: Jennings Brothers, 1870), 14.

    17. Alvord, *8th Semi-Annual Report* (July 1869), 9.

    18. *Reports and Extracts Relating to Colored Schools in the Department of the Tennessee and State of Arkansas. November 30, 1864* (Memphis: Freedmen Press, 1864), 19; Alvord, *5th Semi-Annual Report* (January 1868), 17; *Minutes of the Convention of Freedmen's Commission . . . 1864*, 26. See also Baltimore Association, *2nd Annual Report* (1867), 9; *National Freedman* 2 (April 1866):123, 125; *Appeal of the Western Freedmen's Aid Commission in Behalf of the National Freedmen* (Cincinnati: n.p., 1864), 8–9; Alvord, *4th Semi-Annual Report* (July 1867), 5; *Second Annual Report of the Board of Directors of the Northwestern Freedmen's Aid Commission: Presented . . . April 13, 1865* (Chicago: James Barnet, 1865), [5], 13; and American Freedmen's Union Commission, *The Results of Emancipation in the United States of America* (New York: American Freedmen's Union Commission, [1867]), 31.

    19. *National Freedman* 1 (April 1865):78; *Minutes of the Convention of Freedmen's Commission . . . 1864*, 25; Charles A. Bennett, *History of Manual and Industrial Education up to 1870* (Peoria, Ill.: Manual Arts Press, 1926), 210–265; Friends' Freedmen Association, "Minutes of Instruction Committee," vol. 1, March 13, 1866; Joel Cadbury to George Dixon, 16 February 1867, Friends' Freedmen Association Letterbook, vol. 1, both in Department of Records, Philadelphia Society of Friends.

    20. American Tract Society quoted in M. B. Goodwin, "Schools of the Colored Population," in Henry Barnard, *Special Report of the Commissioner of Education on the Condition and Improvement of Public Schools in the District of Columbia* (Washington, D.C.: Government Printing Office, 1871), 295; William M. Colby to Thomas C. Williams, April 16, 1868, Letters Sent, Arkansas Superintendent of Education, Bureau of Refugees, Freedmen, and Abandoned Lands, RG 105, National Archives (hereafter cited as BRFAL). Excluding the numerous tracts for the freedmen, the curricular material from the American Tract Society included *The Freedman* (monthly, 1864–1868); *The Freedmen's First [Second, Third] Reader* (Boston: ATS, [1866?]); Isaac W. Brinckerhoff, *Advice to Freedmen* (New York: ATS, [1864]); Brinckerhoff, *Gambling and Lotteries* (New York: ATS, [1865]); Brinckerhoff, *A Warning to Freedmen Against Intoxicating Drinks* (New York: ATS, [1865]); Helen E. Brown, *John Freeman and His Family* (Boston: ATS, 1864); Clinton B. Fisk, *Plain Counsels for Freedmen: In Sixteen Brief Lectures* (Boston: ATS, 1866); *Lillie Rose Brown* (Boston: ATS, [1865?]); Lewis C. Lockwood, *Mary S. Peake, the Colored Teacher at Fortress Monroe* (Boston: ATS, [1863]); [Israel P. Warren], *The Freedmen's Spelling Book* (Boston: ATS, [1866]); Jared Bell Waterbury, *Friendly Counsels for Freedmen* (New York: ATS, [1865?]); Waterbury, *Southern Planters and the Freedmen* (New York: ATS [1866?]); Waterbury, *"Out of the House of Bondage": For the Freedmen* (New York: ATS, [1866?]). See also Isaac W. Brinckerhoff, *The Freedmen's Book of Christian Doctrine* (Philadelphia: American Baptist Publication Society [1864]).

    21. For illustrations from and analyses of this instructional material, see Morris, *Reading, 'Riting and Reconstruction*, 174–212, and Butchart, *Northern Schools, Southern Blacks, and Reconstruction*, 135–168.

22. *American Freedman* 1 (May 1866):32; Mary Atwater to R. L. Harper, October 26, 1868, Letters Received, Records of the Superintendent of Education for Alabama, BRFAL; L. Maria Child, *The Freedmen's Book* (1865; rpt. New York: Arno, 1968); *Freedmen's Torchlight* 1 (December 1866).

23. William C. Child to R. M. Manly, June 1866, Letters Received, Records of the Superintendent of Education for the State of Virginia, BRFAL; [John Alvord] to William C. Child, March 21, 1867, Letters Sent, Records of the Education Division of the Bureau of Refugees, Freedmen and Abandoned Lands, BRFAL. James M. McPherson claims that Child's book was used as a primer and textbook in freedmen's schools, but makes no effort to compare its use with that of ATS material. Although there is no doubt that it was used in a few schools, I have yet to find it mentioned in any of the extant documents from the schools and the teachers, whereas various ATS materials were mentioned relatively frequently.

III

BLACK ADULT EDUCATION, 1890–1980

5

Booker T. Washington and George Washington Carver: A Tandem of Adult Educators at Tuskegee

Felix James

After the Compromise of 1877, the retreat from Reconstruction produced many disgruntled blacks in the South. Life for them was most difficult, since southern cities offered few jobs for blacks. Even when they moved to the North, usually they found similar problems. As founder and principal of Tuskegee Institute, Booker T. Washington responded to this dilemma by encouraging blacks to "cast down your bucket where you are," and he proceeded to create programs in adult education to aid them in living.

During its formative years, Tuskegee Institute increased its extension activities. Central to Tuskegee's program was Washington's belief that education should be "made common," to meet the needs of the masses. He wanted the school to touch the lives of a larger number of people throughout the South. Each student was taught that when he left Tuskegee, he would go forth as a missionary to improve his community. He was to carry the spirit of Tuskegee with him and strive to build a community that would be devoid of ignorance and poverty. In this way the entire black population, youth as well as adults, would become enlightened.[1]

In preparing each student to become a missionary, the extension work consisting of the Tuskegee Negro Conference, teachers' and farmers' Institutes, Work of the Business League, and all other extension activities became an important part of the educational scheme. Through these activities the student became thoroughly acquainted with the real problems of Tuskegee Institute. He learned, for example, that the problem was not so much to educate "a few hundred or a few thousand boys and girls, as to change conditions among the masses of Negro people." Washington was one of the first educators to advocate teaching the black masses outside the classroom.[2]

The adult education programs that evolved under Washington were twofold. The first was his individual initiative in promoting his ideas through his "Good Will Tours," or public speeches; the second was institutional adult educational activities usually promoted by Tuskegee Institute with Washington's support. Moreover, as one examines Washington's role in its broader range, it is plausible to suggest that he was striving to establish a model not only for American blacks, but also for blacks all over the world.[3]

ADULT EDUCATION IN AFRICA

Although Washington never went to Africa, his faculty and students became actively involved in Africa in 1900. James N. Calloway, a faculty member, led a group of students to Togo at the request of the German government. Togo, a German colony, wanted to train its farmers in the cotton culture. Specifically, they wanted to experiment with the interbreeding of local and imported cotton to develop a commercially successful variety. By selecting and crossing American and native cotton, they obtained a new variety and successfully launched an experiment station. During the first year "they grew, processed and shipped to Germany a small crop of twenty-five bales." Four years later 950,000 pounds of cotton were sent out, and the process became stable. The expedition gained "international recognition" as France and England adopted essentially the team's methods and processes.[4]

TUSKEGEE NEGRO CONFERENCE

In 1892 Washington sponsored a Tuskegee Negro Conference that consisted of farmers, mechanics, schoolteachers, and ministers. Five hundred persons attended the first meeting. The conference continued to increase in attendance until Washington's death. A sizable number of the men and women in attendance were former slaves. While they attended the conference on the Institute's campus, "it pleased the conference participants greatly to see their sons and daughters matriculating at the institution—an endeavor which was impossible for their generation."[5]

Instead of hearing lectures on agriculture, the farmers were urged to describe both their families and their successes. From the discussions they generally agreed that the main problem of black farmers was economic dependence. When Washington asked how many owned their homes, fewer than 1 percent raised their hands. Several of them freely admitted that they "often bought articles they could produce themselves," which led to their crushing burden of debt. Many farmers noted that they had been able to free themselves from debt by carefully handling their limited resources. They finally agreed to adopt a set of resolutions in which they vowed to work for economic independence and improvement of their homes, schools, and churches.[6]

Because of the enthusiasm this kind of conference engendered, Washington was persuaded to make the meeting an annual affair. Attendance doubled the next year and continued to increase, until thousands attended. Washington expanded the conference to two days, with the first day being the Farmers' Conference and the second, a Workers' Conference. After the farmers had thoroughly discussed their problems and recommendations for self-help, interested educators, ministers, and others met the next day to discuss what they could offer to aid the farmers in achieving their objectives.[7]

Washington spent much time and energy recruiting the best faculty possible for Tuskegee Institute. One such faculty member was George Washington Carver, from Ames, Iowa. In fact, Carver, who joined the faculty as director of agricultural research in 1897, was the "most significant investment made in the history of the school." A casual perusal of his records would immediately reveal that he made an outstanding contribution to the world as a scientist. After Carver's arrival, the conferences continued to increase in attendance and attracted farmers and workers from all over the South, as well as interested whites from both the North and the South. Each year several farmers proudly reported that they had bought land and built homes. One farmer was very thankful for the conferences because they were "giving [the farmers] homes."[8]

With Carver's innovative leadership, the activities of the conference increased. For example, he was able to obtain free garden seeds from the U.S. Department of Agriculture (USDA). Originally, these seeds were distributed by U.S. congressmen to their constituents and "frequently went to farmers who could help the congressmen get reelected, not to those who most needed them." With the direct grant of seeds to Carver for distribution at the conferences, the USDA not only made it possible to encourage farmers to grow their own food and discontinue purchasing it, but also provided the means of doing so. In 1903 the USDA supplied 2,500 packets containing ten packages of various kinds of seeds gathered from the experiment station plot, including Carver's hybrid cotton.[9]

WORKERS' CONFERENCE

At the close of each Tuskegee Negro Conference, Washington organized a smaller, more intimate conference composed of white and black teachers in educational institutions for blacks in the South, preachers, local leaders, and professional businessmen of both races. This conference was designed to reflect on what had taken place the previous day and to encourage teachers and people in other fields to explain and facilitate Washington's effort of total enlightenment of black adults.[10]

AGRICULTURAL SCIENTIST AND EXTENSION WORKER ARRIVES AT TUSKEGEE

Before Carver's arrival at Tuskegee, extension work of the Institute consisted of no more than Sunday afternoon rides by Washington into the countryside. On these trips he wanted to establish a rapport with the black farmers. After he won their friendship and trust, Washington advised them on how to improve their living conditions.[11] These trips helped Washington to realize that the Tuskegee Negro Conference was not reaching a sizable portion of the rural people.

There was a need for a more definite means of reaching the masses, especially those who did not come to the Tuskegee Negro Conference, many of whom remained away because of self-consciousness, inclement weather, and the imaginary discomforts they experienced in mingling with "educated Negroes." To solve this problem, Washington conceived the idea of itinerant demonstrators or "A Movable School."[12]

This idea extended the new techniques of farming and inspired the black people of Macon and its adjacent counties. Washington appointed a committee chaired by Carver to draw up the plans. Among the demonstration materials were a wagon designed for carrying dairy utensils, farm machinery, farm seeds, and other exhibits showing the possibilities of the local farms. Funds were obtained from Morris K. Jesup, a New York philanthropist, and the first operator of the "Jesup Wagon" was George R. Bridgeforth, assistant to Carver.[13]

The year Carver arrived at Tuskegee, Washington persuaded the state legislature to finance the Tuskegee Agriculture Experiment Station. Carver became the director of the experiment station. Believing that "your laboratory is in your head," Carver performed what was viewed as "magic" at the station. Through scientific experimentation, he produced cotton with "longer, finer staple; more prolific and disease resistant; less abusive to the soil; and, maturing early enough to escape the boll weevil." The experiment station was designed to give practical demonstrations of what improved cultivation techniques could produce. Farmers were taken on tours of the station plots, where the various experiments were carefully explained to them.[14]

With the Jesup Wagon, Carver's scientific discoveries were shared with farmers in the surrounding Tuskegee community. When he took trips with Bridgeforth and later with Thomas Monroe Campbell, first agricultural extension agent for the USDA, Carver carried along jars and showed them nutritious ways to prepare and season foods. Farmers were taught how to cure and how to preserve their meat for future consumption.[15]

Demonstrations on how starch and bluing for laundry could be created from potatoes were also given. Carver wrote bulletins on how to raise peanuts and "one hundred and five ways" of preparing them for the table. In addition, these bulletins advised the farmer how to "save his sweet potatoes" and prepare them for human consumption.

Although a number of meetings were held on Saturday, sometimes they were held on Sunday because the congregation of a church was a ready-made audience for a demonstration. Then, too, Carver frequently walked into town on Saturday and talked to farmers as they sold their produce in the town square. On a number of occasions he spent the night with families in the countryside. Farmers' wives took pride in serving Carver food that he had taught them how to prepare. When he returned to his laboratory on Sunday night, he would usually bring several items that he had gathered for experimentation.[16]

When Carver was not available to travel with the Jesup Wagon, Washington himself would occasionally travel with the wagon. The new farm implements were usually made available for the farmers. After he had plowed a number of furrows, Bridgeforth would demonstrate one of the improved plows and would ask observers to compare the amount of work done and the kind of furrow. After these demonstrations, Bridgeforth could hardly get away. Oftentimes the farmers tried to borrow the implements, and one man invited them to remain at his house until he could plow over his cotton.[17]

Sometimes the visiting agents found farmers' wives and children scattering fertilizer in the fields. "A fertilizer distributor demonstrated that there was a quicker and better way which would free members of the families to perform other tasks." Washington also urged the farmers to make their own fertilizer. Several black farmers rented land for $2.50 an acre and paid $1.50 an acre for fertilizer. The wagon carried samples of the various kinds of fertilizer. Farmers were taught the amount of fertilizer needed by their land for various kinds of crops and how to mix it.[18]

Like Carver, Bridgeforth was just as concerned about the kitchen as he was about the field. Experience proved that the wife needed instruction as well as the husband if improvements were to be made in the home. Only a few of the people had vegetable gardens. The wagon carried with it the best vegetables grown in Macon county. Bridgeforth demonstrated how every family could raise enough vegetables on a quarter of an acre, thereby gaining $100 or more for other purposes. Farmers were taught which vegetables could be grown each month in the year, and just how and when to plant, cultivate, and harvest them. The women were introduced to the superior efficiency of the revolving churn over the old "dasher" churn, and informed how the use of butter molds would make the butter more salable.[19]

Bridgeforth often found it necessary to teach the simple lessons of poultry-raising. This was also true with the raising of hogs. Each farmer was urged to purchase at least two hogs for each member of his family, and the wagon carried charts showing the relative merits of different breeds of hogs. Bridge-forth also demonstrated how they could be raised on pasture and on waste land. In this way, farmers learned that a 300-pound hog was more valuable than a bale of cotton, and less costly. The staff taught farmers to raise their own food supply so that their cotton crops could bring in a cash surplus.[20]

After the Jesup Wagon had made the rounds of the various farms of a community, a mass meeting was held in the open air at some central location. These meetings were usually well attended by the farmers and their families. Successful farmers in the community were persuaded to bring samples of their products and to speak at gatherings. Moreover, Bridgeforth gathered samples of poorer crops to exhibit for comparative purposes. "Problems— such as the question of how much one could expect to produce on a given acre—were discussed in Sunday School fashion." For instance, farmers were asked about the best way to grow different crops. After listening to replies, the staff recommended smaller acreage and a variety of crops. At one meeting, the farmers agreed not to work more than twenty acres with each mule. They also agreed that the best method would be to plant ten acres of potatoes, peas, sugar cane, and peanuts.[21] Washington was thoroughly convinced that demonstrations of this kind made lasting impressions on the farmers.

These meetings provided an ideal opportunity to stress another aspect of the philosophy of the Institute, that is, "every Black man should own his farm or home." Ownership provided for a stable family life and eliminated wandering from place to place, which occurred primarily because, when a tenant improved the farm, the landlord would increase the rent. On one occasion, a member of the audience stated that he had built up two farms and then had to move. "Now I let the place run any old way and I can keep it."[22] The important question was, how was land to be obtained? Farmers were instructed to first buy a mule and then the necessary equipment. Then they were told to purchase a few acres of land and "when the land was paid for, and not earlier, to build a good home." The staff noted that this meant frugality and self-denial, and the concerned audience was informed of special cases in which blacks had paid off debts of $1,000 and more with a single crop. Many planters had unused land on which they were paying taxes. Washington believed that if a frugal tenant stayed on the land for a number of years, he should make arrangement by which he would eventually purchase a few acres, although planters were not always eager to sell small tracts of land.[23]

Several white farmers from communities in the area attended the meetings and took an interest in the movement. They listened as attentively as their black neighbors. Planters who owned large plantations invited the Jesup Wagon to visit their tenants. These planters were quite active in publicizing the meetings. They could easily see and understand that a movement of this nature had a direct bearing on the welfare of the entire community and would enhance their own prosperity.[24] Consequently, the Jesup Wagon improved race relations while serving as a school for the farmers.

PHELPS HALL BIBLE TRAINING SCHOOL

According to a survey Washington conducted, moral standards in the community were quite low. The general progress of blacks demanded that efficiency of the minister and church had to be increased to keep pace with the progress of the people. The minister needed to have a better understanding of his duties and opportunities and better equipment for good service. Further, the church needed to improve its organization and methods for reaching and influencing the masses.

In September 1890 Olivia E. Phelps Stokes, heiress of a "family long interested in the Negro," offered Washington a $2,000 permanent scholarship fund to aid in educating "colored men of good moral character, particularly those who have the ministry in view." From this period on, the Stokes sisters, Olivia and Caroline, took a notable interest in the religious life of blacks in Tuskegee. They eventually contributed the money to build Phelps Hall, a nonsectarian chapel, that also housed the Phelps Hall Bible Training School to educate black ministers.[25]

The Bible Training School, which was opened in 1882 with the Rev. Edgar J. Penney in charge, was operated to meet this need. Courses were organized not only for candidates for the ministry, but also for Sunday school workers, social workers, and all who dealt with problems of religious, moral, and social advancement of blacks. An agent was employed to organize local conferences in various communities in Alabama to encourage and direct blacks in their efforts to build local schools to improve family and community life.[26]

TWO-WEEK SCHOOL FOR FARMERS

A course in agriculture organized in 1910 by the agriculture department had eleven students. The second year the number rose to 17, the third year to 70, and the fourth year to 490. In earlier years farmers came from three to six miles to attend; many came on horseback or in buggies and wagons. The ones who lived too far to commute on a daily basis secured board near the school for $2.50 a week. The staff gave lectures and talks to the men and boys on farming, livestock, dairying, and poultry-raising. Special lectures on poultry-raising, dairying, sewing, and cooking were prepared by the home economist for the women and girls.[27]

TEACHERS' INSTITUTE

Meeting quarterly, the Teachers' Institute gave county teachers an opportunity to associate with one another and with the Institute teachers. In addition to general classroom methods, the following subjects were discussed: methods of adjusting classroom work to the needs of the community in which the school was located; teaching of cooking in rural schools; methods of improving social life of the community; methods of supplementing the public school funds; management of a school farm; professional reading for rural teachers; and correlation and adjustment of academic and industrial teaching in the rural school. These meetings benefited the teachers because they could share ideas with one another and in general made a contribution to the schools and communities.[28]

THE FARMERS' INSTITUTE

Iowa State College had for a period of time held monthly Farmers' Institutes to meet the educational needs of the farmer. In 1897 George Washington Carver transplanted this idea to Tuskegee. The first Farmers' Institute was organized at Tuskegee on November 11, 1897, and Charles Green was elected president. Instead of annual meetings, the Farmers' Institute met monthly in the Agricultural Building, which permitted farmers in the surrounding area to attend and return home by sundown. The Institute differed from the Conference, since its members received specific agricultural advice instead of inspiring remarks and general suggestions. The Institutes dealt with the "kind of fertilizer to use, the kinds of crops that are adapted to particular kinds of soils, how to build up worn out soil, the rotation of crops," and the proper time for planting. In short, the participants became students while continuing as full-time farmers.[29]

Attendance at the meeting was voluntary, and usually twenty-five to seventy-five farmers were present. Students were asked to "bring samples of crops, soils, and fertilizers with which they had experienced success or failure." In analyzing the soil, Carver was always able to explain the causes of their results. On a number of occasions Carver took the farmers out to the experiment station plots, where they could see for themselves the value of scientific agriculture. Some of the farmers even accepted Carver's invitation and visited the experiment station when the Institute was not in session.[30]

FARMERS' INSTITUTE FAIR

One result of the Farmers' Institute was an annual fair on the Tuskegee campus. The first Farmers' Institute fair at Tuskegee was held in 1898 to provide an arena for the farmers and their wives to exhibit the fruits of their labor. The quality of the displays increased until highly praiseworthy samples of all kinds of livestock and crops, as well as needlework and prepared foods, were displayed. By 1915 the attendance had grown from a few hundred to thousands, and the duration of the fair was expanded from one day to several days. The success of the Institute "fair attracted the attention of local whites, and in 1911 the white and black county fairs" merged to produce one fair under the direction of the biracial Macon County Fair Association. In keeping with the sentiments of the times, provisions were made for separate facilities such as ticket booths and bathrooms.[31]

SHORT COURSE IN AGRICULTURE

Despite previous success, George Washington Carver believed that more could be done to help local farmers, especially in the "dull winter season." At the beginning of December, in 1903, he recommended that a "lecture course and some practical work" would be helpful to the farmers in the county. A solution was found when the first "Short Course in Agriculture" was held at the Agricultural Building for six weeks in January and February 1904. The short course, which was finally shortened to two weeks, was designed as a school for farmers during the winter months, when many had spare time. Its sessions lasted from midmorning to midafternoon to enable farmers to come and return home the same day. Inexpensive accommodations were eventually made available for those who lived too far away for daily travel.[32]

NATIONAL NEGRO BUSINESS LEAGUE

The idea of a National Business League was born in the mind of William E. Burghardt Du Bois, a professor of sociology at Atlanta University, who had recently turned down an offer to teach at Tuskegee Institute. Although Du Bois was later to become Washington's most forceful critic, at the turn of the century they were not yet as far apart as they believed themselves to be. One of Du Bois' interests at Atlanta was the organization of annual conferences on various phases of race relations. In 1899 the topic was "The Negro in Business," and when the conference ended, Du Bois became a member of the committee that drafted a call for organizing the "Negro Business Men's League," to eventually become a national organization. In his report to the conference, Du Bois recommended a "buy black" sentiment that was an important feature in the Business League. He felt that blacks' dollars should be spent in black businesses, and urged the end of "one-sided development." Black people, he believed, should enter into the industrial and mercantile spirit of the period.[33]

Booker T. Washington organized the National Negro Business League in 1900 to sustain and encourage the development of black businesses. Local leagues were established, but the organization was actually run from Tuskegee and supported with funds contributed by Andrew Carnegie, a wealthy philanthropist. The League was so successful that blacks searching for a way to improve themselves swelled the attendance to 1,200 at its 1906 meeting in Atlanta. The delegates at this meeting reaffirmed their faith in the progress that the "race had and could make in business." They declared their belief that blacks, like all races, must depend for their uplift solely on their ability to "make progress in constructive, visible directions by laying a foundation in economic growth, and resolved that Negroes should emphasize their successes and opportunities more than their failures and grievances." After being used as political pawns in the previous century, they obviously were not interested in political and civil rights. They were primarily concerned with stimulating the philosophy of self-help and racial solidarity.[34]

There was always an unusual amount of enthusiasm at the annual meeting. Applause came frequently as speakers described their rise from poverty to prosperity with emphasis on success. It was obvious that confidence played an important role in bringing about success. While businessmen exuded confidence, members of the League generally believed that anyone who tried could succeed. In 1914 a successful Okmulgee businessman, who had settled in Oklahoma as a homesteader in 1891 with $69 in his pocket, was thoroughly convinced that any black "with ambition and industry, backed by character . . . will positively succeed. . . . Work will accomplish anything." It was believed that there were advantages in the disadvantages of segregation and discrimination. Washington presided over the League's conventions until his death in 1915. At his death, there were approximately 600 local leagues in the national body. Black businesses enterprise grew from 20,000 in 1900 to 45,000 in 1915.[35]

NATIONAL NEGRO HEALTH WEEK

Washington's primary purpose for organizing the National Negro Health Week was to assure the general public that there should be a common bond between the two races. He spent a tremendous amount of time trying to get blacks and whites to collaborate in promoting National Negro Health Week. This program was promoted on a national level by using such instructional techniques as demonstrations, lectures, sermons, and school talks.[36]

CONTRIBUTION TO THE FIELD OF ADULT EDUCATION

Washington and Carver were making contributions to adult education long before twentieth-century educators considered it a discipline worthy of scholarly inquiry. In the developmental stages of adult education, it is probably safe to conclude that scholars did not fail to notice the work of practitioners like Washington and Carver.

Ironically, many well-respected principles of adult education today were espoused by Washington and Carver in the late 1800s. Although deprived of the body of knowledge of their present-day counterparts, somehow these practitioners appeared most astute in the intricacies of adult learning, program planning, needs assessment, program evaluation, teaching strategies, and human relations. More specifically, the actions of the tandem seem to have been supported by the following principles[37]:

1. One is never too old to learn.

2. Adult education leaders must be capable of relating to their constituency.

3. Adult education leaders must adjust instructional strategies to the intellectual level of their clients in order that maximum benefit might be obtained.

4. It is often desirable to take adult education programs to the community, particularly if clients are of the low socioeconomic level.

5. Many adult education projects require the cooperation of several staff members if success is to be achieved.

6. Goals and objectives of the adult education program must flow from needs of consumers.

7. Adult education personnel should make maximum use of all available resources.

8. A continuous effort should be made to improve the adult education program.

9. All adult education instructional programs do not have to be conducted in a formal setting.

10. Intellectual enlightenment is vital to social and economic upward mobility of individuals.

11. Dedicated personnel is a vital element in effective adult education programs.

SUMMARY

The eagerness of Washington and Carver to eliminate poverty, illiteracy, and disease within the human race, especially among people of African descent, was remarkable. They had an unusual charisma that allowed them to continuously motivate men and women to engage in one practical project after another in an attempt to remove the adverse conditions that surrounded them and eventually improve their social and economic status. They brought hope and a new direction to a sizable number of farmers and their wives through the movable school–type of extension work. The practical instructional approach used by Washington and Carver helped farmers from various areas of Alabama to grasp their messages. One of the primary factors that contributed to the success of these leaders was their ability to relate to the masses.[38]

Although Washington spent a tremendous amount of time on speaking and fund-raising tours, he maintained an excellent relationship with the "adult population—farmers in particular." A large part of his success is attributed to his ability to relate to the masses—a skill that several leaders failed to master.[39] For at the heart of his program, Washington believed that education should be made common, to meet the needs of the masses. Each student was groomed to become a missionary to improve his community.

In preparing each student to become a missionary, the extension work became an important part of Tuskegee's educational scheme. The student learned that the problem was not so much to educate a few hundred or a few thousand boys and girls, as to change conditions among the masses of black people. Washington was striving to establish a model not only for American blacks, but also for blacks all over the world.

NOTES

1. Philip H. Nash to George Washington Carver, October 15, 1904, in George Washington Carver Papers (hereinafter cited as GWC Papers), Tuskegee University Archives, Tuskegee, Alabama, Box 5; Carver to Booker T. Washington, February 2, 1912, in GWC Papers, Box 9; J. W. Ranson to Carver, September 1, 1904, in GWC Papers, Box 5; O. B. Martin, "A Decade of Negro Extension Work, 1914–1924," U.S. Department of Agriculture, Miscellaneous Circular No. 72, (October 1929):1–6, GWC Papers, Box 5; Velma L. Blackwell, "A Black Institution Pioneering Adult Education: Tuskegee Institute Past and Present (1881–1973)," (Ph.D. diss., Florida State University, 1973) 31; Leo McGee, "Booker T. Washington and George Washington Carver: A Tandem of Adult Educators at Tuskegee," *Lifelong Learning* 9 (October 1984):16; Linda McMurray, *George Washington Carver: Scientist and Symbol* (New York: Oxford University Press, 1981), 112–113.

2. Martin, "A Decade of Negro Extension Work, 1914–1924," 49–50; McGee, "Booker T. Washington and George Washington Carver"; McMurray, *George Washington Carver*.

3. Blackwell, "A Black Institution Pioneering Adult Education," 51; Louis R. Harlan, "Booker T. Washington and the White Man's Burden," *The American Historical Review* 62 (January 1966):444–445.

4. Blackwell, "A Black Institution Pioneering in Adult Education," 61; Harlan, "Booker T. Washington and the White Man's Burden," 443–444.

5. Blackwell, "A Black Institution Pioneering in Adult Education," 66–67; Felix James, "The Tuskegee Institute Movable School, 1906–1923," *Agricultural History* 45 (July 1971):201; McGee, "Booker T. Washington and George Washington Carver," 16; McMurray, *George Washington Carver*, 115.

6. McGee, "Booker T. Washington and George Washington Carver"; McMurray, *George Washington Carver*.

7. McGee, "Booker T. Washington and George Washington Carver"; McMurray, *George Washington Carver*.

8. Carver to Washington, March 3, 1904, in GWC Papers, Box 5; Carver to Washington, July 20, 1904, in GWC Papers, Box 5; McGee, "Booker T. Washington and George Washington Carver"; McMurray, *George Washington Carver*.

9. Carver to Washington, March 18, 1904, in GWC Papers, Box 5; McGee, "Booker T. Washington and George Washington Carver"; McMurray, *George Washington Carver*.

10. Blackwell, "A Black Institution Pioneering in Adult Education"; McGee, "Booker T. Washington and George Washington Carver," 17; McMurray, *George Washington Carver*, 115.

11. Blackwell, "A Black Institution Pioneering in Adult Education," 74; James, "Tuskegee Institute Movable School," 202.

12. R. C. Bruce to Carver, May 13, 1904, in GWC Papers, Box 5; Thomas Monroe Campbell, *The Movable School Goes to the Negro Farmer* (Tuskegee, Ala.: Tuskegee Institute Press, 1937), 90–91; Blackwell, "A Black Institution Pioneering in Adult Education"; James, "Tuskegee Institute Movable School"; McGee, "Booker T. Washington and George Washington Carver"; McMurray, *George Washington Carver*, 114.

13. Carver to Washington, November 16, 1904, in GWC Papers, Box 5; Campbell, *Movable School*; Blackwell, "A Black Institution Pioneering in Adult Education," 74–75; James, "Tuskegee Institute Movable School"; McGee, "Booker T. Washington and George Washington Carver"; McMurray, *George Washington Carver*.

14. "Adams Act" in GWC Papers, Box 7; James Wilson to Carver, March 20, 1906, in GWC Papers, Box 7; Wilson to Carver, December 10, 1910, in GWC Papers, Box 8; Carver to Wilson, ca. June 5, 1911, in GWC Papers, Box 5; Carver to Washington, March 18, 1904, in GWC Papers, Box 5; O. H. Barnhill to Carver, November 28, 1904, in GWC Papers, Box 5; McGee, "Booker T. Washington and George Washington Carver," 18; McMurray, *George Washington Carver*.

15. Booker T. Washington, "A Farmer's College on Wheels," *World's Work* 13 (1906):8352; James, "Tuskegee Institute Movable School," 202–203; McGee, "Booker T. Washington and George Washington Carver."

16. McGee, "Booker T. Washington and George Washington Carver."

17. George R. Bridgeforth to Carver, June 1906, in GWC Papers, Box 7; Washington, "Farmers' College on Wheels."

18. Declarations of the Twenty-fifth Annual Tuskegee Negro Conference, Tuskegee, Alabama, January 19, 1916, in GWC Papers, Box 7; Washington, "Farmer's College on Wheels," 8353; James, "Tuskegee Institute Movable School," 202–203.

19. Washington, "Farmers' College on Wheels"; James, "Tuskegee Institute Movable School," 203.

20. Washington, "Farmers' College on Wheels"; James, "Tuskegee Institute Movable School."

21. Bridgeforth to Carver, June 9, 1904, in GWC Papers, Box 7; Washington, "Farmers' College on Wheels," 8354; *Southern Letter*, July 1911; James, "Tuskegee Institute Movable School," 203–204.

22. Washington, "Farmers' College on Wheels"; James, "Tuskegee Institute Movable School."

23. Washington, "Farmers' College on Wheels"; James, "Tuskegee Institute Movable School."

24. Washington to Carver, March 13, 1911, in GWC Papers, Box 8; Washington, "Farmers' College on Wheels"; James, "Tuskegee Institute Movable School."

25. Blackwell, "A Black Institution Pioneering in Adult Education," 66; Louis R. Harlan, *Booker T. Washington: The Making of a Black Leader, 1856–1901* (London: Oxford University Press, 1972), 194–197 passim.

26. Blackwell, "A Black Institution Pioneering in Adult Education"; Harlan, *Booker T. Washington*.

27. Blackwell, "A Black Institution Pioneering in Adult Education," 69–70.

28. Ibid., 71.

29. Ibid., 72; McMurray, *George Washington Carver*, 117.

30. Blackwell, "A Black Institution Pioneering in Adult Education"; McMurray, *George Washington Carver*.

31. Blackwell, "A Black Institution Pioneering in Adult Education"; McMurray, *George Washington Carver*.

32. Blackwell, "A Black Institution Pioneering in Adult Education"; McMurray, *George Washington Carver*, 118.

33. Blackwell, "A Black Institution Pioneering in Adult Education"; McMurray, *George Washington Carver*, 119.

34. Fred R. Moore to Washington, March 1906, in Booker T. Washington Papers (hereinafter cited as BTW Papers), Tuskegee University Archives, Tuskegee, Alabama, Box 20; Harlan, *Booker T. Washington*, 266–267.

35. Moore to Washington, February 20, 1906, in BTW Papers, Box 19; Moore to Washington, April 2, 1906, in BTW Papers, Box 21; August Meier, *Negro Thought in America 1880–1915: Racial Ideologies in the Age of Booker T. Washington* (Ann Arbor: University of Michigan Press, 1969), 124.

36. "What the National Negro Business League Has Helped to Accomplish," in BTW Papers, Box 18; Moore to Washington, March 8, 1906, in BTW Papers, Box 20; Moore to Emmett J. Scott, February 20, 1906, in BTW Papers, Box 19; McGee, "Booker T. Washington and George Washington Carver," 18; Meier, *Negro Thought in America*, 124–125; Emma Lou Thornbrough, ed., *Great Lives Observed: Booker T. Washington* (Englewood Cliffs, N.J.: Prentice-Hall, 1969), 14.

37. McGee, "Booker T. Washington and George Washington Carver," 31.

38. McGee, "Booker T. Washington and George Washington Carver"; James, "Tuskegee Institute Movable School," 202.

39. McGee, "Booker T. Washington and George Washington Carver."

6

Education in the Black Monthly Periodical Press, 1900–1910

Michael Fultz

Writing in the *Voice of the Negro* in July 1904, John Henry Adams, Jr., a young black artist and a faculty member at Morris Brown College in Atlanta, presented the first in a series of pictorial essays titled "Rough Sketches" that he would author for this journal. The piece was a short lyrical ode dedicated to the beauty of the "New Negro Woman." Adams did not highlight educational concerns in the text of this article, but two of the captions under his drawings implied its significance. The first captions noted: "This beautiful eyed girl is the result of careful home training and steady schooling. There is an unusual promise of intelligence and character rising out of her strong individuality." The second read: "You cannot avoid the motion of this dignified countenance. College training makes her so."[1]

In October, Adams' second article, on "The New Negro Man," gave education, culminating at the postsecondary level, even greater symbolic prominence. Adams wrote:

To find the new Negro man, one must take the narrow, rugged, winding path as it leads from the humble one room cabin, through the cornfields and the cotton field, pass the county school shanty onto the quiet village in the dale. There, the broader pathway leads from the rough frame cottage, through the smoky, dismal quarters of hirelings; pass the shopping district to the humble academy over the hill . . . to the signal railway station. Tell the conductor you want to get off at Atlanta. Arriving there, take the electric car for any one of the Negro institutions of higher learning, thence to the Negro modern home locality on the broad and sunny avenue, where on either side the playing of innocent colored children, dressed in white laundered jackets and dresses, out upon the green lawns amid blossoming flowers, reveals the meaning of progress peculiar to the black folk.[2]

Although this romanticized scenario was far removed from the restricted realities that confronted the vast majority of African Americans at the turn of the century, Adams' vision of the New Negro man captures, in idealized form, the myths and aspirations of those who would enter the equally new black middle class and professional group. It suggests that education played an important role, albeit embedded, in the "meaning of progress" for this segment of the black population.

In a similar vein, writing in *Alexander's Magazine* in 1908, S. Laing Williams, a Chicago attorney and a key midwestern ally of Booker T. Washington, presented an essay on "The New Negro." "It is sometimes said that the Negro race in America is on trial," Williams commented, using a common argument of the decade, "and it might be as fittingly added that the jury is packed and the verdict made even before the evidence is heard. Hence the burden of our plea always is, hear the evidence." Then, noting that "the test of a race's worth is the kind of men it is capable of producing," Williams presented his "significant and compelling" evidence.

Education has been the controlling passion of the Negro race. Within forty years they have overcome quite sixty percent of their illiteracy. Thousands of young Colored men and women have won academic degrees in many of the best colleges and universities of America and Europe. . . . In other words, the man who forty-five years ago was a chattel has become in some instances a lawyer, a physician, a theologian, an artist, a poet, a journalist, a banker, a diplomat, a linguist, a soldier unafraid, an ardent patriot and a man who dares to have courage in the midst of discouragement.

Thus, for Williams, "the race problem of today, in spite of the people who think, feel and act as if it were the same as in 1860, is a new problem and may be defined: What shall be the status of this educated, high-spirited, ambitious and deserving man of the Negro race or this new Negro?"[3]

Adams' and Williams' depictions of the New Negro man and woman form an important conceptual backdrop for a consideration of the treatment of education and educational issues in the black monthly periodical press between 1900 and 1910. Idealization, exaggeration, pride, and a sense of struggle and uplift are all major components in this formulation. So, too, do Adams and Williams reveal a persuasive faith in education generally and college-going in particular. Both refer to higher education's integral role in demonstrating black achievement in the face of a nation's hostile doubts, a role enhanced by its ability to carve out a unique status for the black middle class.

It is particularly significant that Adams and Williams could converge to such an extent in this singular vision of the New Negro, given that they were poles apart in their personal politics. Adams was closely associated with the radical *Voice of the Negro*, wrote highly admiring sketches for that journal on W. E. B. Du Bois and Atlanta Baptist College's maverick president, John Hope, and even into the 1920s provided cover drawings for the National Association for the Advancement of Colored People's (NAACP's) *Crisis* magazine, edited by Du Bois. Williams, on the other hand, was a confirmed

Bookerite. He served Booker T. Washington faithfully throughout the decade, spying on the Niagara Movement, bargaining for the Tuskegeean's secret purchase of a Chicago black weekly newspaper, and actively promoting the Republican presidential candidacies of Theodore Roosevelt and William Howard Taft.[4] Their relative agreement on the importance of higher education, however, reflects common views of Negro progress and indicates that the commonalities of turn-of-the-century black thought might outweigh ostensible political differences.

The shadow of Booker T. Washington looms large over any consideration of black life and social thought during the 1900–1910 period, and the discussion over industrial education permeated this decade. From his nationwide public platform as principal of Tuskegee Normal and Industrial Institute, as well as through his private machinations as fulcrum of the influential "Tuskegee Machine," Washington dominated the debate over the "Negro Problem" between 1900 and 1910, forcing other blacks to respond, in one way or another, to his pronouncements and policies. Yet it would be quite incorrect to maintain that the context for the discussion of black social, economic, and political issues was established solely or exclusively by the "Wizard of Tuskegee." Looming larger than Washington were the powerful economic and social forces of American racism.

As August Meier has argued persuasively, blacks turned inward in their response to the extreme racism and oppression of the late nineteenth and early twentieth centuries, never giving up their quest for citizenship rights, yet developing a racial creed of their own that emphasized self-help, racial solidarity, and social uplift.[5] Moreover, the ongoing migration and urbanization of the black population, spreading slowly from the 1880s, began to lay the foundation for urban lifestyles and mass Negro markets that would become more fully developed in the aftermath of the unprecedented "Black Diaspora," of the World War I period. As W. E. B. Du Bois observed as early as 1901, the new black community of the period "formed a world among themselves. They are so organized as to come into contact with the outer world as little as possible."[6] Along with the complex pressures that altered the external realities of black America, then, were concomitant shifts within the race's internal structure, signaling the growth and development of the numerically small but socially significant black middle class and professional group, who were coming into their own around the turn of the century. Unlike the vast majority of American blacks, for whom sharecropping and agrarian life patterns meant virtual peonage and "enforced ignorance," this educated, articulate segment of the black population sought to define themselves and the struggle of their people through, in part, the creation of new institutional and organizational frameworks. A wide variety of nationally based middle-class protest and professional organizations arose, for example, during the progressive era, including the Afro-American League in 1890, the National Association of Colored Women in 1896, the National Negro

Business League in 1900, the National Bar Association in 1903, the National Association of Teachers in Colored Schools in 1904, the NAACP in 1909, and the national Urban League in 1911. In this regard, the burgeoning of the black press between 1880 and 1910 was no surprise. Through their own literature, blacks, as always, might "plead [their] own cause," as the first black newspaper, *Freedom's Journal*, commented in 1827. In addition, the black press, as a forum of protest and self-definition, provided vehicles for a form of adult education in black communities, allowing readers to absorb and to articulate new values and meanings appropriate for a social milieu vastly more complex than their forbears had known.

The four black monthly periodicals that form the data base for this chapter—the *Colored American Magazine*, the *Voice of the Negro*, *Alexander's Magazine*, and *Horizon*—represent institutionalized aspects of these trends of migration, urbanization, middle-class development, and adult education. All were published between 1900 and 1910, edited by blacks, and intended for a general reading audience. None were specifically geared to educational issues, although as will be discussed, a variety of educational issues were prominently featured.[7]

COLORED AMERICAN MAGAZINE (MAY 1900–NOVEMBER 1909)

The *Colored American Magazine* was founded in Boston in the spring of 1900 by four young former Virginians who sought to establish a journal "distinctly devoted to . . . the development of Afro-American art and literature" that would also "intensify the bonds of that racial brotherhood."[8] The magazine experienced financial difficulties and underwent several organizational changes during its first few years.[9] Short stories, poems, and serialized fiction appeared regularly, as did articles discussing the general political and social conditions confronting blacks, profiles of noteworthy individuals, and features ranging from "Famous Men [and Women] of the Negro Race" to "Fascinating Bible Stories." Particularly prominent among its authors was Pauline E. Hopkins (she occasionally used the pseudonym Sarah A. Allen), who rose in status from literary editor to general editor in 1902–1903. Aside from her own fiction, which frequently dramatized the "tragic mulatto" theme, Hopkins stressed the value of biography: "We delight to honor the great men of our race because the lives of these noble Negroes are tongues of living flame speaking in the powerful silence of example."[10]

All this changed in the spring of 1904 when Booker T. Washington, in his ongoing efforts to control the contours of black debate, purchased the *Colored American Magazine* and swiftly moved it to New York. Fred R. Moore, then the national organizer and recording secretary for Washington's National Negro Business League, was installed as publisher and general manager.

Moore repeatedly denied that Washington had bought or unduly influenced the journal, insisting that he was merely the Tuskegeean's friend and ardent supporter. In 1907 Moore also became editor and publisher of the New York *Age*, in another undercover attempt by Washington to manipulate and control the black press.[11] Under its new leadership, the journal mostly abandoned its literary pretensions, favoring instead "the doings of the race along material lines."[12] As a result, the magazine became far more political than it had been in its early years.

A total of 108 issues of the *Colored American Magazine* were published during its nine-year run, with the monthly offerings averaging more than sixty pages. At its height under Moore's stewardship, the journal is reported to have reached a circulation of between 15,000 and 17,000.[13]

VOICE OF THE NEGRO (JANUARY 1904–OCTOBER 1907)

Arguably the best edited of the periodicals to appear in the 1900–1910 decade—and hailed by Du Bois as "the greatest magazine which the colored people had had"[14]—the *Voice of the Negro* featured a wide range of articles on the political, social, and economic concerns of the race, along with occasional poetry, humor, and artwork. A 1905 editorial stated: "In a special manner we are set to state the cause of our down-trodden race, and we shall advocate everything for the elevation of the race from a pick-axe and a plow to a telescope and a spectroscope; from a bank-book to a Bible-book; from a common school and industrial education to a college training, a university course and a professional degree."[15]

Based in Atlanta, the *Voice of the Negro* was hampered by the relentless efforts of Booker T. Washington to bring the journal into his orbit. As Louis Harlan has observed, "Washington first tried to force the *Voice* to sing his song and then tried to silence it."[16] Eventually he succeeded.

For the first half of its existence, the *Voice of the Negro* was divided in its editorial opinion. Its primary editors were J. W. E. Bowen, a friend of Washington and a professor (later president) at Gammon Theological Seminary in Atlanta, and J. Max Barber, a recent graduate of Virginia Union University. Washington's confidante and personal secretary, Emmett Scott, was also initially on the editorial board. Although politically independent at first, Barber repeatedly locked horns with Scott over the journal's editorial direction, and gradually moved into the Du Bois camp. (Scott was not listed as an associate editor after August 1904.) Barber was a founding member of the Niagara Movement, and the magazine became sort of an unofficial mouthpiece for that militant civil rights organization. Although Washington and Scott repeatedly sent letters of protest to the journal's publishers (who were white), it was Barber's attempts to repudiate anti-black explanations for the

1906 Atlanta riot that finally led to the downfall of the *Voice of the Negro*. The young editor was given a choice: serve a sentence on a Georgia chain gang or leave town immediately. Barber attempted to reestablish the magazine in Chicago—shortening its name to the *Voice*—but was plagued by financial difficulties that resulted from the relocation as well as by calculatingly malicious, Washington-inspired rumors of cowardice for leaving Atlanta.[17]

In all, forty-two issues of the *Voice of the Negro* were published, with individual copies running about fifty or more pages in its prime. According to Barber, its maximum circulation was 15,000 for the May 1906 issue.[18]

ALEXANDER'S MAGAZINE (MAY 1905–MARCH/APRIL 1909)

In early 1904 Charles Anderson, a graduate and former employee of Tuskegee, was teaching printing at Wilberforce University. At Washington's behest, he returned to Boston (where he had once published a journal named the *Monthly Review*) to take over a failing weekly the Tuskegee was secretly subsidizing to counteract William Monroe Trotter's relentlessly acerbic Boston *Guardian*. A little over a year later, backed with funds from Washington, the Boston *Colored Citizen* was transformed into *Alexander's Magazine*.[19]

Similar in content to the post–1904 *Colored American Magazine*, but a bit more conservative, *Alexander's* was a rather nondescript general race periodical, featuring articles on colleges and industrial schools, discussion of current issues, along with some poetry and book reviews. Although the journal flirted with the Niagara Movement—Archibald Grimke was briefly employed as editor—and toward the end of its existence actively promoted the emigrationist movement through an organization known as the Liberian Development Association, *Alexander's* remained, for the most part, a firm exponent of the Tuskegee cause.[20]

Most of the forty-seven issues of *Alexander's Magazine* ran over forty pages. Its circulation was estimated at 5,000 in 1907.[21]

HORIZON (JANUARY 1907–JULY 1910)

The *Horizon: A Journal of the Color Line* was W. E. B. Du Bois' second attempt at journalism during the 1900–1910 decade. In December 1905, with the help of two Atlanta University graduates, he had established the *Moon Illustrated Weekly* in Memphis; it lasted until the summer of 1906.[22]

The *Horizon* was published in Washington, D.C., in association with Lafayette Hershaw and F. H. M. Murray. Its general theme was "Seek the Seldom Sought," although it occasionally proclaimed itself "Discursive, Disquisitional and 'Different.' " The journal, characterized later by Du Bois as a "miniature monthly," carried virtually no feature articles.[23] Rather, discussion of topics of interest proceeded within three sections: "The Over-

Look," written by Du Bois, touched on any topic the senior editor thought newsworthy; "The Out-Look," by Hershaw, focused mostly on domestic concerns and the white press; and "The In-Look," by Murray, surveyed the black press. Throughout these sections was considerable gossip about the political leanings of various men and women in the black middle class.

Thirty-one issues of the *Horizon* were published; none were issued between November/December 1908 and October 1909. Between 1907 and the end of 1908, the journal was twenty-four to twenty-six pages in length; from November 1909 until its demise, it was twelve pages an issue. No data are available on circulation, but undoubtedly it was quite low.

As can be readily discerned from these brief descriptions, the four periodicals published between 1900 and 1910 fell within pro-Washington and pro-Du Bois camps, with the *Colored American Magazine* and *Alexander's Magazine* lined up with the Tuskegeean, while the *Voice of the Negro* and *Horizon* formed the opposition. Yet the many similarities in their coverage of education, in particular, speak to a prevailing ideology not explained solely by reference to the famous Washington-Du Bois debate. This can best be demonstrated in terms of how the journals addressed three concerns: (1) purposes of education and the overarching issue of "character"; (2) higher education; (3) elementary and secondary education.

THE PURPOSES OF EDUCATION

Many of the writers on black social issues during the 1900–1910 decade were highly prescriptive. They touted education, broadly conceived, as a primary means for racial "uplift" and envisioned far-reaching benefits to individuals and to the race as a whole as a result of schooling. Take, for example, an article on "The Power of Education" that appeared in the *Colored American Magazine* in November 1903. In concentrated form, the author of this brief, three-and-a-half-page essay touched on several of the purposes and benefits commonly ascribed to schooling:

Education lifts men heavenward. The man who becomes truly educated becomes less like a man more like a god. . . . The educated slave is as great as the educated king. Education knows no social line. . . . Education is power itself. The true education not only brings out what is great and noblest in a race, but it will also put us in the front rank of civilization. . . . Education is the motor power which carries in its train all those civilizing and beneficial agencies that distinguish the civilized man from the savage of the forest. . . . The progress of any race depends upon its educated, trained, consecrated, unselfish leaders. . . . The scholar must be the leader of the nation. . . . Only will education wield that power and influence that it ought to wield when it is made possible for the humblest boy or girl in the Republic. Larger opportunity for each and all comes with general education. . . . The great sociological problems of the day, the problem of the races, are all being slowly and surely solved by the power of education. . . . What the Negro race needs today more perhaps than anything else is educated men and women who have race pride enough to unify and blend the race into one harmonious whole.[24]

Yet even this exuberant characterization only begins to scratch the surface of the many advantages that authors throughout the decade attributed to education. Despite considerable overlapping that confounds precise boundaries, several major themes can be discerned from the polemical discussions presented in the journals.

"Ignorance is the cause, the curse, the ever present and ever outstanding brand of inferiority. Remove ignorance and equality among men will prevail."[25] Although what might be called basic skills acquisition was a somewhat neglected issue for most commentators of the period, the prevailing illiteracy among blacks was a frequent topic of concern. Many agreed with the view that "to multitudes of colored people illiteracy is a continuous night without a ray of light,"[26] while expressing the belief that "when we fully survey our faults, our mistakes and our vices, we shall find that ignorance is at the bottom of them all."[27] In fact, a variant of this view was sometimes used as an argument for the provision of education in appeals to recalcitrant Southern whites and Northern philanthropists. As a group headed by W. E. B. Du Bois stated in a memorial to the state of Georgia, "nor is this duty of public education a matter of mere charity or almsgiving: it is, first, a wise measure of self-defense to guard the state against the errors and crimes of sheer ignorance."[28]

Admonitions on the issue of overcoming black illiteracy were common, ranging from standard provisos that "it is brains that will tell nowadays"[29] to statements that "the colored man will do more and be more as he thinks more."[30]

"The Negro must stand alone and prove his case."[31] There was considerable commentary throughout the decade asserting that blacks must "measure up" in one form or another, must "place [themselves] in the proper light before the world," and that such demonstrations of abilities would lead whites to change their convictions of Negro inferiority.[32] "There is a battle to be fought," charged the Afro-American Council, "not with swords and guns on bloody fields, but in the arena of public opinion."[33] Indeed, within this notion often lay the parallel thought that "public sentiment in this country is higher than the law."[34]

Given this point of view, grounded in political and social realities that appeared to be worsening at every turn, education was one of the sole means available to prove wrong the detractors. Black achievements in business and higher education were most often cited as examples of prowess, as were the accomplishments of prominent blacks, particularly Phyllis Wheatley, Frederick Douglass, Kelly Miller, T. Thomas Fortune, Booker T. Washington, and W. E. B. Du Bois. Even literally menial educational feats were pointed to with pride, as did a correspondent in the *Colored American Magazine* in 1907, who noted: "It means no little to us as a race that six prominent white women of our own state [Georgia] express the opinion that with proper training, the Negro race can and will furnish as efficient and as high-class servants as can be secured from any other race."[35] Educational institutions run by blacks were particularly lauded. In this regard, Tuskegee was the standardbearer, "the triumph of the whole Black citizenry of America against the defamation of its accusers."[36] Indices that demonstrated declining rates of illiteracy among blacks were frequently marched out to furnish unequivocal data, for given the advancements since the benchmark days of the Civil War, "who can then say [that blacks] are a race of ignoramuses?"[37]

"Equal opportunity for all men is the spirit of the age."[38] Charles Alexander, editor of *Alexander's Magazine*, likened equal opportunity to Theodore Roosevelt's popular campaign slogan, "The Square Deal," noting that neither was possible, and that the nation's most cherished principles were mocked "when one part of the population remains in poverty and dense ignorance, and the other part is enlightened and prosperous."[39] Such arguments for schooling on the basis of its citizenship functions are, of course, quite common in the history of American education, but for black writers at the turn of the century appeals of this type carried a special rhetorical value. On the one hand, they served to define education's mission, which was, for many, "not only to unshackle the mind from the debasing and malodorous influence of intellectual bondage, but to form, to fashion and to raise all to the full height and high purpose of American citizenship."[40] Second, they provided the basis for a sustained critique of the nation's ostensible commitment to its own exalted traditions; an appeal to the democratic conscience systematized years later in Gunnar Myrdal's famous *An American Dilemma.*[41]

Equality of opportunity was a major theme even apart from its connections to citizenship concerns, for it expressed the race's commitment to its aspirations in an era of seemingly unmitigated hostility to black people's hopes and ambitions. "Give the black boy a chance!" cried Du Bois, and even Booker T. Washington noted that "what the Negro does ask is, *equality of opportunity*" (emphasis in original).[42] So strong was this demand that at one point William Pickens angrily challenged American society:

We simply dare the Caucasian to offer the Negro *equality of opportunity*. As the Southern pickaninnies say when they are in "dead" earnest: "I double-dare you!" I double-dare you to give the Negro child in the public school dollar for dollar with the white child instead of one dollar for every four to the white. In your requirements for citizenship set up any moral or intellectual standard you please, require sainthood and Sanskrit if you wish, and I dare you to apply the test impartially to white and black. Not one inch do we ask that the standard be brought down to us, but we demand an impartial opportunity to come up to the standard.[43]

"Education means service; and service means nobility."[44] Service to the race was an ongoing refrain in the literature of the decade, an essential element

in programs of uplift, and one of the foremost purposes and benefits of education cited by black commentators. Just as Booker T. Washington could say that "in the long run, the badge of service is the badge of sovereignty," Wilberforce University's respected classics professor W. S. Scarborough remarked that "the destined work of the college is to produce men and women of the race fitted for *service to the race*," adding that without this trait, "there would be no justification for any kind of training—in culture, in knowledge—in professions or trades" (emphasis in original).[45]

Proponents of industrial or higher education differed, however, in the way they played on the concept of services as uplift. For those favoring industrial education, such training would increase a person's "usefulness," and the value of their institutions would be "in the service rendered to the communities in which these young people go to live and labor."[46] Thus "Tuskegee is the very foundation-stone of what we are pleased to term useful education; that is, the correlation of the book with the problems of life, . . . service plus culture."[47] Advocates of higher education were more apt to point to the leadership aspects of service, asserting that one central purpose of black colleges was to "raise up leaders, and let those Negro leaders lift their own masses."[48]

Such differing emphases, however, only elaborated on this pervasive theme, and demonstrated its links to such key notions as self-help and racial solidarity. A statement by the National Negro Baptist Convention in 1903 strongly underscored its importance: "The education that does not draw out our love for service . . . is a Christless, useless gift, that is a curse, rather than a blessing to the possessor."[49] According to an article in the *Voice of the Negro*, "education, wealth, business, standing, and even high church relation on the part of the few cannot save them from the ignominy which is sure to come if they forget their less fortunate brethern."[50] Likewise, Roscoe Conkling Bruce's commencement address on "Service by the Educated Negro" at M Street High School in Washington, D.C. made education's links to middle-class notions of responsibility and duty even more explicit with his closing remark: "Remember—*noblesse oblige!*"[51]

"The aim of education is to lead the recipient into a larger, fuller, richer, nobler, higher life."[52] Within a social context in which blacks were commonly characterized as "brutes" and faulted for their alleged immorality, it is not surprising that the moral value of schooling was consistently promoted. Authors referred to the need for, and desirability of, a "Christian education," while citing the "refining" qualities and "cultivating influences" of schooling.[53] Some asserted that "education is a means by which we rise above the degrading influences in life," while others made the connection between "obtaining knowledge, and thereby cultivation."[54] Often used terms extolled the virtues of an education that inculcated the principles of "right living" and "correct notions of life."[55]

Commentators ranging from the archconservative Loyal Legion of Labor to the liberal/radical W. E. B. Du Bois also pointed to education's role in alleviating what they considered a troubling "ignorance on matters of life."[56] As Du Bois put it, "the Negro problem, it has often been said, is largely a problem of ignorance—not simply of illiteracy, but a deeper ignorance of the world and its ways; of the thought and experience of men; an ignorance of self and the possibilities of human souls."[57] Uniting proponents of this view was a conception of slavery as having destroyed the ideals of a positive home life for many blacks, with subsequent social development made difficult by the perils of poverty and powerlessness.

In addition to these major themes, other purposes and benefits of education were promulgated by the black periodical press. For example, schools of all types, from Talledega College in Alabama to Manassas Industrial School for Colored Youth in Virginia, claimed that their institutions acted as a "harmonizer of racial differences" in the community or town in which they were located.[58] Educational opportunities would raise cooking and housework "from the rank of contemptible drudgery, degrading to the persons who do it, to a science and a profession," just as they would increase the "efficiency" of Negro work in a variety of endeavors.[59] Schooling would stem the migration of blacks from rural areas to the southern cities or to the North.[60] Finally, education might also serve to "awaken a spirit of unrest and discontent in any unworthy station."[61] In the latter regard, as an author put it, "it is the fundamental business of the schools to enlarge the range of the students' interests and wants, to stir up a divine discontent."[62]

Although the journals displayed near unanimous agreement on these purposes and benefits of education when taken as a whole, occasionally voices of dissent were raised. For example, the themes of racial pride and solidarity to be gained from education sometimes superceded and clashed with notions of its assimilative functions. This strain of social thought called on blacks to develop "a line of individuality and race standards that [meant] something to [them]."[63] Thus a 1905 editorial in the *Voice of the Negro* warned of "a great danger in the present method of educating the Negro. We are in danger of spoiling the Ethiopian and making a miserable excuse of a white man. . . . We plead . . . for changing the mind of the Ethiopian and this can be done by setting before him different ideals of heroism, beauty and power than are now set before him by the stereotyped methods of education used to educate the whites."[64]

A second form of dissent was also tied to themes of racial pride and solidarity, but in this instance the emphasis in the call for self-help shifted from help or service to the race, to self. Respected journalist T. Thomas Fortune, editor of the influential New York *Age*, most forcefully articulated this point of view. In a 1904 article in the *Colored American Magazine* titled "False Theory of Education Cause of Race Demoralization," Fortune criticized the tendency of "educating the student away from the principle that the first object in life should be the building up of his individual character and material well-being, substituting instead the necessity of devoting all his time and talents to the building up of the character and material well-being of his race." Only blacks and Indians are taught this "false theory," Fortune argued, noting that however well intentioned the motives, their education was designed by those "who regard the Indian and Afro-American people as a peculiar people, not like other people, who require peculiar standards of education, as they are to occupy a peculiar place in the life of the American citizenship." This overwhelming emphasis on service and racial uplift, Fortune charged, led many blacks to have exaggerated feelings of self-importance that in turn stifled organized movements for social change because everyone wanted to be a leader. "The individual must lift himself before he can lift up the race," Fortune concluded.[65] A follow-up commentary in the *Colored American Magazine* extended this argument: "A race of educated men devoting their time and talents to the herculean task of lifting up their fellows and neglecting entirely the supreme business of lifting up themselves, have only a basis in poverty to build upon, and by the nature of the case must develop a race of beggars and hypocrites who cannot respect themselves... and who cannot command the respect of mankind."[66]

If, on occasion, individual authors disagreed over some specific in the litany of panegyrics lavished on the purposes and benefits of education, dissent disappeared with regard to the issue of "character." Character was a ubiquitous ideal in the 1900–1910 decade, elusive and amorphous in meaning yet unmatched in social significance. Along with intelligence and industry, it was considered one of the "trinity of graces."[67] It was the "mainspring of civilization," capable of both elevating the race and indicating that prejudice and discrimination were unjustified: "More can be done in the matter of removing the mountain-high obstacles which confront the Afro-American in every part of this broad land, by cultivating character, than can be accomplished by any other agency."[68] As educator and women's activist Josephine Silone Yates put it, "in the ultimate analysis, character is all."[69]

In a sense, character was the sum of the many purposes and benefits attributed to schooling, yet it also stood somewhat apart from education, resting on conceptions of ethical norms and moral righteousness. Character was perhaps best defined as "the moral force or influence which permeates the individual or race and makes them individuals of strong moral traits, which means the estimate attached to them by the community in general."[70] As with other morality/respectability issues in turn-of-the-century black middle-class thought, discussions of character often mentioned the home and the school as the two social agencies most influential for its formation and development, although in this era of self-made men it could also be "a product of years of self-denial and struggle."[71]

Between the home and the school as contributing factors, opinion was mixed. For several authors, the foundation of character was laid in the Negro home, where it was nurtured by "proper parentage" in an atmosphere that fostered "self-culture."[72] Parents, particularly mothers, were cautioned to "give special consideration and attention to the elements which go to make up true manhood and a perfect character": "We should be careful and see that we cultivate the sensibility that does not weaken the intellect, the intellect which does not dwarf the affections, the affection that does not vitiate the conscience, the conscience that does not unnerve the will, and the will that does not misdirect moral action."[73]

For W. S. Scarborough, on the other hand, character was "*the educated will*," while another author asserted that "the end and aim of all education is the development of character."[74] From this perspective, an education without character-building functions "would be like a solar system without a sun."[75] This goal, in fact, often assumed primary importance in the education of blacks; for James Merrill, the white president of Fisk University, just as for William Holtzclaw, the black principal of Utica Normal and Industrial Institute, "to shape character is a higher aim than to train the intellect."[76]

HIGHER EDUCATION

For the *Colored American Magazine*, the *Voice of the Negro*, and *Alexander's Magazine*, feature-length profiles of black colleges and universities were the jewels in the crown of their treatment of educational issues. All told, the periodicals published features on close to twenty institutions of higher education for blacks during the 1900–1910 decade. Blacks who attended "Northern" colleges and universities were also a topic for occasional discussion, while lesser consideration was given to the "colored" agricultural and mechanical institutions created by the 1890 Morrill Act. Interestingly, it was the post–May 1904 issues of the *Colored American Magazine*—that is, those editions of the journal after it was taken over by Fred Moore and Booker T. Washington—that provided the most extensive coverage of black higher education.

These profiles of black colleges had much in common. A "thrilling history" of the institution was typically provided, starting, as with Rust University, "while the roar of the belching cannon of the Civil War was just dieing [sic] away in the distance."[77] These overviews almost always included effusive praise for the school's abolitionist founders and its initial teaching cadre, often citing "unswerving fidelity" to the aims and goals of a prominent founder or early president.[78] Wherever the school was originally situated— be it the former slave-selling pen called Lumpkin's Jail where Virginia Union University was started, or Fisk's famous Army barracks, or the damp basement of Father Quarles' dilapidated Atlanta church where classes at Spelman Seminary were first held—the institution was eventually located in an "ideal site."

The text of these profiles also typically presented counterarguments to criticisms of black higher education. On the one hand, authors spoke of the need to "dispel this gigantic illusion about over-education, which already threatens to blot all Negro hopes and mental achievements from the map of human possibilities."[79] Likewise, the "noble work" and "positive influence" of alumni/ae were consistently extolled. Statements to the effect that graduates were never convicted of a crime were something of a staple; Spelman's "careful record" showed that 94 percent of its graduates "turn out well."[80]

Information on campus life was sketchy at best. Thus it was only by inference, if at all, that the reader would realize that the vast majority of students attending black colleges and universities during the 1900–1910 decade were enrolled in academic areas other than the college course. In fact, only one article published in the journals surveyed during this decade provides even partial data on this point, and that article aggregated the information for the five Atlanta higher education institutions. In "Our Atlanta Schools," published in the *Voice of the Negro* in January 1904, respected educator John Hope noted that the five Atlanta schools had a total enrollment in 1903 of 2,104 students; of these 126 (5.9 percent) studied in college departments, 1,337 (63.5 percent) were "in the grades," and 557 (26.4 percent) were in the academic or normal course (the equivalent of secondary school).[81] These figures were roughly comparable to data compiled by W. E. B. Du Bois in his 1900 Atlanta University study of "The College-Bred Negro." As Du Bois commented, "in most cases the college departments of these institutions are but adjuncts, and sometimes unimportant adjuncts, to other departments devoted to secondary and primary work."[82] No equivalent statement was found in the black monthly periodical press for this period. Perhaps these discussions of college-going had such positive symbolic value that misinterpretations favoring the race were welcomed. As Atlanta University president Horace Bumpstead commented in 1902 on higher education's incentive value among blacks, "the masses may not be able to go to college, but they may send their representative to college, and when he comes home they may be wise by proxy."[83]

Of all the black colleges and universities that received individual profiles, Fisk University in Nashville was unquestionably considered "the very foremost school in the South for the higher education of colored people."[84] As a 1906 commentary in the *Colored American Magazine* exclaimed, "Fisk University relatively occupies the same position to the colored people of the South that Harvard does to New England. It is their one great university."[85] Its founder and first president, Erastus Craveth, was hailed as "the pioneer of Negro education," and its history and subsequent growth were always highlighted by tales of the Fisk Jubilee Singers, students who rescued the institution from financial ruin during its early years by embarking on a triumphant worldwide fund-raising tour during which "the most cultured audiences were taken captive; crowned heads wept."[86]

The five profiles of Fisk published during the decade all celebrated the fact that the school offered a "full education"; as one article commented, "it was established on the American basis, 'dedicated to the proposition' that the colored youth should have the very best education that he can take and make use of."[87] That graduates of Fisk's college department could enter Harvard and Yale without taking entrance examinations was prominently mentioned, as was the fact that its alumni included W. E. B. Du Bois and Booker T. Washington's wife, women's leader Margaret Murray Washington. Yet, as with profiles on other black higher educational institutions, intellectual goals at Fisk were consistently downplayed. President James G. Merrill, for example, remarked in one article that "the chief aim at Fisk, however, is not scholarship. Manhood is the goal. Christian men and women are its product."[88] Likewise, other articles pointed out that "character before training of any kind is correct education," and that "its highest aim is a Christlike life."[89] More than was the case with other profiles of black colleges, features on Fisk prominently mentioned the school's production of teachers as a central accomplishment. These remarks were made in the context of the leadership and service qualities exemplified by Fisk's alumni/ae. As one commentator summed it up, "Fiskize the Southern Negro, and you have from the point of view of the colored race solved the problem of the race."[90]

Morris Brown College in Atlanta was the only other black college profiled in at least three periodicals. Unlike Fisk, however, Morris Brown was not considered a top-flight academic institution; a 1907 reprint in the *Colored American Magazine* of an editorial written in the *Atlanta Independent* stated that Morris Brown ranked last among the five Atlanta schools "in the public estimation,"[91] whereas Du Bois' and Dill's 1910 study of "The College-Bred Negro American" ranked it twenty-ninth among the thirty-two black institutions doing college work.[92] Its prominence in the periodical press underscores the observation that academic prestige was not a decisive criterion in determining which black colleges and universities received publicity.

The reasons for Morris Brown's publicity are probably linked to the perspective, as one title proclaimed, "The Negro at Self-Help." As the flagship institution of the African Methodist Episcopal Church, Morris Brown had an entirely black faculty and board of trustees. Thus discussions of the school highlighted that it was a "leading exponent of Negro self-assertion," and that it "proposes first to inculcate spirits of self-effort, of independence, of race potency."[93] Articles also noted that before the Reverend R. D. Stinson assumed the position of vice-president and financial commissioner around 1902, "what had been collected for the support of the work came in pennies and nickels and dimes... from the hard-earned wages of the cooks and washer-women and butlers and porters and domestics in general throughout the state of Georgia."[94] As Charles Alexander explained with pride, "the government and development of Morris Brown College typifies the ability of the Negro to manage institutions successfully without the intervention or support of his white neighbors."[95]

Spelman Seminary maintained a unique place in the pantheon of black higher education institutions. Founded in Atlanta in April 1881, and supported, in part, by the American Baptist Home Mission Society and the John D. Rockefeller family, Spelman was the largest and most prestigious school for black women and girls. It was widely publicized as "the Mount Holyoke of the South," and was poetically considered "the flower of the race's educational institutions."[96] Profiles of Spelman highlighted the school's teachers' professional department as particularly sound, along with its nursing program and its Christian Workers' course for those intending to be missionaries in the South or in Africa.[97]

Strangely, the journals only barely touched on black attendance at "Northern" colleges and universities. Perhaps the reason for this limited treatment lay in the limited propaganda value of such matriculation. Whether or not attendance at Northern campuses had a heightened status for some, intellectual attainments for the individual were less significant than the romantic aura or feelings of racial pride and self-help that flowed from articles on the black colleges. Unlike articles on predominantly black campuses, for example, which embellished on a grand institutional history, articles on blacks at Northern colleges tended to focus on a single student's individual struggles and achievements.[98]

ELEMENTARY AND SECONDARY EDUCATION

In contrast to the extensive treatment given to higher education, and the encomiums lavished on black colleges, elementary and secondary education received relatively meager attention in the journals of the period. Grossly unequal allocations of state and county monies, proposals to divide these funds according to taxes paid by race, short school terms, the dismal state of rural schooling, the need for new schools and overcrowding in existing ones, and the deplorable lack of public secondary facilities were the issues of the day for black precollegiate education. Du Bois' 1901 study of "The Negro Common School" in fact elaborates on all of these points, while the 1911 follow-up investigation notes in its introductory resolutions that "it is [the investigators'] firm belief that the Negro common schools [were] worse off than they were twenty years ago, with poorer teaching, less supervision, and comparatively fewer facilities."[99] Yet few of these issues were emphasized by the periodicals of the decade. The question of racially mixed versus segregated schools in the South was, with a single exception, never raised,[100] while mention of the need for high schools for blacks was virtually nonexistent.

Of the litany of protests that might have been raised, two issues, typically discussed in tandem, received the most publicity: opposition to dividing school funds by taxes paid by race, and complaints about discriminatory funding. Several articles took issue with the "mischievous fallacy," as the 1906 Negro Young People's Christian and Educational Congress put it, "that the white race voluntarily imposes taxes upon itself for the education of the Negro."[101] Commentary on this subject decried the "powerful public opinion that regards the Negro common school rather as a burden than as a great work of public utility."[102] To counter these charges that black common schooling was an unfair drain on the pocketbooks of white taxpayers—which besides further heightening hostility to black education also fostered images of black dependency and "shiftlessness"—commentators pointed to two considerations: (1) that when indirect taxes were taken into account, even if allocated by race, black schools did not receive their due; and (2) that "every system of political economy recognizes that the laborer, the tenant, and the consumer pay every charge."[103] As Du Bois succinctly phrased this latter point, "wealth is a social product."[104] Combined with data detailing discriminatory funding of black schools, these arguments summed to the position taken in a 1906 editorial in the *Voice of the Negro*: "There is nothing philanthropic or benevolent about the way the white man treats our people. He is stealing from us every day."[105]

In a related theme, the journals displayed what might be described as an undercurrent of support for federal aid to alleviate illiteracy, yet, again, this trickle hardly constituted an outpouring of concern. Calls for national aid for common schooling in the South cropped up in the resolutions and messages of the Afro-American Council, the Niagara Movement, the National Association of Teachers of Colored Youth, and the Negro Young People's Congress, and the *Voice of the Negro* once noted editorially that Southern white sentiment on the subject seemed to be favorably changing. Nevertheless, not once during the decade did a full-length article elaborate on the need for such a congressional measure.[106]

BOOKER T. WASHINGTON AND INDUSTRIAL EDUCATION

As much as the journals displayed the broad consistencies of middle-class black thought on such issues as the purposes of education and the prestige of higher education, they also highlighted the fundamental division that marked the decade—attitudes toward industrial education in general and Booker T. Washington in particular. From the premier issue of the *Colored American Magazine* in May 1900, in which the editors called on New England blacks to "forbear the spirit of criticism" and support Washington's efforts, to the May 1910 issue of the *Horizon*, in which Assistant Editor L. M. Horshaw flatly states, "I find myself out of harmony with Booker T. Washington," discussion of and debate over the legendary Tuskegean continued unabated.[107]

Acrimony was common. Supporters of Washington called him "a revolutionist" for his educational theories and spoke of his sincerity of purpose, and labeled detractors "perpetual windjammers," who accomplished nothing for the race.[108] Opponents, on the other hand, decried Washington's views as outrageously materialistic, and on one occasion characterized him as "the Arch-Tempter . . . smooth-tongued and cynical, with gold."[109] As longtime Howard University faculty member Kelly Miller observed in his celebrated 1903 essay on "Washington's Policy," "Mr. Booker T. Washington is the storm center around which controversy rages. Contending forces have aligned themselves in hostile array, as to the wisdom or folly of the doctrine of which he is the chief exponent."[110]

The 1900–1910 period saw Booker T. Washington at the height of his power as a political kingpin and saw Tuskegee Institute, the institution that he made synonymous with the idea of industrial education, lavishly funded, greatly honored, and closely imitated. During the early years of the decade, Washington made significant inroads in capturing the allegiance of the Northern black middle class and professional group, a consequence of his close ties with the Roosevelt presidency, his manipulations of the black press, and his shrewd and timely establishment of the National Negro Business League. These activities added the final, fourth wheel to the tenuous coalition that the Wizard assembled among moderate Southern whites, Northern philanthropists, and the rural black peasantry, allowing the Tuskegee Machine to roll into the twentieth century as revved up as one of Henry Ford's new-fangled cars. To be sure, a vocal and articulate opposition refused to be awed or steamrolled, and rose up to challenge Washington's haughty position, whether as driver or as chauffeur. But ultimately, it was not until after the founding of the NAACP in 1909 that the Tuskegeean's commanding presence shifted from foreground to backdrop.

Pro-Washington sentiment in the periodicals was widespread: in glowing biographical profiles; in accounts of Tuskegee, Hampton, and other industrial schools; and in articles and speeches written by him. Overall, Washington's views as presented in the monthly periodicals are consistent with those presented in his book, *The Future of the American Negro.* Thus Washington advocated a program of industrial and agricultural education that would appeal to the self-interest of moderate Southern whites as well as address "the problem of teaching the Negro to stand on his own feet" by "laying the foundation in the little things of life that are immediately at the door."[111] Blacks, he said, must "put brains and skill into the common occupations that are about him, and . . . dignify common labor."[112] He was quick to remark that he favored "the highest and most thorough development of the Negro's mind," and that he "would not have the standard of mental development lowered one whit, for with the Negro, as with all races, mental strength is the basis of all progress." However, just as quickly, he added a significant qualification: "But I would have the larger proportion of this mental strength reach the Negro's actual needs through the medium of his hand."[113] As he remarked on another occasion, "the mere pushing of abstract knowledge into the head, if it is to end there, means little. . . . Our knowledge must be harnessed to the things of real life."[114]

Washington was a thoroughgoing utilitarian who believed that "in the last analysis, the world judges a race by its ability to show definite results, by its ability to achieve a high degree of usefulness."[115] The force of this logic extended in two directions. On the one hand, it reinforced what might be called Washington's "better mousetrap" theory of race relations: the Negro farmer who could dramatically increase his yield per acre, or the Negro mechanic with particularly skilled hands, would be sought out and respected by his white neighbors: "There is almost no prejudice against the Negro in the South in matters of business."[116] On the other hand, it reined in and provided a sense of direction to the black middle class, whom Washington argued should receive "that training which will best fit them to perform, in the most successful manner, the service which the race demands."[117] This small but growing professional group, Washington pointed out, was inextricably linked with the larger black laboring class: "The professional class will be helped in proportion as the rank and file have an industrial foundation so that they can pay for professional services."[118]

To use contemporary terms, Washington advocated a "bottom-up" theory of social development and of higher education's role within that process. His "gospel of wealth" dictated that "nearly all opportunities and privileges rest upon an economic and industrial base,"[119] and only from this primary foundation, this Rock, could his "gospel of the toothbrush" be effectively spread. There was more to it than just his quip, "it is not an easy thing to make a good Christian of a hungry man."[120] Rather, Washington forcefully answered his critics, rhetorically asking, "But would you confine the Negro to industrial life, to agriculture?" and then responding with his broader vision:

No; but I would teach the race that here the foundation must be laid, and the very best service which any one can render to what is called the higher education, is to teach the present generation to provide a material or industrial education foundation. On this industrial foundation will grow habits of thrift, the love of work, economy, ownership of property, and a bank account. Out of it, in the future generations, will grow classical education, professional education, positions of public responsibility. Out of it will grow moral and religious strength. Out of which will grow that wealth which brings leisure, and with it opportunity for the enjoyment of literature and the fine arts.[121]

If Washington's message was often tempered with what his critics charged were accommodationist tendencies, he did have a knack for making these statements seem as if constructive optimism was superior to criticism, that discretion was the better part of valor. "Our duty is to face the present and not to wail over the past,"[122] Washington would remark in one of his stock phrases, explaining to a graduating class at Hampton:

I hope you will not yield to the temptation of becoming grumblers and whiners, but will hold your head up and forward march bravely, meeting manfully and sensibly all the problems that may confront you. Place emphasis upon your opportunities rather than your disadvantages; place emphasis upon achievement rather than upon the injustices to which you will be subjected. . . . It often requires more courage to suffer in silence than to retaliate; more courage not to strike back than to strike; more courage to be silent than to speak.[123]

Washington's views summed to a powerful argument. The "Negro problem," as he saw it, was one of powerlessness—"Weakness invites injustice."[124] As he repeated again and again, "a foundation must be laid." Industrial education, in Washington's views, was not advocated "as an end, but as a means"[125]: "It is not stepping-stones alone, the mere matter of the Negro learning this or that trade, for which I plead; but . . . out of the trade or industry I want to see evolved the full-fledged, unhampered, unfettered man. I plead for industrial development, not because I want to cramp the Negro, but because I want to free him."[126]

Louis Harlan has written that Washington's program appealed to a broad cross section of the black population because it had "considerable social realism," while August Meier has maintained, in attempting to assess Washington's influence on turn-of-the-century black thought, that his contribution lay chiefly in terms of "reinforcing tendencies already in the foreground."[127] These comments go far in correcting the errors of either elevating criticisms of Washington into all-embracing dismissals of his social philosophy or regarding the Tuskegeean as an isolated figure who mouthed self-serving platitudes for, at best, a small group of passive, sycophantic followers. As numerous articles in the periodical literature of the decade demonstrate, various aspects of Washington's agenda struck a responsive chord among the black middle class because, at least in part, his ideas were theirs too.

There was widespread acceptance of the gospel of wealth as a road to racial uplift among the rising black middle class. Perhaps nowhere is this more clearly expressed than in articles relating the progress of the National Negro Business League. Supporters of the League claimed in the standard rhetoric of the times that "instead of begging for opportunities, they [the members] have made them, and instead of petitioning for rights, they are laying a foundation whereon they may stand and demand rights."[128] Likewise, an absence of protest at meetings was justified: "They uttered not one word concerning the franchise, mob violence, or any degrading customs. This was a masterly silence. . . . They understood themselves. It was a silence not from fear . . . [but] to stimulate their people throughout the country towards business. When this purpose bears its full fruitage, the Negro will be heard, for he will be sought."[129] Even the *Voice of the Negro* could be supportive of League efforts, editorializing on one occasion, "The League cries to the race, 'To work, Negroes, and economize, invest, and save your money. What we have lost in politics, like the Jews, let us gain in wealth!' "[130]

Pro-Washington sentiment was also presented in the dozens of articles on Tuskegee, Hampton, and other industrial schools that appeared in the pages of the *Colored American Magazine* and *Alexander's Magazine*. For the most part these articles did not concentrate on the ideological justifications of industrial education, but allowed these points to be raised while recounting a "success story." As with the profiles on black institutions of higher education, the stories on industrial schools followed a common formula: data was provided that indicated the growth of the institution in terms of buildings, number of teachers, and number of pupils; the trades and domestic arts taught were listed; and a glowing account told of triumph over trials and tribulations by the principal, who, along with his supportive wife, strove to "keep the faith" in the South's Black Belt. Extension work in the surrounding community was highlighted, while the school's moral atmosphere was frequently extolled.

Whereas Hampton Institute was given rather perfunctory acknowledgment in the periodicals, the reportage and rhetoric bestowed on Tuskegee proliferated. If Washington was the man of the hour in promoting the cause of "progressive" education for blacks, then Tuskegee was, for this decade and for these journals, the definitive "school of tomorrow."

High among the kudos consistently lavished on Tuskegee was the assertion that it represented "the conspicuous example of the constructive effort of a black man for black people."[131] Critics may have shaken their heads at the school's flashy charisma, but even for them there was no denying that it existed. With a total attendance by the early 1900s of more than 1,500 students, courses of instruction in thirty-seven industries, eighty-three buildings on the grounds, a plant that included 2,300 acres of land, and an endowment fund of more than $1 million, Tuskegee was an impressive facility—even on the printed page.[132]

A few articles provided a broad overview of Tuskegee's operation. The student body was divided into night students and day students. The former group worked all day, every day, at various trades to which they were assigned, and attended classes in the evening. Their daily labors paid for their boarding expenses and allowed them to accumulate enough credits to cover their subsequent matriculation as day students. The day students were divided into two groups who alternately attended academic classes every other day for three days a week and attended industrial classes for another three days. In a rare statement on academic proficiency, the school's academic dean, Roscoe Conkling Bruce, told a Boston audience in late 1904 that seniors at Tuskegee were about at the level of first or second year students in a New England high school.[133] In addition to the main body of the school's work, Tuskegee also conducted a kindergarten and training school for about

200 children, a night school in the town of Tuskegee, and social settlement work for women and young girls in the town and at a nearby plantation, headed by Mrs. Washington. The school and its various operations were open all year long. Around 150 officers and teachers were employed.[134]

Ranking in almost equal importance to articles on the school itself were stories on the famous Tuskegee Negro Conferences. Initiated in 1892, these annual two-day, mid-February affairs were a significant part of the grist for the school's propaganda mill, and evidently, judging from this propaganda, a significant component in Tuskegee's appeal among rural black farmers. These articles would highlight, as one headline proclaimed, Tuskegee's role in the "Social Development in the Black Belt." Washington would personally orchestrate the conferences in the manner of a spirited religious revival. More than 1,000 black families would gather on the school's grounds and listen as, one by one, individual farmers would provide firsthand accounts of conditions in their particular locale and tell of their hard-won success in overcoming obstacles. "Proudly they wave in the air paid off mortgages, or exhibit enviable samples of products, or display well constructed plans for new homes," one account of the proceedings related. "The slothful, on the other hand, witness these manifestations of thrift and yearn for a like distinction."[135]

Accounts of the Negro Conference accomplished two mutually reinforcing ends. First, Tuskegee was said to stand for the idea that "culture is service," and that this extension work defined the institution as much as the program for students.[136] Thus the uplift of the rural Black Belt was credited to Washington and his school. Second, all articles on the Tuskegee Negro Conferences reprinted, in whole or in part, the declarations adopted at the meetings' conclusion. These resolutions, following Washington-inspired themes, served as annual indications that Tuskegee was in tune with its people— and vice versa.

OPPOSITION TO BOOKER T. WASHINGTON

An appropriate point of departure in considering the criticisms leveled against Booker T. Washington and his program of uplift is in the differential reactions of the journals to the major national black social event of 1906– Tuskegee's 25th Anniversary Celebration. The April 4–6 celebration drew thousands to the school to join in the festivities and to honor its founder. *Alexander's Magazine* issued a Tuskegee Souvenir Number in May, reprinting the speeches of several enthusiastic participants, including those by Washington's Southern Education Board president Robert Ogden, philanthropist Andrew Carnegie, Harvard University president Charles William Eliot, and President Theodore Roosevelt's personal envoy, Secretary of War William Taft. The *Colored American Magazine* in its March issue announced the upcoming celebration in a rather snide editorial comparing Fisk's fortieth birthday with Tuskegee's twenty-fifth. The thrust of the piece was to the effect that "Fisk represents the genius of the white man; Tuskegee represents the genius of the black man."[137] Its coverage of the event itself was a laudatory article written by Washington's former speechwriter and soon-to-become nationally renowned sociologist Robert E. Park.[138]

Like the other two journals, the May 1906 issue of the *Voice of the Negro* carried extensive photos of the festivities, and even headlined the anniversary above its masthead on the front cover. But the *Voice*'s intent—the article is not attributed to any author but must have been written by J. Max Barber— was not to praise Tuskegee, but to deliver a stinging critique.

The power of this essay, similar, in a way, to Du Bois' chapter on Washington in his *Souls of Black Folk*, lay in its balanced, yet pointed approach. The article began by crying out against "the moral awryness of the times," asserting that "economic culture is more potent than mental or spiritual culture, and Tuskegee is its thermometer." Democracy was crumbling and "out of the wreck and chaos of old ideals is the tendency towards a sordid utilitarianism." But even these charges could not obscure the fact that Washington and his school had done "much good," that Tuskegee "is a blessing to the black belt of Alabama," and that Booker T. himself "possesses some of the elements of greatness and deserves credit." "Any opposition to Dr. Washington is unreasonable," the article stated, "which is based merely upon dislike for industrial schools." Rather, it was his "grave mistakes in public policy" that were the cause for alarm and dismay. Washington's policies, the essay charged, had "almost paralyzed" black higher education and had allowed the South to perpetuate the myth "that what the Negro wanted was not political and civic equality but industrial opportunity." To counter this situation, "high ideals" were needed—"The things which sustain and elevate character are higher in the hierarchy of forces . . . than the things we can handle."[139]

Although such criticism of Washington was not the first to be published in the *Voice*, it does capture the spirit of that journal toward the Tuskegeean for the previous eighteen months. For most of its first year in operation, the *Voice of the Negro* refrained from criticism of Washington. Emmett Scott, Washington's private secretary, served as an associate editor from January through August 1904, when continued run-ins with J. Max Barber caused him to resign.[140] In October 1904 the *Voice* published its first hint of criticism of the Tuskegeean's policies, remarking in otherwise supportive commentary on the National Negro Business League: "The continued assertion by some of our leaders that a man who can labor will not be discriminated against is untrue. . . . It is well enough to ask our people to secure industrial education but it is wrong to place all our ills upon a lack of such training or to recommend industrial education as a panacea."[141]

In December of that year, the *Voice*, undoubtedly Barber, printed a pair of cutting, satiric editorials—"What Is a Good Negro?" and "What Is an

Insolent Negro?"—that unmistakably mocked Washington and established the battlelines. " 'A good Negro' is one who says he does not want the ballot," the editorial began. "He orates before his people and advises them against going into politics. . . . 'A good Negro' is one who says that his race does not need the higher learning; that what they need is industrial education, pure and simple." Continuing in this vein for several paragraphs, the article concluded with a two-by-four on its shoulder, " 'A good Negro,' to speak the truth, the whole truth, and nothing but the truth, is a 'Dead Nigger.' That to the contrary notwithstanding: 'A man's a man . . . ' and 'Right is right, since God is God.' Here we stand."[142]

The battle was joined when, in January 1905, the *Voice* printed W. E. B. Du Bois' controversial assertion that $3,000 in "hush money" was spent in 1904 "to subsidize the Negro press in five leading cities."[143] In February 1905 the *Colored American Magazine* challenged Du Bois to name these publications, stating that until he produced his evidence, it would have to believe that he had "sunk to blackguardism; and that his right eye is an evil one, and his tongue is greased with slanderous oil."[144] The *Voice* did not resort to specific countercharges, but in both February and March 1905, editorials appeared deploring the "moneygetting attitude" of certain black leaders. In its editorial "Shall We Materialize the Negro," Washington's "false theory of race elevation and race recognition" was specifically denounced as contrary to the traditions of American democracy and as "downright soulless materialism."[145]

Although the *Voice*'s criticisms of Booker T. Washington became rather muted after Barber's account of the Niagara Movement's second meeting in late 1906, the *Horizon* took up the cudgels on its inception in January 1907. This "worthy watchman on the wall," as a friendly newspaper called it, kept up a running skirmish with Washington for its entire three-plus years of existence, seldom printing anything substantial, but throwing provocative little barbs in his direction from time to time. In August 1907, for example, under the headline "Whining Again," F. H. M. Murray wrote: "Booker himself imitates Johnnie Dunck of the 'canal boys' who was always doing exasperating and cowardly tricks—being especially given to tattling."[146] On another occasion, Washington was labeled a "Frankenstein" for a quote urging black parents not to let their children read black newspapers because "they see in them too many accounts of Negro oppression" and parents would not want their children to be "soured by such accounts."[147]

CONCLUSION: "EDUCATION IS TO BE OUR SALVATION"[148]

For black America, as for the nation as a whole, the early years of the twentieth century were a time of fluctuation and confusion. A new century called for reflection, and on reflection the situation looked bleak. The age of

Frederick Douglass had passed, and with him, common black perceptions held by his abolitionist colleagues. As the *Voice of the Negro* editorialized, "there has been a general revolution in American thought on the Negro question. The desire to maintain a real democracy crumbles. The old and ancient doctrines of equality have fallen into desuetude."[149]

Black efforts to forge new definitions in this changing social and economic milieu were chronicled, at least in part, by their monthly periodical press. These organs of black thought and discussion created during the 1900–1910 decade a "universe of discourse" of sorts, particularly among the black middle class and professional group, which wrote articles and constituted many of its readers, "a communion [which] served to define the Negro community to itself and to make clearer its relation to the white world across the color line."[150] As Frederick Dentweiler noted with regard to black newspapers in the early 1920s (and as would be equally valid for the periodical literature of the 1900–1910 decade), "instead of merely reflecting 'life,' the newspapers, in setting themes for discussion and suggesting the foci of attention, help powerfully to create that life."[151]

That this middle class and professional group was engaged in a process of self-definition was undeniable. Articles in all four monthlies, for example, presented debate over the name that blacks would call themselves. "Who Are We?" asked *Voice* editor J. W. E. Bowen, "Africans, Afro-Americans, Colored People, Negroes, or American Negroes?" After six pages of etymological discussion, Bower concluded that "Negroes" was the "most fitting race designation."[152] No! replied New York *Age* editor T. Thomas Fortune caustically: "We are Afro-Americans. The term Negro has not even a respectable tribe in Africa to dignify it, and the term 'colored' . . . may be dismissed from any consideration whatsoever. . . . I always feel a sort of merciful contempt for the goody-goody Afro-American who insists that he is a 'colored person.' "[153] For *Horizon* editor F. H. M. Murray, "somehow there seems to sling a taint to the term Afro-American. From its very birth it has been the chosen totem of the fakir and Janus-faced; of those who seek to live by 'treason, strategem' and 'spoils.' Good men and good measures regard it as tapu [sic]."[154] Both Booker T. Washington and Charles Alexander sided with the term "Negro," with Washington equivocating somewhat by acknowledging that some blacks preferred "Afro-American."[155] (*Alexander's Magazine* even published an article calling on the race to "Make the Name 'Nigger' Honorable."[156])

This chapter has already discussed the widespread agreement expressed in the journals over the purposes and benefits of education. Even acknowledging that sometimes linguistic ambiguities masked subtle differences, concerns such as equality of opportunity, proper recognition of ability and worth, service, leadership, and "right living" pervaded the literature and, along with the general terms of self-help and racial solidarity, formed a set of core values for this black middle class and professional group.

Many of these racial and class-based social concerns converged around an emphasis on "character." Insofar as character merged and blended issues of morality, education, struggle, family life, worthiness, and respectability, it is easy to see why a chorus of voices sang its praises. This attention to the issue of character helps to explain two dominant features of the periodical literature of the decade. One was the preponderance of biographical profiles on individual blacks—businessmen, editors, and others, achievers all—that appeared in all of the journals except the *Horizon*. A good deal of high-minded rhetoric was heaped on these entries. As one author stated, "the right purpose of biography is to lead, to teach, to inspire men; is to give hope to the faint heart, promise to the young and undeveloped character, strength to the weak and easily beset ambition . . . and more, biography is a beacon light to the shipwrecked, the sinking, the almost lost; is a thunder voice speaking through the trumpet of example."[157] These profiles not only fulfilled a recognition and modeling function, but they also displayed what many considered most important of all, "the power of character."[158] For William Pickens, biography was even more important than history, since "history deals with the development of principles; biography with that of character." As he explained, "the best biographies are perhaps those which set before us the characters, even more than the histories, of their subjects."[159]

Second, character's links to education, and particularly to ethical qualities, directly tied in with the extraordinary concern and commentary on black morality issues. Just as blacks' intellectual capabilities were under attack by white supremacists, and by the nation as a whole, so, too, was the race's morality on trial. The improvement of morality was part of the program of uplift of all black organizations, and in fact constituted a *raison d'être* in the philosophies of both industrial and higher education.[160] Commentators vehemently disputed assertions that education increased black criminality or that blacks were inherently an immoral people.[161] As one author commented, speaking for an entire people, "why the black man's moral infirmities are always a subject for platform speeches, for newspapers, for magazine articles, and of conversations is beyond my comprehension."[162] From these types of discussions sprang articles on the importance of proper family life, the necessity of homegetting, and other dictums that unified both middle-class norms and rural aspirations. These discussions also generated considerable commentary arguing that blacks were morally superior to whites. Just as Booker T. Washington could tell the race to take "a [moral] position way upon the high ground,"[163] so, too, could the *Voice of the Negro* argue that "the Negro has a higher sense of justice than the white man; he has never manifested half the avarice and inhumanity . . . ; he believes more in the Christian religion . . . ; and the Negro does not share equal responsibility with the white man for the unblushing profligacy which has thrust upon us an army of mulattoes."[164]

All of these considerations elevated the issue of character to the forefront of discussion during the 1900–1910 decade. There may have been minor disagreements over its relation to commercialism—with the *Voice* taking the lead in asserting that "the greatest need of the hour is not money, but character"[165]—but no one disputed its overall significance. As E. Franklin Frazier has explained, "there was one point on which the proponents of industrial education and higher education were agreed: the Negro student should strive to be respectable."[166]

Character and respectability served as the centerpiece for a number of issues and values uniting the black middle class. Even W. E. B. Du Bois and Booker T. Washington, the two archtypes of the division that rocked this group, held common views on key concerns. Both Du Bois and Washington could agree, for example, that, as Du Bois put it, "the responsibility for their own social regeneration ought to be placed largely upon the shoulders of the Negro people."[167] Both could agree on the need for a Negro Business League (although Du Bois rightly claimed credit for, and Washington never acknowledged, an 1899 investigation that preceded Washington's establishment of the League in 1900[168]). Both could agree on the necessity of carefully studying the conditions of Negro life, and that the "facts" uncovered through such investigations would immeasurably contribute to a program of uplift.[169] And both could agree on the importance of education's role in the social development of the black population—although they disagreed over how.

In a very real sense, the celebrated Washington-Du Bois dispute can be considered as an argument between the right and left wings of the black middle class and professional group over their differing approaches to social uplift for the race—the right wing depreciating protest somewhat while strongly favoring individual business advancement; the left wing advocating "manly," aggressive protest, and what they considered "higher ideals" than those implied in a self-first, wealth-first philosophy. Education was a key issue in these conflicting visions, not because protagonists essentially disagreed over the importance of education or that all forms of training were needed, but because their conflicting approaches gave priority to one form of education—industrial or higher—over the other.

As Meier has noted, and as Harlan concurs, Washington's program made considerable inroads among the black businessmen—and, by extension, the emerging black middle class and professional group—because of his ability to "transmute the laissez-faire individualism of the Gilded Age into the key for racial salvation."[170] In 1903 even W. E. B. Du Bois reluctantly had to admit to the growing influence of black commercial interests, remarking: "The old leaders of Negro opinion . . . are being replaced by new; neither the black preacher nor the black teacher leads as he did two decades ago. Into their place are pushing . . . the businessman, all those with property and money. And with this change, so curiously parallel to that of the Other-world, goes too the inevitable change in ideals."[171] These circumstances explain the dominant voice of the Bookerites for most of the decade.

If Washington and his wing maintained that a "foundation must be laid," if "the Negro needs industrial education in eminent degree, because . . . the very first step in social advance must be economic,"[172] then Du Bois and his allies came at things from the opposite direction. "Upon the foundation-stone of a few well-equipped Negro colleges of high and honest standards," the Atlanta University professor maintained, "can be built a proper system of free common schools in the South for the masses of the Negro people; any attempt to found a system of public schools on anything less than this— no narrow ideals, limited or merely technical training—is to call blind leaders for the blind."[173] If Washington can be said to have advocated a "bottom-up" program of social development, then Du Bois' program was "top-down." For Washington, it worked this way: "Without industrial development there can be no wealth; without wealth there can be no leisure; without leisure, no opportunity for the thoughtful reflection and the cultivation of high arts."[174] For Du Bois, the process went like this: "The very first step toward the settlement of the Negro problem is the spread of intelligence. The first step toward wider intelligence is a free public-school system; and the first step toward a public-school system is the equipment and adequate support of a sufficient number of Negro colleges."[175]

Washington and his supporters urged individual entrepreneurs to follow quietly the Protestant work ethic in a hypothesized meritocracy in which good would be rewarded, spreading the gospel of "usefulness" and industrial efficiency. Du Bois and his less numerous cohort countered that "necessary as it is to earn a living, it is more necessary and important to earn a life."[176] (As one poem in the *Voice* put it, "the life we live is more than meat/Beware the creed your lips repeat."[177]) Du Bois and his supporters would counsel the value of agitation, and would assert the foolhardiness of the belief "that those who toil and accumulate will be free to enjoy the fruits of their industry and frugality, if they permit themselves to be shorn of political power."[178]

For the most part, Du Bois did not often refer to his famous formulation of the "Talented Tenth" in the periodical literature of the decade. Rather, he hammered away at what he called the "educational heresy" that "makes the earning of a living the centre and worm of human training." "Wonderful ideals" were needed, Du Bois maintained, in a situation characterized by "an insistence on the practical in a manner and tone that would make Socrates an idiot and Jesus Christ a crank."[179] Occasionally he could be downright angry. In accusing the South "of seeking the perpetuation of ignorance under the name of 'Industrial Education,' " he bitterly exclaimed:

In educating a child one of the prime and indispensable things is to give him the key to further knowledge by teaching him to read, write and cipher. Without this, and with how much so ever else he may learn he is shut to eternal darkness and ignorance of modern life. Yet today our children are being taught to cook and whittle before they can read, and thousands never learn to read decently because they are busy learning "scientific agriculture." To Hell with such lying deception of the young and helpless.[180]

It was on these themes, and, of course, vigorous opposition to the Tuskegee Machine's system of spoils and patronage, that Du Bois and his wing staked their claim in the periodical press. The two were often indistinguishably interwoven. Du Bois and his colleagues were not totally adverse to industrial education, nor in fact did Washington's wing object absolutely to higher education. Most commentators throughout the decade would have agreed with that part of the resolutions adopted by the Negro Young People's Christian and Educational Congress in 1906, which stated: "The Negro requires every kind and degree of education to meet the wide circle of his needs. The question of industrial, higher or professional training is merely one of ratio and proportion, and must be left to individual aptitude, inclination, and opportunity.[181]

This fundamental tension—never exclusionary, but rather over appropriate balance within moderately conflicting theoretical approaches—played itself out throughout the decade, accompanied by varying degrees of acrimony and name calling. Education was only one component of black social uplift, although all agreed on its importance. As the *Voice* once stated, "it takes a hatfull [sic] of keys to unlock our problem."[182] As Kelly Miller put it, "the rise of educational, industrial and moral movements must be accorded their proper places in the 'up-push' of the race. . . . There is no difference among Negroes on fundamental principles, but on methods of accomplishment."[183]

Education was undeniably essential, but the periodical literature of the decade did not focus on this factor exclusively. Given the broad parameters of black social thought during the decade, each issue of each periodical would contain a wide variety of articles on current events and other topics viewed from a race perspective—in any given month, education might go unmentioned. In fact, the argument can be made that education was not the priority of the day in terms of overall black goals. Simply put, education was always on their broad civil rights agenda, but it was seldom number one. If anything, that top spot was reserved for justice. As the *Colored American Magazine* asserted in its opening issue, "What we desire, what we require, what we demand to aid in the onward march of progress and advancement is justice; merely this and nothing more."[184] Within this political framework, education was only one of many issues of injustice.

In terms of social uplift, as distinct from political demands, education was matched only partially by morality as a key concern, and linked with it through such notions as "character." Higher education was prominently featured—as opposed to elementary and secondary schooling—since its attainment played a critical role in demonstrating achievement, demanding proper recognition, establishing status, and pointing a route toward progress and respectability. But, equally important, an examination of the black monthly periodical literature of the 1900–1910 decade clearly indicates that all educational endeavors were prized. "Educate! Educate! Educate!" cried the *Voice of the Negro.* "Get all the knowledge within reach. Then use it for the good of the race."[185]

NOTES

1. John H. Adams, Jr., "Rough Sketches: A Study of the Features of the New Negro Woman," *Voice of the Negro* 1 (August 1904):324.

2. John Henry Adams, "Rough Sketches: The New Negro Man," *Voice of the Negro* 1 (October 1904):447.

3. S. Laing Williams, "The New Negro," *Alexander's Magazine* 7 (November 1908):18–19.

4. See Louis R. Harlan, *Booker T. Washington: The Wizard of Tuskegee, 1901–1915* (New York: Oxford University Press, 1983), 98–99, 330. See also Louis R. Harlan and Raymond W. Smock, eds., *The Booker T. Washington Papers*, vol. 8, 1904–1906 (Urbana: University of Illinois Press, 1979), 324, 524–525.

5. See August Meier, "Negro Class Structure and Ideology in the Age of Booker T. Washington," *Phylon* 23 (Fall 1962):258–266.

6. W. E. B. Du Bois, *The Black North in 1901* (1901; rpt. New York: Arno Press, 1969), 40.

7. See Charles S. Johnson, "The Rise of the Negro Magazine," *Journal of Negro History* 13 (January 1928):7–21; Abby Arthur Johnson and Ronald Maberry Johnson, *Propaganda and Aesthetics* (Amherst: University of Massachusetts Press, 1979); Penelope L. Bullock, *The Afro-American Periodical Press, 1838–1909* (Baton Rouge: Louisiana State University Press, 1981). It should also be noted that for the purposes of this article, the *Southern Workman*, a monthly journal published by the white administration of Hampton Institute, is not considered a black periodical. Frederick G. Detweiler in *Negro Press in the United States* (repr., College Park, Md.: McGrath, 1968) also explicitly excludes the *Southern Workman* as a Negro publication (p. 40), while neither Johnson mentions it nor Du Bois ("The Colored Magazine in America," *Crisis* 15 [November 1912]:33–35) in his overview of black periodical literature.

8. "Editorial and Publishers' Announcements," *Colored American Magazine* 1 (May 1900):60. See also R. S. Eliot, "The Story of Our Magazine," *Colored American Magazine* 3 (May 1901):43–69; William Stanley Braithwaite, "Negro America's First Magazine," *Negro Digest* 6 (December 1947):21–26.

9. See "Constitutional Rights Association of the United States," *Colored American Magazine* 1 (October 1900):309–311; "The Loyal Legion of Labor, USA," *Colored American Magazine* 5 (June 1902):111–117; "Loyal Legion of Labor, USA," *Colored American Magazine* 5 (August 1902):303–307; "Biographies of the Officers of the New Management of Our Magazine," *Colored American Magazine* 6 (May-June 1903):443–449; Pauline E. Hopkins, "How a New York Newspaper Man . . . " *Colored American Magazine* 7 (March 1904):151–160.

10. Pauline E. Hopkins, "Famous Men of the Negro Race—Robert Morris," *Colored American Magazine* 3 (September 1901):337. See Hopkins' reply to letter writer Cornelia A. Condict regarding her fiction, *Colored American Magazine* 6 (March

1903):399–400. See also "Pauline Elizabeth Hopkins: A Biographical Excursion into Obscurity," *Phylon* 33 (Spring 1972):22–26; Abby Arthur Johnson and Ronald M. Johnson, "Away from Accommodation: Radical Editors and Protest Journalism, 1900–1910," *Journal of Negro History* 62 (October 1977):325–338; Braithwaite, "Negro America's First Magazine," 24–25.

11. See August Meier, "Booker T. Washington and the Negro Press: With Special Reference to the *Colored American Magazine, Journal of Negro History* 38 (January 1953):67–90; Emma L. Thornbrough, "More Light on Booker T. Washington and the New York *Age*," *Journal of Negro History* 43 (January 1958):34–49. On Moore's denial of Washington's ownership, see "Publishers' Announcements," *Colored American Magazine* 7 (September 1904):606, and "In the Editor's Sanctum," *Colored American Magazine* 7 (November 1904):693. There is some question as to the date of Moore's first issue of the *Colored American Magazine.* Moore states that it was the June 1904 issue (p. 71), and this was the first issue to be published in New York and to list Moore as general manager; see "Publishers' Announcements," *Colored American Magazine* 7 (June 1904):458. Yet the May 1904 issue is the first to display the editorial page masthead "In the Editor's Sanctum," which then became a regular feature of the journal, and the lead editorial of that issue bears the unmistakable imprint of Washingtonian philosophy; see *Colored American Magazine* 7 (May 1904):382. Moore's own public account of his takeover of the journal is hazy on specific dates, but it implies that he bought the magazine in May 1904; see "Retrospection of a Year," *Colored American Magazine* 8 (June 1905):342–343.

12. "Publishers' Announcements," *Colored American Magazine* 7 (September 1904):606.

13. See Penelope L. Bullock, "The Negro Periodical Press in the United States," (Ph.D. diss., University of Michigan, 1971) 185; Charles S. Johnson, "The Rise of the Negro Magazine," *Journal of Negro History* 13 (January 1928):12; Du Bois, "The Colored Magazine in America," 33–35.

14. Du Bois, "The Colored Magazine in America," 33. Even Washington held the *Voice* in high esteem, believing that in "breadth, dignity and form" it was a better journal than the *Colored American Magazine*; see Harlan and Smock, *Booker T. Washington Papers*, vol. 8, 571.

15. "Discussion Not Crimination," *Voice of the Negro* 2 (April 1905):272.

16. Louis R. Harlan, "Booker T. Washington and the *Voice of the Negro*, 1904–1907," *Journal of Southern History* 45 (February 1979):46.

17. See J. Max Barber, "Why Mr. Barber Left Atlanta," *Voice of the Negro* 3 (November 1906):470–473; "Our Name Changed," *Voice of the Negro* 3 (November 1906):464; "Who Founded the *Voice*" and "Who Owns the *Voice*," *Voice of the Negro* 2 (March 1905):192–194; "The Voice Publishing Company," *Voice of the Negro* 3 (June 1906):398–399; Harlan, "Booker T. Washington and the *Voice of the Negro*," 45–62.

18. See letter from Barber to Du Bois, March 2, 1912, in Herbert Aptheker, ed., *The Correspondence of W. E. B. Du Bois*, vol. 12 (Amherst: University of Massachusetts Press, 1973), 176–177.

19. Bullock, "Negro Periodical Press," 161–165; Louis R. Harlan, *Booker T. Washington: The Wizard of Tuskegee*, 58–61.

20. See Bullock, "Negro Periodical Press," 161–165; Edwin Redkey, *Black Exodus: Black Nationalism and Back-to-Africa Movements, 1890–1910* (New Haven, Conn.:

Yale University Press, 1969). For an example of support for the emigrationist movement, see "Ten Strong Reasons Why Thrifty and Enterprising Negroes of the United
States Should Take Up Land in Liberia," *Alexander's Magazine* 5 (February 1908):75–
76. See also *Horizon* 4 (August 1908):18–19. Grimke edited *Horizon* from September
through November 1907.
21. Bullock, "Negro Periodical Press," 162.
22. Paul G. Partington, "The Moon Illustrated Weekly—The Precursor to the
Crisis," *Journal of Negro History* 48 (July 1963):206–216.
23. W. E. B. Du Bois, *Dusk of Dawn*. (1940. Repr. New York: Schocken Books,
1968), 93.
24. Samuel Barrett, "The Power of Education," *Colored American Magazine* 6
(November 1903):808–811.
25. J. H. Adams, "A Sign of Work," *Colored American Magazine* 13 (July 1907):25.
26. Fannie Barrier Williams, "Industrial Education—Will It Solve the Negro
Problem?" *Colored American Magazine* 7 (July 1904):493.
27. "The Chief Need of the Southern Negro," *Alexander's Magazine* 1 (March
1906):15.
28. W. E. B. Du Bois et al., "An Appeal for the Colored Schools in the State
of Georgia," *Colored American Magazine* 2 (February 1901):262.
29. John Edward Bruce, "Industrial Education: Will It Solve the Negro Problem?" *Colored American Magazine* 7 (January 1904):21.
30. "An Old and Worthy Institution," *Colored American Magazine* 14 (January
1908):432.
31. William Pickens, "Southern Negro in Northern University," *Voice of the Negro*
2 (April 1905):234.
32. "Loyal Legion of Labor, U.S.A.," *Colored American Magazine* 5 (August
1902):305. See also M. F. Hunter, "The Alabama Conference," *Colored American
Magazine* 1 (June 1900):104–108; George Gilbert Walker, "Our Ideals," *Colored American Magazine* 14 (April 1908):183–185.
33. Cyrus Field Adams, "The Afro-American Council," *Colored American Magazine* 6 (March 1903):332.
34. "What Things the Race Should Emphasize," *Colored American Magazine* 12
(June 1907):407.
35. Carrie Thomas Jordan, "A Plea for Right Education," *Colored American Magazine* 13 (December 1907):443.
36. "The Twenty-fifth Anniversary of Tuskegee," *Colored American Magazine* 10
(March 1906):154. See also R. R. Wright, "Agricultural and Mechanical Colleges,"
Alexander's Magazine 1, no. 8 (1906):19.
37. "Negroes Crowding the Schools," *Colored American Magazine* 11 (November
1906):286.
38. Du Bois et al., "Appeal for the Colored Schools," 263.
39. "When Ignorance Is Bliss," *Alexander's Magazine* 1 (October 1906):47.
40. G. W. Forbes, "The Last Act," *Colored American Magazine* 1 (June 1900):109.
41. See Gunnar Myrdal, *An American Dilemma* (New York: Harper & Row, 1944).
42. Du Bois et al., "Appeal for the Colored Schools," 263; Booker T. Washington,
"The Storm Before the Calm" *Colored American Magazine* 1 (December 1905):210.
43. William Pickens, "The Educational Condition of the Negro in Cities," *Voice
of the Negro* 3 (October 1906):430.

44. R. C. Murray, "Fisk University, A Light Upon a Hill," *Colored American Magazine* 8 (April 1905):210.

45. Booker T. Washington, "Abraham Lincoln," *Colored American Magazine* 16 (April 1909):238; W. S. Scarborough, "The College and the Student," *Colored American Magazine* 14 (October 1908):545.

46. References to "usefulness" filled the literature. See, for example, "What Hampton Students are Doing," *Colored American Magazine* 10 (June 1906):365; Williams, "Industrial Education—Will It Solve the Negro Problem?" 495; Roscoe Conkling Bruce, "Does Tuskegee Educate?" *Colored American Magazine* 8 (January 1905):18.

47. "Twenty-fifth Anniversary of Tuskegee," 154.

48. William Pickens, "Talladega College," *Colored American Magazine* 10 (April 1906):244.

49. Woolford Damon, "Twenty-third Annual Session of the National Negro Baptist Convention," *Colored American Magazine* 6 (November 1903):788.

50. "A Message to the Race," *Voice of the Negro* 2 (January 1905):696.

51. Roscoe Conkling Bruce, "Service by the Educated Negro," *Colored American Magazine* 6 (December 1903):857. Service to the race was probably a popular theme in graduation addresses. See also "Commencement Address by the Hon. W. H. Lewis to Graduates of M Street High School," *Colored American Magazine* 14 (July 1908):425–429.

52. Kelly Miller, "Religion and Education," *Voice of the Negro* 1 (April 1904):164.

53. See, for example, George Jenifer, "The Study of Literature in Colored Schools," *Voice of the Negro* 3 (February 1906):135–137; J. Milton Waldron, "Inside View of the Conditions and Needs of the Colored People of the South," *Colored American Magazine* 6 (October 1903):716–717; Mabel Parsons, "Spelman Seminary," *Colored American Magazine* 14 (February-March 1908):140; Josephine Silone Yates, "The Equipment of the Teacher," *Voice of the Negro* 1 (June 1904):251.

54. S. Ward, "Education, a Means Rather Than an End," *Colored American Magazine* 6 (September 1903):665; Pauline E. Hopkins, "Famous Women of the Negro Race, VII," *Colored American Magazine* 5 (June 1902):129.

55. See, for example, Emily A. Harper, "The Hampton Summer Normal," *Colored American Magazine* 5 (October 1902):403; Pauline E. Hopkins, "Famous Women of the Negro Race, VI," *Colored American Magazine* 5 (May 1902):42; Nannie H. Burroughs, "Industrial Education—Will It Solve the Negro Problem?" *Colored American Magazine* 7 (March 1904):189.

56. "A State Convention of the Loyal Legion of Labor," *Colored American Magazine* 6 (January 1903):22.

57. W. E. B. Du Bois, "Industrial Education—Will It Solve the Negro Problem?" a reprint of his "The Training of Negroes for Social Power," *Colored American Magazine* 7 (May 1904):334.

58. See Archibald H. Grimke, "Talledega College," *Alexander's Magazine* 1 (September 1905):5; Mary W. Ovington, "Industrial School for Colored Youth," *Colored American Magazine* 14 (May 1908):277.

59. "The Woman's Central League Training School," *Colored American Magazine* 3 (June 1901):148; Josephine Silone Yates, "Lincoln Institute," *Colored American Magazine* 12 (January 1907):26–27.

60. See, for example, Washington, "Storm Before the Calm," 203; "Causes and

Remedies for the Negro's Flocking to the Cities," *Voice of the Negro* 1 (May 1904):209–210.

61. "Virginia Union University," *Colored American Magazine* 2 (January 1901):172.

62. Bruce, "Service by the Educated Negro," 854.

63. "Negroes Hurrahing Over Heroes the White Man Makes," *Colored American Magazine* 14 (June 1908):328.

64. "Can the Ethiopian Change His Skin?" 127.

65. Timothy Thomas Fortune, "False Theory of Education Cause of Race Demoralization," *Colored American Magazine* 7 (July 1904):473–478.

66. "The Way of the World," *Colored American Magazine* 7 (September 1904):569.

67. Charles H. Moore, "State Agricultural and Mechanical College," *Colored American Magazine* 4 (December 1901):148.

68. R. M. Hall, "The Future of the Afro-American," *Colored American Magazine* 3 (July 1901):204; Daniel Murray, "Cyrus Field Adams," *Colored American Magazine* 4 (December 1901):148.

69. Josephine S. Yates, "Education Department," *Colored American Magazine* 12 (June 1907):442. See also Alexander Crummell, "Character: The Great Thing," in W. E. B. Du Bois, *Some Efforts of American Negroes for Their Own Social Betterment* (1898, Atlanta University Publications, No. 3; rpt. New York: Arno Press, 1969), 36–39.

70. Hall, "Future of the Afro-American," 204.

71. "After Graduation What?" *Voice of the Negro* 1 (June 1904):257.

72. See, for example, "Self-culture as the Keystone of Education," *Colored American Magazine* 11 (November 1906):324–326; Annie E. Tucker, "Formation of Child Character," *Colored American Magazine* 2 (February 1901):261; Oliver W. Curtis, "Character-Building," *Colored American Magazine* 15 (March 1909):145–146; Mrs. J. W. E. Bowen, "The Nation's Nursery," *Voice of the Negro* 1 (March 1904):113–114.

73. "Self-culture as the Keystone of Education," 325.

74. Scarborough, "College and the Student," 546; Edith Millan, "Discipline in Modern Education," *Colored American Magazine* 13 (December 1907):425.

75. Clarence Miller, "The True Object of Education," *Voice of the Negro* 1 (July 1904):315.

76. James Merrill, "The Work of Fisk University," *Alexander's Magazine* 1 (June 1905):4; William Holtzclaw, "The Growth of the Normal and Industrial School Idea," *Colored American Magazine* 11 (August 1906):118.

77. N. R. Clay, "40th Anniversary of Rust University," *Voice of the Negro* 3 (July 1906):481.

78. See, for example, Murray, "Fisk University," 207.

79. Forbes, "Last Act," 111.

80. Parsons, "Spelman Seminar," 140.

81. John Hope, "Our Atlanta Schools," *Voice of the Negro* 1 (January 1904):10–16.

82. W. E. B. Du Bois, "The College Bred Negro" (1900; rpt. *The Atlanta University Publications*, New York: Arno Press, 1969), 16. Percentages calculated by author.

83. Horace Bumstead, "Higher Education of the Negro—Its Practical Value,"

in *Report of the Commissioner of Education for the Year 1902*, vol. 1 (Washington, D.C.: Government Printing Office, 1903), 227.

84. "Some Schools That Need Help," *Colored American Magazine* 8 (February 1905):62.

85. "The Fortieth Anniversary of Fisk," *Colored American Magazine* 10 (February 1906):85.

86. See Murray, "Fisk University," 209–210; Henry Hugh Proctor, "Forty Years at Fisk," *Voice of the Negro* 15 (March 1906):181.

87. "Fisk University," *Colored American Magazine* 14 (January 1908):53.

88. Merrill, "Work of Fisk University," 4.

89. "Fisk University," 54.

90. Proctor, "Forty Years at Fisk," 182.

91. "What Is the Matter with the Atlanta Schools," *Colored American Magazine* 13 (November 1907):333.

92. W. E. B. Du Bois and Augustus G. Dill, "The College-Bred Negro American," in *The Atlanta University Publications* (1910; rpt. New York: Arno Press, 1968), 13.

93. John Henry Adams, "The Negro at Self-help," *Voice of the Negro* 4 (March 1907):122; Adams, "Sign of Work," 18.

94. Adams, "Negro at Self-help," 124.

95. Charles Alexander, "Morris Brown College," *Alexander's Magazine* 1 (March 1906):123.

96. See Roscoe Simmons, "Spelman Seminary, 'The Mount Holyoke of the South,' " *Colored American Magazine* 11 (June 1906):42–50; "Two Great Schools," *Voice of the Negro* 13 (April 1906):289.

97. Hope, "Our Atlanta Schools," 14; Parsons, "Spelman Seminary," 134–135.

98. See, for example, Pickens, "Southern Negro in Northern University," 234–236; C. C. Poindexter, "Some Student Experiences," *Voice of the Negro* 3 (May 1906):335–338. For an interesting debate between William Pickens and social settlement leader Mary White Ovington over objections to black students on white campuses, see Ovington's response to Pickens' April 1905 article, "Disagrees with Pickens," *Voice of the Negro* 2 (July 1905):469, and "Pickens' Reply to Miss Ovington," *Voice of the Negro* 2 (August 1905):559–560.

99. See W. E. B. Du Bois, *The Negro Common School* (1901; rpt. New York: Arno Press, 1969); W. E. B. Du Bois and Augustus Dill, *The Common School and the Negro American* (1911; rpt. New York: Arno Press, 1968), 7.

100. See criticism of Seth Low's address at the 1905 meeting of the Conference for Education in the South, "Separate Education in the South," *Colored American Magazine* 8 (June 1905):292–293.

101. "The N.Y.P.C.E. Congress," *Alexander's Magazine* 2 (September 1906):21.

102. Du Bois et al., "Appeal for the Colored Schools," 262.

103. L. M. Hershaw, "Who Pays the Bill," *Horizon* 2 (August 1907):11. See also William Pickens, "The Educational Condition of Negroes in Cities," *Voice of the Negro* 3 (October 1906):427–430; William Pickens, "Negro Public Education in Alabama," *Voice of the Negro* 3 (September 1906):641–644. See also Charles Coon, "Public Taxation and Negro Schools," in *Proceedings of the Twelfth Conference for Education in the South* (Nashville: Executive Committee for the Conference, 1909), 157–167.

104. W. E. B. Du Bois, "Compulsory Education and the Negro," *Horizon* 6 (July 1910):5.

105. "The Atlanta Public Schools," *Voice of the Negro* 3 (March 1906):165.

106. See N. F. Mossell, "The National Afro-American Council," *Colored Magazine* 3 (August 1901):293; Archibald Grimke, "A Brief History of the Niagara Movement," *Alexander's Magazine* 4 (September 1907):252; "N.Y.P.C.E. Congress," 21; J. R. E. Lee, "The National Association of Teachers of Colored Youths," *Voice of the Negro* 2 (June 1905):385; "Senator Blair Vindicated," *Voice of the Negro* 1 (April 1904):167.

107. "Editorial and Publishers' Announcements," *Colored American Magazine* 1 (May 1900); L. M. Hershaw, *Horizon* 5 (May 1910):10.

108. Holtzclaw, "Growth of the Normal and Industrial School Idea," 118; "The 'Niagara Movement,' " *Colored American Magazine* 13 (October 1907):248.

109. "Shall We Materialize the Negro?" *Voice of the Negro* 2 (March 1905):194; W. E. B. Du Bois, "The Lash," *Horizon* 1 (May 1907):5.

110. Kelly Miller (written under the pseudonym "Fair Play"), "Washington's Policy," *Colored American Magazine* 6 (November 1903):824.

111. "Speech of Dr. Booker T. Washington," *Alexander's Magazine* 2 (May 1906):62.

112. Booker T.Washington, "The Negro's Part in the South's Upbuilding," *Voice of the Negro* 1 (January 1904):30.

113. Washington, "Industrial Education—Will It Solve the Negro Problem?" 90; Washington, "Negro's Part," 29.

114. Washington, "Storm Before the Calm," 204.

115. Washington, quoted in J. W. E. Bowen, "Doing Things at the Tuskegee Institute," *Voice of the Negro* 2 (April 1905):250.

116. Washington, "Industrial Education—Will It Solve the Negro Problem?" 89.

117. Washington, "Storm Before the Calm, 204.

118. Washington, "Industrial Education—Will It Solve the Negro Problem?" 89.

119. Washington, "Storm Before the Calm," 206.

120. Washington, "Industrial Education—Will It Solve the Negro Problem?" 92.

121. Washington, "Storm Before the Calm," 204–205.

122. Ibid., 201.

123. Washington, quoted in E. Jay Ess, "Work of the Hampton Institute, *Alexander's Magazine* 1 (May 1905):12–13.

124. "Speech of Dr. Booker T. Washington," 63.

125. Washington, "Industrial Education—Will It Solve the Negro Problem?" 92.

126. Washington, "Storm Before the Calm," 205–206.

127. Harlan, *Booker T. Washington*, x; August Meier, *Negro Thought in America, 1880–1915* (Ann Arbor: University of Michigan Press, 1963), 18.

128. Roscoe C. Simmons, "What Has the Negro Business League Accomplished?" *Colored American Magazine* 9 (August 1905):449.

129. George E. Stevens, "Wealth Maketh Many Friends," *Colored American Magazine* 2 (November 1900):25.

130. "The National Negro Business League," *Voice of the Negro* 3 (September 1906):667.

131. "Twenty-fifth Anniversary of Tuskegee," 150.

132. "Annual Report of Principal B. T. Washington," 284–286; "Tuskagee's An-

nual Report," *Voice of the Negro* 2 (December 1905): 873; for criticism, see "Tuskegee's Twenty-fifth Anniversary," *Voice of the Negro* 3 (May 1906):316.

133. See, for example, Bruce, "Does Tuskegee Educate?" 17–21.

134. R. C. Bedford, "Results of Twenty-one Years Work at Tuskegee," *Colored American Magazine* 5 (July 1902):117–225.

135. G. David Houston, "The Tuskegee Negro Conference," *Alexander's Magazine* 3 (March 1907):242.

136. Bowen, "Doing Things at Tuskegee," 251.

137. "Twenty-fifth Anniversary of Tuskegee," 151.

138. Robert E. Park, "Tuskegee and Its Mission," *Colored American Magazine* 10 (May 1906):347–354. For Park's relationship with Washington, see Fred H. Matthews, *Quest for an American Sociology: Robert E. Park and the Chicago School* (Montreal: McGill-Queen's University Press, 1977).

139. "The Twenty-fifth Anniversary of Tuskegee," 315–322.

140. See Louis R. Harlan, "Booker T. Washington and the *Voice of the Negro*," 45–62.

141. "The Negro Business League," *Voice of the Negro* 1 (October 1904):435.

142. "What Is a Good Negro?" *Voice of the Negro* 1 (December 1904):619.

143. W. E. B. Du Bois, "Debit and Credit," *Voice of the Negro* 2 (January 1905):677.

144. "Mr. Du Bois in a New Role," *Colored American Magazine* 8 (February 1905):67.

145. "Shall We Materialize the Negro?" 193, 195; "Character-Training," *Voice of the Negro* 2 (February 1905):126.

146. F. H. M. Murray, "Whining Again," *Horizon* 2 (August 1907):22.

147. "Frankenstein," *Horizon* 1 (May 1907):25.

148. W. S. Scarborough, "The Negro's Program for 1906," *Voice of the Negro* 3 (January 1906):48.

149. "Tuskegee's Twenty-Fifth Anniversary," 315.

150. David Gordon Nielson, *Black Ethos: Northern Urban Negro Life and Thought, 1890–1930* (Westport, Conn.: Greenwood Press, 1977), 50.

151. *Negro Press in the United States*, 268.

152. J. W. E. Bowen, "Who Are We?" *Voice of the Negro* 3 (January 1906):31–36.

153. T. Thomas Fortune, "Who Are We?" *Voice of the Negro* 3 (March 1906):194–196.

154. F. H. M. Murray, *Horizon* 1 (April 1907):22.

155. "Negro or 'Colored,' " *Colored American Magazine* 11 (July 1906):709; "Naming a Race," *Alexander's Magazine* 2 (June 1906):5. See also William Pickens, "Biography," *Voice of the Negro* 4 (January/February 1907):60–61.

156. T. N. Carter, "Make the Name 'Nigger' Honorable," *Alexander's Magazine* 1 (June 1905):7–8.

157. John Henry Adams, "Rough Sketches: W. E. B. Du Bois, Ph.D.," *Voice of the Negro* 2 (March 1905):176.

158. Murry, "Cyrus Field Adams," 149.

159. Pickens, "Biography," 60.

160. See, for example, Bruce, "Does Tuskegee Educate?" 17; Murray, "Fisk University," 210.

161. See, for example, W. E. B. Du Bois, "Vardaman," *Voice of the Negro* 3 (March 1906):189–194.

162. Robert W. Carter, "In Defense of the Race," *Colored American Magazine* 1 (September 1900):252–253.

163. Washington, "Storm Before the Calm," 207.

164. "The Logic of the Liar," *Voice of the Negro* 3 (February 1906):93.

165. "Character-Training," 126.

166. E. Franklin Frazier, *Black Bourgeoisie* (New York: The Free Press, 1957), 76–77.

167. Du Bois, "Industrial Education—Will It Solve the Negro Problem?" 333.

168. W. E. B. Du Bois, "The Growth of the Niagara Movement," *Voice of the Negro* 3 (January 1906):45.

169. See, for example, W. E. B. Du Bois, "The Atlanta Conferences," *Voice of the Negro* 1 (March 1904):85–90.

170. August Meier, "The Emergence of Negro Nationalism," Part II, *Midwest Journal* 4 (Summer 1952):104; Louis R. Harlan, "Booker T. Washington and the National Negro Business League," in *Seven on Black: Reflections on the Negro Experience in America*, ed. William G. Shade and Roy C. Herrenkohl (Philadelphia: J. B. Lippincott Co., 1969), 73–91.

171. Du Bois quoted in Harlan, "Booker T. Washington and the National Negro Business League," 89.

172. Bruce, "Does Tuskegee Educate?" 17.

173. Du Bois, "Industrial Education—Will It Solve the Negro Problem?" 335.

174. Washington, "Storm Before the Calm," 205.

175. Du Bois, "Industrial Education—Will It Solve the Negro Problem?" 335.

176. W. E. B. Du Bois, "The Hampton Idea," *Voice of the Negro* 3 (September 1906):635.

177. Benjamin G. Brawley, "The Education," *Voice of the Negro* 2 (May 1905):319.

178. Reverdy C. Ransom, "The Spirit of John Brown," *Voice of the Negro* 3 (October 1906):416; W. E. B. Du Bois, "The Value of Agitation," *Voice of the Negro* 4 (March 1907):109–110.

179. Du Bois, "Hampton Idea," 634.

180. W. E. B. Du Bois, "J'Accuse," *Horizon* 5 (February 1910):1–2.

181. "N.Y.P.C.E. Congress," 20.

182. "The National Negro Business League," *Voice of the Negro* 2 (October 1905):724.

183. Kelly Miller, "Come Let Us Reason Together," *Voice of the Negro* 3 (January 1906):46.

184. "Editorial and Publishers' Announcements," 61.

185. "A Message to the Race," 696.

7

Education for Life: Adult Education Programs for African Americans in Northern Cities, 1900–1942

V. P. Franklin

During the first three decades of the twentieth century, southern black migrants to northern urban centers were pushed by the absence of economic opportunities in the rural South and pulled by the possibility of economic advancement in the North. As was the case with other unskilled agricultural workers and "country folk," the large industrial and port cities had many attractions, not the least of which was the possibility of "making it big." There were many similarities in the initial experiences of Southern black and white migrants to northern and southern cities. Poor Southern blacks and whites arrived almost penniless in an area where a relative or friend from the point of origin was already settled. The relative or friend helped the migrant find housing and employment, usually in the same neighborhood. Indeed, the initial experiences of Southern and Eastern European immigrants also came to resemble this broad pattern of "chain migration." Older residents and anxious newcomers were bound together by cultural ties and familial relationships formed in their homelands. These relationships and connections cushioned the adjustment of the black migrants and white immigrants to Pittsburgh, Philadelphia, Buffalo, and other northern cities.[1]

Migrant and immigrant assistance programs were usually part of the system of mutual benefit societies previously started by the members of the social or cultural groups already residing in the urban centers. This "social network" existed for immigrant as well as religious and racial or cultural groups in the city, and included the private and public immigrant aid societies and municipal agencies that assisted new arrivals in finding temporary housing and employment. The effectiveness of these Progressive social welfare programs, as well as the motivations behind the educational projects aimed at poor immigrant and migrant families and individuals, has been the subject of much debate recently among social and educational researchers.[2]

Given these initial continuities in the experiences of black and white migrants and immigrants in the cities, there soon began to develop significant discontinuities in the experiences of blacks and whites in both northern and southern cities. The employment patterns and occupational distribution of native-born whites and European immigrants began to converge in the manufacturing and industrial sectors of the urban economy, while black migrants were overwhelmingly employed in the domestic and service sector. Even when blacks were employed in trade and transportation or in industry, they were confined to the low-status, unskilled positions.[3]

European immigrants spent one or possibly two generations in the slums and tenement districts, while the black migrants and their children were limited to preexisting black residential areas, which were often slums and back alleys in congested industrial districts, especially along the waterfronts. Blacks were usually forced to remain in these sections for several generations. The public schools serving these predominantly black residential areas were often the oldest, least equipped, and most overcrowded schools in the entire system, and the black high school graduation rates remained well below those of other groups.[4]

Given the depressed and depressing economic and public educational circumstances for black migrants seeking work in urban America, even during periods of prosperity, it should come as no surprise that when specialized educational programs were offered to adult blacks in Chicago, Philadelphia, Pittsburgh, New York City, Detroit, Cleveland, Cincinnati, Boston, and Baltimore, they responded enthusiastically. However, from the beginning a major problem was the generally shaky financial support for these adult education programs, especially before the end of World War II, whether they were sponsored by African American cultural institutions, organized philanthropy, or the state. Impoverished and underemployed urban blacks could not afford to pay for private schooling or the fees needed to maintain many locally sponsored adult training activities, so the programs had to be subsidized.

In surveying the specialized educational programs for black adults in northern cities from the onset of the Great Migration to the beginning of World War II, we find that black cultural institutions, organized charity, and the local, state, or federal government provided the bulk of the financial and educational resources. However, the implementation and success of these programs usually depended on the skills of black professionals who shared the educational and cultural commitments of the African American population.

AFRICAN AMERICAN CULTURAL INSTITUTIONS

The Great Migration placed severe strains on black religious and social institutions, and identifiable "class tensions" have been documented within the evolving black communities of Chicago, New York City, Cleveland, and other cities.[5] However, the predominant motivation behind black self-help efforts in the early decades of this century appears to have been religious, and social welfare and adult education programs were usually sponsored or subsidized by black churches and other religious institutions. This religious and cultural commitment managed to overcome potential class tensions. In November 1907 the Reverend Richard Robert Wright, Jr., touched on this issue in an essay on "Social Work and Influence of the Negro Church," which he contributed to a special issue of *The Annals of the American Academy of Political and Social Science* devoted to "Social Work of the Church."

In his introductory essay to the special issue, the Reverend Edward Judson, pastor of Memorial Baptist Church in New York City, contrasted the inspirational church, in which the ministers and parishioners come into contact only once or twice a week during regular religious services, with the institutional church, in which the ministers meet "the same people in small groups, at close quarters, and many times during the week." The objective of the institutional churches in impoverished urban areas was to supplement their standard fare of "prayer and praise and preaching . . . with a system of institutions, educational and philanthropic, through which [they] may touch in a helpful way man's physical, mental, and social nature." Rev. Judson believed that the "true missionary spirit" required the institutional churches to work with the Salvation Army, the Young Men's and Young Women's Christian Association, the Board of Education, and settlement houses because "the churches need to feel more of that social compunction which is the high water mark of modern civilization; that spirit which impels cultivated people to dwell in settlements among the poor."[6]

Wright surveyed social work activities within the African Methodist Episcopal (AME) Church, the African Methodist Episcopal Zion, African Union Methodists, Colored Methodists Episcopal, and National Baptist Convention, and found that the proliferation of colleges, universities, seminaries, and other educational institutions sponsored by these black religious denominations demonstrated a real "social commitment and influence." However, at the local level, especially in the large cities, "the chief work of the Methodist denominations has been the building of a strong central organization; and much that might have been hoped in the way of social work by the local church has been omitted. . . . The very independence and isolation of Baptists has retarded their social work."[7]

Wright was in a position to know, for he had come to the Department of Sociology at the University of Pennsylvania from Chicago, where he had served as a pastor of one of two "experimental" AME institutional churches in Chicago. "Seven years ago [1900] the AME Church made a definite attempt to minister to the city environment through the specially established Institutional Church in Chicago." These churches attempted to provide social services, including literacy training and commercial courses, open to all "regardless of the church affiliations of the individuals making it up." Both experiments were abandoned, however, because of a "clash of ideals" between those who held big-city and small-town ideals. These Negro churches "do an immense amount of unsystematized charity and social work, but it is largely done to secure money to pay Church debts and not for social uplift."[8]

As far as Wright was concerned, African American churches in rural areas provided little or no social services, for children or adults. The small-town church provided the standard and served as a cultural center, encouraging "talent in music, dramatic art, and other fields," and maintained a "bureau of charities." "In an unofficial way it cares for the sick and makes provision for the poor. . . . Attached to it are often benefit societies, orphan homes, and families who will take orphaned children."

In the large cities, however, "the Church has no monopoly" on social activity and cultural entertainment; and the larger, more successful churches were dominated by "the personality of the pastors and their peculiar method of preaching" and were not dependent on social services for attracting members. Wright argued that "in New York, Chicago, Philadelphia, Baltimore, Washington, New Orleans, and other cities there are Negro churches whose membership is from 1,000 to 2,500 persons. . . . Negro churches are composed almost entirely of working men [and women], and there is not room enough." Wright concluded that in 1907, "the wisest of the leaders of the Negro churches in the large cities [saw] the need of ministering to the larger social needs of the Negroes who flock to their midst."[9]

Specialized educational programs for black adults were offered in Wright's Trinity Mission AME Church in Chicago, and earlier at the Institutional Church and Social Settlement, which was opened on the South Side by the Reverend Reverdy C. Ransom in an old concerted Railroad Mission in 1901. Ransom's Institutional Church became a place where "men and women met for the betterment of humanity and for the uplifting of the race." A kindergarten, social groups for young boys and girls, a Men's Forum, and a Women's Club were started. Unfortunately, as was later the case with Wright's church, Ransom's social settlement "was bitterly fought by some of the leading [AME] Negro clergymen in Chicago," and Ransom had to seek financial support from wealthy white capitalists in Chicago. When Ransom made public his opposition to the policy gambling racket which "waxed bold enough to ply their trade among [the] Negro children on Chicago's South Side," he and his church were physically attacked by racketeers. On May 3, 1904, the Institutional Church was dynamited, and substantial damage was inflicted on the church building. This event solidified AME opposition to Ransom's work, and he was soon transferred to a church in New Bedford, Massachusetts.[10]

The Reverend Matthew Anderson, pastor of Berean Presbyterian Church in Philadelphia, was much more successful in developing his institutional black church. Anderson took over the church in 1884, and aware of the need for industrial and commercial training for blacks in the city, he opened a school that offered manual training courses for black adults and received a great deal of support from the religious and secular community. A graduate of Oberlin College and Princeton Theological Seminary, Anderson worked to improve the "economic problems of Negro city life." A free kindergarten was started in the church in 1884, a building and loan association was established in 1888, and the Berean Manual Training and Industrial School was opened in 1899. By 1907 the school had enrolled more than 200 adult students who were taking courses in carpentry, upholstering, millinery, plain sewing and dressmaking, stenography, cooking, and tailoring. These specialized programs were not only for members of the church; "any one [could] secure benefit from them without obligating him to the Presbyterian creed."[11]

In other northern cities there were large and famous black churches that sponsored social service and educational programs for black adults. In New York City the Abyssinian Baptist Church was known for the dynamism of its pastor, the Reverend Adam Clayton Powell, Sr., and for its social and educational programs, beginning in 1922. The Abyssinian Community House sponsored numerous adult educational programs, and in the 1930s donated its facilities for adult educational programs sponsored by philanthropic groups and the federal government. Metropolitan Baptist Church in Washington, D.C., was known for its leadership training classes, community study groups, and other educational programs. In Chicago, Congregationalist Church of the Good Shepherd, under the pastorship of the Reverend Arthur D. Gray, became a community-centered church in 1925, and provided employment counseling and vocational guidance, health education, and library facilities, and later established Parkway Community House, where adult training programs were offered.[12]

Black churches and public and private schools serving the expanding northern black communities also provided the facilities for specific educational campaigns aimed at black adults, such as National Negro Health Week. Major R. R. Moton, the successor of Booker T. Washington at Tuskegee Institute, noted in 1928 that Negro Health Week was "another movement of large public significance which has met with gratifying success and which also originated within the race."[13] The idea for a public health education campaign aimed at blacks seems to have come from the Negro Health Society of Virginia in 1913, but was popularized by Booker T. Washington, who devoted one session of the Annual Tuskegee Negro Conference in April 1914 to "The Conservation of Negro Health." Washington participated in several public health conferences, where he argued that "the entire South is dependent in a large measure upon the Negro for certain kinds of work. A weak body, a sickly body, is costly to the whole community and to the whole State from an economic point of view."[14]

Diseased and sickly Southern black migrants to northern cities became the concern of white public health officials as well as of older black residents. The extremely high tuberculosis rates among blacks in northern cities assisted the speedy adoption of National Negro Health Week as an annual affair. In Philadelphia, New York City, Chicago, Cleveland, and other large cities, the second week in April was designated as the time for health checkups for children and adults, for public health exhibitions to be mounted in predominantly black public schools, and for physicians and nurses to be available to answer questions and give advice about health concerns. The broad objective was "to stimulate the people as a whole to cooperative endeavor in clean-up, educational and specific hygienic and clinical services for the sanitary improvement of the community and for health betterment of the individual, family, and home."[15]

During its early years, the National Negro Health Week movement was supported by the Julius Rosenwald Fund, and beginning in October 1927, the U.S. Public Health Service began sponsoring the Annual Health Week Conference in Washington, D.C. Because of its growth, in 1932 the National Negro Health Week offices were moved from Tuskegee Institute to larger facilities provided in Washington, D.C., by the Public Health Service. Two years later the Office of Negro Work was established, and began publishing a quarterly bulletin, *National Negro Health News*. However, at the local level, the Negro Health Week programs were sponsored and promoted by a wide array of black cultural institutions, especially the local chapters and branches of the National Negro Business League, National Medical Association, National Dental Association, National Negro Insurance Association, National Council of Negro Women, the Negro Elks, the Mystic Shrine, Alpha Phi Alpha and Omega Psi Phi fraternities and Delta Sigma Theta sorority.[16]

Coming on the heels of the increasing success of Negro Health Week was Negro History Week. Launched in Washington, D.C, in February 1926 by the Association for the Study of Negro Life and History, the week's activities celebrated the contributions of Africans and people of African descent to American and world history. Exhibitions were mounted depicting the exploits of black soldiers from the Revolutionary era to World War I, the history of black religious denominations, as well as the social and economic advancements made since the general emancipation. Black churches and schools in cities with branches of the Association, including Baltimore, Washington, D.C., New York City, Philadelphia, Chicago, St. Louis, Kansas City, and Cleveland, sponsored lectures and dramatic presentations for black adults and children in the community at large. Negro history courses were offered, and study groups were formed in black churches and community centers as part of the adult educational programs available in these institutions.[17]

Local branches of the Young Men's (YMCA) and Young Women's Christian Association (YWCA) also sponsored specialized programs for black adults on a regular basis. Although at the national headquarters for the associations there may have been only a few black professionals, the executive boards and staff of the local black branches of the YMCA and YWCA were completely staffed by black professionals who recognized the need for ongoing adult educational programs. There were at least thirteen separate black branches of the YMCA in the United States in 1924, and by 1938 the number was forty-six, housed either in their own separate buildings, constructed through generous support from the Julius Rosenwald Fund; or in facilities donated by black churches. Adult educational classes offered by the black branches of the YMCA included trade education, commercial subjects, and black history; the YWCA specialized in courses in domestic sciences, millinery, sewing and crocheting, and art, as well as in lectures on black womanhood, religion, and black history. The educational programs sponsored by black women's clubs and church organizations were often held at the local branch of the YWCA.[18]

The local branches of the National Urban League (NUL) and the National Association for the Advancement of Colored People (NAACP) sponsored numerous adult educational programs during their first thirty-five years. The NUL was founded in 1911 and stressed "interracial cooperation" in assisting black residents to find employment in the cities. As one League official put it, "the Board of Directors and the important committees in each League city included Negro and white persons whose very working together made for an enlightening program of adult education." Founded in New York City in 1910 to assist Southern black migrants to northern cities, the NUL "help[ed] these newcomers to adjust themselves to the trying pace of living in large overcrowded cities" and was "for a long time a major enterprise in many Urban League affiliates." The League's programs were aimed at black migrants to Chicago, Cleveland, Columbus, Detroit, Milwaukee, Newark, Pittsburgh, and St. Louis; they stressed literacy, and training and instruction in trades and commercial subjects that would lead to suitable and long-term employment.[19]

The Chicago branch of the NUL, for example, was concerned about "raising the standard of living" of black migrants, which had plummeted in the 1930s, owing to urban forces "creating family and neighborhood disintegration." "We thought the Negroes could do many things to help themselves," noted Frayser T. Lane, a Chicago NUL official, in 1945. The League launched and participated in political educational programs aimed at black adults, forums on juvenile delinquency, and "a vigorous campaign to encourage Negro citizens to take advantage of all training programs that would equip them for skilled employment." The Chicago branch prepared black workers for "integration on a large scale and in a variety of industries."[20]

The Board of Directors and national headquarters of the NAACP were more interracial in composition than the local branches in both the North and the South. At the local level, NAACP branches thrived and languished in desuetude, usually depending on the quality of local leadership. The local organizations were usually headed by prominent black ministers and lawyers, and the characterizations of branch activities and programs ranged from moribund to activist, conservative to progressive, elitist to mass-based.[21]

The NAACP's commitment to adult education at the local level took the form of leadership training conferences, which provided "intensive instruction in basic techniques and procedures for developing and carrying out local programs of action." The conferences were held in the early 1940s in New York City, Cleveland, Indianapolis, Atlanta, Kansas City, and San Francisco. Ongoing specialized adult training programs similar to those of the YMCA and YWCA were generally not sponsored by NAACP branches, where "large mass meetings, prominent speakers, radio programs and parades" were used to promote "programs of action and education at the local level."[22]

The sponsoring of educational programs for black adults by the local branches and affiliates of the NUL, NAACP, and Association for the Study of Negro Life and History (ASNLH) and by black churches, schools, and fraternal organizations in northern cities was considered part of their "social service" agenda, and represented an important cultural commitment to self-help and collective social advancement in urban America.

ORGANIZED PHILANTHROPY

Informal adult educational programs and formal instruction in a wide variety of areas were available in the settlement houses that served black neighborhoods in many northern cities. Before 1930 black settlement houses were found in Chicago, Philadelphia, Boston, Milwaukee, Buffalo, Indianapolis, Gary, Cleveland, Columbus, and other northern and midwestern cities and towns, and should be considered the main sources for educational programs for black adults sponsored by organized philanthropy. The Julius Rosenwald Fund, the Anna T. Jeanes Fund, the Southern Education Board, and the General Education Board financed county training schools, adult agricultural extension programs, and other educational projects for *Southern* blacks. In northern cities, however, secular and religious reformers imbued with the spirit of progressivism opened settlement houses for both black and white migrants that offered programs in literacy training and basic adjustment to the urban environment. The settlement houses also offered instruction in a number of areas, including musical training, domestic science, foreign languages, health education, art, and dramatics.[23]

Black settlement houses were products of the attempts of organized charity, religious and secular, to adjust black migrants to the realities of urban life as perceived by these progressive reformers. Reform-minded social agencies provided much needed services to impoverished and underemployed black migrants and longtime residents of the cities, and the formal instruction available in many skills and vocational subjects prepared black workers to

seek employment in areas where few blacks were found. The adult educational programs provided by black settlement houses were much needed,
but the number and proportion of black workers reached was usually quite
small. Although many of the settlement house activities were unique, the
greater part of the specialized educational programs available to black adults
in northern cities were provided through black social and cultural institutions.
Before the 1930s the role of organized charity in the provision of black adult
education in northern cities was important, but less important than black
self-help activities.[24]

The limitations of organized philanthropy in meeting the adult educational
needs of urban black communities become apparent when we examine the
educational programs for urban blacks sponsored in the 1930s by the American Association for Adult Education (AAAE). Despite the limited success
of "experimental" black adult educational programs, organized philanthropy
was either unable or unwilling to finance on a wide scale black adult educational programs in northern or southern cities. Francis Keppel, president
of the Carnegie Corporation, convened the first national conference on adult
education in 1924, and the AAAE grew out of the second conference in May
1925. The areas of activity for the adult education movement included workers' education, parents' education, prison education, women workers' education, as well as adult vocational and industrial training. The AAAE served
as a clearing house for information on the adult education movement nationally, and maintained strong links with religious organizations, labor
groups, civic societies, and city governments that were interested in providing specialized educational programs for adults.[25]

A perusal of the minutes and proceedings for the annual meetings of the
AAAE, and the publications issued between 1926 and 1930 reveals little or
no concern with specialized educational programs for blacks adults. In 1930,
however, the AAAE agreed to financially support, with the assistance of the
Julius Rosenwald Fund, two experimental black adult educational projects
to be housed in libraries in Harlem and Atlanta. In New York City the
Harlem Adult Education Committee was formed "to stimulate adult minds
to a greater desire for knowledge and the preparation for fuller life." The
Harlem Experiment operated out of the 135th Street branch of the New
York Public Library, later the Schomburg Center for Research in Black
Culture, and sought to expand the "cultural, vocational, and social" horizons
of black residents in Harlem. Discussion groups on contemporary literature,
drama, modern social thought, art appreciation, and radio education were
held, and lecture courses on parent education, black history, and industrial
efficiency were offered. The art workshop and studio was conducted by artist
James Lesesne Wells, and included free art classes held at the library from
July to September 1933 and sponsored by the Harlem Adult Education
Committee. The Committee also sponsored the Harlem Experimental Theatre, which offered an eight-week course in dramatic training. The course

was geared toward acting in community theaters and provided dramatic training for church groups.[26]

Alain Locke, philosopher, literary critic, and educator at Howard University, was asked by the AAAE to evaluate the black adult educational projects,
and in the third year of the experiment (1934) he published a statement in
the AAAE's *Journal of Adult Education*. Locke made his integrationist biases
clear from the outset. "A proper adult education program for Negroes is . . .
one that includes all the basic and common objectives, aims, and values of
adult education, and includes them as fully as is humanly possible." "Separate or truncated programs" for blacks were unnecessary, but to be successful "certain special slants and emphases may be found suitable and
advantageous." Locke was a staunch supporter of the campaigns by the
NAACP, NUL, and other groups to break down barriers to the further
integration of blacks into the public institutions of American society. Thus
he went out of his way to note that despite the fact that two experimental
black adult educational projects in Harlem and Atlanta were conducted in
separate black libraries, "the programs in general have an interracial spon-
sorship, management, and participation; and in the southern center the work
has even had a modicum of interracial appeal and effect." The content itself
emphasized "universal values."

Locke did not believe that there was any contradiction between his support
of the separate black adult educational programs and more universalistic
values. His support for the extension of the black experimental programs,
which emphasized African and African American culture and experience,
reflected a basic cultural reality: that "in educating adults we find that their
vital, concrete, particular interests provide the strongest and most effective
motivations for serious study. This principle holds for all groups, whether
the group is based on racial, class, professional, sectarian, or just local community interests."[27] The converse was, of course, also true, and the failure
to incorporate programs, leaders, and institutions of these various groups
into adult educational programs would greatly limit their effectiveness.

The Atlanta Experiment was conducted at the Auburn branch of the
Atlanta Public Library and was overseen by an interracial committee. The
director organized study and discussion groups, developed reading materials
for use in literacy classes, and sponsored lectures at the library that were
open to the entire community. In his final evaluation of two projects in 1935,
Locke noted that despite the small staff, lack of supervision by the Atlanta
Adult Education Committee, inadequately trained volunteer assistance, and
lack of participation in many lecture and discussion programs, the program
at the Auburn Library made "a real contribution to the technique of adult
education work."[28]

Social scientist Ira D. A. Reid, in his study *Adult Education Among Negroes*,
published in 1935, was not quite as sanguine about the results in Atlanta.
Indeed, he suggested that some may consider the Atlanta Experiment a

failure because it brought "little of permanent value as to methods of organization" and because of the limited participation of the black churches.

> The church is by far the foremost social institution among Negroes. It did not participate to any great extent in the Atlanta experiment. . . . There is no doubt that the Atlanta experiment was handicapped by its conforming to the standards and program of the Negro branch of the Carnegie Library in Atlanta.

Reid believed that in order for adult educational programs to reach the black community, "an effective working arrangement between schools, churches and the library is very necessary."[29]

Whether or not the Carnegie Corporation, the Julius Rosenwald Fund, or other philanthropies believed that the experiments in Harlem and Atlanta were successful, they were not replicated in other cities. Indeed, these two projects as well as the adult educational programs funded by organized philanthropy and offered in the black settlement houses had to be taken over by New Deal adult educational programs by 1934 and 1935. With the coming of the Great Depression, it became clear that organized philanthropy was unable to provide the funds necessary to meet the adult educational needs and demands of northern black or white communities. In the 1930s the great philanthropies were reduced to sponsoring conferences and small experimental projects. The economic dislocations in the 1930s required massive government intervention. Fortunately the privately funded experimental programs to assist unemployed and underemployed workers in business, agriculture, industry, and education often served as the models and examples for governmental programs implemented on a national scale through Franklin Delano Roosevelt's New Deal program.[30]

STATE-SUPPORTED ADULT EDUCATION

With the creation of the Federal Emergency Relief Administration (FERA) in 1933 and the Works Progress Administration (WPA) in 1935, there was a significant increase in specialized educational programs available to black adults living in the large northern cities. Before the implementation of the New Deal programs, public schools systems in northern cities provided adult education for blacks primarily in evening classes held in separate black schools.[31] Under Harry Hopkins, the director of the FERA, the Emergency Education Division was created, and by the fall of 1933 all of the states had received authorization to develop programs in literacy and citizenship training, vocational rehabilitation, nursery education, and general adult education. Many local programs were specifically designed to provide work for unemployed teachers, but no Emergency Education Program (EEP) could duplicate existing educational arrangements and programs at the local level.[32]

At the Washington Conference on "The Economic Status of the Negro" in June 1933, black leaders and educators made it clear that (a) the economic conditions for black workers were grim, with unemployment in many areas reaching more than 50 percent of the employable black population; and (b) efforts to relieve the social distress must be conducted on a nondiscriminatory basis. The Joint Committee on National Recovery, a black leadership group formed in 1933 to monitor the provisions made for blacks to participate in New Deal programs, began collecting reports about discriminatory practices of federal relief agencies, especially those operating in southern states. When the FERA's emergency education program was announced in June 1933, John P. Davis, the executive secretary for the Joint Committee, inquired about the new federal agency plans for providing "Negro adult education." The federal response was that the general administration and implementation of all educational programs was under the control of state, rather than federal, authorities.[33]

Political pressure was brought to bear on federal officials, and led to the appointment of Ambrose Caliver and Forrestal B. Washington, two black social scientists, to the FERA in September 1933. Their job was to stimulate interest among blacks in the emergency educational programs, and they were greatly assisted in their endeavors by the actions of Aubrey Williams, assistant to Harry Hopkins, who issued a policy statement in October 1934 that guaranteed "complete equity" in the distribution of relief funds. Specifically, with regard to resources for "Negro adult education," the FERA order declared that "since educational opportunities for Negroes are notably inadequate, equity demands that educational relief to Negroes be at least at the level of their percentage of the population in each State." The order also stated that "Negro teachers should always be employed to teach Negro pupils and Negro adults in States maintaining segregated school programs for the two races."[34]

The erosion of the public school system's tax base during the early years of the economic depression meant that many school systems, especially in the large northern cities, had laid off many elementary- and secondary-school teachers. The EEP funds were first used to rehire previously laid off public-school teachers, both black and white. A few "emergency classes" for adults were begun by public school systems in some cities, but the greater part of the increase in the availability of specialized educational programs for black adults came with the Works Progress Administration, later Works Projects Administration (WPA), which took over the EEP programs in May 1935. Between 1935 and 1938 more than one million illiterate adult Americans were taught to read and write a letter. Several million more adults were enrolled in art, music, dramatics, science, handicrafts, and physical education classes. The popular response to state-supported adult educational programs was overwhelmingly favorable.[35]

From the outset, WPA officials pledged themselves to a policy of non-discrimination in which "all elements of the population would share in the benefits of the program." James Atkins, a black educator who served as an educational consultant for the WPA, filed a report on "The WPA and the Negro" in March 1937, which concluded, among other things, that from January 1934 to January 1937, 300,000 blacks were taught to read and write, 40,000 black adults were trained in industrial skills, 10,000 black men and women had enrolled in workers' education classes, and 5,000 blacks were employed as teachers in these adult education programs.[36]

Adult educational programs for blacks in northern cities, sponsored through the FERA, EEP, WPA, or other state-supported agencies, were considered extremely popular. However, whatever success they enjoyed must also be attributed to the skills and cooperation of black professionals and cultural institutions in these northern cities. In 1933 and 1934 EEP classes were sponsored by individual "school districts" at particular sites, such as public schools, churches, lodges, community centers, and settlement houses within the neighborhoods. In Chicago, for example, between June and December 1933 the EEP classes were started in facilities donated by educational, fraternal, and social welfare organizations and the public school system. Black professionals, many of them unemployed teachers, realized that the only way they could gain (or regain) teaching positions was through the authorization of particular facilities on Chicago's South Side as sites for EEP classes. In January 1934 black professionals formed themselves into the South Side Committee on Adult Education, not only to spread the news to potential students about the classes, but also to work with African American cultural institutions on the South Side to donate space for EEP classes. The South Side Committee was able to locate facilities within the black community for thirty-five separate EEP adult education projects, enrolling an estimated 3,000 black students.[37]

In Harlem there were similar programs initially in locating sites for New Deal adult educational programs. The lack of facilities hampered the WPA classes until Abyssinian Baptist Church and St. James Presbyterian Church led the way by agreeing to establish in their church facilities EEP adult education classes in literacy, music, arts, dramatics, and dressmaking. They were soon followed by St. Phillip's Episcopal Church and Salem Methodist Episcopal Church, which also offered classes in shorthand, typing, and interior design.

An adult vocational guidance center was set up in a facility provided by the New York Urban League, and it served to direct clients to the appropriate WPA classes that would prepare them for employment in specific areas. By the spring of 1936 the Harlem Labor Center was offering WPA-sponsored workers' education classes. The all-black staff not only examined the history of the working classes, but also included the contributions of black workers to American economic development.[38]

The Harlem Community Center, opened in November 1937, was the result of a unique federal-local partnership wherein the WPA Arts Projects agreed to supply the Center's teaching staff, while the Citizen's Sponsoring Committee, led by A. Phillip Randolph and Bill (Bojangles) Robinson, agreed to pay for the Center's rent and upkeep. Day and evening classes were available in painting, costume design, lithography, block printing, and photography. Local black artists gave lectures and exhibitions both at the Center and in neighborhood public schools. By January 1938 the WPA was operating thirty-four centers in Harlem alone, employing 127 black teachers and enrolling up to 6,000 students per week.[39]

In Philadelphia the coming of the EEP adult educational programs led to the revitalization of several black educational institutions. The earliest EEP adult evening classes were held in the predominantly black public secondary schools, Barratt and Sulberger, and employed black elementary- and secondary-school educators who had been laid off in an earlier budget crunch. In Philadelphia the lack of funds from private donations meant that the educational and recreational programs available at the Christian Street YMCA and Southwest-Belmont YWCA had to be severely curtailed. Regular staff had been reduced in budget cuts, but in 1934 EEP-sponsored teachers were able to provide classes for black adults in arts, handicrafts, sewing, tailoring, and other subjects.[40]

Philadelphia's black settlement houses, including the Wharton, St. Simon, and Eighth Ward houses, had to make significant cutbacks in staff and programs in the early years of the Depression, but through WPA- and National Youth Administration (NYA)-sponsored programs, teachers were hired to offer courses in vocational training, business, art, music, and physical education. By January 1937 adult education programs were being offered in forty-three publicly and privately sponsored centers in the city's three largest black neighborhoods, enrolling more than 12,500 students. As was the case in Chicago and Harlem, black professionals and cultural institutions in Philadelphia were essential to the early success of EEP and WPA programs.[41]

The addition of state resources for adult educational programs changed the entire black adult educational landscape in Harlem, Chicago, Philadelphia, and other northern and midwestern cities. The federal programs provided new educational opportunities, and ensured the continuation of preexisting programs organized by black social and cultural institutions and organized philanthropy. But the state-supported programs were not a complete success. While the new literacy classes, art and dramatics, black history, workers' education, and commercial courses were attracting large numbers, the vocational and industrial education and trades programs were floundering. As was the case with the EEP classes, vocational education programs were developed locally by public school officials in cooperation with community sponsors who provided the facility and equipment, while the state covered the salaries of the instructors. Courses in tailoring, millinery, mechanical and building trades, restaurant service, agricultural techniques, and handicrafts were offered; by December 1938 forty-four states had WPA vocational education programs, enrolling more than 250,000 students per month.[42]

From as early as January 1936, when the federal government appropriated $234,000 for the Office of Education to conduct a survey of "Vocational Guidance Among Negroes," it was clear that there was extreme underrepresentation of blacks in the vocational education programs. Ambrose Caliver was asked to conduct the study, and he hired assistants in fifteen cities and towns in thirty-four states. The final report revealed that there was great indifference on the part of black youth and adults to trade and vocational education programs because of the absence of employment opportunities for blacks in most industries that required these skills and trades. In many parts of the country blacks were discouraged from enrolling in trade classes in areas where apprenticeship programs were closed to black workers.[43]

This lack of black participation in vocational education programs, and discriminatory treatment in general in federally funded education programs in many southern states, served as the stimulus and justification for a series of annual conferences on "Adult Education and the Negro," sponsored by the AAAE between 1938 and 1942. At the first conference, at the end of October 1938, held at Hampton Institute, Alain Locke; Ambrose Caliver; Mary McLeod Bethune, director of the Office of Negro Affairs in NYA; and John W. Studebaker, the U.S. Commissioner of Education, were among the speakers and participants.[44] Most of the discussion dealt with the educational conditions for blacks in the South and the progress in literacy training and social education in that region. Several speakers did mention the need for increased "vocational training with the modern frontage of vocational guidance and job placement."[45]

The only discussion relevant to the adult educational conditions for blacks in the North was provided in several detailed reports on WPA and NYA for blacks in Washington, D.C. Ten trades were offered in the district public schools, including shoe repairing, printing, automobile mechanics, welding, and electricity. Unfortunately, as of October 1938, black students enrolled in vocational courses constituted only 13 percent of the total of 3,885. The largest number of students were enrolled in the general adult department.[46] In its overall recommendations, the conference participants agreed that "the most pressing problem confronting Negroes is their economic problem. But vocational education must be accompanied with political competence." It suggested that educators "stick close to the fundamental needs of the race. . . . This would give culture for culture's sake a secondary place. Vocational and political education should come first."[47]

The Second Annual Conference on Adult Education and the Negro was held January 22–24, 1940, at Tuskegee Institute, and the theme was "The World Crisis and the Negro Masses." World War II had broken out in 1939, and the conference participants hoped to "interpret conditions and trends in adult education among Negroes in relation to the present world crisis." As was the case with the first meeting, most of the discussion revolved around "the problem of Negro education in the South," and examined extension education, literacy classes, and agricultural courses offered at black colleges and universities.

In a forum on "New Programs, Procedures, and Materials in Adult Education," James Atkins, special assistant for Negro Affairs in the Office of Education, examined in great detail "Special Training Needed by Adult Education Teachers," especially those teachers who worked in communities that were organizing black adult education programs. Atkins believed that the adult education teacher, black or white, should be instructing black adults to make use of the "vital stuff on Negro life." These educators should have knowledge "of the deep longings of the race, of its achievements and contributions, of its failures and wasted opportunities, of its visions and larger hope." Alain Locke called for "further cooperation of the workers in the field of adult education among the Negro." "Popularized literature" should be used "to better inform the white constituency with respect to the Negro . . . and maybe even more important to have the Negro constituents well informed about themselves."[48]

Howard University served as the host for the Third Annual Conference on Adult Education and the Negro, held in Washington, D.C., January 30–31, 1941; the theme was "The Negro in the National Defense." In his opening remarks, Morse A. Cartwright, the AAAE's executive secretary, noted that "this conference is the second in a series of some sixteen arranged for the present year in every part of the United States." An entire session was devoted to "The Negro and the National Defense," and Robert C. Weaver, representing the Council on National Defense, pointed out that "there will be increasing demands for workers in certain occupations." Black workers required training for these new employment opportunities and the National Defense Advisory Commission, working with the two most powerful labor organizations—the American Federation of Labor and Congress of Industrial Organizations—would have to pursue a policy of "non-discrimination in defense employment." Weaver believed that it was necessary for the blacks to avail themselves of "every opportunity to increase their occupational qualifications. Once trained, [they would] be in a better position to demand [their] rights under the laws and policies affecting the defense program."[49]

When the Fourth Annual Conference on Adult Education and the Negro convened at Atlanta University on March 5–6, 1942, the United States had been at war for three months, and "National Defense and the Negro" was the important topic. The WPA programs were being streamlined, and defense training programs replaced general adult education courses throughout the country. In 1941 the NUL branches in New York City, Philadelphia, Chicago, Boston, and other cities spearheaded campaigns in conjunction with the local public school systems to encourage blacks to enroll in the defense training classes. In many instances, black trainees as clerks, typists, and community workers were transferred to military installations for training defense work. The participants at the Fourth Annual Conference on Adult Education and the Negro were assured that the military defense required the training of *all* citizens. The conference "resolved that all discrimination of every type be promptly eradicated from all branches of our armed forces in order that America will be able to say to the world we practice what we preach—we are a democracy in action!"[50]

In November 1942 a special U.S. Senate Committee investigating the national defense program recommended to President Franklin Roosevelt that "the WPA should be eliminated entirely and the money thus saved channeled into the war effort." President Roosevelt agreed, and orders were issued to all the state WPA agencies to have the final reports in by January 1, 1943. It should be noted that the numerous evaluations of the employment status of blacks enrolled in national defense training courses in Philadelphia, New York, Chicago, Cleveland, and other cities between 1939 and 1942 revealed that more than 75 percent of blacks who graduated from or attended and dropped out of defense training had found employment by 1943. This was primarily due to the severe wartime labor shortages in many cities. Unfortunately few blacks who enrolled in defense training programs were employed in areas for which they were trained. The wartime employment crisis allowed black workers to be hired in sectors of the economy where they were previously barred, but they still were locked out of the better paying skilled and semiskilled positions by discriminatory practices of defense employers and labor organizations.[51]

In surveying the specialized educational programs available to black adults who were longtime residents or recent migrants to northern cities between 1900 and 1942, it is clear that of three social agencies providing these programs—black cultural institutions, organized philanthropy, and the state—the most significant, in terms of numbers of programs made available and students enrolled, were the state-supported adult education programs of the New Deal social agencies. It is also clear that black self-help activities were important in the provision of adult education programs by black cultural institutions, organized charity, and the New Deal and national defense training programs.

Black churches, public and private schools, and local branches of the NAACP, NUL, ASNLH, fraternal organizations, and women's groups provided the greater part of adult educational programs for blacks in northern cities before the 1930s. Organized philanthropy entered the picture with the opening of settlement houses in black neighborhoods during this same period, and offered adult literacy, trade, and commercial courses. In most instances, these programs were devised and administered by both black and white professionals. With the coming of the New Deal social programs to northern cities, it was the black educators and professionals who lobbied for the creation of programs in black neighborhoods for black adults. Black cultural institutions provided the facilities and equipment for these state-supported adult education programs.

Northern black communities responded to the need to provide literacy training and specialized educational opportunities to black adults and migrants. This social and cultural response reflected the core values of "black self-determination" and "education" that were deeply embedded in African American culture and experiences.[52] African Americans recognized that if they were to advance themselves in American society, they would have to take responsibility for their own lives and educational destiny, and take advantage of educational opportunities provided by the state and organized philanthropy. Although there is little evidence that enrollment in and graduation from adult education programs raised the occupational status of most black workers in northern cities, the positive response of northern blacks to these programs represented a strong cultural commitment to self-improvement and social advancement in an oftentimes hostile urban environment.

NOTES

1. "Chain migration" is examined in Virginia Yans-McLaughlin, *Family and Community: Italian Immigrants to Buffalo, 1880–1930* (Ithaca, N.Y.: Cornell University Press, 1970); John Bodnar, Roger Simon, and Michael P. Weber, *Lives of Their Own: Blacks, Italians, and Poles in Pittsburgh, 1900–1960* (Urbana: University of Illinois Press, 1982); Allen Ballard, *One More Day's Journey: The Story of a Family and a People* (New York: McGraw-Hill, 1984), which examines Southern blacks' migration to Philadelphia; and Peter Gottlieb, *Making Their Own Way: Southern Blacks' Migration to Pittsburgh, 1916–30* (Urbana: University of Illinois Press, 1987).

2. Contributions to the debate over the amount of social control exercized over the black and white poor by progressive social welfare and educational programs have been made by Robert Bremer, *From the Depths: The Discovery of Poverty in America* (New York: New York University Press, 1956); Lawrence Cremin, *The Transformation of the School* (New York: The Free Press, 1964); Allen F. Davis, *Spearheads of Reform: The Social Settlements and the Progressive Movement, 1890–1914* (New York: Oxford University Press, 1967); Diane Ravitch, *The Great School Wars: New York City, 1836 to Present* (New York: Basic, 1971); Clarence J. Karier, *Shaping of the American Educational State, 1900 to the Present* (New York: The Free Press, 1975); Samuel Bowles and Herbert Gintis, *Schooling in Capitalist America: Educational Reform and the Contradictions of Economic Life* (New York: Basic Books, 1976); Paul Violas, *Training of the Urban Working Class: A History of Twentieth Century Education* (Chicago: Rand McNally, 1978); Don S. Kirschner, "The Ambiguous Legacy: Social Justice and Social Control in the Progressive Era," *Historical Reflections* 2 (Summer 1975):69–88; Michael B. Katz, *Poverty and Policy in American History* (New York: Academic Press, 1983).

3. U.S. Department of Commerce, *Thirteenth Census of the United States. vol. 4: Populations: Occupational Statistics* (Washington, D.C.: Government Printing Office,

1914), 588–590; Niles Carpenter, *Immigrants and Their Children* (Washington, D.C.: Government Printing Office, 1927).

4. Thomas Philpott, *The Slum and the Ghetto: Neighborhood Deterioration and Middle Class Reform, Chicago, 1880–1930* (New York: Oxford University Press, 1978); and V. P. Franklin, "Continuity and Discontinuity in Black and Immigrant Minority Education in Urban America: A Historical Assessment," in *Educating an Urban People: The New York City Experience*, ed. Diane Ravitch and Ron Goodenow (New York: Teachers College Press, 1981), 67–83.

5. Allen Spear, *Black Chicago: The Making of a Negro Ghetto, 1890–1920* (Chicago: University of Chicago Press, 1967); Gilbert Osofsky, *Harlem: The Making of a Ghetto, Negro New York, 1890–1930* (New York: 1966); Kenneth Kusmer, *A Ghetto Takes Shape: Black Cleveland, 1870–1930* (Urbana: University of Illinois Press, 1976); see also August Meier and Elliott Rudwick, *From Plantation to Ghetto: A History of Negro Americans* (New York: Prentice-Hall, 1966).

6. Edward Judson, "The Church in Its Social Aspect," *The Annals of the American Academy of Political and Social Science (The Annals)* 30 (November 1907): 1–13.

7. R. R. Wright, "Social Work of the Negro Church," ibid., 81–93.

8. The Reverend R. R. Wright, Jr., presented some detailed information on his work with the institutional church in his autobiography, *87 Years Behind the Black Curtain* (Philadelphia: Rare Book Company, 1965), 100–115.

9. For negative assessments of northern black churches, see Ira de A. Reid, "Let Us Prey," *Opportunity* 4 (September 1926):274–278; and Harold M. Kingsley, "The Negro Goes to Church," *Opportunity* 7 (March 1929):90–91.

10. Reverdy C. Ransom, *The Pilgrimage of Harriet Ransom's Son* (Nashville: Sunday School Union, [1949]), 103–139. Ransom included articles from the *Chicago Tribune* that reported the dynamiting of his church; see pp. 119–134.

11. Wright, "Social Work of the Negro Church," 91–92. For additional information on the Reverend Matthew Anderson and the Berean School, see R. R. Wright's *The Negro in Pennsylvania: A Study in Economic History* (1912; rpt. New York: Arno Press, 1969), 116–21; and V. P. Franklin, *The Education of Black Philadelphia: A Social and Educational History of a Minority Community, 1900–1950* (Philadelphia: University of Pennsylvania Press, 1979), 170–172.

12. George E. Haynes, "The Church and Negro Progress," *The Annals* 140 (November 1928):264–271; Samuel L. Gandy, "The Negro Church and the Adult Education Phases of Its Program," *The Journal of Negro Education (JNE)* 14 (Summer 1945):381–384; Seth Scheiner, "The Negro Church and the Northern City, 1890–1930," in *Seven on Black: Reflections on the Negro Experience in America*, ed. William G. Shade and Roy Herrenkohl (Philadelphia: J. B. Lippincott, 1969), 92–117.

13. Major R. R. Moton, "Organized Negro Effort for Racial Progress," *The Annals* 140 (November 1928):257–263.

14. Booker T. Washington quoted in Roscoe C. Brown, "The National Negro Health Week Movement," *JNE* 14 (Summer 1945):555.

15. Ibid., 555–556. For additional discussion of Negro Health Week activities, see Eva C. Mitchell, "Adult Health Education and Recreational Programs: National, State, and Local," *JNE* 14 (Summer 1945):363–373; Franklin, *The Education of Black Philadelphia*, 96–97.

16. Roscoe C. Brown, "The Health Education Programs of Government and Voluntary Agencies," *JNE* 14 (Summer 1945):377–387.

17. Luther P. Jackson, "The Work of the Association [for the Study of Negro Life and History] and Its People," *The Journal of Negro History (JNE)* 20 (October 1935):385–396.

18. George Arthur, "The Young Men's Christian Association Movement Among Negroes," *Opportunity* 1 (March 1923):16–18; Jesse E. Moorland, "The Young Men's Christian Association," *JNH* 9 (April 1924):127–138; John Hope, "The Colored YMCA," *The Crisis* 31 (November 1925):14–17; Campbell C. Johnson, "Negro Youth and the Educational Program of the YMCA," *JNE* 9 (Winter 1940):354–362; Ralph W. Bullock, "The Adult Educational Program of the YMCA Among Negroes," and Dorothy I. Height, "The Adult Education Program of the YMCA Among Negroes," *JNE* 14 (Summer 1945):385–395; Lillian S. Williams, "To Elevate the Race: The Michigan Avenue YMCA and the Advancement of Blacks in Buffalo, 1922–1940," in *New Perspectives on Black Educational History*, ed. V. P. Franklin and James D. Anderson (Boston: G. K. Hall, 1978), 129–148; Franklin, *Education of Black Philadelphia*, 244.

19. Alphonse Heningburg, "Adult Education and the National Urban League," *JNE* 14 (Summer 1945):396–397; see also George Edmund Haynes, "Conditions Among Negroes in the Cities," *The Annals* 49 (September 1913):105–119; Eugene Kinkle Jones, "Social Work Among Negroes," *The Annals* 140 (November 1928):287–293. Two general histories of the National Urban League are Guichard Parris and Lester Brooks, *Blacks in the City: A History of the National Urban League* (Boston, 1971), and Nancy Weiss, *The National Urban League, 1910–1940* (New York: Oxford University Press, 1974).

20. Frayser T. Lane, "An Educational Program for the Adjustment of Negroes to Urban Living," *JNE* 14 (Winter 1945):117–122. Lane was the director of the Chicago Urban League. See also Alvarh E. Strickland, *A History of the Chicago Urban League* (Urbana: University of Illinois Press, 1966).

21. Charles Kellogg, *NAACP: A History, 1909–1920* (Baltimore: Johns Hopkins University Press, 1967), presents some information on local branches, but really concentrates on the activities of the national office. There is a real need to examine at least a large sampling of these branches to determine how they operated.

22. Roy Wilkins, "Adult Education Program of the NAACP," *JNE* 14 (Summer 1945):403–404.

23. Inabel B. Lindsay, "Adult Education Programs for Negroes in Settlement Houses," and Anne M. Cooke, "The Little Theater Movement as an Adult Education Project Among Negroes," *JNE* 14 (Summer 1945):347–352; 418–424.

24. For information on black settlement houses before 1930, see Osofsky, *Harlem*, 53–67; Kusmer, *A Ghetto Takes Shape*, 214–215; Jeffrey A. Hess, "Black Settlement House, East Greenwich, 1902–1914," *Rhode Island History* 29 (January 1970):113–127; Julius F. Nimmons, "Social Reform and Moral Uplift in the Black Community, 1890–1930: Social Settlements, Temperance, and Social Purity" (Ph.D. diss., Howard University, 1981); and Judith An Trolander, *Professionalism and Social Change: From Settlement House Movement to Neighborhood Centers, 1886 to the Present* (New York: Columbia University Press, 1987).

25. Morse A. Cartwright, *Ten Years of Adult Education* (New York: Macmillan, 1935), 23–31. The early years of the AAAE are fully documented in the first four volumes of *The Journal of Adult Education (JAE)*, the organization's official publication.

26. *Harlem Adult Education Committee Program* and other pamphlets, brochures,

and publications of the Harlem Adult Education Program may be found in the microfilmed records at the Schomburg Center for Research in Black Culture. Reports on the Harlem Experiment and the Atlanta Experiment may be found in *The Journal of Adult Education*, "Negro Adult Education," 8 (April 1936):205; (October 1936):419; 9 (June 1937):367; 10 (June 1938):355–356; "Education for Negroes," 11 (January 1939):100.

27. Alain Locke, "Reciprocity Instead of Regimentation: Lessons of Negro Adult Education," *JAE* 6 (October 1934):418–420. See also Eugene C. Holmes, "Alain Locke and the Adult Education Movement," *JNE* 34 (Winter 1965):5–10.

28. Alain Locke quoted in Ira de A. Reid, *Adult Education Among Negroes* (New York: The Associates of Folk Education, 1935), 28.

29. Ibid., 28–29; see also Gordon W. Blackwell, "Evaluation of Present Programs of Adult Education for Negroes," *JNE* 14 (Summer 1945):443–452.

30. William Leuchtenberg, *Franklin D. Roosevelt and the New Deal, 1932–1940* (New York: 1963); James Patterson, *The New Deal and the States* (Princeton, N.J.: Princeton University Press, 1969); Nellie Seeds and Margaret Stanley, *The WPA's Education Program* (Washington, D.C.: Federal Works Agency, 1943).

31. George N. Redd, "Adult Education for Negroes Under Public School Auspices," *JNE* 14 (Summer 1945):312–321.

32. U.S., FERA, *The Emergency Education Program* (Washington, D.C.: Government Printing Office, 1935), 2–10; Seeds and Stanley, *WPA's Education Program*, 20–44; Lewis Alderman, "The Emergency Education Programs," *Opportunity* 13 (January 1935):18–19.

33. "The Washington Conference on the Economic Status of the Negro," *Monthly Labor Review* 37 (July 1933):43–44; see also "The Position of the Negro in Our National Economic Crisis," *JAE* 7 (June 1935):335–336; and James Atkins, "The Participation of Negroes in Pre-School and Adult Education Programs," *JNE* 7 (July 1938):345–356.

34. Aubrey Williams, FERA administrator, to state relief administrators and school officers, October 27, 1934, quoted in Melvin R. Maskin, "Black Education and the New Deal: The Urban Experience" (Ph.D. diss., New York University, 1973), 81.

35. Seeds and Stanley, *WPA's Education Program*, 3–7.

36. James Atkins, "The WPA and the Negro," U.S. Works Progress Administration, [March] 1935, quoted in Maskin, "Black Education and the New Deal," 108–109.

37. Lester B. Granger, "The Urban League in Action," *Opportunity* 14 (March 1936):94–96.

38. Adam Clayton Powell, Jr., "Agencies for Adult Education," *JAE* 12 (Fall 1940):499–500; Maskin, "Black Education and the New Deal," 159–200; and Charlotte T. Morgan, "Finding a Way Out: Adult Education in Harlem During the Great Depression," *Afro-Americans in New York Life and History* 8 (January 1984):n.p.

39. Bessie Johnson, "A Study of Free Adult Education Interests as Applied to WPA Adult Education, Harlem" (1937; mimeographed). This survey of WPA programs was conducted from October 1936 to June 1937. Schomburg Center for Research in Black Culture, Adult Education Files.

40. Priscella Clement, "The Works Progress Administration in Pennsylvania, 1935–1940," *Pennsylvania Magazine of History and Biography* 95 (April 1971):244–260; Franklin, *Education of Black Philadelphia*, 111–117.

41. Franklin, *Education of Black Philadelphia*, 111–115; see also Frank S. Horne and Corienne K. Robinson, "Adult Education Programs in Housing Projects with Negro Tenants," *JNE* 14 (Summer 1945):353–362; Maskin, "Black Education and the New Deal," 293–298.

42. Seeds and Stanley, *WPA's Education Program*, 39; see also "Adult Education and the Works Progress Administration," *School and Society* 48 (November 1938):693–694.

43. Ambrose Caliver, *Vocational Education and Guidance of Negroes: A Report of a Survey Conducted by the Office of Education* (1937; rpt. Westport, Conn.: Negro Universities Press, 1971); see also Thomas Hawkins, "Guidance for Negroes," *Occupations* 13 (May 1935):749–750; "Vocational Education Survey," *JAE* 8 (June 1936):205; T. Arnold Hill, "The Plight of the Negro Industrial Worker," *JNE* 5 (January 1936):40–47; Maskin, "Black Education and the New Deal," 779.

44. The official sponsors of the "Adult Education and the Negro" conference were the American Association for Adult Education, Associates for Folk Education, headed by Alain Locke, and the Extension Department of Hampton Institute. The conference probably received support from the Carnegie Corporation. *Findings of the Conference on Adult Education and the Negro* (Hampton, Va., 1938). The mimeographed versions of the proceedings of the four conferences on "Adult Education and the Negro" may be found at the Moorland-Spingarn Collection, Howard University ibid., 9.

45. Alain Locke, "Negro Needs as Adult Educational Opportunities," in ibid., 9.

46. Mrs. T. E. Bohannon, "A WPA Adult Education Program," in ibid., 59–64. Mrs. Bohannon was the supervisor for WPA adult education in Washington, D.C.

47. "Panel Discussion: What Should Be the Major Objectives?" in ibid., 67.

48. "The Problem of Adult Education in the South," *Findings of the Second Annual Conference on Adult Education and the Negro* (Tuskegee, Ala.: Tuskegee Institute, 1940):29–36.

49. *Findings and Recommendations of the Third Annual Conference on Adult Education and the Negro* (Howard University, 1941), 31–34.

50. *Findings and Recommendations of the Fourth Annual Conference on Adult Education and the Negro* (Atlanta, 1942), 60–61, 63–71. See also "Negroes and Defense," *JAE* 13 (June 1941):321, 331.

51. Maskin, "Black Education and the New Deal," 313–330; Franklin, *Education of Black Philadelphia*, 111–117; Christopher G. Wye, "The New Deal and the Negro Community: Toward a Broader Conceptualization," *The Journal of American History* 59 (December 1972):621–639.

52. V. P. Franklin, *Black Self-Determination: A Cultural History of the Faith of the Fathers* (Westport, Conn.: Lawrence Hill & Co., 1984), 147–185.

8

Black Communities and Adult Education: YMCA, YWCA, and Fraternal Organizations

Lillian S. Williams

On the eve of the twentieth century, African Americans in the South began to migrate in unprecedented numbers. The earlier wave of migration, which had gotten under way after the Civil War ended, was characterized by the movement of blacks to southern cities and to the West, with just a trickle wending their way to northern urban centers.[1] The new migration began a major shift of the black population to the urban centers of the North. This movement was sparked, in part, by the economic decline in agriculture in the South and, at the same time, by the industrial jobs in the North that beckoned blacks, particularly after the outbreak of World War I. Equally important in precipitating the movement was the blacks' perceptions of the North. Migrants had some notion of what life was like in the North, for most of them followed in the footsteps of family and friends who had preceded them and who kept them apprised of the conditions that they could expect and helped them find housing and jobs on their arrival.[2] Exaggerated though many of the claims might have been, the North symbolized freedom for them—the locus of their quest for self-actualization as blacks and Americans. In the northern environment they hoped not only to secure good jobs, but also to escape the violence of the racist South and to secure greater access to home ownership and education. Their success depended on the timing of their move and the character of the city to which they moved.[3] Most black migrants, however, found that "life was no crystal stair" in the North and, despite hard work and diligence, found themselves doomed to a life of poverty and its accompanying social ills. Although many blacks previously had lived in southern cities, most were inadequately prepared for the world in which they now found themselves. Agricultural skills left them marginally prepared for other jobs at the same time that white racism set barriers that virtually excluded them from the dynamic growth industries or relegated them to the lowest rungs of the economic ladder.

As African American urbanites faced the twentieth century, little did they know that their lives would begin a course that would shift the major center of the black population from the South to the North and, in the process, destroy Jim Crow laws in the South, grant blacks full citizenship rights under the law, and change forever their relation to the power structure. Regardless of the convoluted nature of their struggle for equality and first-class citizenship, African Americans perceived education as the weapon for attaining their goals.

Steeped in a tradition that protected the interests of big business and invoked a policy of laissez-faire for the masses, governmental structures were not designed to attack head-on the problems that urban blacks faced. Nor were government officials receptive to addressing the social problems that blacks experienced in the cities. This failure meant that other social agencies and community organizations would have to assume an inordinate responsibility.

Blacks had perceived education as a vehicle for liberation from second-class citizenship and economic oppression.[4] Therefore, they already had an infrastructure that placed high value on education. Black churches, fraternal organizations, and social clubs designed pragmatic educational programs to attack specific problems. Blacks also helped to shape policy for the local chapters of national, predominantly white—established and—financed organizations in their neighborhoods—like the Young Men's Christian Association (YMCA) and the Young Women's Christian Association (YWCA). In the process they helped to create viable educational programs to meet the needs of an urban-based population plagued by economic deprivation, political repression, and social isolation.

The greatest numbers of blacks during this period arrived in the North after the outbreak of World War I and on the tail end of the "new wave" of Southern and Eastern European immigration. Initially, blacks shared with the immigrants an inability to secure a solid foundation into the economy of the city. But these displaced groups were not destined to become allies in their quest for empowerment. Indeed, in some sectors, such as domestic service, once a haven for black employment, blacks now faced stiff competition from the immigrants. The black experience differed from that of the "new" immigrants, in that race, rather than religion or ethnicity, proved to be a greater determinant of success. And in just one or two generations many immigrants succeeded in carving out an economic niche for themselves and began the process of dispersal from the areas of first settlement of all newcomers to the city into the more comfortable contiguous areas. Most blacks, on the other hand, remained locked in "enduring ghettos."[5]

Immigrants benefited from the timing of their arrival and the enlightened attitudes of scholars, government officials, and journalists. Progressive era reformers explored ways in which to improve the living conditions of immigrants. They promoted good health by supporting building code legislation. They also sponsored legislation that restricted the use of child labor and limited the work hours of women and children.[6] The promotion of such social legislation, coupled with educational programs specifically designed to address immigrant problems, proved successful in improving the status of sizable numbers of foreign newcomers.[7]

Adult education programs also were a key element in the reformers' blueprint for immigrant adaptation to the city. The adult education movement included in its curricula courses on such topics as health, recreation, and, most important, job training. These programs successfully aided immigrants in their quest for economic and social advancement. Yet the adult education movement virtually ignored African Americans.[8] Thus blacks, not a priority for most white reformers, used their own social institutions to design programs addressed to the specific problems they confronted in the cities.

YMCA AND ADULT COMMUNITY EDUCATION

The YMCA was a notable exception to the foregoing, for it became interested in working with the black population at an early date, and increased its activities after Julius Rosenwald, in 1912, offered financial support for "Y" work among black men and boys. The YMCA, founded in England in 1844 and transplanted to the United States in 1851, was one of the earliest benevolent organizations, with a mission to provide community education programs, grounded in Christianity, for the masses.[9] An examination of its educational policies and programs indicates the ways in which it attempted to address black concerns. As will be seen, even in these institutions black men shaped pragmatic education policy.

Separate branches of the YMCA were established for blacks in New York, Detroit, Buffalo, Washington, D.C., Chicago, Los Angeles, and other cities across the nation where the size of the population warranted it and where blacks petitioned to have "Y" work undertaken in their communities.[10] The support of the black community was essential to secure the funds needed to conduct "Y" work among blacks, and they responded by sponsoring fundraisers and publicizing the advantages of membership in the YMCA. Indeed, their overwhelming support was noted by outsiders. The editor of a Buffalo newspaper observed that the enthusiasm for "Y" work among blacks in Buffalo was unsurpassed, and noted that the white community could benefit from the lessons taught by the blacks.[11] Black endorsement of the YMCA also was essential because the structure of the organization required that a Board of Managers consisting of prominent citizens—usually businessmen—from the targeted area create and supervise viable programs to help alleviate social problems within the community.

Adults were an important constituent of the "Y". One of the major tasks of the Board of Managers of black branches of the YMCA was to design pragmatic education programs for black men and boys. Each of the branches devised detailed curricula and other programs to foster education for them. Popular projects consisted of public lectures, recreation programs, including team sports, and vocational and leadership training. Each component of the education program fostered specific goals. The responsibility for planning and implementing education programs was left to the education committee of each branch.

The Michigan Avenue YMCA of Buffalo, New York, the African American branch, illustrated the extent to which the education committee of black YMCAs stressed adult education.[12] Founded in 1923, it accommodated the black communities of Buffalo and Lackawanna, the site of the Bethlehem Steel Mill, one of the largest employers of blacks in the area. The black population of Buffalo was primarily a migrant population. The 1910 federal census recorded 1,773, 0.4 percent of the population in the city, yet by 1920 this population had increased to more than 4,500, 0.9 percent, as many blacks joined the Great Migration that had wended its way from the South to the North in search of economic opportunities.[13] Many brought with them marginal occupational skills and little knowledge with which to confront their new urban environment. The Michigan Avenue YMCA Board of Managers targeted this group in its efforts to uplift the entire black community.

Executive director William Jackson, formerly of Orangeburg, South Carolina, and a veteran YMCA official, observed that the education of the migrants, especially factory workers, was one of the major needs of Buffalo's black community.[14] Dr. Ivorite Scruggs, Howard University Medical School graduate and a native of Mississippi, was also a member of the Michigan Avenue YMCA Board of Managers. He described, in 1925, the challenge facing administrators of the all-black institution.

We must choose between fear of segregation on the one hand and on the other, racial progress; we must choose between developing the best within us in our own institutions, built along the lines of other groups and a means of self-expression for us, or merely content ourselves with becoming a minor part of institutions fostered by other groups. . . . This is the adjustment period. In the years to come we will have furnished a foundation upon which to develop a superstructure of our own civilization. We must build so that the edifice will be strong and inspiring.[15]

Mortician Wardner H. Jones, chair of the Board of Managers in 1937, endorsed Scruggs' sentiments, and observed that "the great value of the 'Y' is that it is an independent organization which gives the individual a fine opportunity to ally himself with a constructive program of benefit in his own life and community."[16] This was the policy of the "Y" from its inception, but only with the construction of a modern facility in 1927 did the Board have the physical plant to carry out its mandate.

The sentiments of the leaders of the Michigan Avenue YMCA indicate their theoretical perspectives regarding the uplift of their race and the role that blacks must play in the process. They believed in an "ethos of mutuality" that dictated that blacks protect and support one another. Black branch managers across the nation shared these beliefs, and in 1925 Channing Tobias, national director of the black YMCA, summoned them to Washington, D.C., to discuss the conditions of the urban migrant population and to formulate strategies by which the "Y" could help to alleviate the pressures this group faced. Delegates clearly perceived their role as a special one that the tenets of the "ethos of mutuality" demanded.[17]

Among the Michigan Avenue YMCA's most popular programs was physical education, which offered courses in swimming, calisthenics, contact sports, and health. Developing the body comported with Christian philosophy, for if one's body is a temple of God, one must follow a regimen of exercise and proper diet and avoid abuse. Moreover, the physical education program of the "Y" addressed one of the critical shortages in the Buffalo black community—the paucity of recreational facilities. Young men who arrived in the city and found work in local factories were doomed to a life of drudgery, for few employers in Buffalo at the turn of the twentieth century advocated socially enlightened policies. Workers lacked recreational facilities on the job, and racism barred them from most programs in the city. The Central Branch of the "Y" did not permit blacks to use its pool and other physical education facilities. The Michigan Avenue YMCA's educational programs filled a major void in the lives of these young men. Observers noted, too, the relation between involvement in the YMCA and a decline in crime. The physical education programs were often the introduction to the "Y" for many newcomers. Once they enrolled in its courses, "Y" officials often introduced them to other educational programs. These youths became loyal followers, and many later joined the Board of Managers or served in other leadership capacities within the agency.[18]

Religious education pervaded all programs of the Michigan Avenue YMCA. The Association scheduled a symposium, "Studies in the Teachings of Jesus: Finding a Religion to Live By," in 1931. It targeted the young migrant and young adult populations for its programs, for it was concerned about religious and moral teachings. The Board of Managers believed that this population was most at risk to the attacks of urban blight and poverty, and set up a series of lectures and classes for them. Sunday morning sessions were mainly designed for residents in the dormitory, with afternoon sessions open to the public. Topics included "The Golden Rule," "What Is Christianity?" and "The Bible as a Living Document." Concerts, movies, and other forms of entertainment were part of the religious department's program. Participants found that they learned religious philosophy at the same time they experienced rewarding recreational activities.[19]

Black ministers were an integral component of Michigan Avenue YMCA programs. Sydney O. B. Johnson of Lloyd Memorial Congregational Church; Elijah J. Echols, Shiloh Baptist Church; Henry Durham, St. Luke African

Methodist Episcopal Church, and others served in various capacities, such as members of the Board of Managers or its committees. Johnson and Echols were both migrants from Mississippi. That ministers were an integral component of the "Y" is not surprising, for this reflected the traditional role that black clergy played in their neighborhoods. Not only were they the spiritual leaders, but they also were counselors and the acknowledged spokespeople for their community. Because they owed their allegiance solely to the black community, they were in a position to decry the racism that blacks experienced. They also became one of the most effective gatekeepers through which outsiders had to come to seek employees or to disseminate information.[20]

The sense of shared experience and concern that characterized African American communities across the nation was nowhere more prevalent than in black churches, which prided themselves on the fact that they supported their own. With migration, the problems blacks faced took on mammoth proportions, and their churches' resources were taxed beyond the limits. In northern communities, like Buffalo, the number of storefront churches with barely literate ministers who had been "called" to preach the gospel, but who had little expertise to deal with contemporary urban problems, increased. In view of the changing characteristics of the black clergy and the increased demands made on them, the Michigan Avenue YMCA initiated the Ministers' Institute. The Institute provided a network for ministers to discuss the social problems that their parishioners experienced on a daily basis and, simultaneously, a place to devise strategies to solve them. It also gave the participants an opportunity for fellowship and enrichment. Johnson had a wealth of practical experience. In Meridian, Mississippi, he worked at the Lincoln Community Center, and under its auspices he had established an employment bureau for blacks, a night school for World War I veterans, and special education programs for black women and children. William Jackson, a veteran YMCA official, also had a rich background in social work. Leading clergymen, such as Mordecai Johnson, president of Howard University, addressed the group.[21]

Begun in 1928, the Adult Education Forum was also a popular and successful program of the Michigan Avenue YMCA. These forums introduced black and white audiences to nationally prominent black intellectuals. Lecturers reflected an African American value system and became role models for the blacks in Buffalo. African American history was an essential component of their messages, for they seemed to be imbued with the age-old adage that those who do not know their history are condemned to repeat it. Or, as contemporary black historian Bernice Johnson Reagon says, "we acknowledge that we are here because of something someone did before we came."[22]

In March 1930 a standing-room-only audience filled the "Y's" auditorium when Charlotte Hawkins Brown, president of the Palmer Memorial Institute, an academy that she founded to provide pedagogically sound education for black youngsters in Sedalia, North Carolina, addressed the forum.[23] She emphasized the steps that African Americans needed to take to obliterate racial discrimination. Brown, also a vice president of the National Association of Colored Women and president of the North Carolina State Federation of Negro Women's Clubs, in her lecture focused primarily on black women. Like many of the Forum's other guest speakers, she stressed the importance of black history and inquired of the women in the audience if they understood the meaning of slavery for black women. Brown then invoked the name of their spiritual foremother, Josephine St. Pierre Ruffin, founder of the National Federation of Afro-American Women in 1895, whom she identified as the emancipator of black women.[24] She argued that "emancipation of the Negro woman did not follow Lincoln's Emancipation Proclamation, but some 50 years later and has come through women's clubs and is still in progress. To attain the full [realization] of this freedom, more and effective club work among Negro womanhood is demanded."[25] Brown warned black women that, unlike their liberated white sisters, they could not afford the luxury of indulging in the popular pastimes of tobacco or alcohol, for "no one would be there to pick them up when they were [ostracized] by society." This moralizing tone was also typical of the blacks who addressed YMCA forums.[26]

Charlotte Hawkins Brown's warning was echoed by forum speaker George Schuyler, associate editor of an important black newspaper, *The Pittsburgh Courier*. Schuyler, in his 1942 address to the education forum at the Michigan Avenue YMCA, noted that blacks must be ever vigilant, for the "aim of [public] education is to avoid racial equality." He cited the omission in school textbooks of the contributions of African people to the "maintenance of civilization" as evidence to support his observations. Schuyler informed his audience that blacks, like the military, should learn to use propaganda to their advantage. He further suggested that they should highlight the importance African Americans attach to higher education.[27]

The messages that Brown and Schuyler delivered to Buffalo black audiences were prototypes of those that other blacks gave before the education forums. The list of speakers reads like *Who's Who in Black America*. These lecturers were in great demand and traveled across the nation delivering similar speeches to black audiences. They promoted a value system that was embedded in the African American tradition and reminded them of their historical pursuit of an educational program to support and extend their freedom.[28]

Professor John Overtrea, principal of Tuskegee Institute, told the Manhattan Branch of the YMCA forum that blacks "should develop independence in politics and do [their] own thinking." But Overtrea pleaded his case for a strong program in education and self-improvement. The Reverend W. H. Brooks, of New York's St. Marks Methodist Episcopal Church, in his sermon "Human Perfection or Ideals" reiterated Overtrea's message.

Brooks noted that blacks should strive to attain the best in scholarship, for "[they] are to compare with the highest achievements [of any group]."[29] He reminded his audience that such accomplishments resulted from persistence and diligence.

Education was perhaps the greatest challenge confronting black administrators in the "Y." How could they create an educational program to meet their long-range goals, yet satisfy the immediate goals of securing jobs for their constituents? The Board of Managers of the Michigan Avenue YMCA perceived the adult forums as platforms to provide a solid theoretical foundation for guaranteeing black freedom. To help solve immediate needs, the managers established a series of courses to train blacks to take advantage of the job openings that were available to them. Such offerings were part of YMCA policy. The Central YMCA offered training in auto mechanics, plumbing, and other skilled trades from which blacks were excluded. On the other hand, the Michigan Avenue YMCA's curricula consisted of vocational courses, such as steam furnace operation, and janitorial service. Black adults in Buffalo could also register for courses in English, public speaking, and music. These courses reflected both the kinds of jobs available to black Buffalonians and the kinds of personal enrichment they and the Board of Managers deemed important. The curriculum expanded as a result of the pressure applied by blacks and the changing vocational opportunities open to them. During the late 1930s, when Buffalo businesses began to hire black clerical workers, courses in typing and stenography were added to the curriculum.[30]

Other black YMCAs across the country offered similar courses. But often they provided a broader range of subjects that would prepare blacks to assume service as well as skilled positions. The courses reflected the characteristics of the individual city and blacks' relation to the economy.[31] Working in tandem with other black community leaders, such as the executive director of the National Urban League, "Y" officials sometimes successfully persuaded local business to hire blacks in nontraditional fields. Blacks, thereby, were able to enter fields from which they previously had been excluded, and employers received well-trained workers because the YMCA provided their education.

Jesse Moorland, international secretary of the African American Young Men's Christian Association, noted in 1906 the practical nature of YMCA education programs: "Whatever is helpful to young men in a given community is provided. . . . The policy of the educational department is not to teach arithmetic simply because it is taught somewhere else, but because it is needed by men of a given community."[32] Moorland reported that although the major emphasis in YMCA educational programs was to develop "efficient artisans and businessmen," some facilities also prepared them for professional training. Two of the thirty-two African American branches of the YMCA offered a class to train electricians, while several taught clerical courses. In some instances, students who enrolled in these classes had unskilled jobs and were illiterate. In just one quarter-term, many of these students mastered the rudiments of reading and writing and acquired new skills that would give them an opportunity to acquire steadier, higher-paying jobs.[33]

By 1919 Jesse E. Moorland was senior secretary of the African American Men's Department of the YMCA, and reported on the status of one of its innovative educational programs, the War Work Council, established to conduct work among soldiers on the battlefields of Europe. It appointed black YMCA directors and also assigned a number of volunteer black women, like Mary Burnett Talbert, president of the National Association of Colored Women (NACW) and vice president of the National Association for the Advancement of Colored People (NAACP). These councils offered important services to black soldiers. Religious education was a central part of the training program and helped to boost the soldiers' morale so that they could provide distinguished service for their country. But literacy training was also a key element in the council's mission, for a significant number of young recruits came from the rural South, where they had little access to schooling. Under the auspices of the councils, literacy among black troops increased. Moorland observed that the men expressed feelings of empowerment after they were released from the "shackles of an oppressing ignorance."[34] Lecturers helped to educate the men about the world in which they lived and their place in the larger scheme of affairs. Talbert, also a biblical scholar, frequently lectured on religious topics and African American history. As president of the NACW, she undertook a major project designed to purchase and restore the Anacostia, District of Columbia, home of the venerable Frederick Douglass as a monument to him and the achievements of black Americans. When she returned to the United States in 1919, she carried $1,000 that had been donated by the black troops among whom she worked. Black soldiers, she said, wanted others "to catch the vision" of self-improvement and racial uplift too.[35]

Most YMCA work for blacks was conducted in the urban areas, especially in the North, although YMCA administrators were cognizant of the need for programs in the rural areas of the South as well. Rural blacks often were isolated, and lacked an opportunity for the enrichment offered by educational, cultural, and recreational institutions. In 1913 blacks from Brunswick County, Virginia, organized a County Committee of the Colored YMCA to "take advantage of the religious impetus in the race and [to] join to this the social aspects and educational efforts that characterize the YMCA."[36] These organizers believed that the "Y" movement had the power to "uplift" blacks and increase their economic and social value. The Association planned "to establish centers of influence through local leadership, to interest the boys and men in better methods of farming by getting them to read good agricultural papers and experiment station bulletins and by practical examples, and to endeavor to raise the religious and moral standards of the whole community."[37] This, like the programs promoted by urban "Y's," was "no visionary scheme." Blacks formulated educational programs based on the sociocultural experiences of their constituents and their desire to provide for these people curricula to protect the freedom that they enjoyed and to prepare them to extend that freedom in the future.

YWCA AND ADULT COMMUNITY EDUCATION

The YWCAs in the black communities across the nation functioned in much the same way as their male counterparts, and shared a similar history. Many early branches had been established by black women for black women. The earliest branch, founded in Dayton, Ohio, was independent but enjoyed "a friendly spirit" with the Dayton YWCA. Martha E. Murphy, clubwoman and wife of the editor of the *Baltimore Afro-American*, one of the most important black newspapers, noted that black women in Baltimore received a charter to found a "Y" chapter in 1896. This chapter also was independent, and had as its sole purpose "to help young women in our community to better and truer womanhood, [and] to encourage them to make the most of themselves in body and soul."[38]

After 1906 the YWCA organized both "cultural and geographical" branches to address specific needs of its constituents. In some instances, African American YWCA branches became an integral part of the parent organization. But Isobel Lawson observed that "in all too many instances the branch has been used as a means of exclusion rather than inclusion."[39] In 1913 Eva Bowles joined the national staff to work with African Americans and help shape policy regarding them. After completing degrees at Ohio State University and Columbia University, Bowles enjoyed a reputation as a social worker and teacher. She had come to New York from her native Ohio.[40] In her capacity as director of Colored Work, she was able to hire a number of outstanding black women assistants and secretaries of departments; one of these appointees was Elizabeth Ross, a graduate of Fisk University and the University of Chicago and a teacher in the Normal School at Montgomery, Alabama.[41] Bowles founded the 137th Street Branch of the YWCA, one of the largest and most effective.

The new hiring practices of the National YWCA did not resolve all of the concerns of blacks. In 1921 a group of black women went to the headquarters to voice their frustrations over the difficulty in getting white women to "think black."[42] They tried to clarify the needs of their community, especially in light of the increasing number of young women migrants who arrived daily, and to impress on administrators the need to place additional black women on the national staff of the YWCA. These women merely expressed the sentiment of Margaret Murray Washington of Tuskegee Institute, who earlier had spoken of the exclusion of black women from the YWCA and who also had indicated the importance of providing its services to black women and girls. At the April 1921 staff meeting committee members debated whether the Colored Work Committee's task was "administrative and policy making or interpretive." Subsequent to this meeting, black involvement in curriculum planning and training programs increased. Black social scientist F. B. Washington, in 1924, still criticized both the YWCA and the YMCA because they "only met the needs of the middle and upper classes," rather than those of the majority. However, the membership statistics of 1942 suggest that black members represented a cross section of their communities.[43]

The era 1900–1920 was one of expansion of "Y" work in black communities across the country. The impetus for expansion stemmed from black women's concerns regarding the conditions that young migrant women, traveling to the North alone, experienced. They were troubled by the paucity of sound, safe housing and educational opportunities and the abundance of disreputable labor agents who made false promises to unsuspecting young women. The "good jobs" offered by agents often were in prostitution rings, and if they secured legitimate positions in domestic service, these women frequently experienced virtual slavery.[44] Black women wanted to protect and "uplift" these young women. The YWCA was a vehicle for them to do so.

The "Y" branches varied, but the ones in New York, Brooklyn, Detroit, Philadelphia, Indianapolis, Washington, D.C., and Baltimore had well-developed programs in their own structures. This was of critical importance because the organizers perceived the Association as one of the most significant vehicles for community education and considered their independent status as a safeguard for implementing their policies. They believed that under their auspices, they could assure the moral development of young women, provide them with job training for a future of independence, and establish avenues for their cultural and intellectual expression and development.[45] The black secretaries and managers developed comprehensive programs to educate young women in these areas. They occasionally participated in national YWCA projects when they deemed these projects relevant to their constituents' needs.

The curricula of the adult education programs sponsored by African American branches of the YWCA varied by region, but all stressed religious training. The Bureau of Religious Education at national headquarters understood well the importance of African Americans' religious heritage, and wanted to promote a religious program in the branches that would preserve their heritage. The YWCA produced a book of African American folk songs with religious interpretations to assure that black women and girls would continue to appreciate their rich religious tradition, and would be able to draw on it for sustenance, especially in urban environments. In addition, local branches offered classes on scripture and sponsored lectures and symposia by renowned theologians, who addressed such topics as "A Purpose to Life" and "Christianity: Is It Worth While?" The women's Bible classes had as another goal the training of teachers for the community church school classes. Sunday school classes had always been important sources for literacy training and the inculcation of moral values and an African American cultural awareness. The teacher-training programs aimed to prepare Sunday school teachers who were knowledgeable and prepared to use effective and innovative techniques of instruction. These programs were well attended and helped to alleviate the anomie that some women experienced, and they also extended the YWCA principles to other segments of the black communities.[46]

Black YWCA branches offered vocational training programs for women too. YWCA managers and education committees opted to offer vocational programs that would yield immediate benefits, rather than to chart new paths. Therefore, their domestic training programs were the most well-developed and successful programs. In 1905 the Lexington Avenue YWCA in Brooklyn opened its Domestic Training Department. It announced that women could find "recreation, entertainment . . . and religious and educational advantages." It especially appealed to "Southern girls," for they would be taught in the methods and appliances of "Northern homes." While these "girls" were in training, they were guaranteed the "protection of a good home" and an employment bureau that would be "safe" for them to patronize. Such a program was designed to increase literacy while providing job skills. The Brooklyn "Y's" domestic program was comprehensive, and included courses in "cooking, care of the kitchen, waitress, laundry, housemaids and home nursing . . . , sewing, mending, reading, spelling, penmanship, letter writing, arithmetic, and geography."[47]

The Baltimore YWCA also offered courses along "industrial lines," although its domestic training program was not as comprehensive as the New York program. Martha Murphy, the executive secretary, observed that students were fortunate in having teachers who were trained in the top colleges in the country, including Drexel Institute in Philadelphia and Pratt Institute and Columbia Teachers' College in New York. Black teachers often were unable to secure jobs in the public schools in both the North and the South. YWCA administrators at the national headquarters stipulated that well-educated personnel must staff its branches, and sought black educators as role models, managers, and instructors. Students in the black YWCAs across the country were the beneficiaries of the racism that their teachers encountered. The Baltimore "Y" offered cooking, sewing, and embroidery classes. While observers noted the "tremendous amount of real practical work done by the Association," they felt the need for the branch to establish a laundry. Such facilities, they argued, would enable instructors to train girls from the countryside in marketable skills, while helping to promote the "Y's" financial self-sufficiency.[48]

Some may argue that the domestic training programs offered more benefits to employers than to black women graduates. But the Manhattan Branch at 137th Street reported that it placed 317 of the 458 women who sought employment through its employment bureaus. Officials contended that young women who sought factory jobs unsuccessfully should enroll in their domestic training program, where they could secure marketable skills and, simultaneously, learn to mend their own clothes. Pragmatism seemed to govern the vocational programs of the African American YWCA branches.[49] Sheila Rothman was largely critical of the "Y" movement for this very reason. She argued that "in effect, by joining a YWCA, a middle class woman could gain both a place in heaven and, in addition, a source for respectable help." She further contended that such a policy neglected to train women for independence and skilled office work. This analysis was largely true for black women. But Board members conducted a study of the industrial conditions of black working women in 1918 and discussed the racial prejudice that these women experienced, while some committee members suggested the possibility of offering special training programs for them that would lead to independence.[50]

This emphasis on domestic service was directly related to black women's access to the job market. In many parts of the country, black women were losing their edge in the service sector to foreign immigrants. YWCA personnel contended that the well-trained domestic that they prepared would be in a better position to compete successfully in the domestic service market. Further, black women's organizations advocated domestic training, for they perceived it as part of a comprehensive program to bring about social change. The National Association of Colored Women's Clubs, with a membership of more than 50,000 in 1915, had a domestic service department at its national headquarters that promoted and monitored the working conditions of black women. These club women attached great importance to domestic training, for it was an essential component in their world, but they also advocated that black women study chemistry and other subjects that impacted on their lives. In a 1917 issue of their publication, *National Association Notes*, they contended that

good cooking . . . [is] recognized as fundamental . . . in housekeeping, since the health and happiness of the home are dependent upon them. It is necessary then that the housekeeping be extended to encompass the city. The health and welfare of the public needs such vigilance as only one of domestic training can give. The inspection of city sewers, the care of the city's food and water supplies . . . is extending the family housekeeping into community housekeeping.[51]

This sentiment is consistent with that of other progressive era reformers, and black women perceived it as an important means of community uplift. Although it had limited applicability to women in YWCA vocational courses, this sentiment would become an integral part of the community health education programs that the YWCA and YMCA cosponsored with other community organizations for Negro Health Week.[52]

The vocational and academic courses taught by African American YWCA branches varied with the changing status of blacks. The Lexington Avenue

YWCA offered courses in dressmaking and health and hygiene in 1921. The Phyllis Wheatley YWCA of Washington, D.C., had similar course offerings, with the largest enrollments in typing, English, china painting, and millinery. In addition to the standard curriculum, students at the 137th Street Branch YWCA could take French lessons and public speaking. The Ashland Place YWCA of Brooklyn in 1933 sponsored two clubs of business girls. These clubs allowed unemployed young women to maintain their proficiency in typing and shorthand until they resumed work. While such programs indicate the changing opportunities available to black women, business girls' clubs were established in the white YWCA branches at the turn of the century.[53]

By the 1940s black YWCA officials began to debate policy changes that would involve educating black women for occupations of the future, rather than for the limited ones in which they currently found employment. A model for implementing such an educational program was the Harlem Trade School of the 137th Street Branch. Founded in 1914 and accredited by the New York State Board of Regents, it had an enrollment of more than 1,000 in 1944. Students attended classes in business, garment machine operation, beauty culture, practical nursing, and liberal arts. Students gained practical experience, plus an opportunity to secure vocational guidance and job placement.[54] In her 1937 report, Cecelia Saunders of the 137th Street YWCA noted that adult activities included the study of trade unionism, the Social Security Act, and other legislation that impacted on laborers.[55] Such a course of study was designed to produce successful workers who were cognizant of their rights.

The YWCA and several other community agencies, such as the National Urban League, the NAACP, and the YMCA, sponsored Negro Health Week as part of a national program to highlight the health conditions of black neighborhoods. This collective assault on the deplorable health problems among blacks nationwide was a response to the high mortality rates that blacks experienced. Blacks in Buffalo, for example, had a mortality rate twice as high as that of whites.[56] The Negro Health Week programs included lectures by prominent local and national health care practitioners, such as Dr. Charles Garvin of the National Medical Association, who lectured the Buffalo forum on "Disease Peculiarities Among Negroes" in March 1937. Staff personnel distributed pamphlets on communicable diseases and personal and community hygiene, and they set up special clinics to inoculate youngsters. They also conducted workshops for new mothers on the care of their infants. While these activities were comprehensive and allowed the YWCA to launch a major attack on the health ills of African Americans, most branches sponsored health-related programs as part of their regular curricula. The Patterson, New Jersey, YWCA trained black women in its home nursing program, thereby preparing them to find jobs, as well as to take care of their families.[57]

Cultural programs were a popular component of YWCA adult educational activities. The Phyllis Wheatley Club of the New York YWCA performed

"The Opal Ring," a play written by Frances Keyser of the National YWCA and the NACW.[58] The cultural programming of the YWCA often reflected African American communities' interest in their African heritage and their American experience, as well as the YWCA Board members' desire to educate Americans about that rich cultural experience. In 1932 the national YWCA proposed to its branches a course titled "Study of the Cultural Contributions of the American Negro" and distributed a four-page syllabus for students. In 1938 renowned New York pianist Heppie Ross, attired in African garb, performed the folk songs and contemporary music of Africa in Buffalo. The Ashland Place Branch of the Brooklyn YWCA, in celebration of its thirty-second anniversary in 1935, organized "Cultural Expressions," an exhibit of the works of the eminent sculptor Augusta Savage and lectures by noted Howard University painter James Porter.[59] Such forums provided not only vehicles for community education, but also avenues for cultural expression for black creative artists at a time when their opportunities were circumscribed by racism.

Leadership-training sessions and programs to ameliorate the harsh realities of racism were an important aspect of the mission of the YWCA. Through a series of lectures, workshops, and symposia, national headquarters and "Y" branches undertook to address these concerns. In 1920 the YWCA sponsored two Jersey City extension training courses in which forty-one women learned firsthand about the "Y" and the opportunities for employment in the organization. After completing the extension courses, interested women could apply for admission to the summer training institutes. In 1925 Eva Bowles directed a training session at Hampton Institute in which eighteen high school and college graduates from fifteen states participated. Bowles stated that "the purpose of the instruction [is] to afford the young women a larger vision, preparing them for greater fields of usefulness as executive secretaries, girls' workers and as secretaries to other departments."[60] Topics of discussion included social education, foreign work, girls' work, and administration problems. Panels also focused on YWCA projects and ways to implement them. These training sessions attracted growing numbers of participants, with nearly 13,000 in 1943 alone.[61]

Within the context of U.S. racism and its own segregated institutions, the YWCA, by the 1930s, seemed committed to breaking down social barriers by dispelling racial stereotypes that were deeply embedded in tradition. The national YWCA perceived education as a means of ameliorating inimical race relations and, consequently, sponsored comprehensive interracial education programs.[62] These institutes, conducted by African American staff members, focused on race relations and African American history. Local YWCA branches across the nation established interracial committees to "study the history of the races in America . . . and to discuss frankly and with unbiased minds the problems of the Races."[63] The activities of these groups were effective and drew widespread support. A measure of their success was the conversion of Southern white women, like Jessie Ames, to the antilynching movement.[64]

Mrs. David Wyke's address before the World Fellowship Committee meeting of the National Council of the YWCA in 1942 indicated the administration's increasing awareness of the necessity to focus on the issue of racism at home and abroad. She noted:

The outstanding feature of [the War] is the recognition . . . that we are in the midst of a gigantic worldwide social revolution which is transforming all our relationships. . . .

    This is a struggle for freedom, and 'tho it is not always admitted, the colored people, too, share in this revolutionary struggle. . . . The choice that confronts us is . . . between the extension of Democracy everywhere and its utter destruction.[65]

The next year the YWCA sponsored an Institute of Ethnic Democracy because administrators believed that cultural "diversity is the key ingredient in America's pursuit of democracy." Black scholars and political activists were invited to lecture or to lead workshops. Sometimes these sessions were followed by field trips to historical sites that depicted African Americans' contributions to U.S. history.[66] From their inception, these sessions also were designed to educate women for social action. As Mrs. Charles Davis Boardman informed the Kansas City African American YWCA branch in her 1923 address, "women should be interested in [political activities] because they are taxpayers" and are in a better position "to help secure better measures to the benefit of humanity."[67]

The YWCA was an important source for adult community education for African Americans. It offered a practical program through which participants could secure job skills, improve health conditions, and find opportunities for cultural enrichment. It also provided black women training for leadership and social action. Black women across the nation responded enthusiastically to YWCA educational programs. The 137th Street Branch reported that more than 2,000 students enrolled in its trade school in 1937.[68] Women often composed 5 to 17 percent of the black population of their towns. Yet in 1942 in Montclair, New Jersey, 22.1 percent of black women were members of the YWCA. In New Castle, Pennsylvania, Wheeling, West Virginia, and Denver, Colorado, the figures, respectively, were 22, 37.9, and 35.9 percent; Richmond and Norfolk reported that 2.5 and 3.7 percent of adult black women, respectively, joined the YWCA.[69] The success of the YWCA movement among black adults is the result of the efforts of African American women who understood that community's quest for self-determination and who drew on its religious and educational values in mapping out the YWCA's social agenda. The course offerings, health education and cultural programs, as well as the interracial programs of the 1930s and 1940s are indicative of their influence.

MUTUAL BENEVOLENT ASSOCIATIONS AND
ADULT COMMUNITY EDUCATION

Benevolent associations and fraternal societies were another important source of black adult community education. These organizations had been founded as early as the eighteenth century, but the establishment of fraternal societies among African Americans had its genesis in the African societies from which they had been brought.[70] Benevolent societies, like the Prince Hall Order of Masons, which received its charter in 1784, and the Independent Order of St. Luke, founded in 1867, were organized to provide aid for member families during periods of crisis stemming from illness or death. They especially were committed to the support of widows and orphans. These benevolent associations enjoyed a renaissance during the mid-nineteenth century because of the social constraints that blacks faced. The 1913 self-observation of the St. Luke Order accurately characterized the nineteenth century, and depicted itself thus: "Fraternalism means . . . members of the same family, . . . bound by ties of love and kinship, will stand by one another at all hazards. What we lack by sacred ties of blood we make up by a solemn oath-bound obligation, declaring ourselves sisters and brothers, children of the same Father."[71]

The fraternal societies exemplify the commitment of African Americans to the support of their people, but they were very much more than a social service organization. The fraternals became forums to organize black labor and to promote self-education and community uplift through political and economic advancement. All of this was done in the context of religion.[72] They also joined together blacks from diverse socioeconomic backgrounds and formed a network that spanned the continent and later the globe. The Reverend J. A. Bray, in his 1902 address to the Negro Young People's Christian and Educational Congress, explained:

These secret and benevolent societies are great ducts or avenues crossing each other, honeycombing the mass of the race, and ramifying the race structure so that any directed influence may reach every atom of the race composition—however remote a corner . . . thus furnishing a common ground upon which all may stand and realize the great principle of the "brotherhood of man."

In 1938, James A. Jackson of the Elks commented on this phenomenon too, and stated: "If I were obliged to select a medium for reaching the minds of the whole Negro race, to develop mass interest, to reach the high and the mighty, or the lowly . . . among us, I would make my path easy [by going to the lodge], certain that here is a road that has long been trod by those who have had race progress consistently in mind." It is through such a network that the fraternal organizations were able to educate the black community.[73]

Unlike the YMCA and the YWCA movements among blacks, the benevolent societies seldom offered formal classes for the community. They taught the masses primarily by example and precept. A necessary brief and limited examination of Independent Order of St. Luke of Richmond, Virginia; the Most Worshipful Prince Hall Grand Lodge, Free and Accepted Masons, State of Illinois; and the Eureka Grand Chapter, Order of the Eastern Star, Prince Hall Affiliation, Illinois, will illustrate the nature of their educational programs and their impact on African American communities.[74]

St. Luke's most successful adult education programs occurred through its public forums and business enterprises. Maggie L. Walker, Grand Worthy Secretary, rescued the faltering institution in 1899 and developed it into a well-organized, successful entity that could bear the close scrutiny of any observer. By 1913 the Independent Order of St. Luke had a membership of 29,000 in seventeen states in the North and South and the District of Columbia, and by the mid–1920s the membership was more than 100,000. Black membership in secret benevolent societies nationwide totaled two million by 1938.[75] The black community could learn from the considerable organizational skills of Maggie Walker and the St. Luke family alone. But the charismatic Walker also was a highly visible role model for the African American community. She took advantage of her stature within African America and continually inculcated it with values that she and her contemporaries believed would help blacks to escape the inimical effects of racism and second-class citizenship. Maggie Walker and the other St. Luke officers believed that cooperative economics was critical for the salvation of the race. In a 1901 report to the Grand Council, Walker argued cogently for the establishment of businesses by the order: "We need a savings bank, chartered, officered, and run by men and women of the Order. Let us put our moneys together; . . . let us put our money out as usury among ourselves, and realize the benefit ourselves." Using the biblical analogy, she continued: "Shall we longer continue to bring our talent, which the Lord has given us, wrapped in a napkin and hidden away, where it ought to be giving us still other talents?"[76] Heeding Walker's admonition, the Independent Order of St. Luke established several economic enterprises. These businesses were outward manifestations of the values to which the Order subscribed and with which it hoped to imbue the black community. The St. Luke Penny Savings Bank, founded in 1903, was one of the Order's most effective enterprises.[77] At a time when Jim Crow was further engulfing black Richmond, the bank provided other options for them to secure loans for businesses or homes. Moreover, the Order conducted training sessions for its managerial and clerical staff in its banking and insurance enterprises, and thereby provided employment opportunities for blacks in a sector from which they had been excluded in the community at large. A campaign to encourage blacks to save their money accompanied the establishment of the bank. As St. Luke spokesperson, Walker alone placed some 500 piggy banks in the homes of blacks to promote thrift among the adults and youths of the community.

Business education programs sponsored by fraternals were important, for most business schools in the North and South excluded black students. Blacks acquired bookkeeping and other clerical skills through classes such as those offered by St. Luke, as well as through the experience they gained from conducting the Order's business.

Maggie Walker also advocated the formation of a newspaper by St. Luke. The black press was a chronicler of a collective racial identity. Its inception was predicated on African American historical experiences and contemporary issues that the race confronted. Historian V. P. Franklin has documented the important educational function of black newspapers, noting that they not only helped to mold group solidarity, but also were the leading vehicles for the expression of the objective social, political, and economic interests of all segments of the black community.[78] Walker summed it up thus:

No business, no enterprise which has to deal with the public can be pushed successfully without a newspaper, a trumpet to sound the orders, so that the St. Luke upon the mountain top, and the St. Luke dwelling by the side of the sea can hear the same order, keep step to the same music, march in unison to the same command, although miles and miles intervene.[79]

The St. Luke Herald was first published in 1902. In an editorial, Lillian Payne noted that its first task was to report the news, especially as it impacted on "[the] downtrodden and oppressed people" and "to encourage and inspire [them]."[80] The Herald soon developed a loyal following and became an important vehicle for blacks to decry injustices, ranging from mob violence to the decline of financial support for the education of the black community. By 1903 it already had 3,000 subscribers and the numbers continued to grow.

Through its editorials and features, the Herald hoped to encourage the development of economic opportunities for black women who were losing ground relative to their white counterparts. Black women were employed in a few service jobs, whereas white women worked in 295 of the 303 occupation classifications in 1900. But, more important, black women were excluded from the growth industries. The status of black women had to improve to protect the black family and community from economic deprivation.[81] The Herald disseminated such views and apprised its constituency of the progress that St. Luke had made in its efforts to uplift the race. Other black newspapers also published accounts of the St. Luke economic enterprises, like the Emporium, which the Order founded to provide consumer goods for the black community and job training and employment in the managerial and clerical fields for black women.

As Grand Worthy Secretary of the Independent Order of St. Luke, Maggie Walker had the task of carrying the message of the Order across the nation. She was a frequent guest lecturer at conferences and meetings of black organizations. In her 1906 address to the Negro Young People's Christian and Educational Congress, she continued her campaign to provide for the protection and nurturance of black women. She admonished her audience that "every Negro . . . [and] Negro [institution] should be extending the hand which helps and giving forth the words which encourage—for the path of the colored woman is dark and thorny."[82] Walker reminded convention delegates that black women did not work because they wanted to be "masculine women" or to become the "new woman," but for their family. She further contended that "the greater portion of the married men can't support [their] wife and children—with the wages received by them; hence, the woman who does not want to be a burden on her husband goes out into the world— not for glory and honor—for bread and for her babies."[83]

Such addresses included an appeal to black men and women to take advantage of their purchasing power and to establish businesses that would provide suitable jobs for black women and that also would lead to economic freedom for African Americans. For blacks to succeed in these endeavors, they needed disposable cash. When Maggie Walker addressed the Coronella Woman's Literary Club in 1909, her views on this matter were quite evident as she told them that "it is hardly enough . . . to read papers, recite dramatically, sing divinely, look angelic, and dance perfectly, [for] these are but the showy leaves of the fig tree."[84] She reminded them that they could effect social change in their communities through collective economic action.

The Independent Order of St. Luke educated blacks to subscribe to a value system that stressed self-help and racial solidarity. These values certainly were not unique to the Order, but its emphasis on cooperative economics and its establishment of a successful newspaper, bank, and department store were tangible manifestations of its philosophy, despite Jim Crow. St. Luke employed black architects and builders for its projects, and thereby highlighted the achievements of blacks. Members of the Order gained job skills and leadership training. The Independent Order of St. Luke left a legacy that continues to be a valuable source of adult community education today.

The Prince Hall Order of Masons and the Order of the Eastern Star, both of Illinois, subscribed to the same value system as the Independent Order of St. Luke, and promoted the intellectual, moral, and spiritual development of the African American community. The officers of the Grand Chapter also were respected throughout their community and served as role models for their constituents. Frequently their messages were disseminated through their publications. But many of the formal educational programs of the Prince Hall family were conducted for its members. An examination of the schools that it established indicates the impact of fraternal educational programs on their community.

Training in the rituals and procedures of the Masonic Order was essential, and both the Masons and the Eastern Stars established courses for their members that focused on their distinctive rituals. Much of the literature on initiation and other rituals had to be memorized. This was of obvious advantage to the illiterate, but teaching techniques incorporating visuals and the Socratic method also were used. Those who had not mastered the rudiments of learning benefited from these methods and were able to participate in all aspects of fraternal life.

Melissa E. McClure, Worthy Grand Matron from 1918 to 1919, spearheaded a project to establish a *Book of Instruction* for the Order. The Eureka Grand Chapter of the Order of the Eastern Star of Illinois adopted this *Book of Instruction* at its grand session in 1921. *The Book of Instruction*, in conjunction with *The Macoy Ritual*, assured that the ritualistic work of the Order would be performed in a uniform manner throughout the jurisdiction. Schools of instruction were set up to inculcate members with the knowledge needed to successfully pursue their vows and conduct the business of the Order. *The Macoy Ritual* of the Eastern Stars explained that its lessons are "scriptual; its teachings are moral; and its purposes are beneficent."[85] Membership in the Order was a public manifestation that a person subscribed to these beliefs.

The schools of instruction sponsored by the Masons and Eastern Stars evolved continuously according to the perceived needs of the Order. A Worthy Matron or Grand Master might assume education as the special project of her or his administration.[86] This was a much more frequent occurrence among the Illinois Prince Hall Masons and Eastern Stars after 1940. The Grand Lodge developed the "Knowledge Flower" that represented the major foci of the curriculum and included such topics as African American history and the history of masonry. History was a central component of each organization's educational program. The Grand Master of the Prince Hall Masonic Order in the District of Columbia at the turn of the century explained: "We study the history of the past . . . to inform ourselves . . . [what has been] done in the years gone by, to discover . . . the motives that prompted [our ancestors] to action, and then appropriate the best . . . to the conditions of our times [so that] we may . . . carry upward and onward . . . the great work of the world." The curriculum was also designed to help lodge members implement Masonic law, and included courses in jurisprudence, philosophy, symbolism, and leadership training.[87]

In the 1950s the Illinois Prince Hall family's educational programs emphasized leadership training. Students who enrolled in these courses learned about parliamentary procedures, program planning, budget preparation, proper maintenance of Masonic records, and the essential qualities of good leadership, as well as its perils.[88] Members of the Order who had expertise in the specific subjects conducted lectures and workshops. Often they were public-school teachers or business people in the community. Instructors used such techniques as audiovisual aids and sociodrama to achieve the desired objectives. They organized small-group sessions for those who had not mastered the rudiments of learning.[89] As a result of the instruction they received, many members increased their literacy levels; such training also allowed access to membership to all "good" men and women, regardless of their socioeconomic status or literacy status. The skills that members of the fraternals acquired in the leadership training sessions could be used on the job or in other community social organizations.[90] Consequently fraternals relied on their network across the state and nation to wield tremendous influence in shaping educational programs and philosophy in African American communities.

Fraternal organizations advocated the participation of blacks in politics. Although the Eureka Grand Chapter did not endorse political candidates, it and other grand chapters sponsored symposia on the importance of voting and participating in political activities. Members of fraternals also learned the importance of playing politics and its effectiveness by conducting the organizations' business. James Jackson noted the significance of the training for political participation that lodges afforded African Americans in the 1930s: "Denied the right to vote, to participate in primaries or local caucuses, and without privilege of participation in other community organizations, where else would the Negro have become trained to meet the demands for political and civic intelligence of a political sort, as a race pushed forward into national affairs?" He further observed that the Reconstruction politicians virtually all were products of lodge-room education. Selection of the proper candidate would benefit the Order in implementing its programs. In the political forums, participants were told that the ideal candidate embraced "charity, truth, and loving kindness."[91] Adherence to these values, they argued, would lead to a more humanitarian government that would support the needs of all its citizens. While blacks today have alternative forums for political education, the lodge is still providing essential experience and training for many.

In summation, black fraternals have made important contributions to the education of their constituents. Traditionally, their programs were limited to the sizable numbers who were members. In addition to skills development, the secret benevolent societies taught the power of organization and the value of self-confidence. Through their public forums, they also were able to inculcate blacks with a value system, demonstrate the benefits of self-help, and provide role models for young adults. As the needs of its constituents changed, the Prince Hall family and the Independent Order of St. Luke responded. Today the Prince Hall Grand Lodge of Illinois contributes ten scholarships to worthy students to attend college. The lodge has established a number of programs on drug education for young adults, and it also organized the Assault on Illiteracy Program for Chicago residents.[92] These efforts indicate the benevolent associations' commitment to eradicating ignorance in their communities and to providing people with practical skills and a philosophy of hope.

This exploration of black adult community education programs of the YMCA, the YWCA, and fraternal organizations has demonstrated that African Americans place a high value on education. The educational programs that they supported emphasized self-help and racial solidarity and were designed to allow for individual and community uplift. The men and women architects of the educational programs personified the "core" African American values. While they were cognizant of their community's needs, they designed flexible programming that encouraged constituents' input and placed them at the forefront of black community education.

NOTES

A State University of New York at Albany Faculty grant helped to support the research for this project. The writer also acknowledges the special assistance of Francine Frank, dean of the College of Humanities and Fine Arts at the Albany campus, and Daniel Williams, archivist at the Frissell Library, Tuskegee University.

1. Nell Painter, *The Exodusters: Black Migration to Kansas After Reconstruction* (New York: Norton, 1976); Thomas Cox, *Blacks in Topeka Kansas* (Baton Rouge: Louisiana State University Press, 1982); Gilbert Osofsky, *Harlem: The Making of a Ghetto* (New York: Harper & Row, 1966); U.S. Department of Labor, *Negro Migration in 1916–17* (Washington, D.C.: U.S. Dept. of Labor, 1919).

2. See, for example, Allen Ballard, *One More Day's Journey: The Story of a Family and a People* (New York: McGraw Hill, 1984); John Bodnar et al., *Lives of Their Own: Blacks, Italians, and Poles in Pittsburgh, 1900–1960* (Urbana: University of Illinois Press, 1982); Peter Gottlieb, *Making Their Own Way: Southern Black Migration to Pittsburgh, 1916–1930* (Urbana: University of Illinois Press, 1987); Lillian S. Williams, "A Community Develops: Blacks in Buffalo, N.Y., 1900–1930," in *Afro-Americans in New York Life and History*, (July 1985):7–35.

3. See, for example, Kenneth Kusmer, *A Ghetto Takes Shape* (Urbana: University of Illinois Press, 1976).

4. V. P. Franklin and James Anderson, eds., *New Perspectives on Black Educational History* (Boston: G. K. Hall, 1978); James Anderson, *The Education of Blacks in the South, 1860–1935* (Chapel Hill: University of North Carolina Press, 1988); Robert McCaul, *The Black Struggle for Public Schooling in Nineteenth Century Illinois* (Carbondale: Southern Illinois University Press, 1987); Allen Ballard, *The Education of Black Folk: The Afro-American Struggle for Knowledge in White America* (New York: Harper & Row, 1973); Edward Magdol, "Against the Gentry: An Inquiry into a Southern Lower-Class Community and Culture, 1865–1870," in *The Southern Common People*, ed. Edward Magdol and Jon Wakelyn (Westport, Conn.: Greenwood Press, 1980):203.

5. Gilbert Osofsky, "The Enduring Ghetto," in *The Journal of American History* 55 (September 1968):243–255.

6. Some immigrant women opposed such legislation because they needed to work as many hours as possible to earn money to support their families. For a discussion of the YWCA and children and foreign-born women, see Elsie Harper, *Fifty Years in the YWCA* (New York: National Board, YWCA, 1963), 23–36; also Helen Bittar, "The YWCA of the City of New York, 1870–1920" (Ph.D. diss., New York University, June 1979); *Buffalo American*, June 2, 1921, p. 6. The following works also document immigrant experiences and the efforts of reformers to address their problems: Jacob Riis, *How the Other Half Lives* (1890; rpt., New York: Dover Pub-

lications, 1971); Jane Addams, *Twenty Years at Hull House* (New York: Macmillan, 1910); Ellen C. Langermann, ed., *Jane Addams on Education* (New York: Teachers College Press, 1985); Upton Sinclair, *The Jungle* (1905; rpt., New York: New American Library, 1960).

7. See, for example, James Adams, *Frontiers of American Culture: A Study of Adult Education in a Democracy* (New York: Scribner's, 1944); Lewis Alderman, *Public Evening School for Adults* (Washington, D.C.: U.S. Government Printing Office, 1927); Elsie D. Harper, *Fifty Years in the YWCA.*

8. See Morse A. Cartwright, "The History of Adult Education in the U.S.," *The Journal of Negro Education* 14 (Summer 1945):288–292; Charlotte T. Morgan, "Finding a Way Out: Adult Education During the Great Depression," *Afro-Americans in New York Life and History* 7 (January 1984): 17–29; Ira de Reid, *Adult Education Among Negroes* (Washington, D.C.: Associates in Negro Folk Education, 1936).

9. Laurence Doggett, *History of the Young Men's Christian Association* (New York: International Committee, YMCA, 1922); Elmer Johnson, *History of YMCA Physical Education* (Chicago: Association Press, 1979); Mayer Zald, *Organizational Change: The Political Economy of the YMCA* (Chicago: University of Chicago Press, 1970); Clyde Binfield, *George Williams and the Y.M.C.A.: A Study in Victorian Social Attitudes* (London: Heinemann, 1973); Peter Romanofsky, *Social Service Organizations* (Westport, Conn.: Greenwood Press, 1978).

10. J. E. Moorland, "Educational Work of the Colored Young Men's Christian Association," *Southern Workman* 35 (April 1906):244–246; Baxter S. Scruggs, "A Modern Achievement," *Southern Workman* 60 (September 1926):401–406, in the Collis P. Huntington Library, Hampton University, hereafter cited as SW.

11. For a history of the Buffalo African American YMCA and community education, see Lillian S. Williams, "To Elevate the Race: The Michigan Avenue YMCA and the Advancement of Blacks in Buffalo, New York, 1923–1940," in Franklin and Anderson, eds., *New Perspectives on Black Educational History*, 129–148.

12. Ibid., 132.

13. For a history of the migration of blacks into Buffalo, see Williams, "A Community Develops"; U.S. Census Bureau, *Negro Population of the United States, 1790–1915* (New York: Arno Press, 1969).

14. *Buffalo Forum*, September 1923, p. 7.

15. *Buffalo American*, January 15, 1925.

16. *The Y's Messenger*, November 1937, in the Michigan Avenue YMCA Memorabilia folder at the North Jefferson Branch Buffalo and Erie County Library, hereafter cited as MAYMCA Memorabilia.

17. See, for example, Edward Magdol and Jon Wakelyn, "The Southern Common People," *Crisis* 31 (November 1925):14.

18. Other YMCA branches experienced similar results. The African American YMCA branch in Detroit reported that 21,000 persons used its physical education department, while nearly 3,000 enrolled in religious programs and 2,000 availed themselves of the "Y's" vocational guidance program. Scruggs, "Modern Achievement," 403; Williams, "To Elevate the Race," 143.

19. Williams, "To Elevate the Race," 147, n. 53.

20. Historical accounts of the black church are covered in Carter G. Woodson, *The History of the Negro Church* (Washington, D.C.: Associated Publishers, 1921); and

Benjamin E. Mays and Joseph E. Nicholson, *The Negro's Church* (New York: Arno Press, 1933).

21. *Buffalo American*, June 9, 1921; MAYMCA, "Recognition Week Programs," April 21–27, 1947; MAYMCA Memorabilia, *Buffalo Star*, July 10, 1942.

22. "Sweet Honey in the Rock, Introduction to Fannie Lou Hamer," Redwood Records, 1988 (Emeryville, Calif.).

23. Hawkins Brown founded Palmer Memorial Institute in 1902 and designed a comprehensive educational program to teach black youngsters the liberal arts as well as "practical" skills. Although New England philanthropists funded her school, she maintained control over the curriculum. Charlotte Hawkins Brown Papers, Schlesinger Library, Radcliffe College, hereafter cited as CHB; reel 1.

24. In 1895 Ruffin convened a group of black women who organized the National Federation of Afro-American Women, and was its first president. In 1896 this organization merged with the Colored Women's League of Washington, D.C., to form the National Association of Colored Women's Clubs, Inc. Rayford Logan and Michael Winston, *Dictionary of American Negro Biography* (New York: Norton, 1982), 535–536, hereafter cited as DANB.

25. *Buffalo Progressive Herald*, March 15, 1930, in the Charlotte Hawkins Brown Papers, reel 4.

26. Ibid.

27. MAYMCA newspaper clipping, January 23, 1942.

28. V. P. Franklin discusses self-determination as one of the "core" African American values in *Black Self-determination* (Westport, Conn.: Lawrence Hill, 1984). Forum speakers included W.E.B. Du Bois, Mary Church Terrell, Mordecai Johnson, Channing Tobias, R. R. Moton, and Congressman Arthur Mitchell (MAYMCA, Scrapbook, 1926–1936).

29. Excerpts from Professor Overtrea's speech appeared in the *New York Age*, November 7, 1907, p. 1.

30. Williams, "To Elevate the Race," 141.

31. J. E. Moorland, SW 35 (April 1906):244.

32. Ibid., 245.

33. Ibid.

34. Jesse E. Moorland, "The YMCA with Colored Troops," SW 53 (April 1919):173.

35. Ibid., 175; *National Notes* (January–March 1921), 10, in the Hollis Burke Frissell Library, Tuskegee University, Tuskegee, Alabama, hereafter cited as *National Notes*.

36. SW 43 (August 1943):426.

37. Ibid.

38. Isobel C. Lawson, "Negro Women and the Association Idea," *Woman's Press*, March 1939, p. 2, in YWCA Papers, Box 40, folder 2; Sophia Smith Collection, Neilson Library, Smith College, Northampton, Massachusetts, hereafter cited as SSC. For general histories of the YWCA, see Mary S. Sims, *The Natural History of a Social Institution—The Young Women's Christian Association* (New York: The Woman's Press, 1936); Harper, *Fifty Years in the YWCA*; Bittar, "YWCA of the City of New York."

39. *Woman's Press*, 119, SSC, Box 40, folder 7.

40. DANB, 54.

41. *New York Age*, August 20, 1908.

42. *New York Age*, May 14, 1921, p. 2.

43. Bureau of Colored Work, minutes, April 22, 1921, SSC, Box 40, folder 7; *National Notes* (November-December 1904):5; *Buffalo American*, March 20, 1924. Membership statistics for 1942, SSC, Box 40, folder 6.

44. *New York Age*, July 27, 1935.

45. Black women had to constantly prove their respectability. They founded the National Association of Colored Women's Clubs, in part, to counteract the attacks that whites made against them. See, for example, Gerda Lerner, *The Majority Finds Its Past* (New York: Oxford University Press, 1979), 95; Rosalyn Terborg-Penn in Sharon Harley and Rosalyn Terborg-Penn, *The Afro-American Woman: Struggles and Images* (New York: Kennekat, 1979), 17–27; Charles Wesley, *The History of The National Association of Colored Women's Clubs, Inc.* (Washington, D.C.: National Association of Colored Women's Club, Inc., 1985); Darlene Clark Hine, "Rape and the Inner Lives of Black Women in the Middle West: Preliminary Thoughts of the Culture of Dissemblance," *Signs* 14 (Summer 1989): 912–920.

46. Report of Eva Bowles, SSC, Box 42B, folder 6; *New York Age*, October 24, 1907, p. 3; ibid., January 28, 1915.

47. *New York Age*, October 12, 1905.

48. *National Notes* (October 1908):1; *New York Age*, February 20, 1908, p. 2. For salary discrepancies between black and white teachers in the South, see Ambrose Caliver, *Secondary Education for Negroes*, "National Survey of Secondary Education," Bulletin #17, 1932 (1933; rpt. New York: Negro Universities Press, 1969), 75. It also appeared that the Baltimore YWCA adopted a two-tier training program based on one's geographical origins. An exploration of this topic is beyond the scope of this essay, but a study of the tracking of young women into such programs can shed some light on the class biases that may have existed among some YWCA officials.

49. *New York Age*, October 22, 1921; Elizabeth Wilson, *Fifty Years of Association Work Among Young Women, 1866–1916*, YWCA (1917, rev. New York: Daybon Social Science Publications, 1978).

50. "Industrial Conditions Among Colored Women," November 1918, SSC, Box 41, folder 3; Wilson, *Fifty Years of Association Work*, 7.

51. *National Notes* (January 1917), 12.

52. YWCA branches established in white areas also offered domestic training, but it was subservient to their clerical and factory programs. See Bittar, "YWCA of the City of New York," 52, 80, 102, 106, 114–116.

53. *New York Age*, May 14, 1921, p. 1; SW 56 (January 1922):32; *New York Age*, January 27, 1923; *New York Age*, November 4, 1933.

54. Dorothy Height, "The Adult Education Program of the YWCA Among Negroes," 4–5, SSC, Box 40, folder 15.

55. Cecelia Saunders' 1937 Report, Occasional Papers #3, 1937, 2, SSC, Box 40, folder 16.

56. See Lillian S. Williams, "The Development of a Black Community; Buffalo, New York, 1900–1940" (Ph.D. diss., State University of New York at Buffalo, 1979), 264.

57. *New York Age*, May 26, 1910; for an example of a week-long agenda for Negro Health, see the *New York Age*, March 11, 1922.

58. *New York Age*, February 20, 1908; *Interracial News Bulletin*, January 1932, SSC, Box 41, folder 5; *The Y's Messenger*, December 1938.

59. *New York Age*, June 1, 1935.

60. "Report of Eva Bowles to the Department of Research and Method," SSC, Box 42B, folder 6; *New York Age*, January 7, 1925.

61. *New York Age*, January 7, 1925; Height, "Adult Education Program of the YWCA," 6.

62. Cf. Frances Williams, "A Plan for Interracial Education," *Woman's Press*, October 1938, SSC, Box 40, folder 15.

63. Interracial Committee By-laws, SSC, Box 40, folder 8.

64. Occasional Papers, #1, 1936; Occasional Papers #2, 1937, SSC, Box 40, folder 16; Jacqueline Dowd Hall, *Revolt Against Chivalry: Jessie Daniel Ames and the Women's Campaign Against Lynching* (New York: Columbia University Press, 1979).

65. Mrs. David Wyke, "The Role of the Colored Races in Our Post-War World," December 7, 1942, SSC, Box 40, folder 16.

66. SSC, Box 40, folder 12; also see leadership conferences, June 23–30, 1942, ibid.

67. *National Notes* (May 1923):5–6.

68. Occasional Papers, #3, SSC, Box 40, folder 16; the 1942 statistics on Negro Branches of YWCAs in New Jersey and Elsewhere (omitting large cities), ibid., Box 40, folder 6.

69. Ibid.

70. Betty M. Kuyk, "The African Derivation of Black Fraternal Orders in the United States," *Comparative Studies in Society and History* 25 (October 1983):559–592; John Blassingame, *The Slave Community* (New York: Oxford University Press, 1979); W. P. Burrell, *Twenty-Five-Year History of the Grand Fountain of the United Order of True Reformers, 1881–1905* (Richmond, Va.: Grand Fountain United Order of Reform, 1909); I. Garland Penn and J.W.E. Bowen, *The United Negro: His Problems and His Progress* (New York: Negro Universities Press, 1902).

71. *Fiftieth Anniversary—Golden Jubilee Historical Report of the RWG Council, I. O. Saint Luke, 1867–1917* (Richmond, Va.: Independent Order of St. Luke, 1917), 41, Maggie Walker Biography Project, Howard University, hereafter cited as *Fiftieth Anniversary*.

72. Peter Rachleff, *Black Labor in the South* (Philadelphia: Temple University Press, 1984), discusses the important functions that fraternal societies play in the lives of their members and their communities, see especially pp. 13–33. Kuyk in "The African Derivation" discusses the religious influence on fraternal rituals. For an example of fraternal ritual, see W.M.T. Forrester, secretary, *Degree Ritual of the Independent Order of Saint Luke* (Richmond, Va., 1894), in the Virginia State Library, mimeographed. James A. Jackson, "Fraternal Societies Aid Race Progress," *The Crisis*, (July 1938):235–237, 244.

73. Penn and Bowen, *United Negro*, 191; *Crisis*, (July 1938):244.

74. I acknowledge Dr. Gertrude Marlowe, project director, Maggie L. Walker Biography Project at Howard University, for granting me access to its data bank, and H. Lorraine Williams Jeter, Associate Grand Matron, Eureka Grand Chapter, and the History Committee of the Prince Hall Family of the State of Illinois for compiling much of the data on which this section is based.

75. *Fiftieth Anniversary*, 44; *Crisis*, July 1938, p. 244.

76. *Fiftieth Anniversary*, 23.

77. Ibid., 29.

78. *Crisis*, July 1938, p. 235; V. P. Franklin, "Voice of the Black Community: *Philadelphia Tribune*, 1912–1941," *Pennsylvania History* 1 (October 1984):276, 278.

79. *Fiftieth Anniversary*, 23–24.

80. Ibid.

81. Maggie Walker, "An Address for Men Only," St. Luke Hall, March 1, 1906, Maggie Walker Biography Project, Howard University, hereafter cited as MWBP; *Fiftieth Anniversary*, 55. Elsa Barkley Brown documents the womanist ideas of Maggie Walker in "Womanist Consciousness: Maggie Lena Walker and the Independent Order of St. Luke," *Signs: Journal of Women in Culture and Society*, (March 1989):610–633.

82. Maggie Walker, "Address to the Negro Young People's Christian and Educational Congress, August 5, 1906," 5, MWBP.

83. During the first three decades of the twentieth century, married black women were twice as likely to be employed as their white counterparts. U.S. Bureau of the Census, *Historical Statistics of the United States, Colonial Times to 1957* (Washington, D.C.: U.S. Dept. of Commerce, 1960) pp. D26–45.

84. Maggie Walker, "Nothing But Leaves," Cornella Women's Literary Club, 1909, MWBP.

85. Interview, H. Lorraine Williams Jeter, February 6, 1989, transcript, p. 1; excerpts from *The Macoy Ritual* (1897), 13, mimeographed, Eureka Grand Chapter, Order of Eastern Stars, Prince Hall History Committee Archives, hereafter cited as PHHCA.

86. Interview, Williams Jeter, 1.

87. Administrative Handbook, 44, mimeographed, PHHCA. District of Columbia Grand Lodge, *Freemasons*, 1913–1914–1915, 115, Moorland Springarn Research Center, Howard University.

88. For an example of the leadership-training program, refer to the 1987 Report of the Committee on Education, 1–3, PHHCA.

89. Interview, Williams Jeter, 1.

90. Past Grand Master Archie Senter deemed the leadership-training sessions so important that he established a year-long course during his administration. Interview, Williams Jeter, 1.

91. *Crisis*, July 1938, p. 235. A number of prominent politicians, such as Oscar DePriest, the first post-Reconstruction black congressman, and the late Mayor Harold Washington of Chicago, were members of the Illinois Prince Hall Masons. Interview, Williams Jeter, 3. Participation in politics was a longstanding policy for fraternal societies. The Washington, D.C., branch of the Independent Order of St. Luke, in 1912, urged the black fraternals to unite in a federation to lobby and promote blacks' interests.

92. Interview, Williams Jeter, 3.

9

African American Women and Adult Education in the South, 1895–1925*

Cynthia Neverdon-Morton

African Americans often saw education as a means of escaping poverty, enhancing their ability to secure employment, and redressing social inequalities and injustices. Throughout the period when black educational institutions were developing, whites debated not only the kind of education African Americans should receive, but also whether or not they should be educated at all. The blacks who provided most of the impetus for the establishment of educational institutions saw as issues adequate funding for the schools, establishment of curricula to meet the needs of African Americans, qualifications of teachers and administrators, better physical facilities, and control of schools for African Americans.

Southern women focused on many needs of African Americans: the plight of working women, limited economic opportunities, inferior housing, severe health problems, the political straitjacket of Jim Crowism, care for the aged, and programs for the very young. But the key to solving all these problems, the leaders of black women were convinced, was education of the masses of black citizens. Education was seen as the first step toward racial equality, and racial equality was the essential precondition for development of the individual's full potential. Thus individual growth and group improvement were viewed as inextricably intertwined. In order to structure longlasting, meaningful programs in areas of concern, the women encouraged group reliance. In focusing on the development of skills, the women hoped that their efforts would have a multiplier effect in the black community. Once the individual matured and prospered, her knowledge, energy, finances, and time could be utilized to further the goals of the entire race.

*Portions of this chapter have appeared previously in Cynthia Neverdon-Morton's *Afro-American Women of the South and the Advancement of the Race, 1895–1925*. Copyright © 1989 by The University of Tennessee Press. Used by permission.

To promote mass education, black women formed clubs, founded institutions, became teachers, and created innovative informal educational programs of many types. No matter what type of social service activity was planned, some educational aspect was included. Throughout the period under consideration, the kind and quality of education appropriate for African Americans in the South were subjects of continued debate. Black women participated in the debates, but they also developed educational institutions, designed curricula, helped to formulate educational policies, and taught in the classroom. But much teaching took place outside formal educational settings. The women used whatever forum was available, whether discussing such issues as proper dress, suffrage, or the treatment of black South Africans, or providing practical experiences in gardening, home nursing, sewing, or child care. The home was considered the major focal point of informal education, and every willing family member was included in some aspect of the educational process.

The educational needs and interests of black adults received special attention. Educative program activities for adults were designed to assist the participants in achieving one or more specific objectives. Some of the objectives were as follows:

- To attain basic competency skills, such as reading, writing, and mathematical computation
- To learn specific skills that would assist them in their occupation, such as farming, domestic service, and dressmaking
- To participate in study groups, seminars, and conferences that would assist them in becoming more informed citizens, parents, and workers
- To learn, and therefore practice, better health habits
- To learn and implement better care practices for the young
- To utilize more effectively and to a greater extent natural resources and readily available materials
- To involve themselves in many phases of community activism, thus furthering those goals that sought improvement of the quality of life for all blacks

Assuming the leadership role in the defining of educational goals for women and the creation of program activities to achieve those goals was the educated black woman.

PREPARATION FOR SERVICE

As African Americans debated a number of general issues concerning the educating of the race, whites as well as African Americans attempted to clarify the issue of education for women. Both white and black laypeople and educators, from 1895 to 1925, offered arguments for the kind of education, if any, that would be appropriate for women. Selena Sloan Butler, an educator, civil rights advocate, and 1888 graduate of Spelman Seminary, offered a spirited comment on the traditional male view:

It is argued by most people that women's specific and only mission is that of maternity and obeying the injunction of the wise man, "Train up a child in the way it should go." Since so much is expected of her, is it not right that she should be given opportunity for development in the highest and broadest sense, that her physical, mental and moral nature may be prepared to fill the highest and noblest calling allotted her?[1]

Despite arguments during the progressive era against educating women, more and more white women were gaining formal education beyond the secondary level. The same was true for black women. They continued to receive and promote that kind of educational training that helped to develop in them a sense of racial pride and dedication. The postsecondary education of black women emphasized missionary responsibilities and moral values, while extracurricular activities shaped their personal philosophies and their responses to racial goals.

Believing that black women were ultimately to provide the major support system for the race, black and white intellectuals and educators founded schools to meet what they considered to be the special needs of black women. Among those schools were Haines Normal and Industrial School in Georgia, founded by Lucy C. Laney, a member of Atlanta University's first graduating class; Hartshorn Memorial College in Virginia; the National Training School for Women and Girls in Washington, D.C., founded by Nannie H. Burroughs; St. Augustine's School in Florida; and Palmer Memorial Institute in North Carolina, founded by Charlotte Hawkins Brown. In time, Spelman Seminary in Atlanta would be recognized as the most prestigious all-female institution for black women to attend.

Black women who were able to attend colleges and professional schools were prepared for service to those who did not possess their educational, financial, or moral backgrounds. The educated black woman was instructed to actively seek out the areas of greatest need and go there. The challenge to extend their service beyond the United States to all who formed part of the African Diaspora motivated some young women to live in Africa or the Caribbean.

Fisk University in Nashville, Tennessee, was an institution staffed primarily by whites who believed that "the object of education is service" and that the places to serve were Africa and the rural South.[2] Many of Fisk's women graduates accepted the belief of the faculty and administrators, and chose positions in which they could fulfill the charge.

Althea Brown Edmiston serves as an excellent example of such a graduate. Edmiston earned her B.A. degree from Fisk in 1901, and in 1903 she was sent by the Southern Presbyterian Church to the Belgian Congo. In a letter published in the *Fisk University News* in December 1915, Edmiston told of her activities and accomplishments, some of which involved the adult population.

The work of the Lord continues to grow. There were 1,020 present at our Sunday school yesterday. I have charge of the women's department; I have them divided into nine classes, with native teachers to help do the teaching. Mr. Edmiston keeps very busy everyday. He has charge of the experimental farm, in addition to his evangelical work. He is away from home all day, including Sundays at times. Our dear little boy is growing nicely and speaks the native language fluently.[3]

She and her family remained in the village until after 1925. As of 1929, she was residing in Selma, Alabama. It is significant to note that Edmiston, as did countless other black women, successfully orchestrated a public and private life that seemingly left little time for personal indulgences. Edmiston's life was a testimony to the vision and hard work that so many black women of the period considered necessary.

Others saw that residents of the rural South were as deprived as those in the least technologically advanced nations. Even with families and jobs, countless black women found time to render service to those less fortunate than they. Instead of seeking payment for their services, the women often gave freely of their income to further the causes they supported. The Christian tenets to which they subscribed and the educational institutions they attended taught that to give of themselves and of their funds was part of their responsibility.

MOTHERS' MEETINGS AND HOMEMAKERS' CLUBS

Because the number of black women graduates was restricted, while the need for services was so great, it was essential that more women, with or without formal training, who possessed a commitment to racial advancement become involved in community concerns. Because mothers were in constant contact with the youth of the race, attention was given to providing them with the skills necessary to ensure the continuation of a strong family unit.

Many of the college graduates became teachers in the segregated school systems of the South, continuing their work day after the schools closed. It is impossible at times to fully assess the significance of adult and general education programs started by black women for themselves and others of the race because each improved the quality of life to some degree. Nevertheless, because the mothers' meetings could and did have a multiplying effect on new codes of living and, in many cases, produced leaders who were part of the community, those meetings deserve special attention.

When industrial education was officially declared part of the curriculum for black students in Fulton County, Georgia, the teachers voluntarily extended their duties to include greater community involvement. Cooking, housekeeping, sewing, handicrafts, manual training, gardening, and canning were all subjects that lent themselves to community activism. Clubs were organized for children and parents, especially mothers. Black people in Fulton County raised more than $1,000 for improvements of the schools.

In 1913 Camilla Weems was hired by Spelman Institute to teach industrial courses in the county schools. Her work was concentrated in the schools just outside the city limits of Atlanta. Weems first met with all of the county teachers and residents of the communities. She noted that only a few of the African Americans in the area were farmers; most worked in factories or held public jobs. Some of the residents were truck gardeners who supplied Atlanta markets with fresh vegetables, poultry, and dairy products, but few of the residents had personal gardens at home. Therefore, she took gardens as her first project. When the schools opened in September 1913, school gardens were begun with the cooperation of the teachers. Despite the lack of tools and funds, six gardens were soon planted on land near the schools.

Success with the school gardens led to the planting of home gardens. Weems, the teachers, and the recently formed mothers' clubs worked with the families to show them how to not only sell the projects, but also save some for personal consumption. Girls in eleven of the school communities were organized into canning clubs. The Board of Education was so pleased with the progress of the clubs that it offered in 1915 a prize for the most canned items.

The county, which became fully involved in the efforts initiated by Spelman and Weems, made it mandatory for every child to learn the rudiments of sewing, handicrafts, basketry, mat making, and chair caning. For all of the activities, the children used readily available natural materials. Seven of the fifteen schools supervised by Weems installed cooking stoves. The children raised money for three, and the mothers' clubs raised money for the other four. Food was contributed by the families, and cooking lessons were given in kitchens built by the students. The boys made the furniture for the kitchens; the girls made tablecloths, towels, and curtains; and the mothers donated most of the utensils. Where kitchens were not available in the schools, mothers opened their homes for lessons. Manual-training lessons enabled the boys to build furniture for the schools and generally to improve the facilities. Homemakers' clubs for the children reinforced the skills that were taught and demonstrated the need to attain specific skills.

Mothers' clubs, organized in ten schools, extended their activities during the school vacation months. Some activities raised money to establish playgrounds and acquire materials for sewing. Club meetings included literary programs and discussions of economic matters, school work, handicrafts, and ways to improve the home. The constitution developed for the mothers' clubs stated as their objectives "the betterment of home life, the training of children, and the improvement of the community in every way possible."[4] The teachers assisted in implementing the objectives, even after 1925.

The concept of mothers' clubs and homemakers' clubs as an extension of public education was viable in the cities as well. As an extension of the public school, mothers' meetings were organized by Baltimore's black teachers in 1898. The monthly meetings, beginning on September 24, 1898, were held at the #2 female primary school. Topics of interest to the women were discussed, and homemaking techniques were presented. The objective was not only to assist the women in becoming better mothers, but also to build a support unit for the public schools. The mothers sponsored fund-raising activities for the schools and, when necessary, served as a protest group for improved educational facilities and curricula.

In Baltimore during the summer of 1918, 1,333 girls, 1,064 mothers, and 675 boys enrolled in 228 clubs. The teachers and supervisors visited 1,392 homes, offering canning demonstrations in many. In Alabama the homemakers' clubs were aided by the General Education Board and state authorities. During 1920, 15,000 women and girls enrolled in the clubs. As a direct result of the clubs' formation, local black citizens in the state contributed $43,000 for school improvements and activities.[5]

THE NATIONAL ASSOCIATION OF COLORED WOMEN

Mothers' clubs and homemakers' clubs were among the many programs established for women. They were part of a national effort by women to improve the lives of African Americans. In 1896 the National Association of Colored Women (NACW) was formed as a result of the merger of the National League of Colored Women and the National Federation of Afro-American Women. After consolidation, it was reported that the Association encompassed fifty clubs with 500 members in various states. During the tenure of Mary Church Terrell, the first president, the NACW defined objectives that were realistic, purposeful, and lasting.

The Association not only operated national programs, but also constituted the first cohesive national network of black women. The structure of the organization facilitated communication: local clubs at the base, then state and regional federations, and at the top the national body. Information and influence flowed as freely from bottom to top as in the reverse direction.

By 1913 the NACW was affiliated with organizations in Canada, Liberia, and Madagascar, as well as in the thirty states in the United States. Although most of the members were educated, middle-class women, reform for the masses was seen as the basic goal. Mother's clubs, day nurseries, kindergartens, and schools of domestic science were among the many programs implemented to effect reform. So that all members could keep abreast of local and national programs, Terrell organized biennial conventions to be held in cities where there were large numbers of active members.

By 1913 *The National Association Notes*, the official organ of the NACW, reported more than 500 affiliate groups in existence throughout the United States. It was acknowledged, however, that more groups were needed, especially for rural women. Because of the success of the meetings held in Tuskegee, Alabama, Margaret Murray Washington, founder of the Tuskegee Women's Club, was invited by the editor of *The National Association Notes* to write an article providing simple instructions for the establishment of mothers' meetings and clubs.

The instructions mirrored the plans of action used in Tuskegee. Topics for discussions suggested by Washington included "Girls' Home Responsibilities," "An Ideal Home for a Girl," "When Shall a Girl Be Permitted to Receive Her First Company," and "Mother's Relation to the Teacher."[6] She recommended that the topics be given to the women at least two weeks in advance so that they would have ample time to think seriously about them. In response to the article, inquiries seeking more details came to Washington. Such exchanges promoted networking among black women. Given the isolated conditions that many rural women lived in and the difficulty in maintaining quick, effective communication, any activity that fostered greater exposure of programs and ideas was welcomed.

Washington, in a 1917 speech at the Nashville Women's Club, identified the three key elements of club work: individual or city work, state work, and national programs. The city federation, she said, should be composed of clubs of city women at work in various sections of the city but with one ideal. The state federations were to work on projects for the betterment of all in the state.[7]

The Virginia State Federation of Colored Women's Clubs

Sanctioned as part of the national program of the NACW was the formation of homes at the state level to serve as detention centers and as training schools for young women. It was expected that the type of education, including industrial and agricultural courses, received by the women would prepare them to reenter society as employable, fully participating, socially acceptable citizens. One of the earliest homes was the Mount Meigs Home for Girls in Alabama, organized in 1898 by the Alabama State Federation of Colored Women's Clubs.

The development of a home in Virginia clearly outlines how its formation aided in the structuring and strengthening of the state federation. Addie W. Hunton of New York, a delegate to the 1907 Hampton Negro Conference, had prompted Laura D. Titus, later state organizer for the federation, to assemble the conference women for an initial meeting. In accord with the rules of the NACW, ten clubs had to join the proposed federation before it could be recognized as a state federation and a member of the NACW. By November 1907 twenty-five clubs representing the southeastern part of the state met for one day at the Methodist church in Hampton, Virginia. A number of clubs that had been functioning before the inception of the NACW now saw the possibility of expanding and enriching their programs. At the close of the one-day meeting, the federation decided to undertake one special project through a committee headed by Mrs. I. C. Norcum of Portsmouth, Virginia. The state project, an industrial home for wayward girls, would operate on a different level and with a different focus than the community work. The recommendation was unanimously accepted by the federation, and the first task was to raise funds.[8]

The idea for a home for wayward girls was not a new one. At the Woman's Conference during the 1899 Hampton Conference, Rosa Bowser had reported on the Negro Reformatory in Virginia. Of 1,259 black inmates, 66 were women. Bowser believed that a reformatory for women should be erected in order to "reclaim or save the youth of the race." She suggested that 1,382 acres of land available in Hanover County, with existing buildings and equipment, would serve as an excellent site. She did not believe that this was a task for whites: "It is for us to take the burden upon our shoulders and push the good work forward."[9] Instead of a reformatory for women, the site in Hanover became the Virginia Manual Labor School of the Negro Reformatory Association of Virginia.

Some 1,200 women, representing forty-seven clubs, attended the federation's second annual meeting in Richmond in June 1909. There the federation reaffirmed its goal of establishing a home for "wayward colored girls." At the 1910 meeting in Norfolk, each club pledged $10 for the support of the home; the funds were collected at the June 1911 meeting in Roanoke. By June 1911, $600 had been raised for the home, and land was made available by local businessmen. The fact that the national meeting of the NACW was held at Hampton Institute in July 1911 provided additional stimulus for the project; it had been difficult for many to travel to meetings in the North, but more women from the region were able to attend the national meeting at Hampton.[10]

On January 19, 1915, the Industrial Home for Delinquent Colored Girls was opened at Peake, Hanover County, Virginia, with two girls in residence. The site and three buildings had been purchased by the federation for $5,200 in 1914. A matron and farmer were employed by November 1915; the number of girls was then fifteen. The federation appealed to the state legislature and the community for $2,000 for a new building. The Virginia General Assembly appropriated $3,000 for 1915 and $3,000 for 1916.[11]

When Janie Porter Barrett, earlier cited by the Extension Work Committee of Hampton Institute as the "real power among the colored women of the country," was appointed the superintendent of the institution in early 1916, it was estimated that 500 black women were incarcerated in the state of

Virginia. Only more money and expanded facilities would enable the institution to reach many of the 500 before they became confirmed criminals. Constant appeals to the state for funds brought appropriations of $10,000 for 1917 and $20,000 for 1918. Because the legislature could and would provide the additional funds and support, in 1919 the federation transferred the property to the state, and the school was renamed the Virginia Industrial School for Colored Girls. Barrett remained superintendent, but a governing board of trustees, with Mrs. Henry Lane Schnelz of Hampton as president, was appointed. Cottages and two new buildings were added to the facility, but livestock and farm implements were still needed.[12] Until after 1925, the school continued as the only institution of its kind for black women in Virginia. Even though the federation chose to concentrate on projects on the state level, its very existence motivated other women to continue the community work it had begun on the local level.

Because it was impossible for all interested parties to visit sites where successful activities were being carried on, the federation published guides for community improvement, homemaking, and club organizing. Several of the guides were printed in *The Hampton Leaflets* series. One leaflet, "Community Clubs for Women and Girls," written by Janie Barrett, Caroline D. Pratt, and Ida A. Tourtellot, embodied suggestions and principles adopted by the state workers in the federal extension program.

Founded on the principle that women had responsibilities in and out of the home, women's clubs, according to the authors of the leaflet, should aim "to make the individual, the home, and the community more useful in every way."[13] The women of a community should be brought together on one issue, and the club should broaden as the women's interests did. Suggested foci for organizing clubs were church or missionary work, old folks' homes, jails, schools, the poor, the sick, orphans, community improvement, welfare of children, and self-improvement. Domestic concerns such as sewing, cooking, gardening, poultry raising, house cleaning, and savings were considered part of self-improvement. Each step in the formation of a club, directions for electing officers, and the duties of officers and committees was clearly outlined. The leaflet was reissued in 1914 and then revised and reissued again in 1916.

NIGHT SCHOOLS

Many adults were unable to participate in educational programs and activities offered during the day. In response to the needs of this special population, night schools were established. The Town Night School operated by the Tuskegee Woman's Club clearly illustrates the many achievements and problems of such an educational institution. In 1910, when women were excluded from the annual Tuskegee Negro Conference, Margaret Washington met with twelve other women. The Town Night School developed from this meeting. When it became necessary to keep the children occupied while their mothers were in class, a cooking class was formed for them. At the end of 1910 the Town Night School had eight teachers, two academic and six industrial. Along with basic reading, cooking, and sewing, such skills as carpentry, bricklaying, painting, and tailoring were taught. The cooking classes met twice a week and were designed for women who were heads of families or were hired as cooks for whites. The night school was listed in the official Tuskegee Institute catalog as one of its extension programs.[14]

In 1912 Booker T. Washington announced that Tuskegee was no longer able to support the night school. The woman's club assumed the responsibility for keeping the school open eight months a year. There were 103 night classes and 37 day or cooking classes. Enrollment included 140 boys and girls. The club paid the male head of the school $25 a month. Three persons from Tuskegee—one postgraduate, one student, and one teacher—taught at night without pay. Miss Nunn, a member of the club, taught sewing and other subjects at the school at least twice a week. The clubwomen collected and expended almost $300 in sustaining the school that year. There would not have been enough money for another year had additional donations not been made. Solicitations were made to the men of Tuskegee; George Washington Carver gave $25 and a Mr. Taylor, $5.[15]

Despite the financial strain, the night school curriculum was broadened to include additional academic subjects such as black history. The history course proved so beneficial that the women encouraged the teaching of black history in day and night schools throughout the county. For people who could not afford much time or money, the night school provided an opportunity to secure an education. Children of the town also became an integral part of the program, and received educational experiences that reinforced what they learned in public school or, in some cases, substituted for public education.

SOCIAL WORK

Selected adult education programs were designed to improve the skills and expand the knowledge of those who were formally educated. Often these programs had a service component. In Atlanta, Georgia, a school was organized to train those who were interested in becoming certified social workers. In time, the school offered courses, through extension services, to community residents and undergraduate students. Without the official banner of a discipline, African Americans had practiced the major tenets of social work since the antebellum period. Before and during the progressive era, much of the community work initiated by black women focused on educative, social service activities. Social work, which attracted black women as a discipline and vocation, did not become widely accepted until the early 1900s.

Jessie Sleet became the first accredited social worker in 1910. But as a structured body of knowledge evolved in the discipline, African Americans saw the utility of formal training for members of their race. The Atlanta School of Social Work became the first independent institution to offer such training.

With fourteen students and Gary W. Moore as director, the school opened on October 4, 1920. Moore, a teacher of sociology at Morehouse College, had come to Atlanta in 1912 to serve as a fellow of the National Urban League. His assignment had been to teach economics and sociology, to develop a Department of Social Science at Morehouse, and to foster practical work in Atlanta itself. Moore also hoped to persuade the Neighborhood Union, organized by Lugenia Burns (Mrs. John) Hope, to affiliate with the National Urban League. He did not succeed in this latter objective.

Walter R. Chivers, professor at Morehouse, believed that it was through the efforts of Lugenia Burns Hope that the Atlanta School of Social Work began.[16] As organizer of Atlanta's remarkable Neighborhood Union and a full-time staff member of the Atlanta Anti-Tuberculosis Association, Hope had broad expertise and a firm commitment to racial betterment. She served on the board of the Atlanta School of Social Work and taught the community organization course, which included such topics as publicity, finance, committee organization, social programs, recreation, and community movements.

By 1923 the efforts of the Atlanta School of Social Work to increase the number of accredited social workers were evident. The National Urban League reported that there were 150 black social workers; 75 were women employed at forty local organizations. The League, in an effort to further increase the number of social workers, offered fellowships for study at accredited colleges or universities. The Atlanta School of Social Work was incorporated on May 22, 1924, and offered a one-year course. The list of petitioners for incorporation showed the cooperation of colleges, agencies, foundations, whites, and African Americans.

Individual contributions kept the school alive during its early years; funds were also given by the Rosenwald Foundation and the Laura Spelman Rockefeller Memorial Foundation. Through 1925 the institution continuously sought adequate, stable financial support. Volunteer services proved most beneficial to the new school, as directors of social agencies and members of the medical profession freely gave their time and knowledge. The faculty consisted of a teacher in casework and fieldwork, a number of executives of Atlanta social agencies, and E. Franklin Frazier.

Courses were originally designed after patterns suggested by the National Urban League. The approach focused on casework and human behavior, and stressed benefits to individuals rather than benefits to community units. The school's curriculum reflected social changes and attempted to keep abreast of national trends, but blacks' concerns remained central. By 1924 courses were offered in casework, human behavior, social investigation, physiology, home nursing, community organization, play leadership, social problems, and fieldwork. Students spent three days in course work and two days in the field. In order to be near the social services agencies utilized for practicum experiences, the school in time moved to 239 Auburn Street, the top floor of the Herndon Building. Expanding its services, the school provided extension courses for forty-six public-school teachers, conducted a short course for ministers' wives at Gammon Seminary, and presented two lectures a week to the senior normal students at Atlanta University.

After he became director, Frazier introduced into the curriculum courses that stressed sociology and research. In part because of his innovative approaches to social work, the school was accredited on December 29, 1928, by the American Association of Schools for Social Work, founded in 1919. It was the first school for African Americans to meet the Association's accreditation requirements.

Graduates of the Atlanta School of Social Work, most of whom were women, received certificates that qualified them for a number of positions. The graduates were employed throughout the United States as district agents and executives in "colored" departments of associated charities, as probation officers, as Urban League secretaries and assistants, and as welfare workers in industry, social service departments of churches, the YMCA, and the YWCA. The graduates' activities firmly established the formal framework of social work in the black community. They also assisted in providing educational experiences necessary for the black adult population to improve their skills and enhance their lives.

THE INTERNATIONAL COUNCIL OF WOMEN OF THE DARKER RACES

While struggling to change conditions at home, black women throughout the United States sought ways to broaden their understanding of international affairs and the conditions under which other people of color lived. They were particularly interested in the plight of black people on the continent of Africa. To fulfill their desire to become more aware, to assist in influencing international affairs, and to help improve life for people of color, members of the NACW joined the International Council of Women, an interracial group. In 1920 it was obvious that a separate organization would better enable the women to accomplish their specific objectives; thus the International Council of Women of the Darker Races was formed as an adjunct to the NACW.

The stated purpose of the new council was to assist in disseminating information regarding people of color and to help instill racial pride in people of color. As indicated on the official letterhead for the council, the original membership comprised 100 women of color, 50 American and 50 foreign. Mary Church Terrell and Addie Hunton were vice presidents and Maggie

Walker, Mary McLeod Bethune, and Nannie Burroughs were members of the Executive Council.[17]

In 1922 the council began to hold conventions separate from the general sessions of the NACW. The council's meeting in Washington, D.C., attracted representatives from African nations, Haiti, Ceylon, and the West Indies. A definitive statement of purpose was developed at the 1922 meeting: "The Council has as its object the economic, social, and political welfare of the women of all the darker races."[18] The principal activity for the remainder of 1922 was to be an investigation of the status of the women and children in Haiti. Emily Williams was sent to Haiti to study women there; her trip was partially financed by the council, and her report was submitted to the general body of the NACW at the 1923 convention.

On August 5–8, 1923, when the council met at the National Training School in Washington, D.C., three sections were organized. Mrs. C. Edward Dickerson was to chair the International Relations Section; Lugenia Hope, the Social and Economic Conditions Section; and Margaret Murray Washington, the Education Section. Three resolutions were passed and disseminated to the press: a commendation to Adelaide Casely-Hayford for her efforts to found a school for girls in Sierra Leone, a resolution to study the condition of women and girls in Africa, and a condemnation of the French government for its stand on racial discrimination in African nations.[19] The second resolution was crucial; no longer would the council be merely a fact-finding body. After studying conditions in Africa, the next step would be to work to change conditions. Unfortunately the International Council of Women of the Darker Races never moved far beyond gathering data and proposing solutions. The international political arena was not receptive to black women who attempted to become involved in the internal affairs of colonized nations. By this time the entire continent of Africa and the West Indies were affected directly or indirectly by the colonization activities of European nations or the United States. Nevertheless, the women were able to expand their knowledge of people of color and to aid specific individuals or groups in foreign nations. The women also pressured school superintendents in the United States to order books about people of the diaspora. The Council was especially concerned that black youngsters, as well as council members, be exposed to and understand the history and literature of their people.

To ensure that all its members were as well informed as possible, the Council encouraged the development of study groups. Under the Council's Education Section, the Committees of Seven were formed in 1924 to "study conditions of the darker races of the world." Each community was to form a committee to study problems of African peoples and American blacks. Educational, social, religious, and industrial concerns were suggested as broad areas from which specific topics could be selected. It was also recommended that the women read books about Africa and schedule visits from native Africans and missionaries.[20] Articles, letters, and minutes of club meetings show that the local communities took the suggestions quite seriously and worked to complete the recommended tasks. Janie Porter Barrett, in a letter to Margaret Murray Washington, wrote that evenings were spent on discussions about the women of Haiti, China, Africa, and Japan. According to Barrett, the women in her group modeled their discussions after the ones held at Tuskegee.[21]

CONCLUSION

At the local, regional, national, and international levels, black women were involved in the effort to provide meaningful educational experiences for adults. Class differences, although present, diminished in importance as it became clearer that all black women—rich and poor, urban and rural— would have to work together to achieve racial and individual betterment through education. The women not only established local clubs, but in time formed or joined state, national, and international organizations to share experiences, pool resources, and wield greater influence to achieve common ends. Throughout the period, the NACW served as the coordinating body for many social service and educational programs. Key black women leaders were involved at all levels of social activism.

Because of the nature of the oppressive society in which they lived, black women had to confront issues of gender and race as they structured educational programs for adults. Black teachers, principally women, labored long hours to create educational programs within the schools and as extensions of the schools. They would not permit difficult working conditions or lack of adequate equipment to eliminate advancement and innovation. Although the focus during this period stresses women and their role in nurturing children, men were not entirely excluded. Although it would have been easier for teachers and clubwomen to see only the obstacles to quality education for children and adults, they chose instead to concentrate on such positive factors as community involvement, community betterment, and enriching the lives of blacks.

NOTES

1. Selena Sloan Butler, "Heredity," *Spelman Messenger*, June 1897, p. 2.
2. "Education for Service," *Fisk University News* 11 (June 1919).
3. "From a Letter from Mrs. Althea Brown Edmiston, W. C. Africa," *Fisk University News* 6 (December 1915):27.
4. Camilla Weems, "Supervising Rural Schools," *Spelman Messenger*, November 1915, p. 6.
5. J. Walter Huffington, *Supervision of Colored Schools in Maryland* (Baltimore: McCoy Hall-State Board of Education, 1918) 12; "Alabama Improves Colored Schools," *Southern Workman*, January 1921, p. 7.

6. *National Association Notes*, March, 1913, available in Margaret Murray Washington File, Hollis Burke Frissill Library, Tuskegee University Archival Collection (hereinafter cited as TUAC), Tuskegee, Ala.

7. "Mrs. Booker T. Washington, Honored Guest of Nashville's Women's Club," *Globe*, May 11, 1917.

8. Janie Barrett, "Virginia Federation of Colored Women," *Hampton Bulletin*, September 1911; *Fifteenth Annual Report of the Hampton Negro Conference, The Hampton Normal and Agricultural Institute* (Hampton, Va.: Press of the Hampton Normal and Agricultural Institute, 1911), 45–50.

9. "The Woman's Conference," in *Hampton Negro Conference, No. 3*, ed. Hugh Browne, Edwina Kruse, et al. (Hampton, Va.: Hampton Institute Press, July 1899), 43.

10. Addie W. Hunton, "Women's Clubs: State Conventions," *Crisis: A Record of the Darker Races* (hereinafter cited as *Crisis*), September 1911, p. 11; Barrett, "Virginia Federation of Colored Women," 48; Mrs. John E. Milholland, "Talks About Women," *Crisis*, February 1911, p. 28.

11. William A. Aery, "Helping Wayward Girls," *Southern Workman*, November 1915, pp. 598–604; J. E. Davis, "A Virginia Asset—The Virginia Industrial School for Colored Girls," *Southern Workman*, August 1920, p. 357.

12. W. A. Aery, "Industrial Home School for Colored Girls at Peak in Hanover County, Virginia," *Southern Workman*, October 1919, pp. 473–474.

13. Janie Porter Barrett, Caroline D. Pratt, and Ida A. Tourbellot, "Community Clubs for Women and Girls," in *Hampton Leaflet* (Hampton, Va.: Press of Hampton Normal and Agriculture Institute, 1912), 1, Hampton University's Archival and Museum Collection (hereinafter cited as AMCHU) Hampton University, Hampton, Va.

14. *Twenty-ninth Annual Catalogue, 1909–1910, The Tuskegee Normal School and Industrial Institute* (Tuskegee, Ala.: Tuskegee Institute Press, 1910), 99, TUAC.

15. "Seventeenth Anniversary of Tuskegee Woman's Club," *Tuskegee Student*, June 14, 1913, in Women's Work File, Monroe Work Collection, TUAC.

16. "Morehouse Holds Memorial Service for Mrs. Hope," Neighborhood Union Box 14–A–2, Archives Department, Trevor Arnett Library, Atlanta University, Georgia (now titled the Atlanta University Center Woodruff Library); reproduced by permission.

17. International Council of Women of the Darker Races, Printed Sheet, November 10, 1924, Mary Church Terrell Collection, Box 102–12, Manuscript Division, the Moorland-Spingarn Research Center, Howard University, Washington, D.C. (hereinafter cited as MSRC).

18. "Booker T.'s Wife Heads World Order," *Chicago Defender*, August 26, 1922, in Women's Work File, Monroe Work Collection, TUAC.

19. "World International Council—Darker Races," *New York Age*, August 18, 1923, in Women's Work File, Monroe Work Collection, TUAC.

20. M. M. Washington, International Council of Women of the Darker Races, prepared Statement in Mary Church Terrell Collection, Box 102–12, Manuscript Division, MSRC.

21. Janie Porter Barrett to M. M. Washington, February 12, 1925, M. M. Washington Collection, TUAC.

10

The Southern Literacy Campaign for Black Adults in the Early Twentieth Century

James E. Akenson and Harvey G. Neufeldt

Contemporary adult education makes frequent references to technological changes in the workplace. Changes in technology create a demand for workers with increasingly high literacy skills. Increasingly, tenth-grade and even twelfth-grade literacy levels are mentioned as minimal evidence of functional literacy. Without such literacy skills adults will find themselves without access to jobs that provide them with a living wage. A disproportionate percentage of black adults find themselves without the literacy skills to function successfully within the economic, social, and political systems. Contemporary problems of black illiteracy and efforts to develop adult literacy skills bear a striking resemblance to the problems and solutions posed earlier in the twentieth century.

Efforts to eliminate black illiteracy in southern states during the early twentieth century provide evidence of the political, social, and economic constraints under which adult education must function. The Southern literacy campaign from 1910 to 1930 bears witness to the manner in which adult education programs attempted to remove black illiteracy. Special schooling designed to meet the peculiar needs of Southern black adults took place in cities and rural areas of the South. Southern literacy campaign workers labored with maximum devotion and minimum resources. The objectives of eradicating black and white adult illiteracy and preparing adults for participation in a modern commercial, industrial South failed to be met. Every southern state created an illiteracy commission, conducted adult literacy schools, or in other ways acknowledged the existence of illiteracy. Alabama, Louisiana, and South Carolina exerted particular effort to eliminate black as well as white illiteracy during the early twentieth century.

This discussion sets forth the basic assumptions, the methods of delivering educational services, and the constraints under which the Southern literacy campaign for black adults operated. Particular scrutiny will be given to the

Alabama and South Carolina literacy campaigns and their impact on black illiteracy. The specific structure of black illiteracy in the early 1900s is also identified, analyzed, and related to the structure of funding patterns in southern states. This analysis also discusses the implications of black literacy programs to the contemporary concerns for functional literacy and its impact on individuals, groups, and the economic system.

BLACK SOUTHERN ILLITERACY: THE EARLY TWENTIETH CENTURY

The early twentieth century exhibited substantial, if not staggering, adult illiteracy rates. The 1910 census measured illiteracy by simply asking people if they could read and write their name. More sophisticated measures related to functional literacy did not enter into the equation. For people ten years of age or older the average illiteracy rate of a southern county stood at 19.2 percent split between a 9.6 percent white illiteracy and a 32.1 percent black illiteracy rate.[1] Average county illiteracy rates varied from a total illiteracy of 10.4 percent for Kentucky to 34.3 percent for Louisiana. Black illiteracy greatly exceeded white illiteracy and varied in relation to the percentage of blacks within a given county. Kentucky, with 24.8 percent black illiteracy, also had the lowest percentage (9.6 percent) of blacks in the average county. Louisiana counties, in contrast, exhibited 51.4 percent black illiteracy and 48.7 percent black population.

Age proved to be an important variable in the distribution of black illiteracy. The percentage of black illiteracy increased with each age group in the South. For example, in 1910 the fifty-five-to-sixty-four-year age group registered an 81.0 percent illiteracy rate. This far surpassed the 22.0 percent and 40.8 percent illiteracy rates registered by the respective fourteen-to-twenty and thirty-five-to-forty-four-year age groups. Natural attrition through death promised to improve the South's illiteracy rates among blacks by complementing an increased effort to provide younger blacks with basic education.

The pervasiveness of the relation between race and illiteracy may be observed in several ways. Correlational data provides one form of evidence. Almost 70 percent of the relation between black illiteracy and total illiteracy in southern states can be explained from the standpoint of race. Alabama (r = .82, r^2 = .67) and South Carolina (r = .84, r^2 = .71)[2] fit the overall Southern pattern. Black illiteracy rates tended to increase in counties, especially in Alabama, as the black percentage of the total population increased. Moreover, the high percentage of black tenant farmers in densely black counties demonstrated a link between race and low socioeconomic status and illiteracy. The 171 southern counties that demonstrated above average (29.3 percent) total illiteracy and above average (43.9 percent) black illiteracy rates also demonstrated above average total (66.1 percent) farm tenancy and black (50.1 percent) farm tenancy rates.

Black illiteracy data reflect the impact of inequitable funding practices for public education in southern states. In 1900 national per capita spending stood at $3.66, whereas southern states spent $1.25 per capita.[3] For each eligible child of school age, southern states spent $3.41 as opposed to $12.89 nationally.[4] The inequities suffered by Southern children fell disproportionately on black students. In 1910 white students in heavily black populated counties could count on educational expenditures some 12.5 times that received by their black counterparts.[5] In Alabama the discrepancies were even greater. Lowndes County provided schooling for 82.0 percent of white children aged six to fourteen and 46.3 percent of black children. Lowndes County spent $35.09 to educate a white student compared with $1.26 to educate a black child.[6] In a similar manner, Fairfield County, South Carolina, spent $14.77 per white student compared with 77 cents per black student. Such discrepancies suggest that the actual literacy skills of black adults could be less than indicated by the official census data.

THE SOUTHERN LITERACY CAMPAIGN 1910–1930

The eradication of Southern illiteracy took the form of special schools designed to teach adults basic skills of reading and writing. Adult schools included night schools during the regular school year, cotton mill schools, and intensive schools held during the summer lay-by season of late July and August. Called opportunity schools, lay-by, moonlight, or old-folks schools, the intensive schools provided adults with an opportunity to develop basic literacy skills, receive enrichment in health, agriculture, history and geography, and home economics, as well as socialize with their peers.

Alabama and South Carolina developed strong literacy campaigns that included black adults. Virtually every southern state paid deference to illiteracy, created an illiteracy commission, and initiated a modest program. Cora Wilson Stewart, superintendent of the Rowan County, Kentucky, school system, initiated the first Southern adult literacy schools. The Kentucky literacy campaign, like its counterparts in other southern states, initially focused on literacy for white adults. Twenty-five Kentucky school systems established moonlight schools, and in 1914 the Kentucky legislature created the Kentucky Illiteracy Commission. Funding for the commission followed in 1916.[7] Other states followed suit by establishing illiteracy commissions and creating slogans. South Carolina adopted the slogan "Let South Carolina secede from illiteracy." Alabama used "Illiteracy in Alabama—Let's remove it."

Ten years into the twentieth century Alabama and South Carolina illiteracy mirrored that of the South. In Alabama 22.9 percent of the total population, 9.9 percent of the white population, and 40.1 percent of the black population were classified as illiterate. South Carolina fit a similar pattern, with total illiteracy of 26.6 percent, white illiteracy of 9.6 percent, and black illiteracy of 39.2 percent. Against such a backdrop of substantial illiteracy the emergence of the Alabama literacy campaign makes sense. Cora Wilson Stewart visited Alabama in 1914 to address the Alabama Education Association about illiteracy. By February 2, 1915, the Alabama legislature formally created the Alabama Illiteracy Commission. The legislature provided the Illiteracy Commission with the latitude to "expend any funds or use anything of value which it may receive." Such latitude meant little in the context of receiving "no compensation for their services nor expenses of any kind out of the State treasury."[8]

Beginning in 1915 the Alabama Illiteracy Commission began efforts designed to reduce adult illiteracy. Governor Charles Henderson proclaimed May 6, 1915, as Illiteracy Day, calling on "every literate man, woman, and youth" to consecrate himself or herself to the service of the state and, aided by "the favorable guidance of Almighty God," help "wipe away the black stain" of illiteracy, thereby promoting Alabama's "industrial . . . efficiency."[9] References to "industrial efficiency" suggest that Alabama's literacy campaign contained assumptions about the goal of education: to bring Southern society into the industrial and agricultural mainstream. This required at least simple literacy skills, as the Alabama State Department of Education claimed in 1919.

If in addition to learning to read and write, and perform operations in arithmetic, a person gains the power to read a newspaper, a farm journal, and the Bible, and has developed in him health and civic consciousness, he is well on the way toward a normal life.[10]

The Illiteracy Commission of South Carolina evolved in a manner similar to that of Alabama. As early as 1913 prominent clubwoman Julia Selden organized adult schools in cooperation with cotton mills. In 1914 clubwoman and educator Wil Lou Gray worked out "an interesting experiment in adult education."[11] In cooperation with the Laurens County superintendent of education, the townships with the greatest illiteracy rate became the focus of adult literacy classes conducted by volunteer teachers. By 1916 the legislature appropriated $5,000 for the support of adult literacy schools. In 1917 the South Carolina Federation of Women's Clubs requested Governor Manning to create an illiteracy commission. The productive life of the South Carolina Illiteracy Commission lasted until 1919, when fieldworker Wil Lou Gray became the supervisor of adult schools within the state department of education. South Carolina, like Alabama, quickly institutionalized adult literacy efforts within the existing educational bureaucracy, where it occupied a modest niche.

Launching the Alabama and South Carolina literacy campaigns resulted in the creation of opportunity schools designed to provide adults with an opportunity to develop basic reading and writing skills. Launched in the midst of the Jim Crow era literacy campaigns first served whites. In Alabama, however, black leaders took the initiative in expanding the literacy campaign. Black leaders requested and received permission to raise money for black adult literacy work by making literacy buttons and selling them. Once Alabama authorities provided matching funds, blacks often raised the money required from their own communities when local county boards failed to make the necessary appropriations. Blacks also received money from philanthropic organizations such as the Jones, Slater, Phelps-Stokes, and Rosenwald funds. Responsibility for recruiting and teaching black adults rested primarily on the black supervisors who were funded by the Jeanes Foundation. At first, black teachers were expected to teach adults for little or no extra remuneration. With limited state funding came minimum standards for literacy instruction. Schools were required to meet for a minimum of 120 hours per term. Black teachers were required to hold a normal school diploma.

Despite the introduction of state money, consistency of effort marked but few Alabama counties or cities. Significant variations occurred as to individual counties' participation. Coosa County operated opportunity schools for black adults in 1922–1923 (one), 1923–1924 (six), 1926–1927 (three), and 1927–1928 (three). Bullock County conducted ten black opportunity schools in 1921–1922, 1922–1923, and 1923–1924. Sumter County participated in 1921–1922 (eight), 1922–1923 (fifteen), 1923–1924 (seventeen), 1925–1926 (twenty), 1926–1927 (sixteen), and twenty in each of the school years from 1927 to 1930.[12] No county operated black opportunity schools in every year of the 1915–1930 time period. Even Chambers County, Alabama, which conducted the most extensive black literacy campaign, did not achieve consistency. From the 1921–1922 school year through the 1929–1930 school year, Chambers County fluctuated from a low of sixteen (1921–1922) to a high of forty-six (1929–1930) black opportunity schools. An increase in the annual appropriation to $12,500 in 1921, a temporary appropriation of $50,000 in 1927, and a Rosenwald Fund grant of $22,500 in 1930 could not begin to provide the resources necessary to achieve participation by all sixty-seven counties.

In South Carolina, Wil Lou Gray directed the literacy campaign with tireless personal effort, defended and publicized her bureaucratic territory, and developed a national and international visibility among adult educators. The South Carolina literacy campaign included special schools in cotton mills, night schools during the school year, and lay-by schools in the summer. South Carolina denoted opportunity schools as being the special summer adult schools held at black and white colleges. Opportunity schools held at colleges such as Clemson and Vorhees provided particular visibility to the South Carolina literacy campaign and functioned as a centerpiece. Black adults soon became a substantial target group for the South Carolina literacy campaign. Initially, however, black adults fell outside the focus of the literacy campaign because of political ramifications. Wil Lou Gray reported that Pickens County, South Carolina, initiated summer lay-by schools under her guidance. Gray chose to organize some twenty white adult schools and three black adult schools while dividing her time between Pickens County and her office in the state department of education in Columbia. She indicated that "it was thought best not to push the establishment of negro [sic] schools in the first year."[13] As in Alabama, the political and social climate required that an adult literacy program receive widespread support among whites before blacks could be brought into the process.

Funding for the South Carolina literacy campaign proved to be problem for Wil Lou Gray, despite a funding level more generous than funding for the Alabama literacy campaign. State appropriations for the literacy work totaled $436,748 from 1919 through 1930.[14] Total appropriations fluctuated constantly, ranging from a low of $10,000 in 1919 to a peak of $54,875 in 1930. Such figures exclude modest county contributions as well as Rosenwald Fund contributions. Most significant, the per capita expenditures for blacks and whites are obscured. During the 1929–1930 fiscal year, South Carolina spent $1.68 per adult student. Each white adult student received $3.30, whereas each black adult student received $.85, for a 3.9:1.0 expenditure ratio.[15] South Carolina funded $33,133 of the $90,114 for black adult instruction, whereas the 37,800 black adults outnumbered white adults in the 55,036 adult school population. Thus 36.8 percent of adult school funding supported 68.9 percent of the adult school target population.

CURRICULUM MATERIALS AND GUIDELINES

Once under the administrative wing of the state department of education, Alabama opportunity school teachers and administrators could follow guidelines for the organization and delivery of adult literacy schools. Interviews with informants suggest that the actual point-by-point delivery and coverage of lessons varied somewhat from the official opportunity school guidelines. The formal documents do, however, accurately reflect the basic thrust sought in the Alabama literacy campaign. The *Suggestions for Teachers of Opportunity Schools for Black Adults*, published by the Alabama State Department of Education, in various editions presented a logical organization and content for instruction of adults. Lesson materials for black adults included reading, arithmetic, spelling helps and word lists, writing, letter writing, and health.[16]

The section on reading instruction merits special attention, given the primary mission of the opportunity schools. Basal readers for black and white adults included the first, second, and third books of the *Country Life Readers* and the *Bible Story Reader*. Additional reading came in the form of newspapers, Sunday school literature, the *Alabama Forest News*, bulletins by the Metropolitan Life Insurance Company, and a variety of public signs. The public signs included a practical emphasis on highway signs, street signs, post office signs, courthouse signs, and miscellaneous signs. Specific examples of highway signs included Danger, Dangerous Curve, Detour, Railroad Crossing, Go Slow, State Highway Department, and Stop-Look-Listen. Sections on spelling, writing, and letter writing further reinforced reading instruction by providing opportunities to reinforce sight word recognition and to use words to write recipes, checks, and appropriate friendly and business letters.

Opportunity school guidelines also included an extensive arithmetic section that provided black adults with a progression of basic skills and a variety of word problems keyed to daily life. The first arithmetic lessons for black adults stressed operations such as counting from 1 to 100, writing to 100 by twos, counting to 100 by fives, as well as reading telephone numbers, auto license numbers, highway numbers, house numbers, and price tags. Lessons dealing with addition, subtraction, multiplication, and division included reading practical problems and solving the problems with the correct arithmetic operation. Black adults encountered problems such as "A cotton bail weighing 500 pounds sells for 19⅛C per pound. How much does it bring?" or "Sugar sells for 7½C per pound. Find the cost of 15, 20, 18, 14, 19, 25 lbs." Subtraction lessons included: "Nettie Johnson bought 6 yards of goods. She took 3 yards to make a dress for herself. How many yards are left?"[17]

Significant reading content was included in the *Country Life Readers* series, authored by Cora Wilson Stewart. The series was widely distributed, and its content reveals specific assumptions about rural life. Both black and white adults found sections titled "The Farmer," "Thrift," "Civics," and "Scripture," as well as the more romantically titled sections about "Flowers" and "Birds." Specific selected readings under "The Farm" included "The Value of Tillage" and "Crop Rotation," as well as "Out in the Fields with God."[18] Not every selection applied equally to black and to white adults. The section on "Civics" included the "The Poor Voter on Election Day" by John G. Whittier, which stated:

> The proudest now is but my peer,
>   The highest not more high;
> Today, of all the weary year,
>   A king of men am I.[19]

Nevertheless, both black and white adults found a clear set of messages in the *Country Life Readers*. Hard work, honesty, thrift, cleanliness, use of modern agricultural techniques, belief in modern roads and taxation, and patriotism continuously bombarded the adult reader. Directly addressing injustices of the existing sociopolitical system failed to make its way into Cora Wilson Stewart's view of progress for black and white adults.

Reading material geared specifically to black adults proved to be a rarity in the Southern literacy campaign. The South Carolina literacy campaign did produce one item titled "The Story of My Race." Written for beginning black adult readers, it presented short pieces titled "Africa," "What Africa Gives the World," "Animals in Africa," "Slavery," "Leaving the Old Country," and "Abraham Lincoln." The readings on "Slavery" and "Leaving the Old Country" informed black adults about the events and conditions before the Civil War.

Slavery

There were many kind [sic] of slave owners.
The slaves were treated kindly.
A very few slaves were taught to read and write.
Some slaves were happy.
Some slave owners were cruel.
Slaves were beaten.
Families were separated.
They were not taught to read and write.
These slaves were unhappy.
God heard their prayers.

Leaving the Old Country

White traders went to Africa.
They captured many negroes.
They took them away as slaves.
Some were brought to America.
The first slave ship landed in Virginia in 1619.
Some landed in the North.
It was cold, very cold.
The snow was deep, very deep.
The negroes were brought South.
Here they were sold to the Southern Planters.[20]

The slavery discussion was in keeping with liberal thought in the early-twentieth-century South. Slavery and agrarianism were not in keeping with the New South ideology. Not surprisingly, white supremacy, segregation, and black enfranchisement did not receive treatment in such a text.

IMPACT OF THE SOUTHERN LITERACY CAMPAIGN

Literacy continues to be a Southern and national concern, even in the contemporary United States. The Southern literacy campaign did not end in 1930, but limped along with modest allocations institutionalized within state departments of education. Not until the mid–1980s has there existed a resurgence of awareness of, and interest in, illiteracy similar to the emergence of the Southern literacy campaign. The impact of the Southern literacy campaign may be assessed in terms of the reduction of black illiteracy. Black illiteracy did experience a 12.3 percent reduction from 1910 to 1930 in the average southern county. The degree to which the 12.3 percent decline can be attributed to the Southern literacy campaign, however, is problematic and merits attention.

The specific impact of the Southern literacy campaign in counties that engaged in literacy activities bears scrutiny. Five Alabama counties offer evidence related to the actual impact of black adult literacy instruction on the illiteracy rates. Black illiteracy declined in Butler, Chambers, Covington, Lowndes, and Winston counties, despite their substantial variations in percentage of black population. Each of the counties increased black school attendance by at least 30.0 percent. Most significant, Chambers County, which conducted the most extensive literacy campaign, did not experience the greatest decline in black illiteracy. Alabama counties experienced a decline in the black illiteracy rate, regardless of their participation, or nonparticipation, in literacy programs for black adults. Social and educational changes taking place on a regional basis altered illiteracy rates in Alabama and South Carolina, as they did in all the southern states.

Several constraints operating on the Alabama and South Carolina literacy campaigns point to the reasons for the lack of direct impact on the black illiteracy rate from 1910 to 1930. First, the resources made available for the elimination of illiteracy never matched the magnitude of the task at hand. A $22,500 Rosenwald Fund contribution represented 45 percent of the Alabama state funding for 1930–1931. Funding constraints meant that Alabama black adult literacy enrollment ranged from 1,510 in 1915–1916 to a surge peak of 15,381 in 1929–1930. In a majority of the years between 1915 and 1930, less than 5,000 black adults received literacy instruction annually.[21] In South Carolina a similar pattern evolved. A low of 840 black adults received literacy instruction in 1919, with a surge peak of 37,800 in 1930. With the exception of 1930, black adult literacy enrollment ranged from 1,920 to 6,077.[22] Clearly, the state funding levels would never be adequate to address the massive scope of black illiteracy.

The lack of state funding meant that the Alabama and South Carolina literacy campaigns functioned as minor adjuncts to the existing school infrastructure. As the poor relation grafted on the school systems, the literacy campaigns made use of the school facilities, teachers, and administrative personnel of the county and city schools. Teachers such as Marie Coles in Chambers County, Alabama, taught black adults as a secondary function to their primary school year roles as classroom teachers.[23] Superintendents, school boards, and supervisory personnel also made administrative decisions and carried out communication with the state department of education in order for the opportunity schools to exist. Such tasks, however, came in addition to, incidental to, the major functions assigned them. Opportunity schools would fail to exist without the cooperation of such agencies and personnel. The same agencies and roles would have existed without the opportunity schools. Within state departments of education few positions depended on the existence of the literacy campaign. In Alabama the division of exceptional education included other mandates besides the literacy campaign. In South Carolina, Wil Lou Gray's position as director of adult education evolved from the desire to attract her participation in the literacy campaign. Nevertheless, adult education involved programs beyond the extensive activities of the literacy work.

Realities, then, painted a much less rosy view of the Southern literacy campaign than did the rhetoric that called people to arms to march against the "stain" in the midst of Southerners. Limited resources, a massive task, proliferating objectives, and a secondary status within the existing bureaucracies all worked to limit the success of the Southern illiteracy campaign. The decline of Southern illiteracy from 1910–1930 represented other factors, such as increased schooling and attrition of illiterates through death. The primary objective of the opportunity schools—the removal of illiteracy—took place without an impact by the literacy programs themselves. Numerous successes occurred on the individual level. For a limited number of black adults, the ability to read a Bible, a newspaper, or a road sign or to write one's name marked major triumphs from the condition of illiteracy. The fortunate few, however, proved to be the minority.

CONCLUSION

Adult illiteracy remains a problem in the last two decades of the twentieth century. Compared with the early 1900s, the scope of the problem appears to be a minor irritant on the cultural fabric. Creating a relatively few literate black adults in the 1920s did not result in their participation in the emerging commercial, industrial South with any degree of success. The resources allocated to the task assured the Southern literacy campaign of but modest achievements, most of which came in the form of simple pleasures and a sense of dignity. Similarly, adult literacy programs in the late twentieth century exhibit the same essential characteristics. Limited resources delivered with evangelistic zeal cannot bring a target population into the information age, much less universally guarantee access to positions at minimum wage or better. The successes within the context of constraints do represent real achievements. Illiterate black adults did receive help from professional and lay educators who possessed a sense of mission. Sadly, the needs of the target audience far exceeded the resources that decision makers allocated. The problem of black adult literacy was not viewed as a primary mission of the educational system. As a peripheral enterprise, the reduction of adult illiteracy will remain in the last two decades of the twentieth century what it became in the first decades—a lofty goal beyond the grasp of those who sought it.

NOTES

1. Bureau of the Census, *Thirteenth Census of the United States. Vol. 2. Population. Alabama-Montana* (Washington, D.C.: Government Printing Office, 1913); Bureau of the Census, *Thirteenth Census of the United States. Vol. 2. Population. Nebraska-Wyoming, Hawaii, Alaska, and Porto Rico* (Washington, D.C.: Government Printing Office, 1913). Data for the Southern region are based on 930 counties using the *Statistical Package for the Social Sciences*. Counties in Texas, Maryland, Oklahoma, and West Virginia are excluded from these 930 counties. Data dealing with the decline of illiteracy are also based on or derived from average or individual counties as found in census data.

2. Correlational data are derived by using census data and the *Statistical Package for the Social Sciences*. The variance (r^2) provides insight into the strength of the relation between two variables. A correlation may be statistically significant and yet reflect little strength of association between variables.

3. Wycliffe Rose, *School Funds in Ten Southern States* (Nashville: Press of Foster, Webb, and Parkes, 1909), 30.

4. Ibid., 32.

5. Department of the Interior, Bureau of Education. *Negro Education: A Study of the Private and Higher Schools for Colored People in the United States.* Bulletin No. 39, Vol. 2 (Washington, D.C.: Government Printing Office, 1916), 11.

6. Ibid., 28.

7. Raymond B. Fosdick, *Adventure in Giving: A Story of the General Education Board* (New York: Harper & Row, 1962), 74; Charles William Dabney, *Universal Education in the South, Vol. 2, The Southern Education Movement* (Chapel Hill: University of North Carolina Press, 1936), 357–360.

8. State of Alabama, *General Public School Laws of Alabama, 1915* (Montgomery, Ala.: Brown Printing Co., 1915), 148.

9. Alabama Illiteracy Commission, *Illiteracy Day in Alabama: The Plan, The Proclamation of the Governor, June 7, 1915* (Montgomery, Ala.: Brown Printing Co., 1915), 1.

10. Alabama State Department of Education, *Annual Report* (Montgomery, Ala.: Brown Printing Co., 1919), 111.

11. Illiteracy Commission of South Carolina, South Caroliniana Library, University of South Carolina at Columbia.

12. Derived from annual reports of the Alabama State Department of Education 1918–1930.

13. Illiteracy Commission of South Carolina, "The 'Lay-by' Schools in Pickens County" (1919), 4.

14. Derived from Illiteracy Commission of South Carolina, "Statistical Progress of Adult Schools Scholastic Year 1918–19 Through 1940–41."

15. Illiteracy Commission of South Carolina, State Department of Education, "Financial Statement of the Adult Department Scholastic Year, July 1, 1929–July 1, 1930."

16. State of Alabama, *Suggestions for Teachers of Opportunity Schools for Black Adults* (Birmingham, Ala.: Brown Printing Co., 1930).

17. Ibid., 9, 18.

18. Cora Wilson Stewart, *Country Life Readers* (Richmond, Va.: B. F. Publishing Co., 1917), 5–7.

19. Ibid., 252.

20. *The Story of My Race* (n.d., South Carolina Illiteracy Commission Papers).

21. Derived from Annual Reports of the Alabama State Department of Education, 1915–1930.

22. Derived from *Statistical Progress of Adult Schools Scholastic Years 1918–19 Through 1940–41* (South Carolina Illiteracy Commission Papers).

23. Interview with black opportunity school teacher Marie Coles, Chambers County, Alabama, March 17, 1984.

11

Literacy and Voting: The Story of the South Carolina Sea Island Citizenship Schools

Sandra B. Oldendorf

There will be neither rest nor tranquility in America until the Negro is granted his citizenship rights.

—Martin Luther King, Jr.[1]

This chapter examines empowerment for black adults through a historical case study of the South Carolina Sea Island Citizenship Schools. These schools, sponsored by Highlander Folk School, were established in 1957 as literacy schools to enable black adults to meet the South Carolina voter registration requirements. But the goal of literacy evolved into a more far-reaching aim, that of first-class citizenship.

The immediate program is literacy. It enables students to pass literacy tests for voting. But there is involved the mechanics of learning to read and write and all-round education in community development which includes housing, recreation, health and improved home life. It is open to all people of a community who face problems related to first-class citizenship and want to do something about them.[2]

In this chapter, characteristics of curriculum and teaching for democratic empowerment are analyzed. These characteristics can help to further the discussion about effective educational programs for black adults.

THE CITIZENSHIP SCHOOL STORY

The story of the citizenship schools can be told through three dimensions: the place, the times, and the personalities. The place was the South Carolina Sea Islands. Johns Island, the largest of the islands and site of the first citizenship school, is located six miles south of Charleston, South Carolina.

Early citizenship schools were also started on Wadmalaw and Edisto islands, both south of Johns Island. The geographical theme of the islands is isolation; isolation and its effects contributed to the need for the citizenship schools.

The majority of the population on the Sea Islands are descendants of former slaves who worked on huge rice and cotton plantations. After the Civil War many obtained their own small farms on one to twenty-five acres, and raised vegetables and cotton. As a result of years of isolation, the Gullah language, composed of standard and archaic English, corruptions of English words, and African words, can still be heard.[3] Today many young blacks leave the islands to work in cities. As a result, Emory Campbell, director of Penn Center on St. Helena Island, noted, the black native population "has become the new endangered species."[4]

During Reconstruction, Sea Island blacks had a measure of political power. They elected representatives to Congress and had a strong voice in local political affairs. By the late nineteenth century, however, the islanders could no longer vote. Beginning in 1895, South Carolina joined other southern states by adopting Jim Crow laws. One effect of these laws was the disenfranchisement of blacks. Devices such as the grandfather clause, the white primary, the poll tax, and the literacy test kept most blacks from the polls.[5] The Supreme Court declared the grandfather clause unconstitutional with the 1915 *Gwinn v. United States* decision, and the white primary was declared unconstitutional in 1944 by the *Smith v. Allwright* decision. But it was not until 1964 that the Twenty-fourth Amendment to the U.S. Constitution eliminated the poll tax, and 1965 when the Voting Rights Act outlawed literacy tests for purposes of discrimination.

The times, the 1950s, were characterized by a volatile political climate in the South. In addition to discrimination at the polls, the growing force of the civil rights movement, the 1954 *Brown v. Board of Education* decision, and the resistance by some whites to avoid integration were all part of the highly charged 1950s.

The literacy test as a requirement for voter registration was used to discriminate against black voters in the 1950s in the southern states of Virginia, Mississippi, Louisiana, South Carolina, Alabama, North Carolina, and Georgia. After 1950, prospective voters in South Carolina were required to read and write in English any section of the state constitution or pay taxes on property assessed at $300 or more. By 1956 only 27 percent of the eligible blacks in South Carolina were registered to vote. According to the 1960 census, only 10 percent of the black residents of Johns Island were literate and were registered to vote.[6]

In addition to lack of voting power, people on the Sea Islands in the 1950s suffered from poor education, inadequate health care, few economic opportunities, and discrimination. Schools on Johns Island were old, crowded, and drafty in the winter. Teachers had almost no supplies; children walked distances as far as ten miles to school; attendance was sporadic because of the growing seasons. In contrast, the white teachers had supplies and fewer students, were paid about one-third more than the black teachers, and white children rode a bus. Venereal disease was epidemic. There were many unwed young mothers, most of whom knew little about child care. Poor sanitation led to almost constant cases of hookworm and rashes. Black farmers sold their produce to middle men and were often cheated because of their illiteracy. And, of course, everything was segregated: churches, stores, schools, parks, and beaches.[7]

During the 1950s and 1960s Highlander Folk School, Monteagle, Tennessee, became deeply involved in the issue of segregation. Beginning in the 1930s, Highlander had established a reputation for upsetting the status quo by holding integrated workshops for organizing Southern labor. Before the 1954 *Brown* decision, Highlander began conducting workshops for community leaders who wanted to promote peaceful school integration and to encourage black community leadership that would also address discrimination in housing, voting, and the legal system.[8]

The citizenship school story is also rooted in the lives of four persons who developed the idea for the schools. The story begins with Esau Jenkins, a black bus driver, farmer, and civic leader from Johns Island. Called a Communist by some whites and an Uncle Tom by some blacks, Jenkins' philosophy was stated succinctly on the side of his old Volkswagen bus: "Love is Progress; Hate is Expensive." Born on Johns Island, South Carolina, in 1910, Jenkins left elementary school after four years to help his father, a truck farmer. Jenkins later received four more years of schooling. He learned Greek to facilitate the selling of his vegetables to the Greek merchants in Charleston. In the 1950s he organized citizens to bring a high school to Johns Island, and in 1953, Haut Gap High School was opened.[9]

In 1949 Jenkins organized the Progressive Club, a consumer cooperative and a defense fund. Jenkins wanted to "help the people to be better citizens, give them a chance to get a better education, and know how to reason and look out for themselves, and take more part in political action."[10] One of the requirements for membership was to be a registered voter. However, only 10 percent of the black residents on Johns Island were literate; therefore, blacks were effectively cut out of any voice in their government and membership in Jenkins' club. Jenkins tried to increase the number of voters by teaching island residents the required passage of the constitution. He could not teach 2,000 persons to read and write, however, and fear kept many blacks from even trying. Jenkins needed help in upsetting the status quo on Johns Island, and he found it by accepting Septima Clark's invitation to visit Highlander Folk School in 1954.[11]

The second key figure in the citizenship school story is Septima Poinsette Clark, a black schoolteacher from Charleston. Clark graduated from Avery Institute, established by the American Missionary Association in Charleston in 1865. At Avery she received a classic education in Greek, Latin, Spanish, mathematics, geography, writing, history, music, rhetoric, and literature, and graduated near the top of her class. She took summer courses at Columbia University in reading in 1930, and in 1937 she studied with W.E.B. Du Bois at Atlanta University, who taught her that black people must initiate the steps for social change. She earned her bachelor's degree from Benedict College in Columbia, South Carolina, in 1942 and a master's degree from Hampton Institute in Virginia in 1946.[12]

Because black teachers were not allowed to teach in Charleston, at the age of eighteen Septima Clark began her teaching career on nearby Johns Island. Years later she reflected on her experiences.

I realize it was the Johns Island folk who, if they did not set me on my course, surely did confirm me in a course I had dreamed of taking even as a child, that of teaching and particularly teaching the poor and underprivileged of my own underprivileged race. . . . For in my later years I am more convinced than ever that in lifting up the lowly we lift likewise the entire citizenship.[13]

In 1956, after twenty-five years of teaching, Clark was fired from teaching in South Carolina because of her membership in the National Association for the Advancement of Colored People (NAACP). She arrived at an important realization:

I'm a Negro, born black in a white man's land. . . . I am a teacher. I have spent my whole life teaching citizenship to children who really aren't citizens. They have fulfilled all the requirements for citizenship; many of their fathers and brothers have died for their country; bullets and bombs tear black skin as easily as white. . . . But this is not enough to qualify them to vote, to receive a decent education. . . . I can no longer aid in their education, because I joined in the movement to help them claim their citizenship.[14]

She was immediately hired by Highlander Folk School as their integration workshop director and later became their education director.[15]

Highlander's cofounder, Myles Horton, is the third important figure in the development of the schools. Horton was born in Tennessee, educated at Cumberland University, and worked for the Young Men's Christian Association (YMCA) in his early years. At a YMCA conference in Knoxville in 1928 he discovered that "there was no place—not even the public library"—where he and a black conference participant "could relax and exchange ideas when the conference adjourned." Horton read widely and was influenced by educational philosophers William James and John Dewey. He continued his education at Union Theological Seminary (1929–1930) under Reinhold Niebuhr; at the University of Chicago (1930–1931), where he met Robert Park, Lester Ward, and Jane Addams; and in Denmark (1931–1932) at the Danish Folk Schools.[16]

Horton synthesized ideas from his formal education and his work in the mountains when he and Don West, a Georgia native, started Highlander Folk School, an adult education school, on November 1, 1932. Highlander was established in Grundy County, Tennessee, one of the poorest counties in the country during the Depression.[17] They wanted the school to encourage social change in the South. To accomplish this, they began to organize and train labor leaders in Southern industrial areas.

By the early 1950s it was clear to Horton that the greatest social problem in the South was segregation. In 1954 Highlander sponsored a workshop that brought together black leaders from Charleston, South Carolina, including Esau Jenkins, Septima Clark, and Bernice Robinson. At the end of the workshop, participants were asked what action they would take in their communities when they returned. Jenkins' answer was "adult education." He explained that there were plenty of willing students on the island but no teachers and no place to meet. Although Horton at one time had said Highlander would not be a school for reading and writing, he changed his mind when he realized that teaching adults functional literacy skills could lead to citizenship for social change.[18]

Horton procured the funds for the school from two foundations: the Emil Schwartzhaupt Foundation of Santa Cruz, California, and the Marshall Field Foundation of Chicago. The Schwartzhaupt Foundation had a mandate to build community leadership and participation by addressing problems through democratic methods. The Field Foundation's board, which included the Marshall Field family, Ralph Bunche, and Adlai E. Stevenson as its president, had as one of its primary goals the improvement of race relations.[19]

From 1954 to 1957 workshops for island leaders were held in Charleston and on Johns Island to plan for the literacy schools. In 1956 Highlander lent the money for a place to hold classes. Esau Jenkins tried to buy a county-owned building, but the county sold it to a white man who sold it to Jenkins a week later for a profit. After it was renovated by the islanders, Jenkins opened a cooperative store in front; classes were held in the back to avoid drawing attention.[20] Teaching blacks to read and write in order to vote was a dangerous idea in South Carolina in 1957.

In 1956 Jenkins decided to give black voters something to vote for by becoming a candidate for school trustee. He was the first black to do so in ninety years. One resident, surprised to find Jenkins' name on the ballot, told others, "Man, Esau Jenkins' name on that voting machine. You better go on down there and vote." Jenkins estimated that 99 percent of the blacks voted on that day. He came in third out of four candidates, prompting the whites to change selection of school trustees to appointment instead of by election. Jenkins demonstrated that it was possible to be black, run for office, and not be killed for trying.[21]

Once the citizenship schools had a building, the next step was to find a teacher. Earlier efforts by the public schools to start adult education classes on Johns Island had failed because black adults found coming to a regular school, sitting in student seats, listening to a teacher lecture, and using elementary books to be humiliating.[22] A teacher who was sensitive to the needs of the people was needed. In 1956 Horton asked Bernice Robinson, a black beautician and civil rights worker from Charleston, to teach the first citizenship school class. At first she gave an emphatic "no," but she remembered Horton saying: "We need a community worker to do it who cares for the people, who understands the people, who can communicate with the people and some one who has been to Highlander who knows the Highlander philosophy, so there's nobody to do it but you."[23] Robinson considered this an ultimatum and finally agreed. Although she had no formal education to prepare her for teaching, she did have a good ear, an inventive mind, and a strong commitment to civil rights.

Robinson, the fourth important personality in this story, was born in Charleston, South Carolina, February 7, 1914. She attended Burke High School in Charleston but received her high school diploma in New York. In New York she also took vocational courses and held a variety of jobs (comptometer operator, statistical clerk, and campaign worker), which gave her valuable experience in working with all kinds of people. In 1947 she returned to Charleston because her parents were ill. With little work available in Charleston for blacks with or without an education, she took in sewing and operated a beauty shop out of her home. Robinson, as a citizen of New York, was a voter. But when she returned to Charleston and found the white primary still in effect, she became an officer in the Young Women's Christian Association (YWCA) and the NAACP to combat discrimination and disenfranchisement.[24] These actions brought her to the attention of Myles Horton.

PEDAGOGY OF THE DISENFRANCHISED

The selection of Bernice Robinson as teacher was the most important part of developing the pedagogy of the citizenship schools. In contemplating the nature of teaching, Myles Horton concluded:

There is something creative about teaching. When we stop learning, helping others to learn is impossible. We might be able to pass on facts and pre-digested ideas but could hardly stimulate learning. What I teach must be a part of me if it is to become a part of another human being. What I am and what I believe in and am searching for means more than anything I might say as a teacher.[25]

Horton selected Robinson because he thought that a nontraditional teacher, with no set ideas of how to teach and no set curriculum, was needed to be successful with adults on Johns Island.

Bernice Robinson showed a sensitivity to the people, their institutions, and their pride. She recruited students through the black churches, which were not only the focal point of black religious life, but also the center of black social life on the islands. Robinson realized that illiteracy was a sensitive issue and asked potential students about a "friend" who might be illiterate. She treated her students as adults who brought a wealth of experiences to the classrooms. Most were older than she was (her youngest student was thirty-nine; Robinson was forty-three). She won their confidence by saying, "I'm really not going to be your teacher. We're going to work together and teach each other."[26]

On the first night of class in January 1957, Robinson realized that traditional teaching materials would not do. She came armed only with voter registration applications, the United Nations Universal Declaration of Human Rights, sent to her by Horton, and elementary reading materials loaned to her by her sisters-in-law. The adults found the children's materials insulting. Robinson asked her students what they wanted to learn, and discovered that they wanted to order from catalogues, to count money, to read letters from their families who lived off the island, to read the Bible, to fill out money orders, to read the newspaper, to sew and crochet, and to register to vote.[27]

She taught them to write their names using the kinesthetic method, by having students trace their names on cardboard cutouts. Learning their names was a peak experience for Robinson as well as her students. When a sixty-five-year-old woman recognized her name for the first time, Robinson remembers: "I never will forget the emotion I felt when she got up, took the ruler out of my hand, went up to the board and said, 'There is my name, A-n-n-a, Anna. There's my last name, Vastine, V-a-s-t-i-n-e.' Goose pimples came out all over me."[28]

Robinson used the students' experiences to teach reading. She asked students to tell her stories about their work in the fields and their homes. Then she told them, "This is your story. We're going to learn how to read your story."[29] Robinson seemed to know that this was a good way to teach, without ever hearing of the "language experience" approach to reading.

The students' needs also dictated Robinson's next steps. She made copies of postal money order forms. She developed vocabulary and spelling lessons based on words from the South Carolina constitution and their everyday lives. She hand-printed the voter registration application and tacked it to the board for constant referral. She clipped ads from grocery specials for arithmetic. Her math problems had practical application, such as "How much do you expect to receive when you sell your crops?"[30]

Because of the lack of materials appropriate for adults, Robinson and Clark developed *My Reading Booklet* for use with later classes. Clark credits this idea to Wil Lou Gray, director of adult education in South Carolina. It included information about Highlander, the United States and its government, social security, voting requirements, driver's safety, income tax, cooperatives, and government services and programs.[31]

The lessons, including vocabulary, story writing, filling out forms, writing letters, arithmetic, and manners, were based on what Robinson had learned from her first classes. Vocabulary words included "dollar," "sheriff," "sit-in," "imprisonment," "power," "rebellion," and "register." Stories in the booklet told about people going to register, political action, or taking crops to market. A sample math problem was: "Ten students were arrested in the sit-in movement and were fined $75 a piece. How much fine was paid?" The booklet was later adopted by the Southern Christian Leadership Conference (SCLC) and titled *Citizenship School Workbook*. Additions included the history of the civil rights movement; freedom songs such as "We Shall Overcome," "Keep Your Eyes on the Prize," and "Oh Freedom"; and an evaluation instrument for teachers to follow up on their students' activities after the completion of the classes.[32]

By February 1958 Robinson had taught two classes on Johns Island, and all twenty-six students who had attended all five months registered to vote by reading the required paragraph of the South Carolina constitution and writing their own names. The classes had met only twice a week for two hours a night. Adult students, some of whom could not write their names when they began, passed the literacy test after only eighty hours of classes.[33]

The new voters on Johns Island influenced others to get their certificates. Before long, Johns Island was "infested with voters," and word spread to adjoining islands, Wadmalaw and Edisto, and to North Charleston. Expansion was what Horton wanted, and it coincided with additional grant money from the Schwartzhaupt Foundation. Potential leaders on these islands were identified and sent to a workshop at Highlander.[34]

The class on Wadmalaw was taught by Ethel Grimball, Esau Jenkins' daughter, in a small building that belonged to the Presbyterian Church. Grimball was a college-educated teacher with close ties to the people of Johns and Wadmalaw islands. Although she developed her own methods, Grimball, as Robinson, was tuned in to the needs of the students.[35]

A class was started on Edisto Island in 1958 by Alleen Brewer (now Wood). Brewer was a social worker from the Presbyterian Church, which, in turn, furnished a meeting place. Although thirty-eight men and women enrolled (the largest class so far), Brewer met the challenge by grouping students so that they could help one another. She also taught reading, writing, arithmetic, citizenship, sewing, leather craft, and the history of the United States and the civil rights movement, based on expressed student needs.[36] For many of the students on Edisto, the social part of each class session was extremely important. One man said, "Now we don't have to wait until Sunday to fellowship together."[37]

During the three-month period from December 1958 to February 1959, four citizenship schools were held on Edisto Island, Johns Island, and Wadmalaw Island and in North Charleston. With 106 students enrolled in these classes, ranging in age from fifteen to seventy-six, Bernice Robinson became a supervisor, overseeing the development of new classes. At the end of the school term, eighty-six students were registered to vote.[38]

By 1959 music had become an important part of the citizenship school classes. Bernice Robinson taught the students songs to help them learn. For example, she changed words in "Soldiers of the Cross" to "We are building a better nation through this school and each voter makes us stronger." Beginning in 1959, music became a regular part of the schools through the work of Guy Carawan, who had become Highlander's music director. He recorded songs of the island people and taught them songs that were part of their island heritage, such as "Michael, Row the Boat Ashore," which originated in the Sea Islands in the 1850s. In 1966 Guy and his wife, Candie, published the stories and music of the Sea Islands in a book titled *Ain't You Got a Right to the Tree of Life?* [39]

The students' responses to these early classes were very positive. Student comments were recorded on tape, and some wrote letters to the teachers and to Highlander.

I enjoyed the school very good and I hope it will be a little longer if its able to continue.

—Ms. Wright, Johns Island[40]

The adult school means so much to me I cannot express my appreciation and thoughts by words. The only think I am so sorry the school terms was so short. I would like to thank our teacher Mrs. Brewer for helping us out so wonderful in sewing, arithmetic.

—Minnie R. Washington, Edisto Island[41]

It took whites in the Charleston area until 1959 to discover the schools. Otis Perkins, a reporter for the Charleston *News and Courier*, discovered the schools and their connection to Highlander. He pointed out that Highlander Folk School, because of its efforts in promoting integration, "has been accused of harboring subversive elements and of being a breeding ground for agitators."[42] As a result of the article, Bernice Robinson was shunned by her card group (black) and ignored by friends on the street. Association with the NAACP or integration in Charleston in the 1950s could mean loss of their jobs. But, according to Robinson, Charleston was not Selma, Alabama, or Jackson, Mississippi; although whites opposed integration, violence was not their way.[43]

In 1959–1960, 182 adults enrolled in citizenship school classes on Johns Island, Promised Land (northern section of Johns Island), Wadmalaw Island, and Edisto Island and in North Charleston. Sixty-five became registered voters. By March 1960 there were 200 black voters on Edisto, compared with 40 in 1958. Johns Island black voters had increased by 300 percent from 1956 to 1960. In 1960–1961 classes were held in North Charleston and on Edisto and Wadmalaw islands, and 105 out of 111 black students registered to vote. Bernice Robinson and Septima Clark had also organized eight classes in Huntsville, Alabama, and Savannah, Georgia, by 1960–1961. By the end of this session, 245 students, ranging in age from seventeen to sixty-five, had attended the citizenship school classes, and 232 had registered.[44]

By 1961 Highlander had developed a teacher-training program, based on a workshop format, in which potential teachers were taught by demonstration, not lecture. The basic requirements for new teachers were (a) some high school education, (b) twenty-one years of age, (c) able to write legibly on the chalkboard, and (d) be a community resident. Once identified, potential teachers were required to attend a one-week workshop sponsored by Highlander. The goal was to turn housewives, farmers, union members, dressmakers, ministers, college students, business men or women, and public-school teachers into citizenship school teachers. The workshops were organized around four important ideas[45]:

1. "Learning and purpose go hand in hand." Literacy is an important part of becoming a first-class citizen.
2. Teachers should experience the activities they themselves would be conducting.
3. Teachers should experience teaching as an activity done with others, not in isolation. The teachers should build bonds with the other teachers and the workshop leaders by living at the same place, eating together, and singing together.
4. Teachers should see the "big picture": that, as teachers, they were doing something important, that their work was valuable, and that through them participation in a democracy could increase.

In 1961 the state of Tennessee took away Highlander's charter, charging the school with illegal integration and selling liquor without a license. Anticipating this action, Horton had taken out a new charter in August 1961 for Highlander Research and Education Center in Knoxville.[46] The citizenship schools plus the teacher-training workshops were transferred to the SCLC, with Highlander remaining as a consultant for the program.

As director of the SCLC, Martin Luther King, Jr., was concerned about the appeal that radical black groups had for blacks. He saw the citizenship school program as a promising alternative to radical black politics: "The Citizenship Schools developed by Highlander are the most effective answer to the inroads being made by the Black Moslem movement on the lower social-economic status Southern Negro."[47] Andrew Young, who had joined the Highlander staff earlier that year, and Septima Clark went to the SCLC to work with Dorothy Cotton to organize more schools. Bernice Robinson remained at Highlander and acted as a consultant to the SCLC.[48]

The spread of the schools under the SCLC was rapid. By September 1963 there were 700 teachers and 50,000 new voters who could be traced to the citizenship school movement.[49] These figures represent dramatic growth, considering the humble beginning on Johns Island with fourteen students and one inexperienced teacher. But voter registration is only one part of the story. Highlander's goal was that the citizenship school students would become leaders in their communities, "first-class citizens," who would address problems of health, education, jobs, and discrimination.

FIRST-CLASS CITIZENSHIP

In 1976 Horton pointed out that the main purpose of Highlander's work is to spark further action: "People organizing to do things in their community, taking political action, learning about the world ... [education] was kind of the spark that kept those things ignited."[50] The citizenship schools, too, went beyond literacy to try to empower people to improve their communities and their world. The analysis of the schools' efforts to encourage first-class citizenship is based on three criteria: "turning on a light," becoming skeptical, and taking action.

The initial step to first-class citizenship is what Bernice Robinson called "turning on a light." In other words, the schools opened up a new world for a number of island residents:

I want to thank you for this school ... because it look like it make a light for all colored people, and I enjoyed myself because I've never been to school in my life.
—Ms. Extine, Johns Island[51]

So everybody is jubilant for the Highlander Folk School, who have helped them see the light.

—Esau Jenkins, Johns Island[52]

First-class citizens also need to raise questions. Myles Horton, desiring that students be exposed to ideas with which they could evaluate their own world, sent Bernice Robinson the United Nations Universal Declaration of Human Rights, adopted by the U.N. General Assembly in 1948.[53] She put it on the wall of her classroom, used it to teach vocabulary, and asked students to understand its meaning by the end of three months. Although the United States supported these universal human rights (freedom from discrimination; equal protection before the law; freedom from inhuman treatment or punishment; presumption of innocence; the right to take part in government; and the right to an education) for the rest of the world it was apparent to the students that these rights were not a reality for many poor, black people in the United States.

Students who attended the citizenship schools and the Highlander workshops reported becoming aware of the differences between the ideals of a democracy and the realities.

We learned much of what Democracy means that we did not know before. We had some to register and many who are going to register. We learned what many words meant and a better way of expressing ourself. We were inspired to help others toward first class citizenship.

—Solomon Brown, Edisto Island[54]

[Going to Highlander] was our first rewarding experience in true democracy. There were fifty-three whites and twenty Negroes, eating, sleeping, dancing and working together ever day.

—Florence Singleton, Johns Island[55]

Some students were beginning to be more critical of white domination and to realize that change was possible.

Bernice Robinson taught students to be more skeptical about what they read in the newspapers and the promises made to them by people who wanted their support. She taught lessons on how "to read between the lines" by bringing newspaper articles to the class and discussing what they really meant or what was left out. She was sensitive to the fact that many blacks on the islands had been exploited, and she urged them to take a more critical view of their world and to be less accepting of what white people said. She urged her students to speak up in class, an important step in becoming effective citizens.[56]

The ultimate evidence of first-class citizenship, however, is action. Highlander's measure of success has always been the actions taken by its students when they return to their communities. Community action did result from the citizenship schools' influence on the students, the teachers, and others in the community directly affected by the school.

Although Esau Jenkins was a leader in his own right before he came to Highlander in 1954, through his work with the schools he realized the need for encouraging leadership among others. In a letter to Myles Horton in 1955, Jenkins wrote: "My ideas of community leadership have changed in many ways since my stay at Highlander last year. I found that giving others something to do and helping make better citizens in the community is very important. And we are progressing magnificently. My old ways of doing was slow.[57]" Jenkins encouraged citizenship school students to continue their political education by starting "second step" groups in their communities that would address issues, discuss candidates, analyze political power, and develop strategies for practical problems on the islands, such as driving safety. Second-step classes were organized on Johns, Edisto, Wadmalaw, Yonges, and Awensdaw islands and in Charleston and Maryville, South Carolina, and were active in the early 1960s.[58]

Jenkins' influence spread beyond the islands through the Palmetto Voters Association and the Citizen's Committee of Charleston County. Through these organizations he influenced candidates to listen to black needs. He pointed out that the magistrates on Johns Island now needed black votes to get elected and no longer assumed that blacks were guilty when they entered the courtroom. Jenkins and the Citizen's Committee also helped to defeat South Carolina governor Ernest Hollings, a segregationist, in his bid for the U.S. Senate in 1963.[59]

In 1969 Jenkins was appointed to the school board, thirteen years after he ran unsuccessfully for that same board. Bill Saunders, a black radio station owner in Charleston and civil rights worker from Johns Island, credits Jenkins with being instrumental in establishing racial harmony at St. Johns High School, the integrated high school on Johns Island today. The whites did not leave the school, as they did other Charleston County schools, and both blacks and whites have profited from the integration.[60]

Esau Jenkins, with help from citizenship school students and other island residents, helped to establish a credit union, a nursing home, a low-income housing project, and the Sea Islands Comprehensive Health Center.[61] He also helped to expand adult education and bring a kindergarten to Johns Island. Although Jenkins was killed in an automobile accident in 1972, there are a number of places that bear testimony to his work. The Esau Jenkins bridge between Wadmalaw and Johns islands in particular symbolizes Jenkins' leadership as link between people on the Sea Islands and his work to promote the welfare of all.

Ethel Grimball, the teacher on Wadmalaw Island, also grew in her role as an activist. Her vocational and volunteer work reflected a dedication similar to that of her father, Esau Jenkins. She has been a director for Head Start, a director of programs for migrant families, and an executive assistant for the Economic Opportunity Commission of Charleston County. Alleen Brewer Wood, the teacher on Edisto, led a group to Washington in the late 1950s or early 1960s to protest the local response to school integration: placing black children in trailers and white children in the building on the same school grounds.[62]

After listening to and recording the songs of the people, Guy Carawan helped to promote a Johns Island singing group, The Moving Star Hall Singers. In 1965 they performed in the South, at the Newport Folk Festival in Rhode Island, in New York, and in California. Their records and performances brought the group national attention, a market for their music, and an income.[63]

On Wadmalaw Island an organization called the Board of Concerned Members of Wadmalaw Island was formed by the students of the first citizenship school class. They are credited with helping to raise the number of registered black voters from zero in the mid–1950s to more than 1,000 in 1973. A black woman was also elected as a precinct leader and another elected to the school board in 1973. Willie Smith, one of those first students, wrote to Septima Clark and Ethel Grimball in 1959: "I have learn a little of everything in the line of reading and writing math. and fract. And more about civic organizations. And a fine fellowship with one another."[64] Smith's later work in helping to establish Second Step voter education classes and a community center on Wadmalaw may indicate that the fellowship that he so enjoyed became the core for future civic organizations.

Anderson Mack, Sr., credits the citizenship schools with helping him become a leader. He came to the Wadmalaw Island school as a student in his early twenties with a second-grade education. Encouraged by the citizenship school experience, he took more classes through adult education at Haut Gap High School. Later he helped each of his three children receive a college education. Together with other citizenship schools students, Willie Smith and Mary Steed, he helped to establish a community center on Wadmalaw that sponsors a senior citizens' program. He worked to get home mail delivery, paved roads, a kindergarten, and more parent involvement in the local school. Today he continues as a community leader and is currently employed as a supervisor for the county public works department.[65]

Other students experienced greater leadership roles or greater autonomy in their community as a result of the schools. Alice Wine of Johns Island came to the citizenship schools as a cleaning woman for a white family, but she became proficient enough in reading, writing, and arithmetic to become bookkeeper for the Progressive Club and clerk in the cooperative store. Lula Bligen, a student on Edisto, became an officer in the Voters' Association of Edisto Island in 1961. Tony Daise, a citizenship school student on Edisto, became minister of a large Baptist church on that island. A number of other Edisto students continued their education, became leaders in their churches, and helped to establish a community center. Fifty percent of the students on Wadmalaw pursued additional education; a few went to college. Citizenship school classes often became the basis for the first black civic organization in a number of communities across the South.[66] For some students the main result of the schools was developing personally or gaining socially useful skills. They became less dependent on others and made greater contributions to their families. As Ms. Townsond, a student on Wadmalaw reported: "I am a member of the adult school of Wadmalaw Island and a mother of 10 children befor I came a member of adult school I washing and wonent to lern how to read and figer & sow, since I became a member of the adult school I can make my children close and also read and figer much better."[67]

BLACK ADULT EDUCATION AND EMPOWERMENT

What conclusions may be drawn about effective black adult education based on the example of the citizenship schools? Based on an analysis of the schools, four themes emerge about the nature of teaching and a curriculum that encourages empowerment for black adults.

The first theme emphasizes courage, flexibility, and inspired teaching. Bernice Robinson's confidence came from believing that she had a mission to encourage people to read and write and become active citizens. She was not easily intimidated by whites or other blacks who questioned her actions. Alleen Brewer also exhibited courage. She took on a class of thirty-eight students, some of whom were fearful that coming to the class would mean the loss of their jobs. Her confidence helped students deal with their own fears and continue coming to class. The early teachers were also resourceful. Robinson, for example, began without a prescribed curriculum or text and created many of her own learning materials. These teachers also made creative use of less than adequate facilities (a sewing room, a beauty parlor, the back room of a small building, and a tiny church outbuilding). In addition to being courageous and resourceful, the early citizenship school teachers were inspired people. Although their various agendas included getting streets paved in Charleston, increasing black voter registration, expanding educational opportunities, developing community leaders, and helping students feel connected to the rest of the world, all had first-class citizenship as their goal. They, in turn, inspired their students to experience the citizenship schools as part of an important social movement. Teacher personality traits such as these were identified by James Leming, social studies educator, in his research on good teaching. He observed that "charisma, intellect, energy and character of the individual teacher" were key ingredients in the success of a school and its students.[68]

The second theme in education for empowerment is that a good curriculum reflects the needs of the students and the cultural capital they bring to the classroom. A number of contemporary educators urge that the curriculum reflect cultural factors: Giroux when he discusses cultural capital, Pickles when he talks of commonplaces, and Geertz when he refers to local knowledge.[69] All emphasize that teachers should acknowledge and respect the culture from which the students come. The citizenship school curriculum reflected students' needs, students' culture, and the goals of the teachers. Music, for example, was a big part of the black churches on the islands, and it became part of the citizenship schools. Personal goals of the students, such as learning to sew and filling out catalogue order forms, were recognized by the teachers.

Local teachers who respected the intelligence of the students were asked to teach. Septima Clark pointed out that students were treated "as adults and [given] very challenging responsibilities. We use local people they know as a teacher. So you have a combination of a strong challenge and local people with whom they are familiar."[70] According to Bernice Robinson, "their minds are sharp, and they have experiences that are beautiful." They also had good memories, she noted, because people who can't read and write often compensate by developing their ability to memorize.[71]

The third theme in education for empowerment is that the curriculum should be focused on real human problems. John Dewey also supported this idea: "To learn, a student must sense a real problem or question, must be free to form hypotheses and test them in practice."[72] Robinson and the other teachers taught skills such as reading a grocery ad, figuring costs, and planning purchases at the store. The math story problems were often about selling vegetables, and vocabulary words such as "prison," "magistrate," and "power" reflected the struggles of black people with the law. Special classes and community meetings on topics such as insurance, inheritance, health, and consumerism were organized to follow up on the skills learned in the classes. The teachers emphasized that reading, writing, and other skills led somewhere, to broader and longer-range goals. Students were taught to look not only at their immediate communities and their own problems, but also at the problems of human struggle in the rest of the world. Robinson referred to this process as turning on a light. Grimball talked about expanding educational opportunities. Critical theorists such as Stanley Aronowitz, Henry Giroux, and Paulo Freire encourage a similar goal when they refer to critical literacy as a process in which students begin to see the relation between knowledge and power.[73]

The fourth theme is that the students and teachers learned from each other. Robinson was a teacher in the Highlander tradition, and in many ways she preceded the work of Paulo Freire. In this tradition she created a democratic learning environment, not an authoritarian, teacher-dominated one. In this environment dialogue could take place between students and teacher. Robinson's role was to help free her students to develop their own potential, to take responsibility for their own learning. Myles Horton calls this kind of teacher an "enabler" whose role it is "to promote understanding of the learner's lives, sensitivity to injustices, and future thinking about a better world."[74] The teacher as enabler is based on two assumptions. One is that students are capable and have the potential to take responsibility for their own learning, to address their own problems. The second assumption is that democracy is a process, and therefore people can make a difference, can affect the course of society. George Counts said that the success of a democracy rested on the process of constant reexamination, redefinition, and reinterpretation of the nature of democracy as society changed.[75] We constantly struggle with issues of equal rights, private versus public interests, and economic justice. By teaching democracy and citizenship as a process, students learn that they have a role to play in that process and that they can effect change.

CONCLUSION

First-class citizenship is a process of continued growth and change. Herman Blake, after he studied the effects of the schools in 1969, noted: "It is no longer possible to speak of the citizenship program in terms of the Sea Islands only . . . for the program has reached out to embrace the entire county of Charleston, and its impact is felt statewide since Charleston is the largest county in South Carolina."[76] The citizenship schools got people moving, first on the Sea Islands and then throughout the South. According to Bernice Robinson: "The Citizenship School program became the basis for the civil rights movement because it was through these classes that people learned about their rights and *why* they should vote. They learned something about their government and how it's formed and the importance of their vote."[77] The schools, in Myles Horton's opinion, were probably Highlander's most successful program, a spark that helped to ignite the civil rights movement as it spread throughout the South.[78]

The citizenship schools furnish a historical example of education that is based on the belief that adults have the power within themselves to effect change in their own lives. Although the relation of education and power is the theme of the writings of educators such as Michael Apple and Henry Giroux, there are few examples of schools or programs that have actually attempted to put this belief in action. Paulo Freire's literacy schools in Brazil and the Highlander Folk School are two of the most notable.[79] The citizenship schools, therefore, were unique and, based on the descriptive evidence presented in this chapter, successful in empowering students to gain more control over their own destinies. The schools provide a historical perspective for educators who want to promote black adult education, not as literacy or vocational skills, but as a vehicle to first-class citizenship.

NOTES

1. Martin Luther King, Jr., "I Have a Dream," Washington, D.C., August 28, 1963.

2. *My Citizenship Booklet*, 1961–1962, Highlander Center Archives, New Market, Tenn., Box 2, folder 25, p. 3 (hereafter cited as HC, B [box] & F [folder]; Martin Luther King, Jr., in *Citizenship Education Program* pamphlet (Atlanta SCLC [1961]).

3. J. P. Hayes, *James Island and Related Sea Islands* (Charleston, S.C.: Walker, Evans & Cogswell, 1978), 90; G. B. Tindall, *South Carolina Negroes 1877–1900* (Columbia: University of South Carolina Press, 1952), 100–101; G. B. Johnson, *Folk Culture on St. Helena Island, S.C.* (Chapel Hill: University of North Carolina Press, 1930), 42.

4. "Culture and Community Empowerment," *Highlander Reports*, November 1984, pp. 1–2.

5. See Willie Lee Rose, *Rehearsal for Reconstruction: The Port Royal Experiment* (Indianapolis: Bobbs-Merrill, 1964); C. Vann Woodward, *The Strange Career of Jim Crow*, 3rd ed. (New York: Oxford University Press, 1974).

6. Congress, Senate, Committee on the Judiciary, *Nomination & Election of President and Vice President and Qualifications for Voting*, 87th Cong., 1st sess., pt. 5, 1981; U.S. Civil Rights Commission, "Voting in Mississippi: A Case Study," in *The Negro in 20th Century America*, ed. John Hope Franklin (New York: Vantage Books, 1965): 340–342; Department of Commerce, Bureau of the Census, Census of Population, *Characteristics of the Population, South Carolina* (Washington, D.C.: U.S. Department of Commerce, 1960), 48.

7. Guy Carawan and Candie Carawan, *Ain't You Got a Right to the Tree of Life?*

(New York: Simon & Schuster, 1966), 158–179; Septima Clark, "Notes on Johns Island, S.C.," Social Action Collection, State Historical Society of Wisconsin, Madison, WI: B 67, F 3 (hereafter cited as WHS); J. D. Franson, "Citizenship Education in the South Carolina Sea Islands, 1954–1966" (Ph.D. diss., Vanderbilt University, 1977), 41–42; G. Kearney, "Highlander Folk School Uses Practical Sociology in Facing Racial Integration," 1955, WHS: B 83, F 5.

8. Highlander Folk School, Monteagle, Tenn. (hereafter cited as HFS), Staff conference, January 31, 1958, WHS: B 3, F 1.

9. Carl Tjerandsen, *Education for Citizenship: A Foundation's Experience* (Santa Cruz, Calif.: Emil Schwarzhaupt Found., 1980), 213; Nan Woodruff, *Esau Jenkins: A Retrospective View of the Man* (Charleston, S.C.: Avery Institute of Afro-American History, 1984); Carawan and Carawan, *Ain't You Got a Right*, 158–179.

10. Woodruff, *Esau Jenkins*.

11. Ibid.; Tjerandsen, *Education for Citizenship*, 152.

12. Septima Clark, taped interview by author, Charleston, S.C., January 13, 1986.

13. Septima Clark with L. Blythe, *Echo in My Soul* (New York: E. P. Dutton, 1962), 52.

14. W. A. Parris, "Highlander Folk School, an Adult Education Program with a Purpose," *Negro History Bulletin* 21 (1958):185–186.

15. "School Board Dismisses Clark," *Highlander Reports*, July 1956, WHS: B 1, F 6.

16. Aimee Horton, "The Highlander Folk School: A History of the Development of Its Major Programs Related to Social Movements in the South" (Ph.D. diss., University of Chicago, 1971), 15, 19–34.

17. Frank Adams, *Unearthing the Seeds of Fire: The Idea of Highlander* (Winston-Salem, N.C.: Blair, 1979), 25–36.

18. Carawan and Carawan, *Ain't You Got a Right*, 168; Tjerandsen, *Education for Citizenship*, 140.

19. Field Foundation, *Review of Activities*, Oct. 1, 1957—Sept. 30, 1959 (Chicago: Field Foundation), WHS: B 66, F 6.

20. Septima Clark, interview by Peter Wood, Charleston, S.C., February 3–4, 1981, HC: B 2, F 25 & 26.

21. Carawan and Carawan, *Ain't You Got a Right*, 170; Bill Saunders, interview by author, Charleston, S.C., January 31, 1987.

22. Myles Horton, interview by author, New Market, Tenn., October 26, 1985.

23. Eliot Wigginton and Sue Thrasher, "Reading, Writing and Voting," *Southern Exposure* 10 (1982):28–29.

24. Bernice Robinson, taped interview by author, Charleston, S.C., January 14, 1986.

25. Myles Horton, pre-Highlander notes, 1931, WHS: B 54, F 2.

26. Robinson interview.

27. Bernice Robinson, videotaped speech at HFS workshop, New Market, Tenn., 1979; Robinson interview.

28. Robinson interview.

29. Ibid.

30. Wigginton and Thrasher, "Reading, Writing, and Voting," 29.

31. *My Citizenship Booklet*; Horton interview.

32. *My Citizenship Booklet*, 13, 31.

33. Tjerandsen, *Education for Citizenship*, 163; John Glen, "On the Cutting Edge: A History of the Highlander Folk School" (Ph.D. diss., Vanderbilt University, 1986), 535.

34. Tjerandsen, *Education for Citizenship*, 166.

35. Ethel Grimball, interview by author, Charleston, S.C., January 30, 1987.

36. Teachers discuss methods, Tape 515A, 1961, WHS: reel 205, side 1, part 2; Alleen Brewer, "Final Report of the Edisto Adult School for 1959–60," 1960, WHS: B 67, F 4; Clark, *Echo in My Soul*, 156–167; Alleen Brewer Wood, interview by author, Edisto Island, S.C., March 12, 1988.

37. Clark, *Echo in My Soul*, 159.

38. Tjerandsen, *Education for Citizenship*, 167.

39. Robinson interview; Guy Carawan, Sea Islands work, 1960–61 WHS: B 8, F 9; Edisto Island class, Tape 515A, January 7, 1960 WHS: reel 205, side 1, part 1.

40. Final class, Johns Island, Tape 807A, 1957, WHS: reel 7, part 1.

41. Letters from citizenship school students to HFS, 1959, WHS: B 57, F 5 & 9.

42. O. Perkins, "Classes Here Sponsored by Folk School," *Charleston News and Courier*, March 11, 1959.

43. Robinson interview.

44. Tjerandsen, *Education for Citizenship*, 167–168; HFS, *Quarterly Report*, Winter 1960, HC: B 2, F 25 & 26; HFS, "Charleston and Sea Island Activities," 1960–61, WHS: B 1, F 7; HFS, "Factual Report of Adult School," 1961, WHS: B 38, F 4.

45. Aimee Horton, "Teacher Training Workshop," 1965, HC: B 2, F 25 & 26.

46. Today Highlander Research and Education Center is located in New Market, Tennessee, twenty miles east of Knoxville.

47. HFS, "News Release," May 4, 1961, WHS: B 38, F 2.

48. Glen, "On the Cutting Edge," 568–569.

49. Septima Clark, "Success of SCLC Citizenship School Seen in 50,000 New Registered Voters," *SCLC Newsletter*, 1 (September 1963): 11.

50. Myles Horton, "The Spark That Ignites," *Southern Exposure* 4 (1976):156.

51. Final class, Tape 807A, Johns Island.

52. Carawan and Carawan, *Ain't You Got a Right*, 168.

53. S. Chen, *Basic Documents of International Organizations* (Dubuque, Iowa: Kendall/Hunt Publishing, 1979).

54. Letters from citizenship school students.

55. Florence Singleton, speech, Johns Island Civic Club, August 1955, WC: B 67, F 3.

56. Reading the newspaper, Tape 515A, 1965, WHS: reel 57, side 1, part 2.

57. Esau Jenkins, Johns Island, to Myles Horton, Highlander Folk School, April 28, 1955, WHS: B 67, F 3.

58. HFS, "Factual Report . . . "; "Second Step Voter Education Schools," 1963–1965, WHS: B 68, F 1 & 6.

59. Jenkins and Robinson speak to civic clubs, Tape 515A, June 7, 1962, WHS: reel 223, sides 1 & 2.

60. Saunders interview.

61. Woodruff, *Esau Jenkins*.

62. Grimball interview; Wood interview.

63. Guy Carawan, "Letter to Friends and Folk Song Enthusiasts," November 24, 1965, WHS: B 8, F 9.

64. Letters from citizenship school students.

65. Anderson Mack, Jr., interview by author, Wadmalaw Island, S.C., January 31, 1987.

66. Clark, *Echo in My Soul*, 156–167, Lulu Bligen, Edisto Island, letter to Septima Clark, July 6, 1961, WHS: B 67, F 4; Tjerandsen, *Education for Citizenship*; Wood interview; Mack interview; Grimball interview.

67. Letters from citizenship school students.

68. James Leming. "Rethinking Social Studies Research and the Goals of Social Education," *Theory and Research in Social Education* 14 (1986):150.

69. Henry Giroux, "Writing and Critical Thinking in the Social Studies," *Curriculum Inquiry* 8 (1978):291–310; J. Pickles, "The Role of Place and Commonplaces in Democratic Empowerment," *Issues in Education* 3 (1985):232–241; Clifford Geertz, *Local Knowledge* (New York: Basic Books, 1983), 8–16.

70. Tjerandsen, *Education for Citizenship*, 163.

71. Robinson interview.

72. Cited in David Tyack, *Turning Points in American Educational History* (Waltham, Mass.: Blaisdell, 1967), 319.

73. See Stanley Aronwitz and Henry Giroux, *Education Under Siege: The Conservative, Liberal, Radical Debate over Schooling* (South Hadley, Mass.: Bergin & Garvey, 1985); Paulo Freire, *Pedagogy of the Oppressed* (New York: Herder & Herder, 1972).

74. Myles Horton, "Decision-making Processes," in *Educational Reconstruction: Promise and Challenge*, ed. N. Shimahara (Columbus, OH: Charles E. Merrill, 1973), 334.

75. George S. Counts, *Dare the School Build a New Social Order?* (New York: John Day Co., 1932).

76. Tjerandsen, *Education for Citizenship*, 171.

77. Robinson interview.

78. Horton interview.

79. Henry Giroux, *Theory and Resistance in Education, a Pedagogy for the Opposition* (South Hadley, Mass.: Bergin & Garvey, 1983); Freire, *Pedagogy*; Michael Apple, "The Hidden Curriculum and the Nature of Conflict," in *Curriculum Theorizing: The Reconceptualists*, ed. W. Pinar (Berkeley, Calif.: McCutchan, 1975).

12

Adult Education for Blacks during the New Deal and World War II: The Federal Programs

Nancy L. Grant

The Great Depression affected many segments of the American society, but none more profoundly than blacks in the adult education community. Local and county officials, when faced with financial cutbacks, eroding tax bases, and widespread business failures, sought to trim their budgets in the only ways they knew, through cutbacks in educational funding from preschool to adult education. The result was the closing of thousands of schools, a marked reduction in hours, the elimination of programs, and the laying off or firing of between 80,000 and 100,000 teachers. The South was a disaster. Eighty-five percent of Alabama's public schools closed for lack of funds.[1]

Adult education was hit particularly hard. Viewed by many educators in the best of times as enrichment for the middle class and English instruction for recent immigrants, adult education was not widely supported by public funds. Only eighteen states contributed to the support of adult education in their communities, nineteen states had no communities that offered adult classes, four states had one community each that provided adult classes, seven states had between one and fifteen towns that sponsored some form of adult education.[2]

Blacks were particularly vulnerable to cutbacks in all areas of education. By law in the South and by practice in the urban North, blacks were separated into substandard and ill-equipped schools, inferior in quality and quantity to white schools. Lacking effective state and local political organizations, blacks in 1933 could not effectively lobby against precipitous cuts in spending for black educational resources, not only in Mississippi and Alabama, but also in Chicago and Philadelphia. Given the marginality of the socioeconomic position of blacks, funding for blacks in education during the Depression years on the local and state levels reached crisis levels.

Black churches, fraternal orders, the black branches of the Young Men's

Christian Association (YMCA) and Young Women's Christian Association (YWCA) and other black organizations tried to step in with support for private elementary education, scholarships for needy students, and classes for adult education. The National Association for the Advancement of Colored People (NAACP) and the National Urban League were particularly active in sponsoring adult education classes during the Depression. The Rockefeller Foundation also sought to provide funding on a limited basis for blacks in education, particularly in the South. These efforts, while well meaning and important, were limited in impact and scope and could not alleviate for most blacks the educational deprivation wrought by the Depression and compounded by historic racial and sectional discrimination.[3]

Efforts from the private sector that supported education for all Americans did not begin to fill the void created by the economic collapse. In 1933 Roosevelt established the apparatus to provide federally supported adult education programs through the departments of interior, labor, and defense, as well as through the newly created emergency agencies of the New Deal. Over a five-year period, Roosevelt proposed and Congress enacted a complex structure of overlapping emergency agencies. There were federal agencies to administer grants to states in order to house and feed the destitute, and other agencies to employ the jobless from the unskilled through professional ranks in federal projects, to regulate business and support the farmers, and to support youth aged sixteen to twenty-two through job training or keeping them in school with scholarships and part-time jobs.

Programs that supported adult education were only a small facet of the larger plan to avoid societal crisis. The unemployed and underemployed had to be reoriented, retrained, and reinvigorated through jobs and vocational and citizenship training before they became radicalized, and therefore disruptive. Indeed, Roosevelt and his New Dealers sought to avoid a repeat of disruptive incidents that occurred between 1930 and his inaugural. Between 1930 and 1933 Army veterans marched on Washington demanding immediate payment of their war bonuses, farmers barricaded highways in the Midwest to block food shipment and force up prices, black renters in Harlem blocked forced evictions, and thousands of the unemployed marched on Henry Ford's plant in Dearborn, Michigan, demanding jobs and relief, only to be gunned down by the police.[4]

The unemployed did not easily disappear, nor could they be ignored. An estimated 15 million Americans, roughly 25 percent of the nation's workforce, were unemployed in 1933. Among blacks, unemployment was substantially higher than the national average. Blacks, even during the "prosperous" 1920s, were disproportionately concentrated in semiskilled, laboring, or servant positions. When economic collapse made even these jobs very desirable, whites displaced blacks, sending blacks onto relief rolls. Although only 9 percent of the American people were black, according to the 1930 census, blacks accounted for more than 18 percent of those on relief. In the larger cities black unemployment exceeded 50 percent.[5]

Adult education programs during the New Deal served two functions. One function was to employ some of the thousands of unemployed teachers in positions utilizing their pedagogical skills, if not their specific area of expertise. The other function was to provide vocational training to the unemployed and underemployed, in order to prepare them for more technologically demanding positions in the post-Depression economy.

In keeping with the decentralized, locally controlled character of the New Deal, adult education programs were farmed out to many agencies and departments, often administered under local or state control. There was not one coordinating office. The principal agency handling federal support for adult education was the Federal Emergency Relief Administration (FERA) which administered the Emergency Education Program. In 1935 the principal role was taken over by the Works Progress Administration (WPA). There were also other important adult education programs in the Department of Agriculture under the agricultural extension aegis and vocational training programs in the National Youth Administration, the Civilian Conservation Corps, and the Tennessee Valley Authority. After 1940, with the increased demand for military preparedness, there were also adult training programs handled by the Department of War. The economy shifted from widespread unemployment to a labor shortage and round-the-clock production in defense industries. During World War II there were adult training programs to prepare the unskilled and semiskilled to be useful and productive defense and military workers.

Blacks participated in the adult education programs throughout the New Deal, many in segregated programs of the South and Northeast and in integrated programs in the upper Midwest and West Coast. This chapter examines the goals and programs of this particular aspect of federal support for adult education. Much has been written on racial discrimination in New Deal agencies, and the adult education programs in these agencies certainly had their share of racist administrators and discriminatory practices. Of equal importance for this study is the degree to which these adult programs reflected an effort to correct the deficiencies of a past society, as well as an effort to project positions in a future economy for these black participants. Vocational education has traditionally been not only a corrective for the past, but also a mirror into the future for the class and race of the participants. This study examines adult education programs in the WPA, the Civilian Conservation Corps, the National Youth Administration, the Department of Agriculture, and the Tennessee Valley Administration during the New Deal and examines the changes in the WPA program wrought by World War II, as well as providing a brief look at the defense training programs for civilians.[6]

THE WORKS PROGRESS ADMINISTRATION

The program that had the greatest impact during the New Deal and World War II was the Emergency Education Program, originally in the FERA and then in the WPA after 1935. Harry Hopkins, a former social worker and administrator of the FERA along with Frances Perkins, secretary of labor, pushed Roosevelt to include provisions for educational support in the executive order creating the FERA in August 1933. Under FERA, state relief administrations received grants (a) to employ teachers on a work relief basis in rural elementary schools; (b) to establish and conduct nursery schools; (c) to employ people who were competent to teach adults how to read and write English; (d) to provide vocational training to adults who, without additional training, would remain perpetually unemployable; (e) to give vocational training to physically handicapped unemployed adults; and (f) to teach the unemployed how to become self-supporting citizens.[7]

In October 1933 the Emergency Education Program was extended to include the establishment of emergency nursery schools. This program was a means to employ more teachers and to provide a support system for young children from impoverished or disintegrating families. Its purpose was to improve the morale of the children and their parents through special programs that involved the whole family. This form of day care also freed parents from supervisory care and allowed them to devote themselves full-time to the task of finding a job.[8]

The program was moved with little disruption to the WPA in 1935, when FERA was abolished. Under the WPA the goals of the Emergency Education Program took on a broader, more sweeping and progressive tone, although the function within the communities did not change in any significant manner. Hopkins listed before Congress the following eight objectives:

1. to reduce illiteracy and to provide educational opportunities for persons who [had] been denied the usual privileges of public education
2. to foster and increase understanding on the part of American citizens of the economic, political, and social problems which confront[ed] the nation and affect[ed] the welfare of all citizens
3. to assist in the naturalization of the alien population of the United States by providing education in the fundamentals of American citizenship
4. to strengthen American home and family life through educational services to parents
5. to safeguard the welfare of small children born into underprivileged homes
6. to provide vocational training for unemployed men and women and to assist these unemployed to re-establish themselves on a self-supporting basis
7. to help men and women to develop constructive interests to occupy their leisure time
8. to provide opportunities for continuing education for young people whose educational careers were temporarily cut short by the depression.[9]

These eight objectives represented a political decision to present the program through the broadest possible description in order to create a constituency for adult education. Literacy education already had a constituency, and when expanded to include citizenship training and patriotic instruction, it appealed to the public concerned about the influence of radicals among the unemployed. Family support, as shown in preschool classes and parenting and homemaking classes, also had a broad appeal. Adult education was also defined in the broadest manner to include those individuals over the age of sixteen who were not in school on a regular basis.[10]

The Emergency Education Program was not without its critics, most of whom were from the conservative right. James Truslow Adams, writing in *Frontiers of American Culture*, questioned the federal government's involvement in education, noting that it had been the prerogative of the states. He also expressed concerns about the federal influence on educational content.[11]

One aspect of the program that was singled out for attack from the right was the worker education component. Workers' education was described in the second objective of Hopkins to instruct workers about the economic and social forces around them. The classes were a form of leadership training for industrial workers to expand their horizons through discussion groups and extensive readings. From 1933 until it was abolished along with the rest of the WPA in 1952, workers' education was criticized by Republicans in Congress, investigated by the House Un-American Activities Committee, and criticized by the American Legion, the Liberty Leagues, and the Daughters of the American Revolution for stirring up class hatred, for discussing socialism and communism, and for singing radical songs, including the "Internationale."[12]

There were other critics of the Emergency Education Program, but their complaints were centered on racial discrimination and underrepresentation of blacks in the program. Ira de Reid and Doxey Wilkerson, two black federal employees, criticized the FERA and WPA programs for the underemployment of black teachers and a limitation of opportunities for black students in adult education programs. Statistics were not kept on the number of unemployed black teachers, but estimates noted that these numbers were disproportionately large. Black teachers were employed in large numbers in the poorer rural districts of the Southeast and were most vulnerable to layoffs.[13]

The chief purpose of the program was to give employment to qualified teachers. The program was decentralized and responsibility delegated to state and local officials, with oversight authority given to regional administrators. Local relief administrators were responsible for certifying the names of people who were eligible for employment as "work relief." Local school authorities had final approval over all teachers before any could offer courses. Pay was determined by the WPA, although local school authorities determined the number of hours and the school assignments.[14]

New Deal policymakers were insistent that education should be the function of the states and not the responsibility of the federal government. For

blacks, reliance on state and local authorities, particularly in the South, meant
being placed in the hands of officials many of whom had systematically
established separate and inferior education systems based on race. Of particular concern was the refusal of local school authorities to certify unemployed black teachers. This lack of certified teachers severely limited the
number of adult education classes for blacks in both the North and the
South, for it was the policy of the WPA to employ black teachers to teach
black students in accordance with residential patterns and societal customs
as well as Southern segregation statutes.[15]

The FERA did attempt to forestall underrepresentation in certain regions
by establishing a minimum standard of participation for blacks. Official policy
stated:

Since in proportion to the population unemployment among Negroes is equal to if
not even greater than unemployment among other groups and since educational
opportunities for Negroes are notably inadequate, equity demands that educational
relief to Negroes be at least at the level of their percentage of the population in each
state.[16]

Black employment statistics were kept for sixteen Southern states. The
percentage of black teachers in WPA did not equal their percentage in the
general population. In addition, black teachers in urban centers of the South,
including Atlanta and New Orleans, were overrepresented, whereas black
teachers in rural areas were underrepresented. The problem was particularly
acute in Mississippi, where "a large number of needy unemployed white
people exert[ed] a powerful influence upon any effort that [was] made to
serve two racial groups on a population basis."[17]

There were also few black supervisors, particularly in the rural South.
Resistance to black supervisors was reported in the northern states of Iowa,
Minnesota, and Ohio. Black teachers who lived in predominantly white areas
also suffered discrimination. Few districts were willing to appoint black
teachers to instruct whites in adult education classes.[18]

The WPA acknowledged that the qualifications of black teachers were
equal or superior to the qualifications of white WPA teachers. The high
quality of black teachers was attributed to several factors, all linked to the
economy. In the 1920s the size of black colleges expanded dramatically.
The majority of students were preparing to follow teaching careers, although
a sizable minority elected careers in business, social work, and medicine.
By 1929 few black college students were choosing majors other than education, opting for the "most secure profession." In addition, other college-
trained blacks were losing their positions in business and the professions and
were entering teacher-training institutes in order to be certified to work in
a classroom, thereby swelling the pool of qualified blacks for employment

as teachers. The WPA guidelines were flexible and did not require previous classroom experience.[19]

Another factor was the inability of qualified and experienced black teachers to get placement in permanent positions throughout the Depression and war years. The emergency program specifically stipulated that no relief funds could be used to employ people in substitution of teachers regularly employed or to supplant any educational activity already budgeted in the school systems. There were violations of this provision that prevented black teachers from being rehired. Black teachers remained outside the regular workforce not only through the 1930s, but also into the war years. It was observed that "the economic depression hit the Negro harder than the white as evidenced in the quality of those available to be hired on a relief program."[20]

Black teachers were particularly hard hit by a provision in the Emergency Relief Appropriation Act of 1939 that made it mandatory to terminate workers in the WPA who had been employed in relief jobs for eighteen or more continuous months. Many black teachers had remained in the WPA for more than two years and were forced to leave WPA projects without the prospect of permanent reemployment as teachers.[21]

For blacks who were hired by the WPA, the training programs were important and valuable. An important subtext of the program was to rehabilitate the unemployed teacher and improve his or her skills and morale. Training periods for teachers varied in length from a minimum of two days to a maximum of two weeks in a summer school. The two-week sessions for black teachers were held in historically black colleges, including Atlanta University, Livingstone College, and Fisk University. There were seminars on new methods in teaching, including the use of audiovisual aids. Teaching adults required different methods, and teachers were encouraged to foster discussions in the classroom and de-emphasize learning by repetition. Teachers were also given tips on securing cooperation with the public at large, including advertising techniques to gain larger enrollments. Encouraged to make suggestions, vocational education teachers complained about outmoded instructional machinery and faulty equipment. Several noted with irony that the best equipped classrooms were in the home economics section, which trained black adults for work as domestics. Teachers of general adult education complained that the vocabulary in the reading materials was too simplistic for their adult students. All asked for a wider variety of instructional materials supplied by the WPA. Teachers were provided with reading on black history and culture, particularly during Brotherhood Week, the second week in February.[22]

The teacher-training programs also encompassed discussions on citizenship, interracial relations, and civic responsibility, including voting rights. There were no complaints of radicalism similar to the ones brought against the WPA workers' education classes. The discussions appeared to be carefully controlled. The role of the NAACP was characterized in a negative light, particularly in its fight to desegregate professional schools. The discussion centered on the problems that desegregation might cause black schoolteachers who were dependent on a segregated system. Members of the NAACP were described as troublemakers who fostered and thrived on societal discontent. Cooperation with the white civic organizations was discussed. Teachers were encouraged to conform to voter registration requirements, including paying their poll taxes in areas of the upper South and in southern cities where blacks were allowed to vote.[23]

The Emergency Education Program also had an impact on the thousands of blacks who signed up for adult education courses. About 1 million men and women were taught how to read and write. Literacy classes had been a staple of adult education classes since the turn of the century. Most classes were aimed at an immigrant population that spoke English as a second language. The WPA modified that approach to teach native-born Americans how to read. Informal teaching methods that broke down barriers between teacher and students were encouraged. In Georgia the WPA cited 13,854 blacks who were unable to read and write at the time of their enrollment in adult classes; 12,771 enrollees learned how to read and write within six months. The WPA did not provide a precise definition of the term literate, but if moderately accurate, the program was a significant success. However, the WPA could only begin to address the educational disparity between blacks and whites. The median school grade reached by black adults in the United States in 1940 was 5.7 years as compared with 8.8 years for native-born white adults.[24]

In rural areas of the South, the WPA offered classes in home and family care, hygiene, pest control, sanitation, poultry and swine raising, gardening, home canning, and pottery. There were relatively few WPA classes in rural areas. The extension service of the Department of Agriculture held classes in similar subjects, and both agencies wanted to avoid duplication. The WPA also emphasized cooperation with local authorities and utilized community buildings. Sometimes such facilities were difficult to secure for classes to teach black adults, owing to deep-seated racial enmity in the rural areas of the South.[25]

In urban areas the classes were more varied, and included instruction in art and music. There were clear limitations, however, and blacks were not offered the same choices as whites in vocational training. During the period 1940 to 1943 the restrictions became more pronounced. The WPA in 1940 began to redirect its efforts toward job training for immediate employment opportunities in the defense industries. Because of the increase in defense spending, hitherto moribund industries began to produce armaments. By 1942 industries on the West Coast were desperate for skilled and semiskilled labor. Despite the shortage, blacks were not hired in large numbers. Even after Roosevelt's issuance of Executive Order 8802, which prohibited racial discrimination in hiring and promotion in defense industries and government agencies, plants continued to discriminate.[26]

The WPA cited an improved ability to place white trainees in defense industry positions. Indeed, by 1940 the overall employment picture for whites had improved dramatically. In April 1940, 22 percent of blacks in the labor market were unemployed, compared with 17.7 percent of white workers. In August 1940 the unemployment rate for whites was 13 percent, but the rate for blacks had declined only one-tenth of 1 percent, leaving 21.9 percent still unemployed. Blacks could not be placed, even those who had completed training in such needed skills as welding and tool making. WPA workers in 1941 were instructed to inquire into the acceptability of skilled black workers to potential employers. It was judged better to offer training in areas where blacks could be placed.[27]

The WPA began to offer more courses in domestic and household services in response to a nationwide demand for more black maids and butlers. As white domestics were being hired as unskilled laborers in defense industries, blacks were asked to fill the void. In San Antonio, Texas, the WPA was given the use of the Bellinger estate for the purposes of training maids. Black WPA trainees were instructed in the proper housekeeping techniques and caretaking skills in this elaborate setting. The program was able to place all of its graduates. In a Texas survey conducted by WPA, black participants ranked day care for their children, the school lunch programs, and the adult literacy classes as the most beneficial. Valued most highly in the estimation of employers was the household training program.[28]

The demand for black maids was not confined to the South. In Wisconsin there were more than 160 requests for domestics. The WPA was able to supply only twenty-two, giving as an excuse the reluctance of blacks to enroll in the courses. Blacks preferred to work even as unskilled laborers in the defense plants for higher wages and better working conditions. Wisconsin WPA administrators gave themselves high marks for providing employment opportunities for blacks. Blacks were not so complimentary on the WPA. One elevator operator stated: "The WPA is all right to us but somehow we just don't belong to the permanent things."[29]

It was never intended for the WPA to be permanent. Congress voted to dismantle the WPA in June 1943, citing that the war emergency had solved the unemployment crisis. Congress chose to ignore the significant number of black trainees still on its relief rolls. In December 1942, 24.2 percent of the black trainees had not been placed, whereas only 8.6 percent of whites remained on the rolls.[30]

There were several programs conducted by the government that attempted to supersede the training functions of the WPA. One such program in the Office of Education was the Vocational Training Program for War Production Workers. This program was aimed primarily at adults with minimal educational backgrounds. One segment of the program sought to help skilled workers in war industries improve their knowledge. The other part helped unemployed men and women prepare for war jobs. The program contained a nondiscrimination clause:

No trainee under the foregoing appropriations shall be discriminated against because of sex, race, or color; and where separate schools are required by law for separate population groups to the extent needed, an equitable provision shall be made for facilities and training of like quality.

Black trainees were 12 percent of the preemployment segment, although enrollment statistics in no way indicated the quality of the training or equitable expenditures. Although 12 percent of the training stations were available to blacks, only 6 percent of the equipment was allocated for blacks. Blacks were also enrolled in sham programs. One visitor noted that "in one course for 150 shipfitter helpers . . . the sole shop equipment consisted of some shipyard pictures clipped from *Life* magazine and a 'bathtub navy,' purchased out of the instructor's pocket at the five and ten."[31]

Only 4 percent of the participants in the supplementary training program for skilled workers were black. Many blacks were ineligible for this training because they did not hold skilled positions in defense industries. Despite the efforts of the Fair Employment Practices Committee to encourage the hiring and promotion of blacks and other minorities, many defense industries continued to bar blacks from skilled positions. An officer of the Vultee Aircraft Company spoke for many in his field when he asserted: "We do not believe it advisable to include colored people with our regular work force. We may at a later date, be in a position to add some colored people in minor capacities such as porters and cleaners." The exclusion policies of many skilled craft unions effectively prevented blacks from being employed in the heavily unionized maritime, railroad, aviation, and construction trades, all of which were vital in the war effort.[32]

The educational and training programs of the WPA and related agencies evolved throughout the Depression and World War II to meet demands of the public, the economy, and the war crisis. Blacks did not enjoy the full benefit of these programs because of limitations imposed by WPA officials, state and local authorities, and public and private employers.

THE CIVILIAN CONSERVATION CORPS

The Civilian Conservation Corps (CCC) was another emergency employment agency that contained educational programs. Established in 1933, the CCC was a work program for unemployed young men between the ages of eighteen and twenty-five. Enrollees spent forty hours per week on projects designed to give them useful work in such activities as erosion control, wildlife protection, rural road construction, restoration of historical sites, and national reforestation. The CCC also provided general vocational training and basic instruction in reading and writing.

The CCC was a source of constant criticism from the NAACP and other civil rights organizations for blatant racial discrimination in all facets of its program. The director, Robert Fechner, was a conservative, Southern-born vice president of the American Federation of Labor who segregated CCC camps, not only in the South, but also in the Midwest. In addition, the CCC was the archetypical decentralized organization. The Labor Department selected enrollees, the War Department transported the young men to the camps that it administered, and the Departments of Agriculture and Interior supervised the actual conservation projects. The Office of Education administered the vocational training programs.[33]

Critics of CCC policy had to first understand the chain of responsibility and lobby that agency for change. The CCC was able to use its decentralized structure as a convenient excuse to avoid responses to criticism. When the Julius Rosenwald Fund complained to the Department of Labor concerning treatment of blacks in CCC camps, the Department of Labor replied that it was responsible only for the selection of trainees, not for the administration of the camps. Under pressure from civil rights groups, the enrollments of blacks did increase from a low of 5 percent in 1935 to a high of 11 percent in 1938.[34]

The Office of Education was responsible for advising the War Department on the content of the training programs and the employment of camp educational personnel. Unlike the WPA, which stressed flexibility and creative innovation in the classroom, the CCC stressed a more traditional and structured teaching environment. Teaching personnel were under the supervision of the company commander and were expected to devise programs that corrected deficiencies in education, citizenship, and character. Teachers were told that the enrollees were, as a group, "failures" who had to be instructed in a simple and direct manner. After receiving complaints of poor teaching in the camps, the CCC began in 1936 to require their teachers to attend a four-week training period.[35]

More than 1,200 part-time teachers were engaged in instruction of blacks in segregated camps. The literacy program in the CCC, as in the WPA, was its most successful. The requirement that all enrollees sign their name to receive their paychecks induced thousands to enroll in literacy classes. Black teachers were advised to motivate students by pointing out "successful colored men who have advanced through learning and indicating the obstacles which an illiterate encounters." One camp, Fort Meade in Maryland, was able, through the cooperation of the Association for the Study of Negro Life and History, to receive monthly material on black history.[36]

Those who read above the eighth-grade level could attend evening classes in nearby towns. Opportunities for blacks depended on the availability of high schools or adult schools for blacks. There were few high schools for blacks in the South, particularly in the rural areas. The CCC did allow campers to take correspondence courses through black college extension schools.[37]

Camp advisors described black campers as unrealistic, noting that they all want "white-collar jobs." CCC officials advised blacks to train for jobs available in the workplace, such as janitors, chauffeurs, table waiters, and dishwashers. Advisors noted that few black teenagers did sign up for these vocational classes, and those that did lacked motivation. Blacks continued to press for greater representation in the administration of camps, and better opportunities for vocational training until the CCC disbanded in July 1943.[38]

NATIONAL YOUTH ADMINISTRATION

The CCC was an incomplete response to the problems of young people, catering to the most desperate cases, and was primarily an all-male enterprise. The children of the middle class were also in danger of being lost. The major objectives of the National Youth Administration (NYA) were to provide funds for the part-time employment of needy high school, college, and graduate students aged sixteen to twenty-four, and to provide part-time employment for young people no longer in school but out of work. Both objectives sought to combine work relief, guidance counseling, and vocational training.[39]

Roosevelt appointed Aubrey Williams, a Southern liberal, to be the head of the new agency. Williams elected to rely on grass-roots support and encouraged local control and development. He set only the broadest policy guidelines, allowing state and local officials to fill in the details. He did develop a Division of Negro Affairs headed by black educator Mary McLeod Bethune. She set a broad agenda, which included actively recruiting blacks to the programs and allocating funds for black high schools and colleges to hire NYA students. The student assistance program provided work on college campuses and in the local communities. Students tutored and assisted in classrooms, laboratories, and museums. Others worked as general office assistants. A special fund was allocated for the use of black college students whose needs were not being met through regular appropriations. Another special fund, administered by the national office, gave scholarships to black graduate students. Even with this special infusion of funds, black participation in the student programs was only 7.4 percent, far below the 15 percent representation of black youth in the total youth relief population.[40]

The vocational training program of NYA also actively sought black participation. Of the youth participating in this program, 10.7 percent of the group was black. As with other agencies that relied on local and state leadership, the racial mores of the region determined the degree of participation and the opportunities in NYA. Programs were gender-specific, with girls given courses in home management, child care, domestic service, canning, cooperative purchasing, and marketing, while boys were given projects in house building, playground improvement, and furniture repair. In rural areas boys were given instruction in soil conservation and landscaping. Unlike the WPA and CCC, the NYA was not seeking to develop expertise in these students. Classes were primarily a vehicle for contact with counselors who encouraged students to return to school.[41]

The Division of Negro Affairs suffered most markedly from a lack of black administrators and counselors. A special position of state administrative assistant was created for each state with a sizable black relief population. At the peak of the program in 1938, there were twenty-three black administrative assistants, but their numbers quickly dwindled. By 1940, of the 402 members of administrative staffs in five regions, only 30 (including secretaries) were black.[42]

In 1940 the NYA began to shift away from counseling and unemployment relief to instruction in defense industry work. The NYA recruited heavily among women who were entering the workforce for the first time and blacks, both men and women, who had been underutilized. The NYA was confronted with pressures from defense industries to train blacks in noncompetitive skills. Unlike the WPA and the CCC, the NYA elected to institute an equality of opportunity program that sought to provide blacks with training in welding, radio technology, and aviation mechanics. The NYA received criticism from craft unions and conservative politicians and had difficulty in finding instructors for the trainees. Yet the NYA was able to place blacks trained in skilled trades in plants in Pennsylvania, New Jersey, and Delaware.[43]

THE DEPARTMENT OF AGRICULTURE, THE AGRICULTURAL ADJUSTMENT ADMINISTRATION, AND THE FARM SECURITY ADMINISTRATION

Adult education in agriculture consisted of several programs administered by different agencies and departments, all with responsibilities in farming. The Cooperative Extension Service of the Department of Agriculture was a continuation of a service in place since the passage of the 1914 Smith-Lever Act. Other programs were instituted to instruct farmers on the most efficient means to survive the Depression and how to benefit from the New Deal agricultural subsidies.

During the New Deal the Cooperative Extension Service operated in more than 3,000 counties and employed more than 9,000 extension agents. More than 1 million men, women, and children participated in its program of farm demonstration, home demonstration, and boys' and girls' club work. Farm demonstration work was conducted by agricultural advisors known as county agents. These agents served as teachers without classrooms who showed farmers the latest techniques in production. Agents distributed literature and arranged for local demonstration projects. The county agent became, next to the local politician and the plantation owner, the most important person in the county. The home economics agent worked with rural farm families in demonstrating methods to improve child care, nutrition, family relations, and sanitation. A smaller number of agents worked as counselors for boys' and girls' clubs.[44]

Blacks participated in the extension programs, many living in the South in abject poverty. Indeed, 96 percent of all blacks living in rural areas were living in the sixteen southern states. Contact with the county agent meant the different between access to modern technology and continued isolation and ignorance. Blacks were less likely than whites to have this vital contact. In 1930 there were 2,342,129 white and 881,687 black farm operators. In 1935 there were 1,515 white and 185 black county agricultural agents. The potential clientele of the average black agent was more than three times the clientele of the white agent. Also, county agents instructed farm owners and tenant farmers, who had some responsibility for crop management and selection. Agents ignored sharecroppers, 40 percent of whom were black.[45]

After 1935 the percentage of black agents decreased in part because of the passage of the Bankhead-Jones Act. This legislation increased by 100 percent the federal subsidies to the states for agriculture. States were given discretionary control over the distribution of federal funds. Many southern states elected to expand extension programs only for whites, hire more white agents, and develop cooperative research programs with white agricultural colleges. Although a few black professors from Tuskegee and from Hampton Institute served as consultants to the extension service, black land grant colleges were not formally included in research activities.[46]

The extension service, despite its shortcomings, was considered to be "a marvelous boon to the Negro farmer." When served by a "good or competent Negro extension agent," the quality of life of that individual farmer improved measurably.[47]

The Agricultural Adjustment Administration (AAA) and the Farm Security Administration (FSA) also conducted educational programs in the field. The AAA introduced bureaucratic complexities to the lives of the small farmers who wanted to qualify for a crop reduction program of federal subsidies. The AAA county agents' responsibilities included instruction of compliance regulations, as well as local administration. There were only three black agents in the field. In a survey of black farmers about AAA regulations, many admitted that their understanding was vague because no one explained the instructions.[48]

The FSA, under Will Alexander, a Southern liberal, did employ black agents and supervisors who instructed blacks on how to qualify for loans to retain or purchase farms. Many gave courses on simple bookkeeping and how to fill out forms. In addition, the FSA conducted a limited program of experimental homesteads in which young black farmers could intern on efficiently run modern farms before they moved on to their own farms. More than 1,700 black families lived on FSA homestead projects, which were designated adult educational centers.[49]

The demands of the war also affected farmers and the agricultural education program. Farmers were given quotas to grow crops and raise livestock. Blacks were seldom consulted by local boards that determined quotas of production. Blacks complained that AAA agents were not assisting blacks in acquiring skills necessary to meet their goals. The numbers of AAA and extension agents were reduced by World War II. A proposal to use unemployed black schoolteachers as part-time field agents was rejected. The ranks of black farmers also thinned during the war. Local Southern draft boards were not sympathetic to the plight of the small black farmer, and many black farmers were drafted. County agents did not inform black farmers that they were eligible for deferments as critical labor for the national defense.[50]

THE TENNESSEE VALLEY AUTHORITY

The Tennessee Valley Authority (TVA) incorporated several elements of adult education in its program of revitalization of the seven-state watershed of the Tennessee River. By constructing dams along the Tennessee River, the Authority planned to bring about flood control, improved use of marginal lands for agriculture and recreation, and better navigation on the Tennessee River. The TVA announced that in order to bring about a new industrialized and modern valley, the local inhabitants would have to improve technical and vocational skills. The TVA inaugurated an ambitious program to provide vocational training for all TVA workers and to support public and private educational institutions through subsidies and special TVA-run programs.[51]

Blacks living in the valley were promised employment by the TVA in the same proportion to their number in the total population of the area. Black employment from 1933 to 1945 in these areas averaged 10 percent, close to the 11 percent population for the entire valley. Yet these statistics were deceptive. In the TVA, quotas were filled through hiring blacks in temporary, unskilled positions that lasted for only six months.[52]

The short tenure of employment was one of many factors that limited participation of blacks in the vocational training programs of the TVA. Although the TVA had a small black training staff, it had little input in the development of the training program. The TVA frequently worked with other New Deal agencies to set up a training program for a dam site. At Wheeler Dam, near Chattanooga, Tennessee, the TVA used teachers from the WPA to conduct classes in adult education and agents for the extension service to establish demonstration farms and teach home economics. The TVA also contracted with local colleges to conduct training programs.[53]

J. Max Bond, an educator from Atlanta, headed the Training Division for Negro Workers from 1934 to 1938. Bond was a careful observer of racial conditions in the TVA and sought to bring about changes quietly and effectively. In 1938 he resigned, frustrated over a lack of progress. Bond was particularly upset over the restricted opportunities for blacks in the skilled trades. There were three classes open for black men and one class for black women. Men could take courses labeled "Janitors Training," "Skilled Handymen," and "Automobile Oiling." Women could train to be charwomen.[54]

Black employees were excluded from all apprenticeship programs. The skilled crafts unions that conducted the apprenticeship courses in cooperation with the TVA restricted their membership to whites only. The TVA had signed a series of agreements with the labor unions, promising to use only skilled tradesmen who were members of a union. During World War II, in compliance with Executive Order 8802, the TVA pressured unions to expunge all racially exclusive statements from their by-laws. Although the unions complied, no blacks were made members of the unions.[55]

When the TVA established a program to train white University of Tennessee students for permanent work as technicians and engineers, black leaders in Knoxville called for a similar program for black Knoxville College students. The TVA began a program to train college students to be janitors and cleaning women. Knoxville students were insulted, and boycotted the program, despite the relatively high wages offered.[56]

The relation of the TVA to the black community of Chattanooga was somewhat better. The TVA conducted classes in citizenship as part of its adult education program. In 1935 the TVA sought to transform its teaching into practice. The TVA openly courted black political support for a referendum calling for the city to buy electricity from the TVA. Blacks in Chattanooga had a history of voting in city elections, although the usual turnout was low. To ensure a large turnout, the TVA was able to get the city government to waive the poll tax for this election. Blacks voted overwhelmingly for TVA electricity.[57]

The TVA sponsored the People's College in cooperation with the Chattanooga Community Council, a group of black schoolteachers, ministers, and skilled laborers. The purpose of the college was "to acquaint blacks with their problems, to encourage the organization of permanent study groups, and to develop a group of volunteer leaders." More than 1,100 people attended the lecture and discussion sessions. The largest numbers came to hear Rayford Logan, a black historian, speak on "Fascism, Communism, and Democracy as Each Relates to American Minorities," and Ira de A. Reid, a member of "Roosevelt's Black Cabinet," lecture on "Social Security and the Negro."[58]

The war did not create significant opportunities for blacks in the TVA. Still relegated to unskilled and semiskilled positions, blacks remained out of skilled positions and apprenticeship training programs despite shortages of manpower and the strategic necessity of building dams to supply electricity for the atomic energy research in nearby Oak Ridge, Tennessee. In 1945 vocational training for blacks offered the same courses with one addition: blacks could train for positions as fertilizer plant and chemical plant operators. The TVA had decided to transfer most operations in the fertilizer plants at Wilson Dam over to blacks. Although these jobs were permanent, semi-skilled, and well paying, they were considered undesirable because of the poor working conditions and the noxious fumes.[59]

This analysis of adult education for blacks in the federal government reveals the extent to which adult education served different functions in the New Deal agencies and departments. For the WPA, adult education programs were a means to create employment for out-of-work teachers. That the programs themselves had a positive impact, particularly the literacy classes, was a bonus. Adult education in the CCC served to keep young men busy in their leisure hours and out of trouble. The NYA sought to give enrichment classes and financial support to students in order for them to complete their education. Adult education in agriculture tried to produce better informed and more efficient farmers who, during the Depression, learned how to survive crop reductions and government bureaucracy and, during the war, learned how to meet quotas on production. Adult education in the TVA attempted to provide a better trained workforce for an increasingly technologically sophisticated Tennessee valley.

Blacks tried to benefit from these adult education programs. Whether in the Bethune-led Negro Division of the NYA, the liberal FSA, the cautious WPA, the decentralized CCC, the pro-union TVA, or the conservative-led Agriculture Department, blacks suffered from restricted employment and vocational opportunities. Political pressure from conservative factions and the limited vision of white employers contributed to the problems inherent in the individual programs.

All programs used a population percentage as a standard to measure progress. Most published reports or articles stated that the agency or department had reached its percentage goal in the participation of blacks. Statistics were artfully used to mask low overall percentages of participation of blacks in training and relief programs. In the interest of maintaining a percentage quota, agencies and departments were forced, for the first time, to keep careful records of blacks in the federal government, providing a useful data base for future comparisons.

Contrary to popular image, the war years did not produce a perceptible change in opportunities for blacks, particularly in vocational training. In the case of the WPA, regressive training for domestics superceded training for work in defense plants. Only the NYA managed to train and place skilled workers in defense plants in the Northeast. If adult education in the Depression and World War II was a mirror into the future, then that future, with few exceptions, resembled the past.

NOTES

1. Joyce Kornbluth, *A New Deal for Workers' Education: The Worker's Service Program 1933–1942* (Urbana: University of Illinois Press, 1987), 24–26.

2. Ibid., 24–25; Malcolm Knowles, *The Adult Education Movement in the U.S.* (New York: Holt Rinehart & Winston, 1962), v-vii.

3. Roy Wilkins, "Adult Education Program of the NAACP," *Journal of Negro Education* 14 (Summer 1945): 403–406.

4. Kornbluth, *Workers' Education*, 25; Robert S. McElvaine, *The Great Depression* (New York: Random House, 1984), 81–94.

5. Nancy Weiss, *Farewell to the Party of Lincoln* (Princeton, N.J.: Princeton University Press, 1983), 47–49.

6. For more information on discrimination in New Deal agencies, see Weiss, *Farewell to the Party of Lincoln*; Jack Kirby, *Black Americans in the Roosevelt Era* (Knoxville: University of Tennessee Press, 1985); Raymond Wolters, *Negroes and the Great Depression* (Westport, Conn.: Greenwood Press, 1970); Harvard Sitkoff, *A New Deal for Blacks* (New York: Oxford University Press, 1978).

7. Beulah Amidon, "Emergency Education," *Survey Graphic*, (September 1934): 415–417; James Atkins, "The Participation of Negroes in Pre-School and Adult Education Programs," *Journal of Negro Education* 7 (July 1938):345–348.

8. Atkins, "Participation of Negroes," 346.

9. Ibid.

10. Kornbluth, *Workers' Education*, 24–26.

11. James Truslow Adams, *Frontiers of American Culture: A Study of Adult Education in a Democracy* (New York: Charles Scribner, 1944).

12. Kornbluth, *Workers' Education*, 100–101.

13. Ira de A. Reid, "The Development of Adult Education for Negroes in the U.S.," *Journal of Negro Education* 14 (Summer 1945):299–306; Doxey Wilkerson, *Special Problems of Negro Education* (Washington, D.C.: Government Printing Press, 1939), 134–136.

14. James Atkins, "Progress Report on the Negro Unit of the Education and Training Section," 1940, 1–6, WPA Files, National Archives, Washington, D.C.

15. Ibid.; Forrester B. Washington, "Progress Report on Negro Work in Training Programs and Emergency Relief," 1934, FERA Files, National Archives, Washington, D.C.; Atkins, "Participation of Negroes," 349–350.

16. Atkins, "Participation of Negroes," 349.

17. Atkins, "Field Report, Mississippi, Sept. 8–12, 1941," WPA Files; Atkins, "Field Report, Louisiana, January 17, 1942" p. 5, WPA Files.

18. Atkins, "Report of Field Trips, 1941–1942," WPA Files, Washington, D.C. Atkins, a black educator who served as a consultant for the WPA, traveled extensively throughout the United States evaluating the effectiveness of the training programs for black WPA teachers. A cautious critic, Atkins nevertheless described in detail the programs that worked and those programs that did not.

19. Atkins, "Progress Report on the Negro Unit 1934," 2–4, FERA Files.

20. Morse Cartwright, "History of Adult Education in the U.S.," *Journal of Negro Education* 14 (Summer 1945):289.

21. James Atkins to Dr. Ambrose Caliver, March 1, 1941, 1–2, WPA Files.

22. Atkins Report of Field Trips: Arkansas, February 1941; Oklahoma, February 1941; Louisiana, January 5–8, 1942; Ohio, December 1940, WPA Files.

23. Atkins Report Arkansas February 1941, 2–4; Luther Jackson, "Citizenship Training: A Neglected Area in Adult Education," *Journal of Negro Education* 14 (Summer 1945):477–481. Also see L. D. Reddick, "Adult Education and the Improvement of Race Relations," *Journal of Negro Education* 14 (Summer 1945):492–493. Reddick is very critical of the lack of political content in the citizenship classes conducted in teacher-training sessions. The "red baiting" of the WPA programs produced administrators who chose survival over programs that advocated social change. He observed that "courage and social intelligence found no welcome; caution and optimum loyalty were preferable. Many of the school men who assisted in these endeavors were likewise insecure or markedly conservative."

24. James Atkins to James Simmons, January 9, 1939; Atkins, "Participation of Negroes," 352; Reid, "Development of Adult Education for Negroes," 305.

25. L. R. Alderman, director of the Education and Training Section, "Progress Report 1940," 9,10,16. WPA Files.

26. For a more detailed account of the impact of Executive Order 8802 and the Fair Employment Practices Committee, see Louis Kesselman, *The Social Politics of FEPC* (Chapel Hill: University of North Carolina Press, 1948); Louis Ruchames, *Race, Jobs, and Politics: The Story of FEPC* (New York: Columbia University Press, 1953); Paul Burstein, *Discrimination, Jobs, and Politics*, (Chicago: University of Chicago Press, 1985).

27. Memo, Thelma McKelvey to Martin Carpenter Re: Program Selection in Vocational Training of National Defense Workers, 5, WPA Files; Herbert Hill, *Black Labor and the American Labor System* (Madison: University of Wisconsin Press, 1985), 175–177.

28. Atkins Field Trip, Texas, November 1941, WPA Files.

29. Atkins Field Trip, Wisconsin, June 1941, WPA Files.

30. Memo, William Easten to George Field, December 3, 1942, WPA Files.

31. Herman Branson, "The Training of Negroes for War Industries in World War II," *Journal of Negro Education* 14 (Summer 1945):378–379; memo, Rall Grigsby, Re: "Data on Negro Defense Training," May 2, 1942, 4, WPA Files. Also see Robert Weaver, "The Defense Program and the Negro," *Opportunity* (November 1940).

32. Hill, *Black Labor*, 177; Roy Wilkins, NAACP, to Frank Persons, Department of Labor, May 31, 1933; George Arthur, YMCA to Frank Persons, June 11, 1935, WPA Files.

33. Howard Oxley, "The Civilian Conservation Corps and the Education of the Negro," *Journal of Negro Education* 7 (July 1938):375; for a more critical account, see John Salmond, "The Civilian Conservation Corps and the Negro," *Journal of American History*, 52 (June 1965):75–88; John Salmond, "Civilian Conservation Corps," in *Franklin Roosevelt: His Life and Times* eds. Otis Graham and M. Wander (Boston: G. K. Hall, 1985), 62–64.

34. Garth Akridge, Julius Rosenwald Fund, to Eleanor Roosevelt, April 19, 1935; E. Roosevelt to Frances Perkins, April 1935; Robert Fechner, director CCC to Frank

Persons, April 18, 1935; Akridge to Frank Persons, July 18, 1935. Department of Labor Files, National Archives, Washington, D.C.

35. Samuel Harby, *A Study of Education in the Civilian Conservation Corps Camp of the Second Corps Area, April 1933–March 1937*, (New York: Edwards Brother, Inc., 1938).

36. Howard Oxley, "CCC," 379.

37. Marian Thompson Wright, "Negro Youth and the Federal Emergency Programs: CCC and NYA," *Journal of Negro Education* 9 (July 1940):400–402, 404; memo L. R. Reynolds, June 9, 1933, CCC Files, National Archives, Washington, D.C.

38. Oxley, "CCC," 381.

39. Wright, "Negro Youth," 401; John Salmond, "The National Youth Administration," *Franklin Roosevelt: His Life and Times*, 278–279.

40. The National Youth Administration Final Report, 33–35, FERA Files; Walter Daniel and Carrol Miller, "The Participation of the Negro in the National Youth Administration Program," *Journal of Negro Education* 7 (July 1938):361.

41. NYA Final Report, 33–35.

42. Daniel and Miller, "The NYA," 359–361.

43. NYA Final Report, 129–130, 132.

44. Doxey Wilkerson, "The Participation of Negroes in the Federally Aided Program of Agricultural and Home Economics Extension," *Journal of Negro Education* 7 (July 1938):331–334.

45. Ibid.

46. Wilkerson, "Participation of Negroes," 336–343; John Davis, president of West Virginia State College, to Henry Wallace, Sec. of Agriculture, December 8, 1937; Wallace to Davis, January 28, 1938; memo, James Jardine to P. H. Appleby Re: Extension Service, December 30, 1937, Secretary of Agriculture Files, National Archives, Washington, D.C.

47. Jane McAllister and Dorothy McAllister, "Adult Education for Negroes in Rural Areas," *Journal of Negro Education* 14 (Summer 1945):337–340; memo, Thomas Roberts to Roy Reid Re: Field Trip, February 28–March 24, 1942, Secretary of Agriculture Files.

48. J. D. LeCron to Charles Brown, December 16, 1937; Henry Wallace to Leon Harris, National Federation of Colored Farmers, April 19, 1940; Report of Inquiries and Field Observations Among the Negro Farmers in the Present Emergency, June 26, 1942, Secretary of Agriculture Files.

49. For a general analysis of New Deal agricultural policies, see Paul Mertz, *New Deal Policy and Southern Rural Poverty* (Baton Rouge: Louisiana State University Press, 1978). The best analysis of the Farm Security Administration is Sidney Baldwin, *Poverty and Politics: The Rise and Decline of the Farm Security Administration* (Chapel Hill: University of North Carolina Press, 1968).

50. Report of Inquiries and Field Observations Among Negro Farmers, 4–8.

51. For a critique of the promise of the TVA, see Phillip Selznick, *TVA and the Grass Roots* (New York: Harper & Row, 1966); Michael McDonald and John Muldowny, *TVA and the Dispossessed* (Knoxville: University of Tennessee Press, 1982); Nancy Grant, *TVA and Black Americans: Planning for the Status Quo*, (Philadelphia: Temple University Press, 1989).

52. See Grant, *TVA and Black Americans*, chapter on employment of blacks in the TVA.

53. J. Max Bond, "The Education Program for Negroes in the TVA," *Journal of Negro Education* 6 (April 1937):384–389.

54. Ibid., 384–388. For a detailed analysis of TVA training for blacks, see Nancy Grant, "Government Planning and Education for Blacks: The TVA Experience 1933–1945," in *Education and the Rise of the New South*, ed. Arthur White and Ronald Goodenow (Boston: G. K. Hall Publishing Co., 1981), 215–236. J. Max Bond, before quitting, gave the local chapter of the NAACP material to support their investigations of discrimination in TVA.

55. Bond, "Education Program for Negroes," 386–388.

56. B. B. Evans to Roy Wilkins, April 1942, NAACP Papers, Library of Congress, Washington, D.C.

57. Gilbert Govan, *The Chattanooga County 1540–1976* (Knoxville: University of Tennessee Press, 1977), 456–458; The National Urban League, "A Study of Economic and Cultural Activities of the Negro Population of Chattanooga, 1947," 23–35, 182–183, Special Collections, Chattanooga Public Library.

58. *Chattanooga Times*, March 15, 1938; pamphlet, "People's College," n.d., 7–10, TVA Files, Knoxville, Tennessee.

59. Grant, *TVA and Black Americans*, chapter on employment in TVA.

13

Post–World War II Manpower Training Programs

Edwin Hamilton

At the close of World War II, black soldiers, on returning home, learned once again that fighting for their country brought them no nearer to full citizenship. Many black soldiers were unable to secure employment despite training and technical skills acquired in the Armed Forces. When the war ended in 1945, there were 695,264 blacks in the Army (8.67 percent of its total strength) and 74 percent who were returning from overseas duty.[1] After the war, there was also a steady increase in the unemployment of civilian black workers who had been recruited and trained through a national program for war jobs in American industries. As these industries reduced their labor force and changed production lines, it was mostly black workers, the last to be hired, who were the first fired. Branson provides an analysis of the specific training black workers received that was preemployment training designed to equip people with menial skills for war jobs. This limited training along with continuing discrimination had a dramatic negative impact on transitional employment.[2] However, the resilience of black workers to find other employment was not to be denied as the country experienced a postwar economic boom that raised the demand for unskilled labor in industries in selected cities across the country. This was a period of relatively full employment for all American workers. In 1948 the unemployment rate for black men was 5.8 percent compared with 3.4 percent for white men.

The federal government played a major role in promoting employment for black workers in the years after the war, and expanded that role to include massive manpower training as the country experienced a series of economic recessions that reflected high levels of unemployment among black and white workers.

This chapter describes the major federal manpower programs in terms of policies and objectives in serving unemployed and underemployed black Americans since World War II. After the war there were no national federal efforts to provide large-scale manpower training until the 1960s. This period marks the beginning of the major federal legislation that emerged to respond to national unemployment problems and trends.

FEDERAL MANPOWER LEGISLATION: A BRIEF OVERVIEW

The first major federal legislation that came about as a result of the rise of unemployment during the post-Korean recessions was the Area Redevelopment Act of 1961 (ARA). The purpose of this Act was to provide employers with federal incentives to locate or expand their businesses in depressed areas of the country. One of the bill's key provisions was a program to retrain the unemployed, thus offering a ready-made workforce to a newly arrived employer.[3] ARA was initially funded in the amount of $10 million and was restricted to depressed areas; it involved a separate training project for each employer.

The Manpower Development and Training Act of 1962 was the second national anti-unemployment program legislation. Originally, the heart of this legislation was full federal financing for the first two years, followed by continued full federal support for on-the-job training but providing only 50 percent matching funds for institutional training of the unemployed in occupations for which there were reasonable expectations of employment. Heads of families with at least three years of labor market experience or heads of farm families with annual incomes below $1,200 could qualify for up to fifty-two weeks of training allowances at levels equal to the average unemployment compensation benefit in the state. Limited numbers of youths aged nineteen to twenty-one years could receive training allowances of $20 per week.[4] The Act originally authorized federal funds of $100 million to be allocated among the states. Principal amendments of the Act were made in 1963, 1965, 1966, and 1967.

The Economic Opportunity Act of 1964 (EOA) was the major federal legislation that undergirded the War on Poverty. The Act was administered by a national Office of Economic Opportunity. Its broad purpose was to eradicate poverty by eliminating the factors that cause it. EOA was intended to be a comprehensive attack on the multiple problems directly related to poverty. The central thrust of the Act was to provide employment-oriented programs. Title IB, Comprehensive Work Training Programs, provided a sequence of unbroken useful training and work opportunities together with appropriate remedial and supportive services to target groups of unemployed and low-income people so that they could obtain and hold regular competitive jobs. The original funding authorization for the Act was around $1 billion.

The Adult Education Act of 1966 is the major legislation that supports programs of adult basic education. This Act expands educational opportunity and encourages the establishment of programs of adult public education, enabling all adults to continue their education to at least the level of completion of secondary school and makes available the means to secure training that enables them to become more employable, productive, and responsible citizens.[5]

The Emergency Employment Act of 1971 (EEA) was passed at a time when the national unemployment rate was about 6 percent. For blacks, the unemployment rate was 10 percent. The Act established a new program of subsidized public service jobs. It authorized $2.25 billion in funding over a two-year period for a temporary program of transitional public employment in state and local governments and extended the decision making to a greater degree than any previous manpower legislation. The Act was implemented with remarkable speed. Nearly $1 billion was disbursed in a single year through grants to 650 agents.

At the heart of the original Comprehensive Employment and Training Act of 1973 (CETA) were Titles I through IV. Title I provided a program of financial assistance to states and certain local governments to plan and operate manpower programs. Title II provided for public service employment programs in areas of substantial unemployment. Title III directed the secretary of labor to operate manpower programs for special target groups and to conduct research, evaluation, and labor market information functions. Title IV reenacted the Job Corps program within the Department of Labor. The Act was amended in 1978, which added Titles V (National Commission for Employment Policy), VI (Public Service Employment), VII (Private Sector Initiative Program), and VIII (Young Adult Conservation Corps). CETA reflected the revenue-sharing concept adopted by the Nixon Administration as part of the proposed New Federalism. The premises supporting decentralization were (a) local authorities better understood what the local needs were and how best to respond to them, and (b) to deal effectively with those needs, there needed to be maximum flexibility in the use of manpower resources that would replace the current system of categorical programs.[6] Billions were allocated under CETA. The CETA legislation expired in 1982.

The Job Training Partnership Act of 1982 (JTPA) shifted major job training program responsibilities from the Department of Labor to state governors and, at the same time, made business and industry partners in the planning, administration, and oversight of the program at both state and local levels. Title I establishes the state and local delivery systems and addresses general program and administrative issues. Title II authorizes funding and establishes requirements for two programs: a year-round training program for disadvantaged adults and youth and a summer youth employment and training program. Title III provides a separate, state-administered training and employment program for dislocated workers. Title IV establishes funding and requirements for federally administered activities, such as Job Corps, Native American programs, and migrant and seasonal farm worker programs.

Title V contains miscellaneous provisions and changes to training-related activities in other federal programs, including state employment service agencies and the Work Incentive Program. JTPA funding for program year 1985 totaled more than $3.6 billion.

SELECTED MANPOWER PROGRAMS OF BLACK PARTICIPATION

The major manpower programs that served large numbers of blacks covered a broad spectrum of purposes and intent. They can be classified primarily under one of three categories: (1) basic education/prevocational, (2) vocational and skills, and (3) work experience or on-the-job training.

Federally Sponsored Programs

Neighborhood Youth Corps (NYC). The NYC was established under the EOA of 1964 to provide useful work experience opportunity to unemployed youths, especially those aged sixteen through twenty-one, both in school and out of school. Its objectives were to improve the employability of its enrollees by enabling them to develop sound work habits, learn basic skills, and acquire a record of successful work experience.

NYC served more blacks than any other manpower program. It was an important program in increasing the high school graduation rates of black youth. A study of NYC participants found that the increased earnings compared with a control group over a period of eighteen months accounted for a greater probability of black youth completing high school as compared with the control group *and* NYC white enrollees.[7] NYC programs operated from 1963 through 1973.

Manpower Development Training Act Programs (MDTA). There are three basic types of MDTA programs: (1) institutional training, usually prevocational, is conducted in classrooms or training centers. (2) On-the-job training (OJT) is conducted under contract agreements between a prime sponsor and a private employer or other suitable agency. The OJT program provides learning in an actual work situation and is designed to train workers for available jobs in industry. (3) OJT-coupled projects provide for linking OJT with supplemental or related instruction, as well as with basic education, prevocational training, or pre-apprenticeship training to fit the training needs of the individual. (Studies and surveys during the early stages of MDTA found that the earning power of blacks, particularly black women, was increased as a result of training.) A detailed study in Michigan found that white participants gained more than black trainees, but the social benefits were greater in the case of blacks because of reduced transfer payments.[8] An analysis of training slots by race revealed that black participants were over-represented in institutional training programs (prevocational, low level skills

Table 13.1
Enrollment by Race in NYC and MDTA Programs, 1966

Program	Enrollees White (%)	Black (%)
Manpower Development Training Act Programs		
Institutional	61.8	35.9
On the job	84.6	13.8
Neighborhood Youth Corps		
In school	57.3	37.5
Out of school	46.6	46.4

Source: Manpower Report of the President, 1967. (Washington, D.C: Government Printing Office), Table F-3, p. 278, Table F-4, p. 279.

training) and underrepresented in OJT programs (professional and technical skills training), particularly in the South.[9] During the early stages of NYC and MDTA programs, blacks were enrolled at high levels of participation. Table 13.1 provides a cursory analysis of enrollment distribution percentages among black and white enrollees in 1966.

Concentrated Employment Program (CEP). The CEP was initiated in 1967 to bring together, in one unified effort, all the various manpower programs administered by the Department of Labor that were designed to help people in the worst areas in rural and urban America. Department of Labor programs that were integrated to achieve the concentration of resources needed included MDTA, NYC, Operation Mainstream, New Careers, Comprehensive Work and Training, Work Incentive, and the JOBS program. In addition, linkages with programs of other agencies were sought to provide a truly comprehensive approach to solving complex manpower problems. The proportion of blacks served by CEPs nationally fell from 81 percent in 1968 to 58 percent in 1973.[10] The early CEPs were important to the black community because it had administrative control of the programs.

Job Corps. Originally established by the EOA of 1964, current authorization for the program is in Title IVB of the JTPA. The Job Corps is designed to assist young adults who both need and can benefit from the wide range of services provided in a residential setting. These services include basic education, vocational skills training, work experience, counseling, health care, and related support services. The typical enrollee served by Job Corps is an eighteen-year-old high school dropout who reads at the elementary-school level, comes from a poor family, belongs to a minority group, and has never held a full-time job.[11] The Job Corps has 105 residential centers nationwide and enrolled 44,000 young adults in 1986.

The Job Corps has a long history of serving a large number of blacks. In 1972, 61 percent of the enrollees were black; by 1986 this number declined to 57 percent. These have been mostly hard-core young adults with very poor academic backgrounds and attitudes, which make training and placement difficult. However, numerous studies have indicated a fair to good record in training and referral. Job earnings of black terminees tend to be slightly lower than earnings of white terminees.

Work Incentive Program (WIN).   Sponsored generally by the state and local employment service, WIN is designed to coordinate social service and manpower efforts to expand work and training programs for recipients of Aid for Dependent Children and for children of unemployed parents. WIN participants were also involved in MDTA training and other support from CEP. It basically provides preemployment training for welfare mothers. As a work incentive, participants were able to keep a portion of their welfare payments along with earnings from a job. Started in 1967, the WIN program included basic education, vocational training, child care, and counseling, as well as placement services and referral to some public service jobs.

WIN's limited success is particularly critical to blacks in solving the problem of dependency because blacks are overrepresented on the welfare rolls. Blacks constituted 45 percent of WIN participants in 1973.

Job Opportunities in the Business Sector (JOBS).   The JOBS program was started in 1968 as a partnership program between government and private industry. Its purpose was to stimulate industry to provide training and jobs for the unemployed. Although this program was not targeted for blacks, they represented three-fourths of the participants during the first two years.

The proportion of JOBS participants who were black fell from 75 percent in 1970 to 41 percent in 1973. During this period the quality of training and costs of reimbursements were critical areas of concern. An early study by the General Accounting Office revealed that most of the subsidized jobs were low-level dead-end jobs that participants could have secured on their own. There is evidence to indicate that many participants either quit or were laid off. Given the sharp decline in the black proportion of JOBS participants, it is reasonable to assume a disproportionate failure on the part of blacks to obtain meaningful employment.

Public Employment Program (PEP).   The PEP, established by the EEA of 1971, provided federal funding at the state and local levels for the creation of public service jobs. These were to be transitional opportunities for the unemployed and underemployed, combining work experience, training, job restructuring, and civil service reform to assure permanent jobs for the majority of participants.

An estimated 80,000 blacks were hired through PEP in its first year, 95 percent of whom were unemployed. Most of these blacks were employed in state and local government departments of public works and social services. Of blacks who left the program in 1974, 27 percent moved into permanent employment in the public sector.[12]

Operation Mainstream.   Operation Mainstream was designed to provide

Table 13.2
Black Enrollment in Federal Work and Training Programs, 1972

Program	Black Enrollment (%)
Institutional training under MDTA	33
JOBS and other OJT	34
Neighborhood Youth Corps	
In school and summer	53
Out of school	43
Operation Mainstream	19
Public Service Careers	45
Concentrated Employment Program	61
Job Corps	62
Work Incentive Program	36
Public Employment Program	23

Source: Manpower Report of the President, 1973 (Washington, D.C., Government Printing Office), Table 4, p. 54.

adults (many of them older rural residents) with work and supplemental income. The enrollment level for the program peaked in 1973 as a result of the impetus of the 1972 White House Conference on Aging. Additional funds were provided to support subsidized employment for 5,000 new jobs in public and private nonprofit agencies for people fifty-five years of age or older. During the full course of this program, a relatively small number of blacks were involved in comparison with the other major programs.

Public Service Careers (PSC). The PSC program, initiated in 1970, was a small manpower program that focused on training paraprofessionals to assist professionals employed in but not limited to public service agencies, schools. PSC was coordinated with the Supplemental Training and Employment Program (STEP), which was a temporary effort designed to provide income and work experience for trainees who completed a prior manpower program and could not find immediate or stable employment. PSC enrolled about 40,000 persons during 1971–1972. The program declined in 1973, as it was subsumed under CETA.

Table 13.2 provides an analysis of the percentage of black participation in nine manpower programs in 1972. These were the major programs that contained substantial levels of black participation.

The National Apprenticeship Program. The National Apprenticeship Act of 1937 defined the federal role in apprenticeship. The Bureau of Apprenticeship and Training provides for the formulation and promotion of labor standards necessary to safeguard the welfare of apprentices, for bringing employers and labor together to set up programs, and for providing equal employment opportunity for minority groups and women. In 1977 the percentage of registered apprentices who were black was 9.5 percent. A large percentage were being trained in the following occupations: cement masons (25.9 percent), cooks and bakers (19.5 percent), plasterers (19.5 percent), operation engineers (18.0 percent), and pipefitters and steamfitters (17.8 percent). Apprenticeship training serves a more qualified group of young adults. Mastery of some academic skills is a prerequisite for training eligibility.

CETA National Programs. Administered directly from the national office, three programs accounted for more black participation than the others.

1. The Targeted Outreach Program assisted black youths in obtaining employment in the skilled construction trades and other highly skilled occupations. In 1981 seven labor and national community-based groups secured employment for 7,900 persons. Approximately 50 percent were black. Placement in the construction industry and manufacturing accounted for most of the jobs. Forty-five percent were placed in apprenticed jobs.

2. National OJT was designed to reduce skill shortages in occupations needed in the private sector. There were thirty projects in 1981 with national labor organizations. OJT contractors obtained employment for 10,200 of the 16,000 participants in the program. Of those who got jobs, 63 percent were economically disadvantaged, 40 percent were minorities, and 38 percent were women. These jobs were high-wage and apprenticeable positions.

3. Projects for the Handicapped focused on job training for individuals and personnel serving handicapped workers. Other projects, typically conducted by national advocacy organizations, include promotional efforts to encourage employers to hire handicapped people. In 1981, 12,000 persons participated in the program, and 4,600 were placed in jobs. Seventy-three percent of the placements were low-income, 34 percent were minorities, and 51 percent were women.

CETA Youth Programs. The youth employment and training programs authorized under Titles IV and VIII of CETA provided a broad range of work experience, training, and services to enhance the employability of youth. These programs included the Job Corps, described earlier, the Summer Youth Employment Program (SYEP), the Youth Employment and Training Programs (YETP), the Youth Community Conservation and Improvement Projects (YCCIP), and the Young Adult Conservation Corps (YACC).

SYEP provides short-term part-time employment to low-income fourteen-to twenty-one-year-old youths during the summer months. This has been a major program for black high school youth. Nationally, more than 60 percent of the enrollees are black. Federal outlays for SYEP increased from $721 million in 1980 to more than $825 million in 1984. Because of cutbacks in 1985, many municipalities contributed hard cash to their programs in efforts to increase the enrollment of eligible youths, who otherwise would have been idle during the summer months.

YETP offered a variety of services to youths aged fourteen to twenty-one. The program is targeted to low-income youth who are in school by encouraging them to complete their education while providing training and work experience to help them prepare for the labor market. More than half the enrollees of YETP come from minority groups, with about two-thirds of this group being black youths. In 1981 approximately 393,700 participants were enrolled in YETP, with federal funding of $719 million. Of those leaving the programs that year, 32 percent returned to school and 20 percent entered regular employment.[13]

YCCIP provided unemployed sixteen- to nineteen-year-old youths with opportunities for employment, work experience, and skill training in projects that benefit the community. The intent of these projects is to enable low-income youths (particularly high school dropouts who have had difficulty securing employment) to acquire work habits and skills that will enhance their employability. This was a relatively small program that enrolled about 30,000 youths per year under CETA. Approximately 40 percent of the enrollees have been black youths. Eighty-seven percent of the enrollees were from low-income families.

YACC provided employment and other services to unemployed youths, aged sixteen to twenty-three. Participants engaged in conservation work and assisted in other projects on federal and state public lands and waterways. In 1981 there were 68,000 enrollees at a federal cost of $174 million. Approximately 30 percent of the enrollees were black. The program came under heavy criticism from Congress in 1981 because of its high cost ($12,100 per enrollee year) and poor placement and referral record and for not serving those youths who were most in need. The program was phased out in 1982.

Private Sector Initiative Program (PSIP) of CETA. The PSIP was funded under Title VII of CETA. Its purpose was to bring together the public and private sectors in a joint effort to improve the delivery of employment and training programs. The first year of full operation was 1981. During this year, PSIP served 117,000 participants with a 53 percent job placement rate. Eighty-nine percent of these regular jobs were in the private sector. Classroom training represented the largest program component of PSIP and accounted for 54 percent of program expenditures. OJT was an important component, and accounted for 20 percent of program expenditures. The federal outlay for PSIP in 1981 was $264 million. In 1982, 98 percent of the participants were in the low-income group, 33 percent were under the age of twenty-two, and 49 percent were minorities.

The levels of black participation in the various CETA manpower programs during 1981 are shown in Table 13.3. Excluding Job Corps, the highest level of black participation has been in the youth programs. These programs have primarily provided opportunities for work experience with a limited amount

Table 13.3
Black Enrollment in CETA Manpower Training by Program Titles, 1981

Program Titles	Black Enrollment (%)
Title IIB and C (institutional, OJT, work experience, etc.)	31
Title IID (public service jobs)	34
Title IV* (youth programs)	44
Title VI (employment with public agencies)	33
Title VII (private sector training and employment)	34

*Job Corps is not included.

Source: Employment and Training Report of the President, 1982 (Washington, D.C.: Government Printing Office), Table 2, p. 30.

of skills training. It can be assumed that they met some immediate economic needs of participants, but failed to make a substantial impact on the long-term employment preparation needs of the great majority of the enrollees.

Job Training Partnership Act (JTPA) Programs. Most of the manpower programs that had high levels of black participation when administered by CETA were continued under JTPA. These include Job Corps, Institutional and OJT Training Programs, and the Summer Youth Employment and Training Program. Program coordination also continued to exist between JTPA, WIN, Older Worker Program, and the National Apprenticeship Program. However, the Job Corps and SYEP continued to be the programs with the largest percentage of black participants. With the exception of Job Corps, the bulk of JTPA programs has measurable black participation are administered under Title II. During 1984 JTPA served approximately 936,000 persons under Title II, with total expenditures for these programs of $1.7 billion. Of this amount, 74 percent was spent for training, 11 percent for supportive services, and 15 percent for administrative services. Classroom training was the most common initial assignment for Title II participants, with 38 percent assigned to that activity. Title IIA consists of a variety of significant skills training programs. These are administered by state and local institutions and agencies. Although the nonwhite distribution of participants in 1984 was 48 percent, blacks constituted only 32 percent of the total distribution. Table 13.4 provides a breakdown of participant characteristics in Title IIA in 1984.

Table 13.4
Selected Characteristics of Participants in JTPA, Title IIA, 1984

Characteristics	Percentage
Male	49
Female	51
Age	
Under 22	43
22 and over	57
Education	
High School graduate	59
In school	15
Dropout	26
Race/Ethnic group	
White	52
Black	32
Hispanic	12
Other	4
Economic status	
Low income	93
Receiving public assistance	42

Source: Training and Employment Report of the Secretary of Labor, 1985. Department of Employment and Training Administration (mimeographed), Table 1, p. 11.

Community-based Manpower Programs

Historically, there have been many self-help initiatives in the black community to develop and manage manpower programs for unskilled youths and adults. These efforts have produced mixed results, particularly in the long run, where the perennial problem has always rested on funding capacity and continuity. In the 1960s and 1970s the federal government played a major role in providing grants to a variety of community-based organizations. Since 1982 community-based organizations have faced increasing difficulty in securing sufficient funding from federal sources. Successful community-based organizations have diversified their funding outreach strategies to compensate for this situation. In the black community two organizations have served large numbers of people and have been able to maintain program operations for more than twenty years. These manpower programs are Opportunities Industrialization Centers (OIC) of America, Inc., and the National Urban League (NUL) programs. In addition to federal funds, monies to support their programs come from major corporations, local businesses, labor unions, state and local governments, foundations, community groups, religious organizations, and individual donations.

OIC of America, Inc.   The OIC movement was founded in the black ghetto of Philadelphia by Leon H. Sullivan in 1964. The original program consisted of two components, a "feeder" system and a skills training center. The feeder system screened all applicants and provided adult basic education to those in need, preemployment orientation, referral to other agencies as needed, or enrollment to the OIC skill center. Most enrollments in the feeder program were for two to four months' duration. The skills training varies from six to twelve months, depending on the skill specialty. In 1966 OIC expanded to eight other cities, where demonstration projects were implemented. By 1987 OICs were replicated in seventy cities across the country. The contemporary program design to date has ten components: recruitment, intake assessment, orientation, counseling, feeder/prevocational, skills training, job development, job placement, job follow-up, and support services.

During the more than twenty years of their existence, OICs have serviced more than 1 million persons and trained more than 800,000, with a placement rate of 75 percent entering full employment.[14] In the early years the enrollment of black participants was approximately 80 percent. As the program multiplied in various regions, the enrollment complexion was changed to reflect areas with large populations of unskilled whites and Hispanics. In 1985 the black participant share of OIC was 36 percent. Table 13.5 provides a breakdown of the characteristics of OIC participants.

National Urban League. The NUL has been instrumental in eliminating racial barriers for entry into labor unions and apprenticeship training. In 1966 the NUL reached an agreement with the American Federation of Labor and Congress of Industrial Organizations (AFL-CIO) for a preapprenticeship training program for black youths. The AFL-CIO pledged $10,000 a year for three years to support the NUL program. The League announced that it would "guide Negro youth towards preparation for job opportunities in organized skill trades, assist in the placement of qualified individuals in suitable job categories."[15] Over the years the NUL has been involved in conducting many job training programs that were largely funded by the government. The programs were managed by NUL affiliates throughout the country. On-the-job training was the major method practiced because of the NUL's emphasis of job placement.[16] The NUL's programs expanded under CETA in the 1970s. According to Mirengoff and Rindler, there was a substantial increase in federal funds between 1974 and 1975.[17] The NUL received $10 million for forty-seven projects in 1974, and $16 million for seventy-five projects in 1975. The Labor Education Apprenticeship Program (LEAP) was designed to attract more women into apprenticeship training. LEAP was conducted in fifteen cities across the country from 1974 to 1979. This unique program placed minority women in such nontraditional crafts as asbestos work, bricklaying, carpentry, masonry, electricity, roofing, and welding. Partly because of this effort, the proportion of women among all registered apprentices increased from 1.7 percent in 1977 to 2.2 percent in 1978.[18]

Table 13.5
Characteristics of OIC Participants, 1985

Characteristics	Enrollment (%)
Sex	
Male	44
Female	56
Age	
16–21	26
22–54	70
55 and over	4
Ethnic/Race	
Black	36
White	44
Hispanic	15
Other	5
Education	
Dropout	28
In school	31
High school graduate	41
Labor Force	
Unemployed	93
Employed	7

Source: Annual Report 1985: Opportunities Industrialization Centers of America, Philadelphia.

IMPACT AND CONTINUING ISSUES

The federal manpower programs made their most successful impact on blacks from the 1960s through the mid–1970s. Clearly most of the programs with heavy black participation were geared to work experience and preemployment experience. They benefited individuals and their communities in the short run by providing needed income and activities for practical involvement. Without question, a higher, more intensified level of training and education was needed to tap the motivations and interests of many black participants who were led to believe that their training would equip them with skills for stable and meaningful employment. The growth of the federal outlay for manpower programs ended about 1973. This period marks the beginning of a change in program emphases and reductions in budget appropriations that resulted in a declining percentage of black participation. Even in the early years of federal programs blacks had a mixed success under MDTA. From fiscal 1963 to 1968 the black share of participants rose from 21 to 45 percent. However, by 1973 it had fallen back to 30 percent.[19] As the 1975 recession took hold of the economy, federal initiatives shifted to the training and employment of other minorities (Hispanics, Asian boat people, and so on) and of whites who were displaced by industrial labor force reductions. As of today, blacks have been unable to regain their previous share of manpower training resources.

One of the continuing questions that has been discussed and debated during the past decade is, given the huge expenditure of federal funds, at what level did blacks benefit from the manpower training programs of the past? The critical issue is not the investment of government funds, but the level of outcome. It is clear that some of the programs maintained disproportionately high enrollments of blacks in the early years because blacks unquestionably had the greatest needs. On the other hand, those manpower programs that provided comprehensive skills training tended to reflect a lower proportionate enrollment of blacks, particularly since 1973. For this group the research data suggests that there were substantial long-range benefits. Manpower programs also produced many indirect benefits. This writer has contended over the years that one significant indirect benefit was that these programs provided entry-level employment for thousands of black professionals and paraprofessionals who otherwise would have been unemployed. This mixed employment and training of blacks served to enhance the overall development of the black community.

It is generally perceived that government manpower programs had a minimal impact on black employment. However, this is only part of the total equation. The fundamental difficulty with federal aid is that the federal government is not the primary source of institutional change. The vast control of training and employment remains in the hands of state, local, and private institutions. Traditionally, manpower legislation has addressed this issue, and continuing efforts are needed to induce and encourage these institutions to play a greater role in solving the problem of black unemployment. However, these solutions are always linked with the state of the economy and the political climate.

Despite current efforts, it appears that the black employment rate will never return to its level of 1948. The economic structure of America has undergone massive changes and the shift from heavy manufacturing to a service and information base is expected to continue into the twenty-first century. This has tremendous implications for future strategies for the education and training needs of blacks. In recent years there has been increasing attention on the effectiveness of public school systems as the fundamental sources of career development. This concern is expected to continue because it offers a major promise of reducing the growing reservoir of young blacks who find themselves increasingly unskilled and unemployed. Future interventions will need to focus on prevention and amelioration of the basic sources that feed into the problem. It is also expected that self-help initiatives in the black community will continue to expand, but also a simultaneous outreach to government and private institutions will be required in the struggle to provide ongoing effective education and training for blacks in a competitive labor market.

NOTES

1. B. Quarles, *The Negro in the Making of America* (New York: Macmillan, 1969), 224.

2. H. Branson, "The Training of Negroes for War Industries in World War II," *Journal of Negro Education* 84 (1943):376–385.

3. S. A. Levitan, *Federal Aid to Depressed Areas: An Evaluation on the Area Redevelopment Administration* (Baltimore: The Johns Hopkins University Press, 1964), 13.

4. G. L. Mangrum, *MDTA: Foundation of Federal Manpower Policy* (Baltimore: The Johns Hopkins University Press, 1968), 52.

5. *Adult Education Act*, P. L. 91–230, Section 302.

6. W. Mirengoff and L. Rindler, *The Comprehensive Employment and Training Act: An Interim Report* (Washington, D.C.: National Academy of Sciences, 1976), 389.

7. G. G. Somers and E. Stromsdorfer, *A Cost Effective Analysis of the In-School and Summer Neighborhood Youth Corps*, Working Paper No. 350–52 (Washington, D.C.: Urban Institute, November 1970).

8. J. H. Goldstein, *The Effectiveness of Manpower Training Programs: A Review of the Impact on the Poor* (Washington, D.C.: Government Printing Office, November 1972), 63.

9. Mangrum, *MDTA*, 68.

10. Levitan, *Federal Aid to Depressed Areas*, 259.

11. U.S. Department of Labor, Employment and Training Administration, Job Corps, "Job Corps in Brief" (n.d., mimeographed), 1–17.

12. S. A. Levitan et al., *Still a Dream: The Changing Status of Blacks Since 1960* (Cambridge, Mass.: Harvard University Press, 1975), 262.

13. *Employment and Training Report of the President, 1982.* (Washington, D.C.: Government Printing Office, 1982).

14. *Annual Report 1985: Opportunities Industrialization Centers of America* (Philadelphia, 1985).

15. F. R. Marshall and J. Briggs, *The Negro and Apprenticeship* (Baltimore: The Johns Hopkins University Press, 1967), 227.

16. W. L. Henderson and L. C. Ledebur, "Expanding On-the-Job Training," in *The Economics of Black America*, ed. H. G. Vatter and T. Palen (New York: Harcourt Brace Jovanovich, 1972), 32–39.

17. Mirengoff and Rindler, *Comprehensive Employment and Training Act*, 98.

18. *Employment and Training Report of the President, 1979* (Washington, D.C.: Government Printing Office, June 1979), 26.

19. Levitan et al. *Still a Dream*, 257.

Historiographical Essay

A comprehensive history of the education of the black adult remains to be written. The sources cited in this essay are selected primarily from this book's author citations and from Leo McGee and Harvey Neufeldt, *Education of the Black Adult in the United States: An Annotated Bibliography* (Westport, Conn.: Greenwood Press, 1985).

One difficulty a scholar quickly encounters in analyzing adult education is the definitional problem. Adult education may include formal training provided by governmental or private agencies, or it may include any agency seeking to improve the quality of life for any adult. If the latter definition is chosen, adult education may include anything and everything. The topics studied for inclusion in this book contain a broad definition of adult education. The changing definitions of adult education in twentieth-century America are discussed in Harold Stubblefield, *Towards a History of Adult Education in America: The Search for a Unifying Principle* (London: Croom Helm, 1988). Malcolm S. Knowles provides a useful history of the adult education movement of "white" America in *A History of the Adult Education Movement in the United States* (Malibar, Fla.: Krieger, 1977, revised).

Several excellent studies are available on the slave community. The most comprehensive analysis of adult education within the slave community is Thomas L. Webber's *Deep Like the Rivers: Education in the Slave Quarter Community, 1835–1865* (New York: W. W. Norton, 1978). Webber focuses not only on the efforts of the white community in educating the slave, but also on the attempts of the adult black slaves to create a culture different from that of the white society. Other useful studies on the efforts of black adults in educating slaves are John W. Blasingame, *The Slave Community: Plantation Life in the Antebellum South* (New York: Oxford University Press, 1972), and Eugene Genovese, *Roll Jordon Roll: The World the Slaves Made* (New York: Pantheon, Random House, 1972). Barbara Finkelstein discusses the desire for and importance of literacy for the slave in "Reading, Writing and the Acquisition of Identity in the United States, 1790–1860," in *Regulated Children/Liberated Children:*

Education in Psychohistorical Perspective, edited by Barbara Finkelstein (New York: Psychohistory Press, 1979), 114–139.

The slave artisan has received considerable attention from historians. Marcus Jernigan, in *Laboring and Dependant Classes in Colonial America, 1607–1783* (Chicago: University of Chicago Press, 1931), and Leonard Stavisky, in "The Origins of Negro Craftsmanship in Colonial America," *Journal of Negro History* 32 (October 1947):417–429, describe the training of black workers before 1800. The training of slave artisans after 1800 is discussed in John Hope Franklin, "Slaves Virtually Free in Antebellum North Carolina," *Journal of Negro History* 28 (July 1943):284–310; R. I. Brigham, "Negro Education in Antebellum Missouri," *Journal of Negro History* 30 (October 1945):405–420; and Robert Starobin, "Disciplining Industrial Slaves in the Old South," *Journal of Negro History* 53 (April 1968):111–128. An analysis of the diverse occupations filled by and the high level of skills of slaves is found in Claudia Dale Golden, *Urban Slavery in the American South, 1820–1860: A Quantitative History* (Chicago: University of Chicago Press, 1976). Gloria Hall's *But Some of Us Are Brave* (Old Westburg, N.Y.: Feminist Press, 1982), includes a chapter on the education of the female slave.

The church became an important educational institution for the adult slave. Two excellent accounts of the white mission to the slave are Luther P. Jackson's "Religious Development of the Negro in Virginia from 1760 to 1860," *Journal of Negro History* 16 (April 1931):168–239, and "Religious Instruction of Negroes, 1830–1860, with Special Reference to South Carolina," *Journal of Negro History* 15 (January 1930):72–114. Also useful in analyzing the white mission to the slave are Donald G. Mathews, *Religion in the Old South* (Chicago: University of Chicago, 1977); Edward Loring, "Claude C. Jones: Missionary to Plantation Slaves, 1831–1847" (Ph.D. diss., Vanderbilt University, 1976); and Michael Sternett, *Black Religion and American Evangelism: White Protestants, Plantation Missions, and the Flowering of Negro Christianity, 1787–1865* (Metuchen, N.J.: Scarecrow Press, 1975). On the role of individual churches or denominations in educating the slave, see George C. Whatley III, "The Alabama Presbyterian and His Slave, 1830–1864," *The Alabama Review* 13 (January 1960):40–51; Donnie Bellamy "The Education of Blacks in Missouri Prior to 1861," *Journal of Negro History* 59 (April 1974):143–157; Theodore Rector, "Black Nuns as Educators," *Journal of Negro Education* 51 (Summer 1982):238–253; Thomas Drake, *Quakers and Slavery in America* (New Haven, Conn.: Yale University Press, 1950), and Faith Vibert, "The Society for the Propagation of the Gospel in Foreign Parts: Its Work for Negroes in North America Before 1783," *Journal of Negro History* 18 (April 1933):171–212.

The importance of the black church in educating the black adult slave is analyzed in Webber's *Deep Like the Rivers*, and Sternetts, *Black Religion and American Evangelism*.

There were numerous institutions involved in and approaches to the education of the free black before 1865. The lifestyles and options of and educational opportunities for free blacks in the upper South is analyzed by Ira Berlin in *Slaves Without Masters* (New York: Pantheon Books, 1974). Leonard Curry analyzes the black community's faith in education and moral uplift in *The Free Black in Urban America, 1800–1850: The Shadow of the Dream* (Chicago: University of Chicago Press, 1981). John Hope Franklin discusses the free black's struggle to acquire the rudiments of education in *The Free Negro in North Carolina, 1790–1860* (Chapel Hill: University of North Carolina

Press, 1943). The world of the free blacks in the antebellum South is depicted in Michael P. Johnson and James L. Roark's *Black Masters: A Free Family of Color in the Old South* (New York: W. W. Norton, 1984) and Marina Wikramanayake's *A World of Shadow: The Free Black in Antebellum South Carolina* (Columbia: University of South Carolina Press, 1973).

Churches, moral reform societies, and the convention movement all played important roles in educating the free black adult. Among the churches, the Quakers, led by Anthony Benezet, were among the most influential before 1800. Benezet's work is highlighted in Carter Woodson's *The Negro in Our History* (Washington, D.C.: Associated Publishers, 1922) and discussed briefly by Vincent Franklin in *The Education of Black Philadelphia* (Philadelphia: University of Pennsylvania Press, 1979). The impact of the conventions in educating free blacks on slavery, justice, moral reform, and religion and the importance of education to blacks for self-help and uplift are delineated in Howard Bell's "A Survey of the Negro Convention Movement, 1830–1861" (Ph.D. diss., Northwestern University, 1953) and "Free Negroes of the North, 1830–1835: A Study in National Cooperation," *Journal of Negro Education* 26 (Fall 1957):47–55, and in Bella Gross' "The First National Convention," *Journal of Negro History* 31 (October 1946):435–443. The educational activities of black benevolent and moral reform societies are discussed in Howard Bell's "The American Moral Reform Society, 1836–1841," *Journal of Negro Education* 27 (Winter 1958):34–40; Daniel Perlman's "Organizations of the Free Negro in New York City, 1800–1860," *Journal of Negro History* 56 (July 1971):181–197; and Richard W. Pih's "Negro Self Improvement Efforts in Ante-Bellum Cincinnati, 1836–1850," *Ohio History* 78 (Summer 1969):179–187.

The black press and literary societies played important roles in educating the literate free black adult. Two studies that assess the influence of the nineteenth-century black press are Martin Dann, ed., *The Black Press, 1827–1890: The Quest for National Identity* (New York: G. P. Putnam, 1971), and Penelope Bullock, *African American Periodical Press, 1838–1909* (Baton Rouge: Louisiana State University Press, 1981). Also useful are Renk LaBrie III's "Black Newspapers: The Roots Are 150 Years Deep," *Journalism History* 4 (Winter 1977–1978):111–113, and Lione Barrow, Jr.'s "Our Own Cause: Freedom's Journal and the Beginnings of the Black Press," *Journalism History* 4 (Winter 1977–1978):118–122. An excellent descriptive account of black literary societies and their role in educating the black adult is Dorothy Porter's "The Organized Educational Activities of Negro Societies, 1828–1846," reprinted in August Meier and Elliott Rudwick, ed., *The Making of Black America: Essays in Negro Life and History*, Vol. 1. *The Origins of Black America* (New York: Atheneum, 1969):276–288.

The Civil War and Reconstruction era witnessed massive drives to reduce illiteracy levels. Left unanswered, as Ron Butchart points out, was the kind of education deemed appropriate for the freedmen. In addition to the sources cited in Butchart's essay, black adult education during this tumultuous period is discussed in Leo McGee's "Adult Education for the Black Man in America, 1860–1880: An Historical Study of the Types" (Ph.D. diss., Ohio State University, 1972) and "Twenty Years of Education for the Black Adult: Implications for Teachers and Administrators," *Adult Leadership* 21 (March 1973):291–294.

In discussing the education of blacks during the Civil War, historians have focused primarily on the Union Army and Freedmen's Bureau. Most useful are John Blassingame's account of the Union Army's efforts in "The Union Army as an Educational Institution for Negroes, 1862–1865," *Journal of Negro Education* 34 (Spring 1965):152–159, and Dudley Cornish's "The Union Army as a School for Negroes," *Journal of Negro History* 37 (October 1952):368–382. Studies that focus on the activities of Union Army chaplains and generals are Warren Armstrong's "Union Chaplains and the Education of Freedmen," *Journal of Negro History* 52 (April 1967):104–115, and Robert Bahaney's "Generals and Negroes: Education of Negroes by the Union Army, 1861–1865" (Ph.D. diss., University of Michigan, 1965). Black Union Army chaplains and officers played an important role in educating black soldiers. Their efforts are highlighted by John Blassingame in "Negro Chaplains in the Civil War," *Negro History Bulletin* 27 (October 1963):23, 24, and by Dudley Cornish in *The Sable Arm: Negro Troops in the Union Army* (New York: W. W. Norton, 1966). Margorie Parker discusses the Freedmen's Bureau's supporting role in educating the ex-slave in the "The Educational Activities of the Freedmen's Bureau" (Ph.D. diss., University of Chicago, 1951).

Promoters of black education during the early years of Reconstruction made little distinction between educating children and adults. As Butchart points out, education during these years was almost by definition adult education. Most scholars make at least brief mention of this phenomena, but then move on quickly to discuss formal education in schools and colleges. Excellent studies on the meaning of education for the freedmen are James Anderson's "Ex-Slaves and the Rise of Universal Education in the New South, 1860–1880," in *Education and the Rise of the New South*, edited by Ronald Goodenow and Arthur White (Boston: G. K. Hall, 1981), 1–25, and *The Education of Blacks in the South, 1860–1935* (Chapel Hill: University of North Carolina Press, 1988). In chapter 9 of *Been in the Storm So Long: The Aftermath of Slavery* (New York: Alfred A. Knopf, 1980), Leon Litwack provides an excellent account of the uses of literacy as perceived by the freedmen and the white missionaries. W.E.B. Du Bois' *Black Reconstruction in America* (rpt.; New York: Russell & Russell, 1962) emphasizes the freedmen's thirst for literacy.

Black leadership and institutions played important roles in the education of freedmen. Earl West documents the contributions of black teachers in "The Harris Brothers: Black Northern Teachers in the Reconstruction South," *Journal of Negro Education* 48 (Spring 1979):126–138. Clarence Walker focuses on the black church in *A Rock in a Weary Land: The African Methodist Episcopal Church During the Civil War and Reconstruction* (Baton Rouge: Louisiana State University Press, 1982). James Allen discusses the black press as an educational institution for freedom in "The Black Press in the 'New South': Jessie C. Dukes' Struggle for Justice and Equality," *Journal of Negro History* 64 (Summer 1969):215–228.

Scholars have not reached consensus on the motives and goals of white missionaries who became involved in black adult education during the Reconstruction era. James McPherson, in "The New Puritanism: Values and Goals of Freedmen's Education in America," in *The University in Society*, ed. Lawrence Stone (Princeton, N.J.: Princeton University Press, 1974), II:611–639, argues that despite the cultural imperialism evident in the mission to the slaves, some of the abolitionist missionaries enunciated a goal of eventual equality. Butchart and Anderson, on the other hand, have emphasized the white mission as an educational mission for second-class citizenship.

In addition to Ronald Butchart's *Northern Schools, Southern Blacks and Reconstruction:*

Freedmen's Education, 1862–1875 (Westport, Conn.: Greenwood Press, 1980) and Robert Morris' *Reading 'Riting and Reconstruction: The Education of Freedmen in the South, 1865–1870)* (Chicago: University of Chicago Press, 1981), there are several statewide studies of educational activities. One such perceptive study is Jacqueline Jones' *Soldiers of Light and Love: Northern Teachers and Georgia Blacks, 1865–1873* (Chapel Hill: University of North Carolina Press, 1980). Other state studies include John Meyers' "The Education of Alabama Freedmen During Presidential Reconstruction, 1865–1867," *Journal of Negro Education* 40 (Spring 1971):163–171; Joe Richardson's *The Negro in the Reconstruction of Florida, 1865–1877* (Tallahassee: Florida State University Press, 1964); Roberta S. Alexander's "Hostility and Hope: Black Education in North Carolina During Presidential Reconstruction," *North Carolina Historical Review* 53 (April 1976):113–132; Joel Williamson's *After Slavery: The Negro in South Carolina During Reconstruction, 1861–1877* (Chapel Hill: University of North Carolina Press, 1965); and Joe Richardson's "The Negro in Post–Civil War Tennessee: A Report by a Northern Missionary," *Journal of Negro Education* 34 (Fall 1965):419–424.

The attitudes of Southern whites toward black education is highlighted by Guion Johnson in "Southern Paternalism Toward Negroes After Emancipation," *Journal of Southern History* 23 (November 1957):483–509, and by Joe Richardson in *The Negro in Reconstruction of Florida.*

Agricultural education, including demonstration extension work, has long been an important aspect of adult education. The federal government became financially involved, especially with the passage of the Smith-Lever Act in 1914. A definitive study of the history of agricultural extension up to the passage of the Smith-Lever Act is Roy Scott, *The Reluctant Farmer: The Rise of Agricultural Extension to 1914* (Urbana: University of Illinois Press, 1970). Also useful are Wayne Rasmussen, *Agriculture in the United States: A Documentary History*, Vol. 2, *1869–1914* (New York: Random House, 1975), and Alfred True, *A History of Agricultural Extension Work in the United States, 1785–1923* (Washington, D.C.: Government Printing Office, 1928). Seaman Knapp's contribution to farm demonstration is discussed in Joseph Bailey, *Seaman A. Knapp: Schoolmaster of America* (New York: Columbia University Press, 1945).

Most standard histories fail to analyze farm demonstration within a racial context. Most of the extension work was done in white land grant colleges. Most county agents were white agents working for white farmers. The impact of race on farm demonstration work is addressed in Gladys Baker's *The County Agent* (Chicago: University of Chicago Press, 1939).

Tuskegee's extension and demonstration program was one of the few bright spots in an otherwise bleak picture of black extension. George Washington Carver's contributions to this program are discussed in Linda McMurray's *George Washington Carver: Scientist and Symbol* (New York: Oxford University Press, 1981), and Leo McGee's "Booker T. Washington and George Washington Carver: A Tandem of Adult Educators at Tuskegee," *Lifelong Learning* 8 (October 1984):16–18, 31. The selection of the first two black farm demonstration agents who were placed at Tuskegee and Hampton Institutes is described in Allen Jones' "The South's First Black Farm Agents," *Agricultural History* 50 (October 1976):636–644.

Tuskegee's extension work is depicted in several articles and books. Accounts by participants are Thomas Campbell's *The Moveable School Goes to the Negro Farmer*

(Tuskegee: Tuskegee Institute, 1939), and Booker T. Washington's *Working with Hands: Being a Sequel to 'Up from Slavery' Covering the Author's Experiences in Industrial Training at Tuskegee* (New York: Doubleday, 1904), especially chapter 10. These works present Tuskegee's public image at its best. Also written within this public image is Purvis Carter's "Robert Lloyd Smith and the Farmer's Improvement Society, a Self-help Movement in Texas," *Negro History Bulletin* 29 (Fall 1966):175–177, 190. Other accounts, some of which are more analytical, are Felix James' "The Tuskegee Institute Moveable School, 1906–1923," *Agricultural History* 45 (July 1971):201–209; Louis Harlan's *Booker T. Washington: The Making of a Black Leader, 1865–1901* (New York: Oxford University Press, 1972), and Booker T. Gardner's "The Educational Contributions of Booker T. Washington," *Journal of Negro Education* 44 (Fall 1975):502–518.

Demonstration work, corn and tomato clubs, and industrial education were all part of an attempt to transform the rural Southern community. Harvey Neufeldt, in "Southern Education Reform and the Revitalization of the Rural Community" (unpublished paper, AESA Convention, San Francisco, November 1984), analyzes the role of Northern philanthropists and Southern educational leaders in this movement during the first two decades of the twentieth century. Elizabeth Jocoway provides a critical case study in *Yankee Missionaries in the South: The Penn School Experiment* (Baton Rouge: Louisiana State University Press, 1980). Also useful is Gerald Robbins' "Rossa B. Cooley and Penn School: Social Dynamo in Negro Rural Subculture, 1901–1930," *Journal of Negro Education* 33 (Winter 1964):43–51. Rossa B. Cooley's *School Acres: An Adventure in Rural Education* (New Haven, Conn.: Yale University Press, 1930) is an account by one of the participants.

There are only a limited number of studies available in the history of the education of black women. Documentaries include Gerda Lerner, ed., *Black Women in White America: A Documentary History* (New York: Pantheon Books, Random House, 1972), and B. J. Lowenberg and R. Bogin, eds., *Black Women in Nineteenth Century American Life: Their Words, Their Thoughts, Their Feelings* (University Park: Pennsylvania State University Press, 1976). Cynthia Neverdon-Morton describes the educational activities of black women in the South in *Afro-American Women of the South and the Advancement of the Race, 1895–1925* (Knoxville: University of Tennessee Press, 1989). Black women's clubs' activities are highlighted in Gerda Lerner's "Early Community Work of Black Club Women," *Journal of Negro History* 59 (April 1974):158–167, and Cynthia Neverdon-Morton's "Self Help Programs as Educative Activities of Black Women of the South, 1895–1915: Focus on Four Key Areas," *Journal of Negro Education* 51 (Summer 1982):207–221. The educational activities of the National Association of Colored Women are briefly described in Beverly Jones' "Mary Church Terrell and the National Association of Colored Women, 1896 to 1901," *Journal of Negro History* 67 (Spring 1982):20–33. Isabel Lindsay's "Adult Education Programs for Negroes in Settlement Houses," *Journal of Negro Education* 14 (Summer 1945):347–352, includes a description of programs in job training and racial understanding.

Vincent Franklin's study, *The Education of Black Philadelphia, a Social and Educational History of a Minority Community, 1900–1950* (Philadelphia: University of Pennsylvania Press, 1979), parts of which are summarized in "In Pursuit of Freedom: The Educational Activities of Black Social Organizations in Philadelphia, 1900–1930," in Vincent P. Franklin and James Anderson, eds., *New Perspectives on Black*

Educational History (Boston: G. K. Hall, 1978), 113–128, is a model case study of the voluntary educational activities within a black community in twentieth-century urban America. Also useful are Ira Reid's *Adult Education Among Negroes* (Washington, D.C.: Associates in Negro Folk Education, 1936), and Lillian Williams' "Community Educational Activities and the Liberation of Black Buffalo, 1900–1930," *Journal of Negro Education* 54 (Spring 1985):174–188.

Religious organizations continued to play an important role in the education of the urban black adult in the twentieth century. Descriptions of the black church's efforts in adult education, including literacy training, are found in R. R. Wright's *87 Years Behind the Black Curtain* (Philadelphia: Rare Books Co., 1965), and "Social Work of the Negro Church," *The Annals of the American Academy of Political and Social Science* 30 (November 1907):1–13. Sherman Webster examines educational activities in ten selected Baptist black churches in "A Study of the Patterns of Adult Education in Selected Negro Churches" (Ed.D. diss., Indiana University, 1959). Negative assessments of the black churches' role in community involvement and adult education are found in Samuel Gandy's "The Negro Church and the Adult Education Phases of Its Program," *Journal of Negro Education* 14 (Summer 1945):381–384; Jon Butler's "Communities and Congregations: The Black Church in St. Paul, 1860–1900," *Journal of Negro History* 56 (April 1971):118–136; and Ira Reid's "Let Us Pray," *Opportunity* 4 (September 1926):274–278.

The importance of the black YMCA and YWCA to the black community is beginning to be recognized by scholars. Lillian Williams analyzes the role of the "Y" in a racist society in "To Elevate the Race: The Michigan Avenue YMCA and the Advancement of Blacks in Buffalo, New York, 1922–1940," in Franklin and Anderson, eds., *New Perspectives on Black Educational History*, pp. 129–148. Less analytical accounts are found in J. E. Moorland's "The Young Men's Christian Association Among Negroes," *Journal of Negro History* 9 (January 1924):127–138; Ralph Bullock's "The Adult Education Programs of the YMCA Among Negroes," *Journal of Negro Education* 14 (Summer 1945):385–389; and Dorothy Height's "The Adult Education Program of the YWCA Among Negroes," *Journal of Negro Education* 14 (Summer 1945):390–395.

The role of fraternals in the black community and their importance for adult education is discussed by Peter Rachleff in *Black Labor in the South: Richmond, Virginia, 1865–1890* (Philadelphia: Temple University Press: 1984); William Muraskin in "The Hidden Role of Fraternal Organizations in the Education of Black Adults: Prince Hall Freemasonary as a Case Study," *Adult Education* 26 (1976):235–252; and James Jackson in "Fraternal Societies Aid Race Progress," *The Crises*, (July 1938):235–244.

The Summer 1945 issue of the *Journal of Negro Education* included several status reports on health education efforts undertaken by the black community and governmental agencies. These included Eva Mitchell's "Adult Health and Recreational Programs: National, State and Local," pp. 363–373, and Roscoe C. Brown's "The Health Education Programs of Government and Voluntary Agencies," pp. 377–387. Also useful is Rivers F. Barnwell's "Health Education of Negroes Provided by Press, Radio and Theatre," *Journal of Negro Education* 6 (July 1937):565–571.

The National Urban League and the National Association for the Advancement of Colored People both promoted adult education. Roy Wilkins, in "Adult Education Programs of the NAACP," *Journal of Negro Education* 14 (Summer 1945):403–406, makes brief mention of the NAACP's involvement in this area. Two histories of the National Urban League are by Guichard Parris and Lester Brooks, *Blacks in the City: A History of the National Urban League* (Boston: Little, Brown, 1971), and by Nancy Weiss, *The National Urban League, 1910–1940* (New York: Oxford University Press, 1971). The National Urban League's emphasis on self-help is discussed in Alphonse Heningburg's "Adult Education and the National Urban League," *Journal of Negro Education* 14 (Summer 1945):396–402. The League's activities in Chicago is analyzed by Alan Spear in *Black Chicago: The Making of a Negro Ghetto, 1890–1920* (Chicago: University of Chicago Press, 1967), and by Alvarh Strickland in *A History of the Chicago Urban League* (Urbana: University of Illinois Press, 1966).

The black periodical press played an important role in shaping the discourse among and in the education of a small emerging black middle class during the first three decades of the twentieth century. A useful study of the black middle class is E. Franklin Frazier's *Black Bourgeoisie* (Glencoe, Ill.: Free Press, 1957). The important role of the black periodical press in shaping the discourse among black professionals is discussed in David Nelson's *Black Ethos: Northern Urban Negro Life and Thoughts, 1890–1920* (Westport, Conn.: Greenwood Press, 1977) and in Frederick Detweiler's *The Negro Press in the United States* (Chicago: University of Chicago Press, 1922). The rise of the Negro magazine is discussed in Penelope Bullock's *The Afro American Periodical Press, 1838–1909* (Baton Rouge: Louisiana State University Press, 1981) and Charles Johnson's "The Rise of the Negro Magazine," *Journal of Negro History* 13 (January 1928):7–21. The *Colored American Magazine* is discussed in "Pauline E. Hopkins, Biographical Excursion into Obscurity," *Phylon* 33 (Spring 1972):22–26; in Abby Johnson and Ronald Johnson's "Away from Accommodation; Radical Editors and Protest Journalism, 1900–1910," *Journal of Negro History* 62 (October 1977):325–338; and in William Braithwrite's "Negro America's First Magazine," *Negro Digest* 6 (December 1947):21–26. Booker T. Washington's attempts to influence the black press is analyzed by August Meier in "Booker T. Washington and the Negro Press: With Special Reference to the *Colored American Magazine*," *Journal of Negro History* 38 (January 1953):67–90, and by Louis Harlan in "Booker T. Washington and the Voice of the Negro, 1904–1907," *Journal of Southern History* 45 (February 1979):45–62.

Governmental funding became increasingly important for black adult education after 1930 as part of the New Deal. Harvard Sitkoff, in "The New Deal and Race Relations," in Harvard Sitkoff, ed., *Fifty Years Later: The New Deal Evaluated* (Philadelphia: Temple University Press, 1985), 98–112, and in *A New Deal for Blacks* (New York: Oxford University Press, 1978), provides a positive assessment of the New Deal's impact on blacks. More pessimistic conclusions are found in Nancy Weiss' *Farewell to the Party of Lincoln* (Princeton, N.J.: Princeton University Press, 1983), and L. D. Reddick's "Adult Education and the Improvement of Race Relations," *Journal of Negro Education* 14 (Summer 1945):488–493.

New Deal programs were designed not only to provide relief, but also to stimulate adult education. Joyce Kornbluth provides an excellent study of the New Deal programs for workers' education in *A New Deal for Workers' Education: The Workers' Service Program, 1933–42* (Urbana: University of Illinois Press, 1987), and for female workers' education in "The She-She-She-Camps: An Experiment in Living and Learning, 1934–1937," in Joyce Kornbluth and Mary Frederickson, eds., *Sisterhood and Solidarity: Workers' Education for Women, 1914–1984* (Philadelphia: Temple University Press, 1984), 255–283. Programs for urban blacks are discussed in Melvin Maskin's "Black Education and the New Deal: The Urban Experience" (Ph.D. diss., New York University, 1973). Also useful is Raymond Wolters' *Negroes and the Great Depression* (Westport, Conn.: Greenwood Press, 1970).

Programs within the Works Progress Administration, especially the Emergency Education Program, promoted adult education. Positive assessments of these programs for blacks are found in James Atkins' "The Participation of Negroes in Pre-School and Adult Education Programs," *Journal of Negro Education* 7 (July 1938):345–346. Doxey Wilkerson highlights the program's success in literacy training in *Special Problems of Negro Education* (Washington, D.C.: Government Printing Office, 1939). George Redd's "Adult Education for Negroes Under Public School Auspices," *Journal of Negro Education* 14 (Summer 1945):312–321, provides a negative assessment. Classes to prepare blacks to meet voter qualifications are described in Luther P. Jackson's "Citizenship Training—A Neglected Area in Adult Education," *Journal of Negro Education*, 14 (Summer 1945):477–487.

The Civilian Conservation Corps provided educational activities for young adults. Frank Hill's *The School in the Camps: The Educational Program of the Civilian Conservation Corps* (New York: Associates for Adult Association, 1935) makes some mention of activities within camps for black adults. Howard Oxley's "The Civilian Conservation Corps and the Education of the Negro," *Journal of Negro Education* 7 (July 1938):375–382, provides the "public" image of the camp, omitting any discussion of racial discrimination. Studies that analyze the impact of race in the CCC programs are John Salmond's "The Civilian Conservation Corps and the Negro," *Journal of American History* 52 (January 1965): 75–88; Calvin Gower's "The Struggle of Blacks for Leadership Positions in the Civilian Conservation Corps: 1933–1942," *Journal of Negro History* 61 (April 1976):123–135; and Marion Wright's "Negro Youth and the Federal Emergency Programs: CCC and NYA," *Journal of Negro Education* 9 (July 1940):397–407.

The National Youth Administration not only provided funds for part-time employment of high school and college students, but also underwrote some of the cost of vocational training programs. Studies that discuss this program's importance to black youth are Walter Daniel and Caroll Miller's "The Participation of the Negro in the National Youth Administration Program," *Journal of Negro Education* 7 (July 1938):357–365; John Salmond's "The National Youth Administration," in *Franklin D. Roosevelt: His Life and Times*, edited by Otis Graham and M. Wander (Boston: G. K. Hall, 1985); and Marion Wright's "Negro Youth and the Federal Emergency Programs: CCC and NYA," *Journal of Negro Education* 9 (July 1940):397–407.

The New Deal's support for agricultural and home demonstration programs had implications for adult education for blacks in rural areas. These programs are discussed by Giles Herbert in "Some Recent Developments in Adult Education Among Negroes in Agriculture," *Journal of Negro Education* 14 (Summer 1945):337–340, and by Jane McAllister and Dorothy McAllister in "Adult Education for Negroes in Rural Areas," *Journal of Negro Education* 14 (Summer 1945):337–340. Doxey Wilkerson analyzes the under-representation of blacks in federally funded extension programs in "The Participation of Negroes in the Federally Aided Program of Agriculture and Home Economics Extension," *Journal of Negro Education* 7 (July 1938):331–340.

The Tennessee Valley Authority became actively involved in job training for its new employees. The most comprehensive study of the Tennessee Valley Authority's hiring policies and training programs for black adults is Nancy Grant's *TVA and Black Americans: Planning for the Status Quo* (Philadelphia: Temple University Press, 1989), and Grant's "Government Social Planning and Education for Blacks: The TVA Experiment, 1933–1945," in *Education and the Rise of the New South,* edited by Ronald Goodenow and Art White. Also useful are Max Bond's articles, "The Educational Program for Negroes in the TVA," *Journal of Negro Education* 6 (April 1937):144–151, and "The Training Program of the Tennessee Valley Authority for Negroes," *Journal of Negro Education* 7 (July 1938):383–389.

The impact of racism in educational and employment opportunities for black adults in war industries and the Armed Forces during World War II has been addressed by several scholars. The discrimination and exclusionist policies of the Navy are highlighted in L. D. Reddick's "The Negro in the United States Navy During World War II," *Journal of Negro History* 32 (January 1947):201–219, and of war industries in Doxey Wilkerson's "Section E: The Vocational Education and Guidance of Negroes: The Negro and the Battle of Production," *Journal of Negro Education* 11 (April 1942):228–339, and in Herman Bransom's "The Training of Negroes for War Industries in World War II," *Journal of Negro Education* 12 (Summer 1943):376–385. David Lane provides a brief analysis of a literacy training program for black troops stationed in Europe after World War II in "An Army Project in the Duty-Time General Education of Negro Troops in Europe, 1947–1951," *Journal of Negro Education* 33 (Spring 1964):117–124.

The impact of race on vocational programs that prepared students for skilled-level positions was especially evident in governmental programs during the Depression and World War II. The underrepresentation of blacks in programs that would lead to social and economic mobility is discussed by Ambrose Caliver in *Vocational Education and Guidance of Negroes: Report of a Survey Conducted by the Office of Education* (rpt.; Westport, Conn.: Greenwood Press, 1970); by George Redd in "Adult Education for Negroes Under Public School Auspices," *Journal of Negro Education* 14 (Summer 1945):312–321; by Charles Thompson in "The Federal Programs of Vocational Education in Negro Schools of Less Than College Grade," *Journal of Negro Education* 7 (July 1938):303–318; and by Christopher Wye in "The New Deal and the Negro Community: Toward a Broader Conceptualization," *Journal of American History* 59 (December 1972):621–639. The lack of meaningful programs for physically handicapped black adults is emphasized in Doxey Wilkerson and Lemuel Penn's "The Participation of Negroes in the Federally Aided Program of Civilian Vocational Rehabilitation," *Journal of Negro Education* 7 (July 1938):319–330. Wiley Hall provides a brief description of training programs for blacks undertaken by the CIO in "Adult Education Programs of Labor Unions and Other Worker Groups," *Journal of Negro Education* 14 (Summer 1945):407–411.

Vocational training and apprenticeship programs initiated during the 1960s and 1970s have received considerable attention from scholars. Included are Sam A. Levitan, in *Federal Aid to Depressed Areas: An Evaluation of the Area Redevelopment Administration* (Baltimore: The Johns Hopkins University Press, 1964); S. A. Levitan et al., in *Still a Dream* (Cambridge, Mass.: Harvard University Press, 1975); Garth L. Mangum, in *MDTA: Foundation of Federal Manpower Policy* (Baltimore: The Johns Hopkins University Press, 1968); William Mirengoff, in *The Comprehensive Employment Training Act: An Interim Report* (Washington, D.C.: National Academy of Sciences, 1976), and William Mirengoff and Lester Rindler, in *CETA: Manpower Programs*

Under Local Control (Washington, D.C.: National Academy of Sciences, 1976). On a case study of a local MDTA program, see Dennis Ekberg and Claude Ury, "Education for What? A Report on a M.D.T.A. Program," *Journal of Negro Education* 37 (Winter 1968):15–22.

Several studies analyze different aspects of the management training programs. William Brazziel describes manpower training programs during the early 1960s in "Manpower Training and the Negro Worker," *Journal of Negro Education* 35 (Winter 1966):83–84, while Herbert Hill analyzes the impact of federal training programs on black employment in "Employment, Manpower Training and the Black Worker," *Journal of Negro Education* 38 (Summer 1969):204–217. J. H. Goldstein's *The Effectiveness of Manpower Training Programs: A Review of the Impact on the Poor* (Washington, D.C.: Government Printing Office, November 1972) compares manpower training programs for black and white participants. Bennett Harrison focuses on the problem of training the hard-core unemployed in *Education, Training and the Urban Ghetto* (Baltimore: The Johns Hopkins University Press, 1972).

Racism prevented blacks from participating in many meaningful apprenticeship programs. The importance of apprenticeship programs for black adults is discussed in Ray Marshall and Vernon Briggs' *Equal Apprenticeship Opportunities* (Ann Arbor: University of Michigan Press, 1968); in Ray Marshall's *The Negro and Apprenticeship* (Baltimore: The Johns Hopkins University Press, 1967); and in Ray Marshall's "Negro Participation in Apprenticeship Programs," *Journal of Human Resources* 15 (Winter 1967):51–69. Marshall discusses discriminatory practices used by union officials to exclude blacks from participation in apprenticeship programs, but also highlights successfully integrated programs. Also useful is Marshall Medoff's "Discrimination: Blacks and the Apprenticeship Trade Program," *The Negro Educational Review* 26 (October 1975):147–154, and Thomas Patton II's *Manpower Planning and the Development of Human Resources* (New York: Wiley-Interscience, 1971).

There is a need for research studies that provide a systematic evaluation of literacy programs. Most literacy programs relied more on rhetoric than on monetary support. This is especially true of literacy programs during the first three decades of the twentieth century. The rhetoric of the Southern literacy campaign is analyzed in Florence Estes, Harvey Neufeldt, and James Akenson's "Appalachian and Southern Literacy Campaigns in the Early Twentieth Century: Historical Perspectives in Two Keys," in *Education in Appalachia: Proceedings from the 1987 Conference in Appalachia*, edited by Alan DeYoung (Lexington, Ky.: Appalachian Center, University of Kentucky, 1987), 81–94. Cora Wilson Stewart provides an upbeat account of her literacy work in *Moonlight Schools for the Emancipation of Adult Illiteracy* (New York: Doubleday, 1922), while Harvey Neufeldt and James Akenson provide a critical analysis of the ideology underlying the moonlight schools in "The Southern Illiteracy Campaign, 1911–1930: A Study in Ideology, Southern Progressivism and Victorian Attitudes" (unpublished paper, History of Education Society annual meeting, Atlanta, November 1985) and in "The Social Studies Component of the Southern Literacy Campaign, 1915–1935," *Theory and Research in Social Education* 14 (Summer 1986):187–200. The literacy campaign in Alabama is discussed by James Akenson and Harvey Neufeldt in "Alabama's Illiteracy Campaign for Black Adults, 1915–1930," *Journal of Negro Education* 54 (Spring 1985):189–195.

The citizenship schools represented a more radical position on the uses of literacy. Anthony P. Dunbar, in *Against the Grain: Southern Radicals and Prophets, 1920–1959*

(Charlottesville: University Press of Virginia, 1981), analyzes Miles Horton's place within a conservative racial, political, and economic Southern climate. Miles Horton and the Highlander School are viewed positively by Aimie Horton in "The Highlander Folk School: A History of the Development of Its Major Programs Related to Social Movements in the South" (Ph.D. diss., University of Chicago, 1971). J. D. Franson analyzes the citizenship education programs in "Citizenship Education in the South Carolina Sea Islands, 1954–1966" (Ph.D. diss., Vanderbilt University, 1977).

Paulo Freire's writings are often cited as a theoretical basis for using education, including literacy, as a vehicle for empowerment. Most useful are Freire's *The Pedagogy of the Oppressed* (New York: Seabury Press, 1970) and *The Politics of Education: Culture, Power and Liberation* (Mass: Bergin & Garvey, 1985), and Paul Freire and Doualdo Macedo's *Literacy: Revealing the Word and the World* (Mass.: Bergin & Garvey, 1987). Freire's work relies heavily on evidence that is anecdotal.

The literature on the education of the black adult confirms V. P. Franklin's argument in *Black Self Determination: A Cultural History of the Faith of the Fathers* (Westport, Conn.: Hill, 1984) that education has been one of the major components of the black adult cultural value system. What is also evident is that blacks as well as whites played a major role in promoting and providing educational activities for both the young and adults. What is not clear is the extent to which these educational programs were able to effectively challenge an American value system that viewed the black adult as a second-class citizen.

Index

Contributors

JAMES E. AKENSON is a professor in the department of curriculum and instruction at Tennessee Technological University, where he teaches methods courses and supervises student teachers. His research deals with social studies education and adult illiteracy.

RONALD E. BUTCHART is interested in areas of nineteenth-century social history, particularly the history of teachers and teaching, African American education, and education reform. He teaches courses in the history of American education and social foundations of education at the State University of New York College at Cortland.

V. P. FRANKLIN is currently associate professor of history at Arizona State University. He is the coeditor of *New Perspectives on Black Educational History* (1978) and author of *The Education of Black Philadelphia* (1979) and *Black Self-determination: A Cultural History of the Faith of the Fathers* (1984), as well as of numerous essays and reviews in African American education and history. Among his current projects is a history of the education of Black Catholics in the United States.

MICHAEL FULTZ is an assistant professor of education at the Harvard Graduate School of Education, where he teaches courses in urban education and the history of American education. He is currently working on a research project on "The Educational Vision of the Black Middle Class, 1900–1960."

NANCY L. GRANT is an associate professor of history at Washington University in St. Louis, Missouri, where she teaches twentieth-century U.S. history. Her publications are on the New Deal and blacks, Southern regionalism, and government employment policy toward minorities.

EDWIN HAMILTON is a graduate professor in the School of Education at Howard University in Washington, D.C. He is coordinator of the degree programs in the discipline of adult education and teaches courses to graduate students. His research specialties are program planning, design, and evaluation of continuing education and training.

ELIZABETH L. IHLE graduated from the University of Tennessee at Knoxville in 1976 with an Ed.D. in the history of education. Her specialty is women's education, and in 1986 she published a series of articles on the history of black women's education in the South under a grant from the Women's Educational Equity Act. She currently serves as a professor of educational foundations and as affirmative action officer at James Madison University.

FELIX JAMES is a professor in the department of history at Southern University at New Orleans, where he teaches courses in African American and U.S. history. He has written a number of articles on African American history.

BOBBY L. LOVETT is interim dean of the College of Arts and Sciences and professor of history at Tennessee State University. His research interest includes Civil War and black history. He has published several works on blacks in the American Civil War.

LEO MCGEE is associate vice president for academic affairs at Tennessee Technological University. He has been involved in research in the field of adult education for more than two decades. He has authored or co-authored four books and more than forty articles. These works have primarily covered the history of education for the black adult in America but have also addressed the plight of the black farmer.

HARVEY G. NEUFELDT is a professor in the department of curriculum and instruction at Tennessee Technological University, where he teaches courses in the foundations of education. His research areas include the history of adult literacy and black adult education.

CYNTHIA NEVERDON-MORTON is a professor in the department of history, geography, and international studies at Coppin State College. Her research areas include African American women's history and the history of the African diaspora. One of her most recent publications is *Afro-American Women of the South and the Advancement of the Race, 1895–1925*.

SANDRA B. OLDENDORF is the program officer for the School of Education and Psychology at Western Carolina University. She coordinates field experiences and teaches curriculum development. Her research areas include Highlander Folk School's Sea Island citizenship schools and developing model clinical training programs designed to connect theory to practice.

LILLIAN S. WILLIAMS is a professor of women's studies and African American studies at the State University of New York at Albany. Her research interests are in African American urban and women's history, and she is the author of several articles. She is associate editor of *Afro-Americans in New York Life and History* and currently is preparing a biography of reformer Mary Burnett Talbert.

L. H. WHITEAKER is an associate professor in the history department of Tennessee Technological University, where he teaches courses on the Civil War and American social and cultural history. His research areas include Southern history and the Civil War.